G000123445

North Wales Rock
Selected Rock Climbs in North Wales

Author Simon Panton

Contributions Al Leary, Rob Wilson, Graham Desroy,
Simon Marsh, Mark Reeves and Pete Robins

Editor Simon Panton

Design Allen Williams

Original design template by Mark Lynden/Matrix 10

Printing Northend Creative Print Solutions, Clyde Road, Sheffield S8 0TZ

Distribution Cordee (www.cordee.co.uk)

Publisher Ground Up Productions Ltd.

October 2006

ISBN 978-0-9554417-0-7

Guidebook Disclaimer
The writer and publisher of this book accepts no responsibility for the way in which readers use the information contained therein. The descriptions and recommendations are for guidance only and must be subject to discriminating judgement by the reader. Advice and training should be sought before utilising any equipment or techniques mentioned within the text or shown in any of the photographic images. Climbing and bouldering are activities with a danger of personal injury or death. Participants in these activities should be aware of, and accept, these risks and be responsible for their own actions and involvement.

www.groundupclimbing.com

LLANBERIS GUIDES

Rock climbing in Snowdonia with qualified & experienced guides
Dringo creigiau yn Eryri gyda hyfforddwyr profiadol a chymwys

Cenotaph Corner, Dinas Cromlech, Llanberis Pass. Photo: Ray Wood

www.llanberisguides.com
08707 606 515

or all enquiries
bookings
lease call:

Contents

General introduction	6
Graded List	20
Llanberis + Intro	26
Craig Ddu	28
Clogwyn y Grochan	34
Carreg Wastad	42
Dinas Cromlech	48
Cromlech Boulders	56
Esgair Maen Gwyn/Scimitar Ridge	58
Clogwyn Gafr	62
Dinas Mot	66
Diffwys Ddwr/Craig y Rhaeadr	81
Clogwyn y Ddysgl	86
Diffwys Ddu/Cyrn Las	91
Cwm Glas Bach	96
Clogwyn Du'r Arddu	104
Lliwedd	122
Slate Intro	134
Vivian Quarry	136
Rainbow Slab Area	146
Bus Stop Quarry	160
Dali's Hole Area	166
Serengeti	172
Never Never Land	176
Ogwen + Intro	178
East Face of Tryfan	180
Milestone Buttress	188
Clogwyn Bochlwyd	192
Glyder Fach Main Cliff	196
Clogwyn y Tarw	202
Cwm Cneifion	208
Clogwyn Du	211
Idwal Slabs and Walls	214
Glyder Fawr	226
Clogwyn y Geifr	230
Carnedd y Filiast	234
Craig Lloer	236
Braich Ty Du	240
Llech Du	242
Craig yr Ysfa	248
Clogwyn yr Eryr	256
RAC Boulders	262
Tremadog + Intro	264
Craig Bwlch y Moch	266
Craig Pant Ifan	282
Craig y Castell	290
Craig y Gesail	294
Craig Cwm Trwsgl	298
Craig yr Ogof	300
Y Garn	306
Craig y Bera	310
Craig Cwm Du	312
Castell Cidwm	314
Llechog	318
Clogwyn y Bustach	321
Clogwyn y Wenallt	324
Carreg Hylldrem	328
Carreg Alltrem	332
Craig y Clipiau	336
Craig yr Wrysgan	340
Clogwyn yr Oen	344
Gogarth Intro	350
Yellow Wall	354
Castell Helen	360
Red Wall	366
Left-Hand Red Wall	370
Mousetrap Zawn	374
Holyhead Mountain	380
Upper Tier	388
Main Cliff	396
North Stack Wall	410
Flytrap Area	414
Wen Zawn	418
Easter Island Gully	426
Rhoscolyn	432
Lleyn Intro	442
Trwyn y Gorlech	444
Craig y Llam	446
Trwyn Maen Melyn	448
Pen y Cil	450
Craig Dorys	452
Cilan Head	458
Ty'n Tywyn Quarries	468
Porth Ysgo	472
Llandudno + Intro	474
Mayfair Wall	476
Plumbline Area	480
Firefly Area	484
Excursion Area	488
Chain Gang Wall	492
Yellow Wall	496
Homo Sapien Area	499
Marine Drive Bouldering	500
Lower Pen Trwyn	502
Wonder Wall	509
Castell y Gwynt	512
St Tudno's Upper Crag	519
Upper Craig y Don	522
Great Zawn	526
Castle Inn Quarry	530
Route Index	532
Crag Index	538
Advertising Directory	539
Acknowledgements	540

North Wales Rock

The north-west corner of Wales hosts some of the most celebrated and historically important rock climbs in the world. This spectacular crag-infested landscape, with its rugged mountain valleys and towering sea cliffs has proved an irresistible lure for generations of climbers seeking the thrill and adventure of the Welsh climbing experience.

Within this tight geographical area lies an unrivalled and astounding diversity of crags. From classic mountain routes to wild sea cliff adventures and intense sport climbs, there is something to please all tastes and capabilities.

This guide covers a broad selection, 676 in total, of the finest climbs from all the best areas: the Llanberis Pass, Cloggy, Lliwedd, Ogwen and the Carneddau, Tremadog and the Moelwyns, Gogarth, the Lleyn Peninsula and the Llandudno limestone crags. The grade range runs from classic Diffs right up to E7 test pieces, and from F5+ sport routes up to F8 grade clip-ups. There are also some brief details of the many bouldering opportunities in the area.

An attempt has been made to showcase all aspects of the North Wales crags, whilst remaining focussed upon the simple criterion of quality. There is no star rating system in the book as all the featured routes offer superb climbing of one style or another.

Each of the geographical areas has an introduction section, which includes a large-scale area map and some hints about seasonal conditions. The individual crag chapters are provided with an easy-to-read title bar listing key factors such as aspect, altitude, rock type, climbing style and approach time. A simple colour coded graded list gives a snapshot of what routes are on offer. A quick glance will tell you if a particular cliff fits your requirements for the day.

Further detailed information can then be gleaned from the introduction sections, which give a more in-depth assessment of the nature of the venue. This includes vital conditions advice, approach details, descent information and access restrictions, if any exist. Each crag is supplied with its own approach map, which can be related back if necessary to the large-scale map at the start of the area section. The tabbing system on the edge of the page allows you to quickly thumb through to different sections of the guide. Look out for the additional **B** symbol on the page tabs. This indicates any relevant bouldering information, or in a few cases an overview of the main bouldering venues.

Kim Leyland relaxing after a big route on the West Buttress of Cloggy   photo: John Coefield ∧

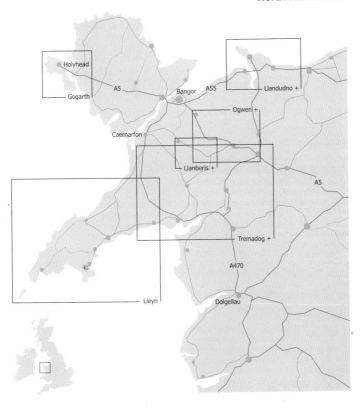

The guide has been divided into five distinct geographical sections which correspond to the navigation tabs on the side of the pages:

Llanberis + The famous Llanberis Pass is the most intensely developed area in the whole of North Wales. Also included in this section are the mighty cliffs of Lliwedd and Clogwyn Du'r Arddu and, of course, the quick-drying Dinorwig Slate Quarries.

Ogwen + The Ogwen Valley has numerous classic crags spread out along its southern side. In addition a number of secluded cliffs in the sprawling Carneddau mountain range can be found in this section.

Tremadog + The popular dolerite crags on the edge of the Tremadog coastal plain provide the focus for this section. A variety of outlying venues across the southern part of the region are also included.

Gogarth & Lleyn Although geographically separate, the wild sea cliffs of Gogarth and the Lleyn Peninsula have much in common. If you want some adventure, this is the place to come.

Llandudno + This section covers the limestone crags in and around the seaside resort of Llandudno, where you will find an abundant mix of classic sport and trad routes.

Mountains and Coast • Access and Conservation

There is a notable split between the weather conditions experienced in the mountain and coastal areas that fits well with the shift of the seasons. Although it is possible to climb on the lower altitude mountain valley crags throughout the year, the winter months yield fewer days when conditions are favourable for climbing. The difference in weather conditions and temperature between the mountains and the coast is often dramatic. Even if it is really lashing it down (or perhaps snowing!) in the Llanberis Pass and the Ogwen Valley, a visit to Tremadog, the Llandudno Ormes, Gogarth or the Lleyn Peninsula will often lead you to a dry and sunny crag.

In summary, the best tactic is to hang out on the mountain crags when the weather is good, and make a swift exit to the coastal crags when the rain clouds roll in. And thus, with a bit of luck and the odd smart decision, you should find dry rock more often than not.

Access and Conservation

Whilst it is true that the overriding majority of crags in the north-west Wales region have well-established access agreements, this should not be taken for granted. It is recommended that prior to your crag visit a quick reference is made to the British Mountaineering Council Regional Access Database which provides dynamic updates of any changes to access arrangements (**www.thebmc.co.uk/outdoor/rad/rad.asp**). For example, a temporary seasonal restriction may be applied if a rare bird is found nesting close to climbing routes. Of course, this restriction will be removed if nesting at the location ceases.

The Countryside Rights of Way Act, which was introduced in Wales in 2005, established a statutory right of access to areas of 'open access' land, i.e. generally, unimproved land above the 'fridd' line (the walled demarcation between improved farmland and open hillside). If you consider that prior to the act there was precious little in the way of access issues relating to mountain crags situated above the fridd, it becomes obvious that nothing much has changed. Nonetheless, many of the crags in North Wales lie on private land outside of the 'Open Access' areas, and consequently it remains imperative that good relations are maintained with the landowners. Bad behaviour from one or two individuals can quickly sour a long-established access agreement. Please be mindful of the sometimes delicate nature of these agreements, and always act in a respectful and considerate manner. If you encounter any problems, please contact the BMC immediately.

A number of the crags in this region are recognised as nationally or internationally important sites for conservation. They have been designated for various reasons relating to the vegetation, bird life or geology. The nesting sites of uncommon or rare birds are protected by seasonal climbing restrictions, which have been agreed with the BMC. Certain cliffs at Gogarth, on the Lleyn Peninsula and on the limestone cliffs around Llandudno have such restrictions, details of which can be found in the crag introduction sections. For easy reference, crags that have an existing access restriction, even it only applies to one or two routes, are marked in the title bar with the ® symbol. Furthermore, each route affected by an access restriction is marked with a ®.

Numerous books have been written about Snowdonia and its wildlife. A quick internet search or a visit to a bookshop will provide you with an extensive choice of background reading.

More detailed information regarding particular conservation and species issues is available from the following organisations:

The Countryside Council for Wales - **www.ccw.gov.uk** 01248 672500

The Royal Society for the Protection of Birds - **www.rspb.org.uk** 01248 363800

The North Wales Wildlife Trust - **www.wildlifetrust.org.uk/northwales** 01248 351541

LLANBERIS +

OGWEN +

TREMADOG +

GOGARTH & LLEYN

LLANDUDNO +

As a general guide to good behaviour, the Countryside Code provides some sensible advice:

Respect • Protect • Enjoy

- Be safe - plan ahead and follow any signs
- Leave gates and property as you find them
- Protect plants and animals, and take your litter home
- Keep your dog under close control or on a lead
- Consider other people

∧ Seasonal restriction notice at Red Wall, South Stack, Gogarth photo: Si Panton

Safety on the crags

Many of the crags featured in this book are situated high up in the mountain environment. Before setting out on the hill, make sure that you have an up to date weather forecast from a reliable source, and that you are suitably equipped to deal with any potentially hostile weather conditions. Waterproofs, food and water, sensible approach shoes (as opposed to 'bendy' trainers) or walking boots, and a map and compass should be considered essential items for a visit to a mountain crag.

The sea cliffs in this region can be equally serious places upon which to climb. Make sure you have either a copy of the tide tables, which are usually available from climbing shops or water sport shops, of which there are many in the North Wales area, or that you have consulted one of the many online tide prediction websites prior to your crag visit. If the approach involves an abseil, it is much safer to use an extra static abseil rope, which can be left in situ as a potential means of escape should it be required.

The majority of routes described in this book are multi-pitch. Consequently it makes sense to use double ropes; these will reduce drag on big pitches and allow quick abseil retreats. You should also keep a pair of prussic loops or rope ascending devices clipped to your harness at all times. These will be of great use in rescue situations and will get you out of all sorts of tricky scenarios should the need arise. If you are used to shorter outcrop style climbing, then you may find that your climbing rack will be inadequate for the big multi-pitch routes typical of this area. For example, on a sea cliff route it is not unusual to take in excess of 15 quickdraws (most of which should be extra long), half a dozen or more 120cm or 60 cm slings, a double set of cams up to size 4, a full double set of wired nuts and some lightweight hexes. You will also need extra gear to set up any abseils.

For a typical mountain route, you could probably drop a set of cams and some of the slings and quickdraws from the above list. There are of course many crags in the area where a more conventional rack will suffice. On the sport routes a single rope and 10 quickdraws will normally be enough, although it is common practice, especially on the limestone crags, to carry some wires.

Silvia Fitzpatrick slotting in another sinking wire on **The Strand** E2 5b, Upper Tier, Gogarth photo: Ray Wood ∧
Helicopter rescue from Main Cliff, Gogarth photo: Graham Desroy ∧

Head injuries are common in climbing accidents, so it seems sensible that all climbers, whatever grade they climb, should consider wearing a helmet. Luckily there is a wide range of lightweight helmet designs currently available. If you haven't got one, go and try one on at your local climbing shop, you'll be surprised how comfortable (and stylish) they are these days.

First Aid: If spinal or head injuries are suspected, do not move the patient without skilled help, except to maintain breathing or if this is essential for further protection.
If breathing has stopped, clear the airways and start artificial respiration. Do not stop until expert opinion has diagnosed death.
Summon help as quickly as is compatible with safety.

Rescue: In the event of an accident, where further assistance is required, dial 999 and ask for North Wales Police Mountain Rescue if the accident occurred inland, and for the Coastguard if the accident occurred on a sea cliff. Give as many details as possible including a grid reference, if possible. Bear in mind that mobile phones cannot always be relied upon to work as signal quality will be found to vary considerably, especially in mountain areas.
In the event of a helicopter evacuation secure all loose equipment, clothing, rucksacks, etc. All climbers in the vicinity should try to make themselves safe. Do not approach the aircraft unless told to by the crew.

Mountain Rescue Teams: The local Mountain Rescue teams are manned by volunteers and funded almost entirely by donations. Please help to support their valuable work by making a donation. Details of how to donate can be found on the following websites:

www.llanberismountainrescue.co.uk
www.ogwen-rescue.org.uk
www.aberglaslyn-mrt.org

Local Accommodation and Facilities • Definitive Guidebooks

The north-west corner of Wales is a popular tourist destination, and as such it is well served with accommodation to suit the weary traveller. All tastes are catered for: campsites, bunkhouses, youth hostels, bed and breakfasts and hotels. The choice is huge, but there are a number of traditional campsite bases popular with climbers. For example, opposite the Vaynol in Nant Peris (or just up the road at Snowdon House), Garth Farm just opposite the RAC Boulders, the Llyn Gwynant campsite, the Gwern Gof Isaf and Gwern Gof Uchaf campsites in the Ogwen Valley, Eric's Café at Tremadog and Outdoor Alternative at Rhoscolyn.

There are numerous cafes, pubs, ice cream parlours, restaurants, and takeaway food establishments in the local villages. Food shopping is well catered for too with various wholefood shops, bakeries, butcher shops and supermarkets in the towns and villages throughout the area.

Llanberis, Capel Curig and Betws y Coed have the highest concentration of climbing and general outdoor shops. But you will also be able to find supplies in Bangor, Caernarfon and Beddgelert.

The two main climbing walls in the area are the Beacon Climbing Centre in Waunfawr (see their advert on page 24) and the Plas y Brenin wall in Capel Curig (see their advert on page 255).

If you are looking for a rainy day alternative to climbing, then mountain bike hire is available from a few outlets, such as the V12 Outdoor shop in Llanberis (see their advert on page 5).

www.snowdonia-active.com provides a whole host of information about local guides, instructors and activity providers, accommodation and campsites, outdoor shops and cafes. Check out the Directory, a geographically specific database covering outdoor orientated businesses in the north-west Wales area. The site is also host to a whole range of downloadable activity and area guides and it has links to numerous weather forecasting websites.

Public Transport: Although the Snowdonia area is well served with a modern road network there are many alternatives to traveling by private car. The Snowdonia National Park, the Lleyn Peninsula and Anglesey are criss-crossed with a network of local and regional buses, and rail links. In the northern part of the National Park the special Sherpa bus service connects the most popular climbing areas to adjacent towns and villages.

Definitive Guidebooks

There is a range of definitive guidebooks covering the North Wales area. These provide a deeper level of coverage than is possible in the pages of a selective guide. Regular visitors to the area may wish to consider investing in one of the following:

Llanberis (Climbers' Club, Iwan Arfon Jones, 2004)

North Wales Slate (Ground Up, Mark Reeves, Pete Robins, due out in 2007)

Clogwyn Du'r Arddu (Climbers' Club, Nick Dixon, 2004)

Lliwedd (Climbers' Club, Kelvin Neal, 1998)

Ogwen and Carneddau (Climbers' Club, Iwan Arfon Jones, 1993)

Ogwen (Climbers' Club, Mike Bailey, due out in 2007)

Tremadog (Climbers' Club, Iwan Arfon Jones, Dave Ferguson, Pat Littlejohn, 2000)

Cwm Silyn and Cwellyn (Climbers' Club, Bob Wightman, Paul Jenkinson, 2003)

Meirionnydd (Climbers' Club, Martin Crocker, John Sumner, Terry Taylor, Elfyn Jones, 2002)

Gogarth (Climbers' Club, Andy Newton, 1990)

Lleyn (Climbers' Club, Iwan Arfon Jones, Dave Ferguson, Pat Littlejohn, 2002)

North Wales Limestone (Rockfax, Alan James, 1997)

North Wales Bouldering/Bowldro Gogledd Cymru (Northern Soul, Simon Panton, 2004)

Welsh language

Welsh is the first language for the majority of local people in this part of Wales. You will hear it spoken as you move around the local villages and towns, and you will notice that most signposts are bilingual Welsh/English.

As a basic introduction some useful words and phrases are shown below:

Croeso – Welcome
P'nawn da – Good afternoon
Nos da – Good night
Diolch yn fawr – Thank you very much
Mae'n ddrwg gen i - Sorry
Paned o de – Cup of tea
Peint o gwrw – Pint of beer
Afon – River
Dyffryn – Valley
Mynydd – Mountain
Clogfaen – Boulder
Congl, Cornel - Corner
Llech – Slab
Crib - Arete
Dringo – Climbing

Bore da – Good morning
Noswaith da – Good evening
Diolch – Thank you
Os gwelwch yn dda – Please
Iawn - Okay
Paned o goffi – Cup of coffee
Llwybr cyhoeddus – Public footpath
Llyn – Lake
Ynys – Island
Craig, Clogwyn – Crag, Cliff
Hollt - Crack
Rhych – Groove
Wal, Mur – Wall
Bargod, Gordo - Overhang
Bowldro - Bouldering

∧ The Parc Padarn bilingual sign, Llanberis photo: Si Panton

A Concise History of Rock Climbing in North Wales

The historical record of climbing exploits in the North Wales makes for inspiring reading. Each generation has left behind a trail of classic routes, which have been absorbed into the treasure chest of must-do climbs. This extraordinary legacy of brilliant routes draws climbers back to the area time and time again.

In the late 19th and early 20th century the mountain crags of Snowdonia provided a training ground for aspirant alpinists. Long rambling routes on Lliwedd and the East Face of Tryfan were all the rage with the well-heeled gents who frequented the Pen y Gwryd hotel.

By the time of the 2nd World War standards had escalated significantly. Menlove Edwards, Colin Kirkus and Jack Longland, in particular, had pushed the boat right out leaving an impressive catalogue of groundbreaking routes in their wake. Routes such as *Western Slabs*, *Shadow Wall*, *Brant* (done in 1940), *Bow Shaped Slab*, *Curving Crack*, *Pinnacle Wall*, *Lot's Groove* and *Longland's Climb* stand as proud testaments to the vision, skill and courage of their authors.

Yet it was in the post-war years when working class climbers from Lancashire arrived on the scene that things really started to change. Joe Brown and Don Whillans, and the close knit Rock and Ice club to which they belonged, established an unprecedented roster of utterly classic routes. Up on Cloggy, and in the Llanberis Pass, the big lines were there for the taking. Joe and the rest of the lads simply got stuck in, whatever the weather. The resulting climbs are now sought after, iconic emblems of a time passed. *Cemetery Gates*, *Cenotaph Corner*, *Surplomb*, *Octo*, *Vember*, *The Corner*, *The Boulder*, *White Slab* – each one an inspirational siren for successive generations of climbers. As the '60s arrived Brown spearheaded a drive for new lines on the fine dolerite crags of Tremadog and throughout the outlying areas. Once more a range of enduring classics (*Vector*, *The Grasper*, *Tensor*, *Ferdinand*, *Dwm*, *Hardd*) emerged.

In the mid '60s the focus shifted to Gogarth, which was soon to be regarded as the most important sea cliff in Britain. A new wave of talent appeared on the scene. Pete Crew, Baz Ingle and Martin Boysen started to make their mark, however Brown remained pivotal to developments, climbing nearly fifty new routes on Gogarth during this period.

As the '70s arrived fresh benchmarks were being set, fitness levels were rising and equipment was improving. In 1974 Pete Livesey climbed *Right Wall* (E5 6a) on Dinas Cromlech; his landmark ascent typified the growing confidence of the new breed. Big bold lines began to fall and an even fitter and more tenacious class of climber showed up. Pete Whillance and Ron Fawcett made E6 a reality with *Midsummer's Night Dream* on Cloggy and *Lord of the Flies* on Dinas Cromlech.

Standards continued to rocket and almost immediately in 1980 John Redhead climbed the first E7, namely *The Bells! The Bells!* on North Stack Wall at Gogarth. The '80s proved to be a busy decade; initially the buzz could be found at Tremadog as a succession of top climbers struggled to make a stylish ascent of *Strawberries* (E6 6b), however the next major surge came in 1983/84 on the bolt protected limestone crags of Llandudno. Jerry Moffatt and Ben Moon broke the magic F8a grade with *Masterclass* and *Statement of Youth*, and soon everybody was clipping bolts and hanging out on the Marine Drive.

By the mid '80s the Llanberis slate quarries were in vogue – a sustained burst of activity yielded a rush of new routes. Johnny Dawes' ascent of *The Quarryman* (E8 6c) in 1986 was a real landmark. Johnny then topped this remarkable route with an outrageous headpoint of Cloggy's last great challenge. Twenty years later *Indian Face* (E9 6b/c) has yet to see a ground up ascent.

Gogarth saw a resurgence of interest in the late '80s, which lasted through into the '90s, when the even more adventurous sea cliffs of the Lleyn Peninsula enjoyed a boom of new lines. In 1990 Jerry Moffatt returned and established *Liquid Amber* (F8c) on Lower Pen Trwyn, then in 1996 Neil Carson produced another desperate sport climb on this crag. *The Big Bang* was rated F9a and ten years later it remains unrepeated.

Liam Desroy setting off on the direct finish of the classic **Cemetery Gates** E1 5b, whilst his dad (Streaky Desroy) belays >
photo: Alex Messenger

The mid '90s were characterised by the rise of bouldering and a spate of fearsome head-point ascents. Leo Houlding's *Trauma* (E9 7a) on Dinas Mot stands out as 'the' route of the time. A toxic mix of desperate climbing and menacing danger, overcome by a very on-form climber.

These days there is a healthy spread of activity across the different crags. Naturally the flow of new routes has slowed, but what is emerging is an inspiring emphasis upon style. There has been a notable shift away from the headpoint ethic towards a more traditional ground up approach – a climbing style that all climbers, no matter what their leading grade, can relate to.

Grades

This guide uses the standard British grading system for traditional runner-protected climbs. This runs in ascendance through the full range of difficulty, from straightforward climbs suitable for beginners, right up to state-of-the-art test pieces: Difficult, Very Difficult, Severe, Hard Severe, Very Severe, Hard Very Severe, and Extremely Severe, an upper range which is subdivided into numbered E grades (E1 to E11, although the hardest climb described in this book is E7). This adjectival grade gives an overall impression of the difficulty of the climb, taking into account factors such as how serious it is, how physically sustained it is and how technically difficult the climbing is. There is also an additional technical grade (4a, 4b, 4c, 5a, 5b, 5c, 6a, 6b, 6c, 7a), which gives an indication of the hardest single move on a given pitch.

Sport climbs are described with the simple linear French system: F5, F5+, F6a, F6a+, F6b, F6b+, etc, right up to F8b, the hardest featured route in this guide.

There is an approximate parity between a given sport grade and a well protected traditional route, however there are so many other factors governing the difficulty of a Welsh traditional route - beyond the physical and technical difficulty, which are covered by a sport grade - that any comparisons should be treated as no more than very rough guides. For example, F6a would be similar to a well-protected E1, but only to someone familiar with placing natural protection and dealing with the myriad challenges of a typical traditional route (e.g. loose rock, navigation of line, etc.).

Boulder problems are described with a split grade of the American 'V' system, which runs from V0- to V16, and the Fontainebleau system, which runs from Font 3 to Font 8c+.

The intro sections to each of the crags gives a colour-coded list of the featured routes, which can be seen below. (The grade conversion table can be used for reference.)

	UK (adjectival - technical)	**French** (sport)	**American**
E6 and above	D	F2	5.2
E3 – E5	VD	F2+,3	5.3/5.4
HVS – E2	S — 4a,b	F3+	5.5/5.6
S – VS	HS — 4a,b,c	F4	5.6/5.7
D – VD	VS — 4b,c/5a	F4+	5.8
	HVS — 4c/5a,b	F5,5+	5.9/5.10a
F7c and above	E1 — 5a,b,c	F6a	5.10b
F7a – F7b+	E2 — 5a,b,c/6a	F6a+,6b	5.10c,d
F6a+ - F6c+	E3 — 5b,c/6a	F6b+	5.11a
F5 – F6a	E4 — 5b,c/6a,b	F6c,6c+	5.11b,c
	E5 — 5c/6a,b,c	F7a,7a+,7b	5.11d/5.12a,b
	E6 — 6a,b,c	F7b+,7c,7c+	5.12c,d/5.13a
	E7 — 6b,c/7a	F8a,8a+	5.13b,c
	E8 — 6c/7a	F8b,8b+	5.13d/5.14a

< Glenda Huxter on **The Bells! The Bells!** E7 6b, North Stack Wall, Gogarth photo: Al Leary

Graded List • Traditional Routes

Here it is; a lifetime's worth of climbing condensed into one humungous list. Time to get ticking!

E7

Dawes of Perception
Kaya
The Clown

E6

Strawberries
Other Realms
Dreams and Screams
Jub Jub Bird
Conan the Librarian
Glyder Crack
Skinhead Moonstomp
Potency
The Disillusioned Screw Machine
The Rainbow of Recalcitrance
Ludwig
Pretty Girls Make Graves
The Cad
Scare City
Foulish Goulish
OlympusTrip
A Midsummer Night's Dream
Lord of the Flies
Gold Rush

E5

Crow
Atomic Hotrod
Quantum Jump
King Wad
Mammoth (Direct)
The Bog of the Eternal Stench
The Nectarine Run
The Kicker Conspiracy
Cystitis by Proxy
Flashdance/Belldance
Cruella Deville
Tufty Club Rebellion
Bananas
Scary Canary
Cockblock
Pyschic Threshold
Hunger
Heading for Heights
Flake Away
Womb Bits
Connie's Crack
Poacher
Heading The Shot
Mr Olympia
Never Never Land
Energy Crisis
The Long Run
Magellan's Wall
Crimson Cruiser
The Thoughts of Chairman Ray
Long Kesh
Mur y Meirwon

Hydraulic Transmission
Schittlegruber
Helmet Boiler
Bittersweet Connection
Jack of Shadows
The Cruise
Splitstream
Death Trap Direct
Nimitz
Plas Berw
Doenitz
Dinosaur
Heart of Gold
Tentative Decisions
Catalyst
Waves of Inspiration
Private Investigations
Call it Black
Major Headstress
Positron
Central Sadness
Honeydew
The Cow
Citadel
The Great Arête
Poetry Pink
More Genius
Run Fast, Run Free
Reactor
Bathtime
The Exile
Chain Gang
Killerkranky
Right Wall
Rimsky Korsakov
Warpath

E4

Vulture (Cilan)
Zangorilla
The Camel
Roc Ness Monster
The Atomic Finger Flake/Void
Zukator
The Skull
Sexual Salami
New Dimensions
Fear of Infection
The Axe
Astoroth Direct Finish
Penal Servitude
What a Difference a Day Makes
Vulture (Craig Bwlch y Moch)
The Boldest/Direct Finish
Fingerlicker
Snowdrop
Ormuzd
Slug Club Special
Resurrection
Wildebeest
Ride the Wild Surf

Great Balls of Fire
Scarlet Runner
Clonus
The Trail of Tears
Clonus Left-Hand
Opal Moon
The Mau Mau
The Viper
Short Stories
Cardiac Arête
Byzantium
Pen Trwyn Patrol
Godzilla
Cream
Non Dairy Creamer
Blue Peter
Arachnid
Great Wall
Beasts of the Field
Katana
Cannibal
Pagan
Dogs of War
Gritstone Gorilla Direct
Rapture of the Deep
Frozen Moment/New Wave
Weasels Rip My Flesh
Nosferatu
Kubla Khan
Electric Blue
Soap on a Rope
Metal Guru/Golden Bough Finish
Strike
The Mermaid etc
Direct Hit
Rapture
The Visionary
Precious Time
Mordor
Jacuzzi Jive
Twisting by the Pool
The Sweetest Taboo
Hyndsight

E3

Vulcan
Quasar
Neb Direct
Stroll On
Sacred Idol
Pulsar
Syringe
West Buttress Eliminate
Samurai Groove
Central Wall
Memory Lane
Foil
20,000 Leagues Under the Sea
T. Rex
Colossus
Television Route

Silly Arete
Supercrack
Scarlet Runner Direct
Manx Groove
Solid Gold
The Burning
Horse Latitudes (Horsing Around Finish)
Stratosphere
Capital Punishment
Demetreus
Bloody Slab
Goose Creature
Oriole
November
Satsuma Special
Geireagle
King Kong/Troubador
Comes The Dervish
El Guide Direct
The Hand Traverse
The Exterminating Angel
Lubyanka
Homicide Wall
Ghosts
Green Wall
South Sea Bubble
This Year's Model
The Rat Race
Sai Dancing
The Cruel Sea
The Assassin
Old Sam
Winking Crack
Gritstone Gorilla
Hysteresis
Wonderwall
Mantrap
Left-Hand Red Wall
Deygo
Redshift
Left Wall Direct Finish
Blue Remembered Hills
Fantasia
The Hole of Creation
The Big Groove
The Moon
Plumbline
Centrefold
A Cry of Angels
Incredible Surplus Head
Klondike
Pocket City
The Path to Rome
Cripple Creek
Rembrandt Pussyhorse
Anchovy Madonna
A New Austerlitz
Firefly
Day of Reckoning
Clear White Light
Goldcoast
The Sind
Kalahari
The Mask of Red Death
Creeping Lemma

E2

Pincushion
Appian Way
The Great Corner
Grond
Nimbus/The Snake
Surplomb
The Wasp
The Sun
Orpheus
Spectrum
Astoroth
Chreon
Left Wall
Never as Good as the First Time
Phoenix
Wendigo
Is it a Crime
The Mostest
Far from the Madding Throng
Ten Degrees North
Silhouette
Daddy Cool/The Sting
Aura/Pinnaclissima
German Schoolgirl
Samurai
Ferdinand
Hebenwi
Bran Flake
Jelly Roll
Jabberwocky
Quietus
The Glass Wall
The Burner
Pull My Daisy
Yellow Wall
The Spider's Web
Fail Safe
Tensor
The Troach
Plastic Nerve
Scorpio
Woubits
The Stebbing
Overhanging Arête
The Savage Sunbird
The Strand
Sterling Silver
Pinnacle Arete
Suicide Wall Route 1
Valor
Holy, Holy, Holy
Zarquon/Resurrection/Erection
Resolution Direct
Rowan Tree Slabs
Shrike
The Thing
Erosion Groove Direct
Extraction
Grasper
Mabinogion
First Amendment
Slippery People
Red and Yellow, etc (R.O.Y finish)
Psychotherapy

Vector
Last Tango in Paris
The Wrack
Trouble with Lichen
The Quartz Icicle
The Monster
Suicide Wall Route 2
Knowing Her etc
Kanly
Atlantis/True Moments/Freebird
White Slab
The Weaver
Hardd
Slape Direct
Torero
The Bardsey Ripple
The Death Wisher
Limestone Lemur
Talking Heads
Flytrap
Toiler on the Sea
Aardvark
The Savage
Massambula
Primate
Merchant Man
U.F.O.
The Eternal Optimist
Rastus
Mousetrap
Excursion
Red Wall
SS Special

E1

Hangover
Octo
Old Holburn
Nexus
The Grooves
Cenotaph Corner
First Slip
Nightride
The Monster Kitten
Diapasan
California Arete
Seams the Same
Fool's Gold
Llithrig
Superdirect
The Groove
Canol
Bella Lugosi is Dead
Fifth Avenue
Park Lane/Doomsville Connection
Penamnen Groove
Barbarian
North-West Passage
The Wall
Vember
Mestizo
Troy
Rampart Corner
Launching Pad
Terminator

21

Graded List • Traditional Routes

Looning the Tube
Devil's Nordwand
The Boulder
Swastika
Emulator
Falcon
Gogarth
Gnat Attack
Breaking the Barrier
One Step in the Crowds
Overlapping Wall
Leg Slip
The Plum
Javelin Blade
Hombre
Bauxed
Efnision
Helsinki Wall
Elliw
Grim Wall Direct
Dwm
Great Feat/Mean Feat
Condor
Anarchist
Sea Panther
Hydro
Cemetary Gates
Tantalus
Precious Metal
Ivy Sepulchre
Nice 'n' Sleazy
The Wild Rover
Connor's Folly
Pale Shelter

HVS

Plexus
Crucible
The Ramp
The Concrete Chimney
Fratricide Wall
Sickle
Wind
Yellow Crack
Green Slab
Spider Wall
Bruvers
King Bee Crack
Phagocyte
The Fang
Jubilee Climb
Gollum
Superdirect
Boot Crack
Herford's Crack
Pedestal Crack
Black Spring
The Corner
Spitting Image
Lighthouse Arête Direct/Blanco
Javelin
Strapiombo
Solstice
Fantan B
Continuation Cracks

Avernus
Diagonal
Central Park
Karwendal Wall
Kaisergebirge Wall
Scavenger
Spectre
A Dream of White Horses
Mental Lentils
Central Route/Scarface/Groove finish
Get Close
Mean Feat
Grey Arete
Flake Wall
West Rib
Lot's Groove
Yob Route
Sheaf
Stromboli
Diadem
Scratch Arete
Meshach
The Gauntlet
Icarus
Lorraine Direct
Bochlwyd Eliminate
Vertigo
Wen
Cordon Bleu
Kirkus Direct
Britomartis
Space Below My Feet
Curver
Gallop Step
Munich Climb
Brant Direct
The Mole
Mur y Niwl/Pinnacle Wall
The Hylldrem Girdle
Merlin/Direct Finish
Great - Bow Combination

VS

Rift Wall
Pigott's Climb
Cobweb Crack
The Direct Route
Striptease
Kirkus's Route (Craig yr Ogof)
Bloody Chimney
Llyn
Shadrach
Touch and Go
Rocking Chair
Double Criss
Bezel
Overhanging Chimney
Ribstone Crack
Phantom Rib
Shadow Wall
Original Route
Zambesi
Javelin Buttress
The Grimmett
Curving Crack

Equinox
Noah's Warning
Fallen Block Crack
Sabre Cut
The Sword/Route 2
Nea
Lorraine
Yellow Groove
Brant
Mallory's Ridge
Seamstress
Belle Vue Bastion
Longland's Climb
Flake Crack
Hawk's Nest Arete
Rap
Tension
Black and Tan
Heather Wall
Kirkus's Route (Craig Lloer)
Grey Slab/Lost Boot Climb
Creagh Dhu Wall Direct
Plumbline
One Step in the Clouds
Grim Wall
Rainbow Warrior
Guillemot's Groove
Oxine
Eagle Finish
Lavaredo Wall
Zigzag
Pinky
Imitator
Red Wall Escape Route
Lightning Visit
Big Gut
Clutch
Scratch
East Wall Girdle
Western Slabs
Slow Ledge Climb
Truant
Princess
Lighthouse Arête

HS

Main Wall
Manx Wall
The Cracks
Zig Zag Climb
Skylon
Direct Route
Dives/Better Things
Wall Climb
Soapgut
Paradise/Black Arête
Creagh Dhu Wall
Christmas Curry/Micah Eliminate
Valerie's Rib
Marble Slab
Adam Rib
Angel Pavement
White Streak/Honeysuckle Corner
Tennis Shoe
Jacob's Media
Slab Climb Right-Hand

S

Monolith Crack
Lazarus
Groove Above
Crown of Thorns
Devil's Staircase
The Gambit Climb
Avalanche/Red Wall/Longland's
Continuation
Crackstone Rib
Slack
Poor Man's Peuterey
Central Route
Gamma
Kirkus's Climb Direct
Chimney Climb
Asahel

VD

Great Gully
Reade's Route
Wrinkle
Parchment Passage
Rectory Chimneys
Sub-Cneifion Rib
Horned Crag Route
Hope
Gashed Crag
Devil's Kitchen Route
Overlapping Rib Route
Spiral Stairs
Grooved Arete
Pinnacle Ridge Route
Direct Route
Ordinary route
Pulpit Route/Ivy Chimney
Ampitheatre Buttress
Chasm Route
Central Arete
Rib and Slab
Pinnacle Ridge Route
Primitive Route
The Arête
Flying Buttress
Outside Edge Route
Eastern Arete
Left Edge
Bramble Buttress
Africa Rib
Y Gelynen

D

Ridge Route (Slanting Buttress)
Arête and Slab
Slab Climb
Ordinary Route (Ogwen)
Lockwood's Chimney
Ordinary Route (Cwm Silyn)
Rowan Route
The Parson's Nose

F8b

Bungle's Arête

F8a+

Menstrual Gossip

F8a

The Medium
Manic Strain
Statement of Youth
Muscle Beach

F7c+

Masterclass
Oyster
The Dark Destroyer
Spong (is good for you)
The Dark Half

F7c

I've Been a Bad, Bad Boy
Gin Palace
Forsinain Motspur
The Magic Flute

F7b+

Libertango
La Boheme Direct
True Clip
Plagued by Fools
Hidden Sign
Needle in the Groove

F7b

La Boheme
White Hopes
Homo Erectus
You've Had Your Chips
Barking up the Wrong Tree
Bloodsports
Dive, Dive, Dive
Mean Mother
Riptide

F7a+

Geordie War Cry
Axle Attack
Homo Sapien
Mayfair
The Bearded Clam
Laura
The Bloods
Captain Fingers
No Arc, No Bark
Night Glue
The Refrain
Face Race
Crunchy Toad IX

F7a

The Pink Pinkie Snuffs It
Mr Chips
Sweet Dreams
The Reflex

F6c+

Excursion Direct
The Pirates of Pen Trwyn
Mad O'Rourke's Kipper House
Clowns of God
Menincursion

F6c

Under the Boardwalk
Contusion
Cakewalk Direct
Route 3
The Cakewalk

F6b+

String of Pearls

F6b

Kaffe Fasset
Heaven's Gate
School Mam

F6a+

Skin Deep
Skin Game

F6a

Route 2
Beauty is Only

F5+

Golden Pond

F5

Route 1

The centrepiece of North Wales climbing, this remarkable crag-infested mountain valley has the highest concentration of classic routes in the whole area. From the colossal, sprawling Dinorwig slate quarries, on up through the rugged steep-sided Pass itself and across to the magnificent cliffs of Clogwyn Du'r Arddu and Lliwedd on the flanks of Snowdon, this is Welsh climbing at its very best.

The climbing is predominantly multi-pitch traditional, although single pitch climbs can be found in various locations. There are some sport routes in the Dinorwig Quarries, although these tend to be in the higher grades.

Seasonal Conditions: Climbing on the bigger and higher cliffs, such as Cloggy and Lliwedd is limited to dry summer spells, however the crags on the sunny north side of the Pass can be climbed on throughout the year. The obvious exception to the rule is Craig Ddu, which seeps with enthusiasm through the winter months. In showery weather the slate quarries are a blessing, they dry extremely quickly, and can be fully climbable, given a fresh breeze, within an hour of rain.

Getting There: On summer weekends both the Pen y Pass car park and the lay-bys in the Pass soon fill up with Snowdon-bound hill walkers. Your choice is to arrive early, or pay to park in the Blaen y Nant campsite. Alternatively park in Llanberis or in the large car park in Nant Peris and catch a Sherpa bus up the Pass. During the week, and particularly out of the school summer holiday period, parking is not usually an issue.

Llanberis, from which Cloggy and the lower slate quarries are accessed, is well provided with parking opportunities.

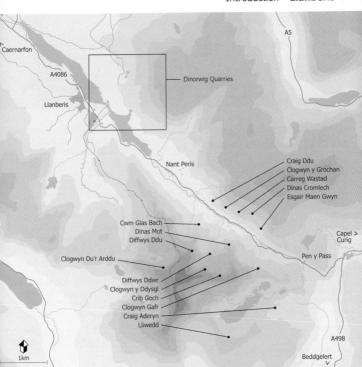

Caernarfon

A5

A4086

Llanberis

Dinorwig Quarries

Nant Peris

Craig Ddu
Clogwyn y Grochan
Carreg Wastad
Dinas Cromlech
Esgair Maen Gwyn

Cwm Glas Bach
Dinas Mot
Diffwys Ddu

Capel ⟩
Curig

Pen y Pass

Clogwyn Du'r Arddu

Diffwys Ddwr
Clogwyn y Ddysgl
Crib Goch
Clogwyn Gafr
Craig Aderyn
Lliwedd

A498

Beddgelert

1km

Al Leary and Matt Perrier stomping up to Cloggy on a hot summer day photo: Si Panton ∧
A shower clears and a rainbow forms, Llanberis Pass photo: Al Williams ⟨

Craig Ddu

Area: Llanberis Pass
Style: Trad (1-3 pitches)
Aspect: South-West
Rock type: Rhyolitic Tuff
Approach: 5 minutes
Altitude: 200m

The Bog of the Eternal Stench	E5
Mabinogion	E2
Orpheus	E2
Yellow Wall	E2
Canol	E1
Sea Panther	E1
Rift Wall	VS
Yellow Groove	VS
Zigzag	VS
Crown of Thorns	S
Rib and Slab	VD

An intriguing jet-black cliff that marks the entrance to the magnificent Llanberis Pass. This, the first and most 'roadside' of the crags on the north side of the valley, is perhaps the least conventional. Craig Ddu is a fascinating, almost surreal, place to climb. In many ways it is a crag of contradictions and contrast: it looks like a slab, but is in fact mostly overhanging, albeit in a gentle fashion. It has a friendly roadside demeanour, yet it is quite a serious cliff. The rock is very compact and smooth but it can be suspect in places. It takes an inordinate amount of drainage, yet it possesses an exceptionally sunny aspect.

Then there are the colours, so vivid in the evening sun: the intense blackness of the rock and the bright green vegetation conspire to mesmerise the uninitiated. All in all a quirky, leftfield venue best approached in a dry spell. You'll either love it or hate it. Indifference is an unlikely response.

Conditions: A very sunny crag, however the central section of the crag does take an exceptional amount of drainage after rain. Luckily, *Mabinogion* and most of the routes on the right side are not affected by the same seepage problem.

Approach: From the layby 100m right of the crag, follow a vague path up leftwards and across the hillside to reach the foot of the routes.

Descent: Walk over the top across grassy slopes, taking care when wet, to descend to the left (looking in) of the main crag.

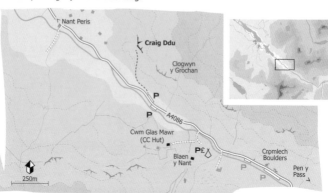

∧ Graham Desroy sampling the exquisite delights of **Mabinogion** E2 5c/6a photo: Si Panton

LLANBERIS +

OGWEN +

TREMADOG +

GOGARTH & LLEYN

LLANDUDNO +

Craig Ddu • Left-Hand Wall

Mabinogion 30m

30m left of the descent path, and level with the base of the main crag, lies a cracking micro route route:

1. Mabinogion E2 5c/6a 14m
A perfect little gritstone-esque route, packing quite a punch.
Climb the attractive diagonal crack with a testing move to gain good finger pockets. Cross the crack leftwards to reach yet another pocket and continue up (difficult at first) to a sloping ledge. The thin crack in the short steep wall above provides a powerful finale.
[W Todd, J Silvester 2.5.85]

2. Sea Panther E1 5b 52m
A fine route (when dry!); a little spooky at first, but superb climbing on the headwall.
P1 5b 37m Climb the wall right of the chimney flake with some spooky crux manoeuvres at around 8m leading to good holds and a system of ledges above. Trend rightwards and follow positive holds up a crack, before moving back left to gain a ramp. Finish up and left to a tree belay.
P2 15m Scramble up or off left to finish.
[D J Roscoe, B M Roscoe 9.5.80]

3. Crown of Thorns S 4a 55m
A pleasant, albeit relatively serious, excursion up a series of connecting ramplines leading to a final moment of reckoning.
P1 30m Start right of the usual watercourse where a boulder protrudes a metre out of the ground. Climb directly to a ledge at 8 metres, then follow the ramp up right, moving back up left to (possible belay) climb the wall above to a sloping ledge. Follow a further rampline up right to an open scoop and belay.

Rib and Slab Area • **Craig Ddu**

LLANBERIS +

OGWEN +

TREMADOG +

GOGARTH & LLEYN

LLANDUDNO +

P2 4a 25m Tiptoe up the flaky slab on the right, before stepping back left above the steep retaining wall to gain positive finger holds; a final tricky move remains. Continue up slabby rock and grass to reach a belay.
[P R J Harding, C W F Noyce 30.1.49]

4. Zigzag VS 4b 77m
A enjoyable and subtle climb shuffling upwards through improbable ground.
P1 4b 37m Start under a prominent overhang 6m up, and about 15m right of the *Crown of Thorns* starting boulder. Climb up leftwards to a grassy ledge at 6m. Go diagonally right to another grassy ledge. Step left into a short shallow groove and climb leftwards crossing an easy ramp-line to the foot of a right-slanting ramp line 3m higher. Follow this to a grassy stance.
P2 4b 40m Continue diagonally rightwards along a ledge system for 6-7m to gain the black groove, an obvious weakness. Steady away up this to the top, bearing left at the final steepness, and leftwards up the grassy slope to gain a belay.
[D Belshaw, J Brown 17.6.52]

5. Canol (with direct start) E1 5b 63m
A great route, with steep and interesting climbing.
P1 4c 18m Start below the right-hand end of a small overhang at 6m, a few metres right of *Zigzag*. Climb the ledgy wall to a move right at 8m. Continue up to reach a large block belay.
P2 5b 24m Scale the short steep wall on the left, behind the belay, to gain and then follow a rightward-sloping ramp. From its top pull through the left side of the overhang and move up to a ledge. A 10m easy traverse leads rightwards to a huge block belay.
P3 4b 21m Climb the obvious groove 2m left of the block belay and finish through the shattered rock gap in the overhangs.
[J Brown, D Belshaw 16.6.52]

Craig Ddu • Right-Hand view

LLANBERIS +

OGWEN +

TREMADOG +

GOGARTH & LLEYN

LLANDUDNO +

6. Rib and Slab VD 76m
A popular outing with superb open climbing.
P1 30m Climb the surprisingly problematic rib, past a steepening, to a broad terrace.
P2 46m Ascend the pleasant slab taking a line just left of centre. Care is needed with the final belay. It is worth staying tied on for the steep scramble, which leads left (facing in) to the descent.
[V J Wiggin, D R Meldrum 29.10.48]

7. Rift Wall VS 5a 60m
An engrossing route with a fierce crux.
P1 4b 21m Start in a bay at a rock step 8m right of an old metal fence post. Scramble diagonally left to a ledge. Move up for a metre or so, then follow a series of steep steps diagonally up and right to reach the base of the slab. Scoot up this to belay beneath the overhanging corner-crack.
P2 5a 27m Tussle up the steep corner, then saunter onwards (a little dazed, no doubt) up the slab to the top of a pedestal.
P3 4a 12m Move up to the bottom of a steep corner. Make an exposed swing onto the left arête on large flakes and finish more easily.
[J M Edwards, K N Davies, F J Monkhouse 27.7.49]

8. Orpheus E2 5b 55m
An absorbing and pumpy route. Take plenty of cams.
P1 5b 25m Start by the two low quartz bands. Move up and left on the grassy ledges below an undercut slab. Climb the left side of this for 2m until a rising traverse rightwards across the slab can be made to reach a small pedestal on the arête. Climb the steep wall above trending very slightly rightwards until final juggy moves lead through the overhanging band at its weakest point. Easily up the slab to belay top right.
P2 4c 15m Climb diagonally right up a short wall, then continue easily to a small bay. Exit from the right end of the bay and move right around a bulge to climb the arête to the top of the pedestal.
P3 4c 15m Move right and ascend a crack and overhang to finish up a groove.
[C J Phillips, R I C Kirkwood, J Arthy 13.6.67]

Craig Ddu

LLANBERIS +

OGWEN +

TREMADOG +

GOGARTH & LLEYN

LLANDUDNO +

9. The Bog of the Eternal Stench E5 6b 50m
A ferocious pitch which strikes a line directly up the impending black wall to break through the top overlap.
P1 20m. As for *Yellow Groove* to the block, then descend the ramp on the other side for 5m.
P2 6b 30m Climb straight up and then slightly left to gain a groove, which is followed to the break. A burly move up and to the right gains a peg at the overlap. Pull on to the headwall and crank with conviction for the top.
[P Pritchard 29.4.87]

10. Yellow Groove VS 4b 36m
A fine steep route blessed with an ample supply of positive holds.
P1 15m Start on the right-hand side of the obvious rock pyramid and scramble easily up to the block at its top.
P2 4b 21m Climb the groove above to an overhang, and move right to a ledge beneath a clean-cut groove. Scale this, then step left to finish up the wall.
[J Brown, D D Whillans 17.7.55]

11. Yellow Wall E2 5b 48m
Another superb route giving interesting, sustained and varied climbing.
P1 5b 27m Start on the right-hand side of the rock pyramid at the foot of the steep wall. Stiff moves precede a rest at 6m. From here, head up leftwards to gain a very shallow groove, which leads to an overhang. Turn this on the right, and go up to a ledge.
P2 5b 21m Traverse left beneath an overhang to a sloping ledge. Make a physical pull through the overhang and wobble up the groove to the top.
[D Yates, D Potts 16.7.62]

Jon Ratcliffe soaking up the sun on P1 of **Canol** (Direct Start) E1 5b
photo: Graham Desroy

Clogwyn y Grochan

Area:	**Llanberis Pass**
Style:	**Trad (1 - 5 pitches)**
Aspect:	**South-West**
Rock type:	**Rhyolitic Tuff**
Approach:	**5 minutes**
Altitude:	**250m**

Cockblock	E5
Quantum Jump	E5
Quasar	E3
Stroll On	E3

First Amendment	E2
Slape Direct	E2
Spectrum	E2
SS Special	E2
Surplomb	E2
Hangover	E1
Brant Direct	HVS
Karwendal Wall	HVS
Kaisergebirge Wall	HVS
Sickle	HVS
Spectre	HVS
Wind	HVS

Brant	VS
Nea	VS
Phantom Rib	VS

A popular roadside crag hosting an impressive array of classic outings and fierce testpieces. The Grochan is an intense uncompromising crag, which has drawn generations of climbers to pit themselves against its many challenging routes. Don't expect an easy ride, especially if you're not firing on all cylinders. The rock itself is invariably clean, but in places there are suspect holds that should be treated with care. The upper slabby section of the crag is more broken and vegetated.

Conditions: Although a very sunny and generally quick-drying crag the upper sections of routes such as *Brant,* and the rock adjacent to Goat's Gully, can be badly affected by drainage after rain.

Approach: A steep path leads up from the lay-by directly beneath the crag.

Descent: It is possible to descend via the steep and tricky gully on the western side of the crag (a finger-stone marks the initial chimney at the top of the gully). However it is common on most of the routes described to abseil back to the base of the cliff. Obviously this requires care, not to mention consideration of other climbers if the cliff is busy.

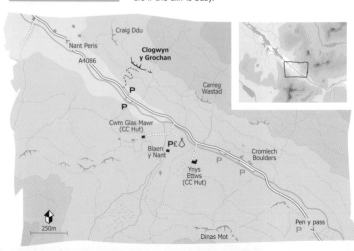

∧ Al Leary romping up P1 of **Spectre** HVS 5a photo: Si Panton
↙ Clogwyn y Grochan from Cwm Glas photo: Al Williams

Clogwyn y Grochan

1. Phantom Rib VS 4c 56m
An enjoyable and exhilarating trip up the line of connecting grooves and ribs left of *Nea*.

P1 4b 12m Start up awkward parallel cracks in the left wall of the gully, next to the start of *Nea*, stepping right and climbing past a tree to a ledge.

P2 4c 12m Go up the groove, and then traverse steeply right and pull up onto a ledge on the rib. Continue up the rib on small holds to gain a stance just above in a corner. Small wires will be appreciated on this thrilling pitch!

P3 4b 18m Walk right to a small corner behind a tree and then follow small ledges rightwards below two hanging grooves to a short groove in the arête. Climb this and step right into another groove, which leads to a large sloping ledge.

P4 4a 14m Traverse right along the ledge and climb the corner. Move back left along a narrower ledge and ascend to a belay directly above the previous stance. From here it is possible to abseil off as described for *Nea*, or finish up P4 of *Nea*.

[G W S Pigott, M Kennedy-Frazer, W H Stock 9.4.49]

2. Nea VS 4b 75m
A popular classic, tackling the obvious curving groove line that cleaves Goat's Buttress.

P1 4b 20m Start by scrambling up the easy gully to a grassy bay. Climb the groove until it divides. Follow the left-hand branch for 5m, and then step delicately right around the rib to gain a crack, which leads to a poky little stance.

P2 4a 23m Romp up the slabby corner-crack until a small chimney leads to a comfortable, albeit stone covered ledge, taking care not to knock any loose material from the ledge.

P3 4b 20m Swing out left onto the deceptively steep wall and climb a series of short grooves trending slightly leftwards to gain a large ledge. (It is common to abseil from here – 50m ropes will get you to the grassy bay at the start of the route).

P4 12m Finish up the steep wall behind. Belay well back.

[N E Morin, J M Edwards 10.9.41]

3. Spectre HVS 5a 78m
A fantastic and satisfying route, linking a series of splendid pitches.

P1 4c 20m Start at the lowest point of Goat's Buttress, 4m left of a square cut chimney. Udge up the innocuous looking thin crack to a ledge on the right. Continue up easier rock on the right, ignoring the ledge at the base of *Nea*, to a holly tree belay below a steep groove.

P2 5a 29m Climb the steep groove with difficulty to a ledge below a butterfly-shaped overhang. Trend leftwards into a hanging groove which leads up onto slabby sweep of rock. Scoot across rightwards to the foot of an intimidating wide crack.

P3 5a 9m The original 'Harding slot' is one of 'the' classic Welsh crack pitches. Gain a standing position in the slot via aggressive layback manoeuvres, a further burst of energy applied to the hand crack/flake should lead you to the respite of the belay ledge at the top of *Nea* P2. (Care is required with loose stones on the ledge.)

P4 4b 20m *Nea* P3. See abseil comment in *Nea* description.

P5 12m *Nea* P4.

[P R J Harding, E H Phillips 4.5.47]

4. Spectrum E2 5c 65m
A strenuous route sporting contrasting pitches: a deceptive first and a classic second.

P1 5b 14m Start 3m right of the square-cut chimney right of *Spectre* below some shattered overhangs. Climb up to the innocuous looking overhangs from the left. Pull directly into a shallow groove with good handholds, which quickly lead to a ledge. A bold and pushy lead.

P2 5c 30m Move right onto the wall and climb thin cracks to the overhang. Pull round this to better holds and follow the crack diagonally right to a ledge. Move diagonally up and left, in a 'goey' position, to pull over the left side of the overhang. Climb a groove to a ledge. Move right to a crack at the end of the ledge and climb it to belay beneath P3 of Spectre.

P3 5a 9m P3 of *Spectre*.

P4 4b 20m *Nea* P3. See abseil comment in *Nea* description.

P5 12m *Nea* P4.

[R Edwards, D Mellor, M Boysen (4 pts) 4.10.65, FFA: G Regan 1975]

5. S S Special E2 5b 84m

A justifiably popular first pitch which dissects the wanderings of *Sickle* directly.
P1 5b 46m Start left of *Sickle*. The right-hand crack of the slabby wall leads to a ledge. Continue up the steep thin right-hand crack to join *Sickle* at the roof. Move rightwards round the roof using a flake to reach easier ground above. Belay in a short corner above slabs. (It is common to abseil off at this point).
P2 4c 18m P3 of *Sickle*
P3 4b 20m *Nea* P3.
[D Roberts, P Williams, B Dunne 20.7.77]

6. Sickle HVS 5b 77m

An interesting route that follows a line of weakness up and across the slabby wall right of Goat's Gully.
P1 5a 21m The huge flake is surmounted by the crack on its right or left side. From its top, step left onto the wall and climb the thin crack to a ledge. Continue to a niche, and traverse right past some blocks to a sloping stance.
P2 5b 18m Step down and move across the wall on the left with difficulty to a groove. Go up this to the overhang (often wet), which is passed delicately on the left. Climb the slab to a stance and belay in a small corner on the right.
P3 4c 18m Cross the slabs on the left and follow a short steep crack in the left wall of Goat's Gully to a stance on *Nea*.
P4 4b 20m *Nea* P3.
[J Brown, D Cowan 30.8.53]

7. Brant Direct HVS 5a 23m

The striking groove line offers a compelling lesson in the art of bridging and jamming. The slightly overhanging groove leads to a junction with *Brant* on the long sloping ledge. Belay on the right and abseil retreat or continue up P2 of *Brant*.
[P R J Harding, J I Disley, P R Hodgkinson, G Dyke 24.4.49]

Clogwyn y Grochan • Central Buttress

Goat's
Gully

8. Cockblock E5 6b 23m

An aggressive and pumpy pitch, that has a habit of spitting off the ill-prepared and the unfit. Bouldery moves gain a ledge at 3m. Move up past a small pillar (good nut), before making a long reach up right. Keep cranking up until easier ground is reached at 15m. Belay on the long ledge above.
[J M Redhead, C Shorter, K Robertson 25.8.80]

9. Slape Direct E2 5c 21m

Another fierce little pitch.

Start about 5 metres down and left of the *Brant* sentry-box. Gain the leftward-slanting crack from the right and climb up to a small quartz ledge on the right. Some tricky manoeuvres and a memorable crank are required to reach a crack and better holds that lie above the bulge. Easier ground leads to a holly belay.
[M W Harvey, D J Abbott (1 pt) 23.9.54]

10. First Amendment E2 5c 45m

A physical P1 precedes an intimidating and initially serious P2.

P1 5c 21m Start a couple metres down and left of the *Brant* sentry box. Climb the strenuous thin crack to the *Brant* traverse. Continue up the corner to the tree.

P2 5b 24m Behind the tree is a large flake. From the top of this, make bold moves up the smooth wall; then continue up the superb, well-protected hanging groove above.
[D Roberts, P Williams 10.5.78]

Si Panton coming up to the belay on P1 of **Hangover** E1/2 5b photo: Graham Desroy **>**

Clogwyn y Grochan

LLANBERIS +

OGWEN +

TREMADOG +

GOGARTH & LLEYN

LLANDUDNO +

11. Brant VS 4c 113m

A devious classic allowing the VS climber to sneak through some impressive territory unscathed (well, relatively!)

P1 4c 21m Start 16m R of the *Brant Direct* groove, on top of blocks and below a sentry-box niche. Move up to the niche, then head leftwards across the wall, making tricky moves between a spike jug and a prominent juggy ledge. Step up and continue left, then up a short groove to a crevassed ledge (in situ slings) shaded by a holly tree. Pull straight up, swinging round left to reach a higher crevassed ledge and belays.

P2 4c 15m Traverse downwards along the sloping ledge, stepping down (all quite entertaining) to gain a short, steep V-groove. Work out which way to face, then thrutch upwards with conviction to reach another ledge system leading back right to a belay not far above where you started!

P3 4a 43m Follow the rising line of ledges leading up leftwards onto a slab. Continue up past an overlap and slabs to gain an obvious corner which leads up towards a large yew tree (this pitch is best avoided if wet). 60m ropes will get you back to the deck in one from here, while 50m ropes will require two abseils – take care with ropes jamming.

P4 4a 34m Follow the main nose of the buttress behind the yew.

[J M Edwards, J E Q Barford 5.8.40]

12. Surplomb E2 6a 39m

A full-on action-packed, must-do route!

P1 6a 24m Start as for *Brant*, but exit the sentry-box with a bouldery traverse right to a finger-jug. Continue boldly up on well-spaced holds, trending right to reach a ledge. The short overhanging V-chimney does not give in easily, but at least the gear is good.

P2 5b 15m Bridge up the chimney until a swing onto the left arête can be made. Continue up a shattered crack to a stance.

[J Brown, D D Whillans (1 pt)1.3.53, FFA: P Gordon 1959]

13. Stroll On E3 6a 40m

An urgent, pulse-quickening romp up the appealing crackline. The crux is pulling round the roof, but above there is little respite for the rapidly pumping leader. Make haste, or plummet.

[R Fawcett, P Livesey 5.5.76]

14. Hangover E1 5b 45m

A fantastic route that weaves in and out of the striking groove line. Could be E2!

P1 5a 21m The main groove doesn't quite reach the floor, so gain it from a further groove on the left. Steady climbing, although initially bold, leads up to a belay on a sloping ledge beneath the steep upper groove.

P2 5b 24m Swing out right past a shallow groove and blast up the steep wall on spaced holds, until a traverse line leads back left into the main groove, which provides a sustained and taxing finale.

[J Brown, R Greenall, M T Sorrell, F Ashton 18.5.51]

Clogwyn y Grochan • Right-Hand Buttress

Lords

15. Quasar E3 6a 37m

An infamous stopper route that is sure to trip up over-confident or careless leaders. Start 5 metres right of *Hangover*. A strenuous groove leads to an overhang. Pull out right to a good flake and resting ledge. The twin cracks above provide a stubborn crux, albeit one with a choice of methods for the canny. Climb the wall (as for *Hangover*) to a ledge on *Kaisergebirge Wall*. Finish up the groove as for that route.

[J Moran, A Evans, E Marshall 12.6.77]

16. Quantum Jump E5 6b 37m

A cracking pitch, coming on like a harder and better version of its neighbour, *Quasar*. Start a few metres right of *Quasar*. Step left and up into a short right facing groove and make a big span to good holds leading to the steep crack to the right of the *Quasar* crux. Swarm up the crack to reach the end of the *Kaisergebirge Wall* ledge. Finish boldly up the shallow scoop right of the finishing groove of that route to gain the 'Lords' ledge.

[R Fawcett 10.79]

17. Karwendel Wall HVS 5b 34m

A good route with a hard crux. Climb the shallow groove right of a small spike to join the *Kaisergebirge Wall* traverse. From the sloping platform, climb up slightly left at first until a stiff move right to a sharp hidden hold gives access to a rising traverse line which is followed rightwards to easy ground and up to Lords.

[H I Banner, J O'Neill, R Beesly 1.8.58]

18. Kaisergebirge Wall HVS 5b 30m

A grand climb that builds to a final moment of reckoning. Follow the obvious rising traverse-line leftwards to a good ledge. Move left again to the foot of a steep shallow groove, which provides a testing crux.

[P R J Harding, J I Disley, A J J Moulam (7 pts) 28.8.48]

19. Wind HVS 5b 27m

An aggressive little pitch, demanding a concerted effort from the leader (i.e. it might be E1). Storm up the steep thin crack with as much conviction as you can muster.

[M E Crook, J Moran 26.5.77]

Matt Perrier contemplating his next move on P1 of **Brant** VS 4c photo: Si Panton **>**

Carreg Wastad

Area:	**Llanberis Pass**
Style:	**Trad (2 - 4 pitches)**
Aspect:	**South-West**
Rock type:	**Rhyolitic Tuff**
Approach:	**10 minutes**
Altitude:	**350m**

Zangorilla	E4

Erosion Groove Direct	E2
Old Holborn	E1
Overlapping Wall	E1
Yellow Crack	HVS

Overhanging Chimney	VS
Ribstone Crack	VS
Shadow Wall	VS
Skylon	HS
Crackstone Rib	S

Wrinkle	VD

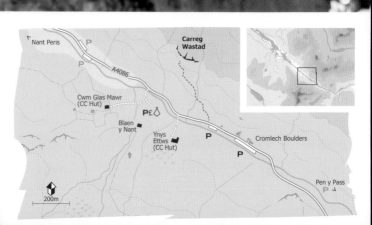

A sunny roadside crag hosting an attractive range of low/mid-grade routes. Although mostly solid, sections of the rock are not beyond suspicion, and should be treated with a degree of knowing caution.

While Carreg Wastad is slightly overshadowed by its popular neighbours, Clogwyn y Grochan and Dinas Cromlech, its routes still exude enough character and charm to draw a regular flow of climbers.

Conditions: Sunny and quick-drying, although some drainage will linger in the cracks after rain.

Approach: From the Ynys Ettws layby, cross the road and follow a narrow diagonal path up/across the steep hillside to reach the crag base.

Descent: Via easy gullies at either side of the cliff.

∧ Becky McGovern on **Shadow Wall** VS 4c photo: Alex Messenger

Carreg Wastad

1. Skylon HS 4b 70m
A delightful route with interesting climbing and good protection where you want it most.
P1 4b 40m Start below a slim groove/crack running up to a small overhang at 20m. Climb easily up to the small overhang and follow the small groove for a few moves before making an exposed step back left above the lip. Move up to a ledge, and then climb up rightwards to a comfortable belay stance.
P2 30m Move leftwards up the large flake then strike a direct line for the top staying left of a steep bulge. Scramble to the top.
[R Handley, E H Phillips 13.4.52]

2. Wrinkle VD 71m
A polished classic, finishing boldly on the upper fluted, slabby walls.
P1 24m Start as for *Skylon*, but move right up slabby steps, and then move back left to below an overhang. Make an airy traverse right to a gangway, leading right for 5m to an accommodating ledge and nut/thread belays in a ragged crack.
P2 20m Follow the wide corner crack at the right end of the ledge, until an awkward move gains a ledge. Traverse the ledge rightwards for 3m to reach a shallow groove slanting back left. Go up this and then continue up a wrinkled slab to a decent ledge.
P3 27m A short crack on the right leads to the top of a small pedestal. Follow the slabby grooves above with care to a ledge, and finish up the broken corner on the right. Be careful with suspect rock and belay well back.
[M P Ward, J E Q Barford, B Pierre - 5.47]

3. Overlapping Wall E1 5b 75m
A good route requiring a steady lead on P2.
P1 4c 27m Start below the chimney of *Overhanging Chimney*, just left of a large overhang. Climb up for 6m, and then traverse right on positive but creaky holds to a ledge. Move up, first left then right to gain the left end of a large quartz ledge. Climb up past a shallow groove and ledges to gain a stance below the large chockstone of *Overhanging Chimney*.
P2 5b 21m Ascend the groove and then gain its left rib. Move left again and break through the overlap at its weakest point. From a good nut, traverse left then go up and follow a groove back right to a ledge. Move right to belay in the corner.
P3 4c 27m Follow a rising traverse line across the right wall and go up onto the rib, which provides an airy finish.
[M G Hughes - 7.48]

4. Overhanging Chimney VS 4c 72m
An absorbing and varied route.
P1 4c 27m As for P1 of *Overlapping Wall*.
P2 4c 15m Ascend the corner and pass the bulging chockstone with difficulty to gain the chimney slot. Traverse out right to reach a belay in a small chimney.
P3 4a 30m Move up and again rightwards, before climbing directly up the wall and cracks left of the upper section of *Crackstone Rib*.

5. Crackstone Rib S 4a 54m
A much photographed classic.
P1 34m Start at the foot of *Erosion Groove Direct*. Climb a short crack to a ledge. A polished traverse line leads leftwards past a depression to the arête. Make a bold step around on to the arête and follow it in an exposed position to a ledge. Climb the short wall to gain a sloping ledge.
P2 4a 20m Ascend the easy groove on the right to a corner. Move up follow the traverse line on the left wall until it is possible to finish up a short steep crack.
[J M Edwards, J B Joyce - 14.7.35]

Carreg Wastad

6. Ribstone Crack VS 4c 52m
A sustained and satisfying crack line.
P1 4c 34m Start as for *Crackstone Rib* up the short crack to a ledge. Step right and work up the steep crack, utilising a variety of techniques along the way. A tricky section leads up into an open groove and then hop over a shoulder on the left to a sloping belay stance.
P2 4a 18m Move back right and finish via a huge flake.
[J I Disley, A J J Moulam (2 pts) - 22.3.51]

Becky McGovern on P1 of **Crackstone Rib** S 4a photo: Alex Messenger ∧

Carreg Wastad

LLANBERIS +

OGWEN +

TREMADOG +

GOGARTH & LLEYN

LLANDUDNO +

7. Erosion Groove Direct E2 5c 55m
This classic Whillans test piece takes the open groove running the full height of the cliff.
P1 15m Scramble up past the first of two holly trees, then step left into a crack that leads to a stance and belay on a huge flake.
P2 5a 20m After a difficult start the corner groove, on the left, leads to a small overhang at 15m which is passed on the left. Continue up the overhanging groove above to a stance.
P3 5c 20m Step right and make a tricky entry to the groove. The wide overhanging crack leads more easily to the top.
[D D Whillans, J Brown - 17.8.55]

8. Shadow Wall VS 4c 47m
A fine route with a thrilling traverse under the large diagonal overhang on P2.
P1 4a 27m Start by scrambling up to the foot of the groove that runs up to the left end of the prominent overhang. Ascend the groove past a holly tree to a belay under the overhang.
P2 4c 12m With escalating difficulty traverse up rightwards under the overhang along a system of 3 ledges. From the top ledge, a final crux move right gains a short groove, which leads to a tree belay.
P3 8m Climb easily to a good ledge.
[J M Edwards, J B Joyce - 14.7.35]

9. Yellow Crack HVS 5b 50m
Classic crack climbing – satisfying and brutal!
P1 12m Follow P1 of *Shadow Wall* to belay at the holly tree.
P2 30m 5b Step right and climb a steep corner crack, which turns awkward at 6m. Swarm up the crack to a large ledge. Make a long step right into the groove on *Zangorilla*. Follow this for a few moves then swing up left to a narrow ledge and a junction with *Shadow Wall* at its crux. Finish up *Shadow Wall*.
P3 8m Climb easily to a good ledge.

10. Zangorilla E4 6a 49m
An intimidating and spectacular route, which climbs through the large overhang above the *Shadow Wall* traverse.
P1 6a 34m Start 3m right of *Shadow Wall*, beside a huge flake. Move up to the steep groove above and follow it and the wall above to the yew tree ledge. Step across left into the steep, smooth, leaning groove. A burst of technical and fingery climbing leads to good holds. Move up left to belay on the ledges of *Shadow Wall*.
P2 6a 15m Undercut wildly out left across the overhang, with an awkward move to get established on the head wall. Finish boldly up the wall.
[A Sharp, C Dale - 2.7.77]

11. Old Holborn E1 5b 81m
Scrappy lower pitches lead to an exposed and rousing finale up the steep tower.
P1 4c 27m Start at a small rib with a groove on either side. Climb the groove on the right side of the rib, then swing left onto the rib. From its top make difficult moves right onto a slanting rake. Follow this and move up to a holly tree stance.
P2 4a 9m Climb the short groove from the left side of the ledge. Move left and pass a large detached flake with care to gain a grassy ledge and ash tree belay below the tower.
P3 5b 27m The steep and sustained groove behind the tree leads to a step right. Go up past a loose block to below the large roof. From a good handhold under the roof, make a daring swing out left to a hidden ledge. Move back onto the steep arête and climb up to small ledges. Poor belays.
P4 4c 18m Climb the wall above, trending right to finish. A bold pitch.
[P Crew, B Ingle, D Potts - 5.63]

Dinas Cromlech

Area:	**Llanberis Pass**
Style:	**Trad (1-6 pitches)**
Aspect:	**South-West**
Rock type:	**Rhyolitic Breccia**
Approach:	**25 minutes**
Altitude:	**400m**

Lord of the Flies	E6
Atomic Hotrod	E5
Right Wall	E5
Resurrection	E4
Foil	E3
Left Wall	E3
Memory Lane	E3
Grond	E2
The Monster	E2
The Thing	E2
Cemetery Gates	E1
Cenotaph Corner	E1
Ivy Sepulchre	E1
Cobweb Crack	VS
Noah's Warning	VS
Sabre Cut	VS
Dives/Better Things	HS
Flying Buttress	VD
Parchment Passage	VD
Spiral Stairs	VD

A dramatic crag, home to several of the finest routes in the area. Dinas Cromlech stands guard over the Llanberis Pass, a proud, turreted fortress that has defined the hopes and dreams of generations of keen craggers. This cliff is steeped in climbing folklore (Joe Brown on *Cenotaph Corner*, Pete Livesey on *Right Wall* and Ron 'Come on arms!' Fawcett on *Lord of the Flies*), and the mighty historical routes that breach its defences are a constant source of inspiration for all climbers.

Although not a big cliff in the traditional sense, its lofty position, perched on the steep slopes of Esgair Felen, afford it an added sense of exposure and grandeur.

The heavily pocketed rhyolite is brittle in places, but generally well-tested on the popular routes.

Conditions: A very sunny and open crag, however drainage persists after rain in the cracks, and typically on the right wall of the corner.

Approach: There are a choice of approaches: the traditional one thrashes up scree-loaded paths leading up to the right side of the crag, whilst a devious, but more pleasant path leads up from the left side of the Cromlech Bouders, cutting back right to reach the left side of the crag.

Descent: For routes that finish at the top of the crag, scramble up around the top of the crag to find a steep but straightforward descent gully leading back down the right side of the crag. For routes that finish on the 'Valley' it is normal to abseil down the wall just right of *Cenotaph Corner*, taking care not to dislodge any stones on climbers below.

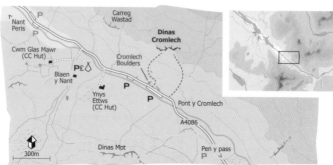

∧ Martin Crook hanging from a sinker jam on **The Grond** E2 5b photo: Ray Wood

↟ Dinas Cromlech photo: Si Panton

Dinas Cromlech • Left-Hand

1. The Thing E2 5b 38m

A compelling historic test piece, with well-protected and interesting climbing.
Follow the rightward-slanting overhanging crack up into an overhanging groove/niche. Undercut up past a hanging flake and move quickly past a pumpy section to gain a sapling; a broken system of cracks leads to the top.
[J Brown, D D Whillans 11.2.56]

2. Parchment Passage VD 36m

An alternately wild, then physical route tackling the leftmost of the three right-facing corners in this part of the crag via a devious and exposed diversion.
P1 13m Scramble up the vegetated ramp beneath/left of the tree to reach a ledge.
P2 23m Move up leftwards to a wild step onto the exposed arête. Follow a sloping gangway running back right into the polished corner, which is followed with sustained difficult climbing (thankfully well-protected), stepping right near the top to a steep finish.
[J M Edwards, O S Bell 27.3.33]

3. Cobweb Crack VS 5a 34m

A satisfyingly steep crack, which succumbs to a variety of techniques.
P1 13m Scramble up the vegetated ramp beneath/left of the tree to reach a ledge (as for *Parchment Passage*).
P2 5a 21m Climb the crack with continuous interest, moving left up the wide diagonal section to a junction with the top of *Parchment Passage*.
[J Brown, M T Sorrell 2.9.51]

4. Noah's Warning VS 5a 67m

A superb route, striking a direct line up the crag.
P1 4c 40m Start by scrambling up ledges to the base of the crack. Climb the steep and tricky crack, using helpful holds on the left wall, to reach a series of interconnected scoops leading up to an overhang. Turn this on the left to reach a ledge.
P2 5a 27m Ascend the obvious chimney/crack above until it steepens. Move up right into a shallow scoop. Pull out of this steeply to reach easier ground, and the top shortly after.
[J Brown, M T Sorrell 3.9.51]

Jon Garside on **Foil** E3 6a photo: Alex Messenger **>**

5. Dives/Better Things HS 4b 64m
A classic route, building to a crescendo on the superb upper pitch.
P1 4a 24m Scramble up above a quartzy slab to a large spike belay beneath a steep hanging corner *(Sabre Cut)*. 3m to the left, a strenuous crack leads up to the black diagonal overhang slanting up right. Climb diagonally right (often wet) beneath the overhang on rough aerated rock to an open ledge (known historically as the 'Forest').
P2 4b 40m The short crack on the left gives access to a V-shaped corner-crack. Sustained, but well-protected climbing leads to an easing as the groove slabs out. Continue up the crack to the top.
[J M Edwards 18.12.31/ T D Bourdillon, J W T Tomlinson 18.04.49]

6. Sabre Cut VS 4c 55m
A superb route, with a tremendous upper corner pitch.
P1 4c 32m Follow the steep hanging corner until it divides, then step out right and climb the wall to the 'Forest'. Continue up to a good belay on its upper right edge.
P2 4b 23m Traverse left and ascend the pleasant, albeit wide corner-crack to the top.
[E Pentir Williams, R G Williams 1935]

7. Foil E3 6a 24m
A spotless and testing pitch up the well-protected finger-crack in the wall right of *Sabre Cut* P2. Starting from the *Sabre Cut* belay, gain and follow the thin crack, which turns hard at 15 metres. Continue to a poor rest at a pocket. More strenuous moves above lead to an uncertain exit.
[P Livesey 1.7.76]

LLANBERIS +

OGWEN +

TREMADOG +

GOGARTH & LLEYN

LLANDUDNO +

Dinas Cromlech • Cenotaph Corner Area

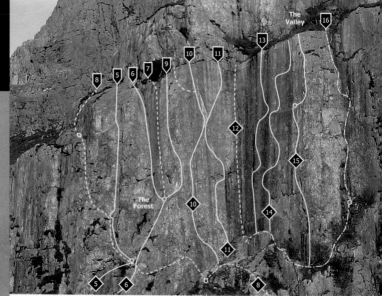

Cenotaph Corner Area

The central Cromlech walls tower over the valley like a huge open book. The opposing sheets of sheer rock, set at right angles across the arrow straight *Cenotaph Corner*, are home to a series of brilliant sort-after climbs.

8. Spiral Stairs VD 84m

A popular and exposed trip searching out a wandering line of weakness. Best suited to equally competent parties, as the traverse on P2 is quite serious to second.

P1 30m Scramble up polished ledges (see topo on page 55 for start), and continue left-wards along the narrow path beneath the vast left wall of the corner to a belay just up on the left, by a short crack.

P2 21m. Go up the crack then along the obvious leftward traverse-line, descending slightly for 15m, until a rib leads up to the 'Forest'.

P3 21m. Move across left to climb a short crack to a ledge on the left. Continue up left-wards on good holds via an easy slab to a poor stance and spike belays.

P4 12m. The chimney/groove leads to easy slabs.

[J M Edwards, S B Darbishire 6.12.31]

Routes 9 – 16 are accessed by scrambling up the polished first pitch of *Spiral Stairs*.

9. Memory Lane E3 5c 46m

A serious and sustained route; hard for the grade. Start at the *Spiral Stairs* belay. Climb the crack directly to the 'Forest'. Step right onto the left wall of the *Corner*, and climb diagonally leftwards to a ledge (crux). Follow the bold and fantastically positioned arête to the top. (It is common to place side runners in *Left Wall* to protect the lower crux.)

[P Livesey, J Lawrence, G Price 7.76]

10. Left Wall E3 5c 40m

A tremendous pitch and a source of inspiration for all climbers working up through the grades. Start on the large sloping ledge below *Cenotaph Corner*. Climb diagonally left to stand on a flaky ledge below the main crack. Follow this on positive holds, past a hard section where it slants up rightwards, to a good resting place below the fork. Regain your composure and prance up the thin left-hand branch, continuing directly with confidence for the top...or scamper out left on a line of hollow jugs after 6m (E2 if you go this way).

[R Moseley, J Smith, J Sutherland (several pts) 6.5.56, FFA: A Garlick 21.09.70]

11. Resurrection E4 6a 44m

An outstanding route which swaggers up the dramatic left wall of the corner to a fingery climax. Start just left of *Cenotaph Corner*. Move up leftwards for 5m, and then ascend directly on pockets (passing an old thread) to The Girdle ledge. Move right and climb up the left side of a flat rib, with a hard move to reach better holds. Move across to join *Left Wall* where the crack forks. Follow the right-hand fork with sustained difficulty to a good spike and runner. The most popular finish continues in the same line on small face-holds, making a big reach for a flat hold, before finishing directly. (The original finish made a long reach left from the good spike to sharp finger-holds leading to a shallow groove.)

[R Edwards, N Metcalfe (4 pts) 1975, FFA: P Livesey, J Lawrence 09.75]

12. Cenotaph Corner E1 5c 37m

A celebrated and duly polished classic, forging a direct line up one of the most striking rock features in Britain. Climb the corner passing a difficult move at 8m, and an obstinate crux section entering and leaving a niche, close to the top.

[J Brown, D Belshaw (2 pts) 24.8.52]

13. Lord of the Flies E6 6a 40m

A classic, but chillingly bold route, snaking up a seemingly blank sheet of rock; *Lord*... is an undeniably serious and lonely lead, demanding both fitness and supreme confidence. Start 3/4m right of the *Corner*, below thin vertical cracks. Climb the cracks until they run out, and then go directly up to a thin ledge. Finger-traverse right along this and make serious moves at its end to gain a large pocket. Continue up leftwards and aim for the next big pocket (crux). Runner in the pocket and also good nut in a short crack out to the right. Step right and ascend to better holds and *The Girdle* ledge. A few tricky moves up the wall gain a finger-ledge leading right to the base of a shallow groove and a sustained finish up the groove past a bomber large nut placement.

[R Fawcett, C Gibb 26.6.79]

14. Right Wall E5 6a 46m

An über-classic pitch that defined the state of the art in the mid 70s; a bold route-finding tour de force that navigates a parallel path to its neighbour, *Lord....* Start at the right-hand end of a grassy ledge at a short wall and short groove. Ascend the short wall to a ledge. Climb the groove, breaking out left up the diagonal crack (good wires). Move back right and continue up the wall on pockets to a narrow ledge and so to a good rest on the right. Step up onto a prominent foothold and climb leftwards to a large broken pocket, or move left a short way and ascend direct. From the top of the pocket, step left and climb up on small pockets to a line of holds rising rightwards to *The Girdle* ledge. Traverse right until directly below a shallow pocket, the Porthole, 6m above. Start up the wall just to its right; make crux moves to gain the Porthole and continue boldly to reach a series of finger ledges leading rightwards to a finish up a thin crack.

[P Livesey 15.6.74]

Dinas Cromlech

15. Cemetery Gates E1 5b 52m
A fantastic route set in an exhilarating position on the edge of this impressive sheet of rock. Start by carefully descending from the top of a huge flake right of *Cenotaph Corner* to a tree belay below the right arête.

P1 5b 34m Climb up first right and then left to the foot of the chimney/crack. Enter this boldly and follow it past an awkward section to a good ledge at 18m. Continue up the crack pulling through some final hard moves to gain The Girdle ledge.

P2 4c 18m From the right side of the ledge, ascend the wide crack for 5m, step round the arête to the right, go up steeply on a series of juggy incuts and reach the top.
[J Brown, D D Whillans 30.9.51]

16. Ivy Sepulchre E1 5b 59m
Another superb Cromlech line that is well-protected and utterly classic.

P1 25m Start by carefully descending from the top of a huge flake right of *Cenotaph Corner* to a tree belay below the right arête. Continue traversing right along the ledge and go up over two rock steps to reach a belay at the foot of the corner.

P2 5b 34m Follow the corner with sustained interest to a large overhung niche. Work up past the steepening (crux) and continue up the corner with a short deviation on to the left wall near the top.
[P R J Harding, E H Phillips (2 pts) 29.8.47]

17. Flying Buttress VD 87m
An essential, if somewhat polished, classic. Steep and exposed, but furnished with the regular occurrence of positive holds. Start just right of the prominent quartz exposure at the foot of the castellated ridge, which forms the right edge of the cliff.

P1 18m Ascend directly on large well-worn holds.

P2 18m Continue up the centre of the ridge to the pinnacles on its summit.

P3 6m. Climb over the pinnacles to belay on the left wall of the gully.

P4 15m Ascend the large rock steps on the left wall, and then step round the corner across a little groove (or reach this point from below, which is harder) to a leftwards traverse line and so to the pinnacle ledge.

P5 15m Climb the steep wall behind the flake to a rightward-slanting gangway. Follow this to belay on a ledge below a chimney.

P6 15m Make a difficult entrance to the chimney, which leads more easily to the top.
[J M Edwards 18.12.31]

Dinas Cromlech

LLANBERIS +

OGWEN +

TREMADOG +

GOGARTH & LLEYN

LLANDUDNO +

Routes 18 – 20 are each reached by linking with a route on the lower walls, or by abseiling in from the top of the crag.

18. Grond E2 5b 15m
One of the best hand crack pitches in the UK. Steep, clean and relatively featureless which means a delight for some and pure horror for others!
Attack the striking right-angled corner-crack with conviction, plugging cams at will (sizes 2.5 – 4).
[D D Whillans, J Smith, D Gray, J Brown 09.58]

19. The Monster E2 5c 21m
Another physical crack pitch: a perfect aperitif for those who enjoyed the challenge of the previous route. A rightward traverse on jams gains the crack, which provides sustained difficulties and a precarious finish where it widens. Exit just left of a perched block.
[M Boysen, E Volar 1972]

20. Atomic Hot Rod E5 6b 21m
A stunning American style finger crack, sure to cruelly expose any technique inadequacies in a prospective leader. Abseil in to the grassy ledge beneath the route. Climb up the corner first, then move left to the foot of the undercut and overhanging finger crack... and away you go!
[R Fawcett, P Williams 11.4.80]

Cromlech Boulders

Area: Llanberis Pass
Style: Bouldering
Aspect: South
Rock type: Rhyolite
Approach: 0 minutes
Altitude: 200m

The Cromlech Boulders sit conveniently adjacent to the Nant Peris – Pen y Pass road, right in the middle of the Llanberis Pass. The easy access guarantees their popularity, as does the attractive spread of problems throughout the grade range. There is something for everybody here, from kid's mini-boulders right up to the mind-boggling grade of V13/Font 8b. There is also an endless supply of arm-destroying stamina link-ups and variations.
The landings are generally okay, but if you have access to a bouldering pad then take it with you.

Conditions: Year-round climbing is possible although it can get a bit chilly in the depths of winter. It's normally possible to find whatever combination of shade and shelter suits the weather of the day. The boulders dry very quickly, although drainage streaks can persist on the roadside face after heavy rain. One or two of the landing areas become water-logged during rainy periods, but the majority are unaffected by drainage problems.

Approach: It couldn't be more simple: pull up in the layby beneath Dinas Cromlech and get out of, or off, your chosen mode of transport. During the summer season you may find it hard to park, particularly on a weekend, although spaces tend to start appearing from mid-afternoon onwards as Snowdon-bound hillwalkers return from Pen y Pass to their cars. It is also possible to park in the Blaen y Nant camping field further down the valley (next to Ynys Ettws, the Climbers' Club hut), although you may be charged for the privilege.

Si Panton pulling through the crux of **The Quickness** V7/Font 7a+ photo: Rich Betts ⋀
Helen John hanging in there on **The Heelhook Traverse** V4/Font 6b+ photo: Gruff Owen ⋀

Cromlech Boulders

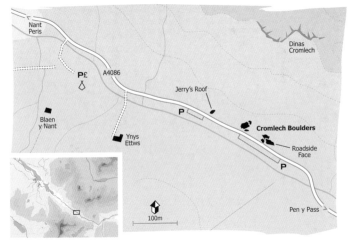

∧ Chris Doyle rocking up on Roadside Face classic **Ramp Left-Hand** V2/Font 5+ photo: Si Panton

Map labels:

Nant Peris · A4086 · P£ · Blaen y Nant · Ynys Ettws · Jerry's Roof · P · **Cromlech Boulders** · Roadside Face · P · Dinas Cromlech · Pen y Pass · 100m

Side tabs:

LLANBERIS + ⓑ · OGWEN + · TREMADOG + · GOGARTH & LLEYN · LLANDUDNO +

Esgair Maen Gwyn (Scimitar Ridge)

Area:	**Llanberis Pass**
Style:	**Trad (single pitch)**
Aspect:	**South-East**
Rock type:	**Basalt**
Approach:	**15 minutes**
Altitude:	**270m**

Killerkranky	E5
King Wad	E5
The Kicker Conspiracy	E5
Tufty Club Rebellion	E5
Roc-Nest Monster	E4

Chreon	E2
Troy	E1

A radical crag with an impressive collection of routes. Perhaps best known for the photogenic upper arête classic test piece *King Wad,* which is a regular take-off point for flying leaders who miss the final slap!

The rock itself bears a curious form, which is quite hard to read on first acquaintance. It is characterised by rather bizarre 'stuck on' plates, which thankfully take runners. The only problem being that these placements are often not spotted until you glance back down to find a foothold. So keep your eyes peeled! There are also number of in situ pegs dotted around the crag – obviously these should be backed up if possible. The routes described are generally quite solid, however some sections of the cliff feel a bit creaky, and should be treated with care.

Conditions: A relatively quick-drying venue that receives plenty of sunshine in the morning. In the summer the afternoon shade may be preferred on some of the harder routes.

Approach: From the Cromlech Boulders a pleasant walk leads along the valley bottom to a large boulder beneath the sudden and somewhat awe inspiring profile of the crag above. Grunt steeply up a choice of vague paths (least unpleasant if you keep mostly to the left) that weave up through the shifting scree to the base of the cliff.

Descent: Go up almost to the top of the ridge, traverse right and cautiously descend the steep scree gully that runs back down beneath the main face. If more than one route is to be done then it is quickest to abseil, then retrieve the kit after the last route.

(*Artemis* VD, the tree-filled groove at the bottom left end of the crag, provides a quick way to the top.)

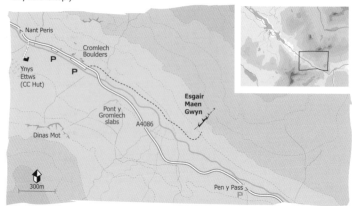

∧ Glenda Huxter going for it on the wild upper arete of **King Wad** E5 6b photo: Ray Wood

↟ Looking down the Pass to Pont y Gromlech photo: Si Panton

Esgair Maen Gwyn (Scimitar Ridge)

1. Roc-Nest Monster E4 6a 24m
A good introduction to the harder routes on the cliff. From 3m up the *King Wad* flake span left on undercuts to a peg, then move directly up on blind layaway holds, clipping a further three pegs as you go. Finish up either the groove or the arête left of the *King Wad* arête.
[E Stone, G McMahon, D Goodey 07.08.90]

2. King Wad E5 6b 30m
One of the best routes of its grade in the area. Spectacular positions and memorable climbing make this a bona fide classic. From initial easy ground move up and layback the obvious detached flake, then follow the groove above to a thread. Continue up and right to a niche, then bridge up to the base of a groove (peg). Take a few moments to rest and recover from the E4 section you've just climbed, then steel yourself for the dramatic finish: swing right onto the arête in a wild position and cruise past another peg to an uncertain glory!
[P Pritchard 18.06.87]

3. Tufty Club Rebellion E5 6a 27m
A tremendous pitch broadly tackling the blunt arête left of *Chreon*. Start at a loose flake 8m down and left of the *Chreon* groove. Climb up and left to good holds on a suspect flake. Pull up slightly rightwards to a slot, and then move straight up to undercuts. Traverse boldly rightwards around the arête to a peg, then move up and left onto the arête proper, which gradually eases to finish in a little black groove.
[A Popp, M McGowan 24.05.87]

4. Troy E1 5b 27m
A fine and exposed climb that follows the ragged wide crack line in the left wall of the groove of *Chreon*. From the base of the groove, step left to gain the crack. (The direct start is E3 6a.)
[J Walker and party 06.79]

5. Chreon E2 5b 26m
The large open groove provides a superb sustained pitch with an exposed finish.
[M Walton and party 06.79]

6. Killerkranky E5 6a/b 27m
This excellent pitch has reasonable protection, assuming you spot it all. It is also the easiest of the E5s here. The route follows the attractive thin crack line right of *Chreon*. A fierce pull through a low overlap leads into a sustained, but steady section gradually easing into an open groove, which runs to the top.
[M E Crook, N Thomas 04.10.86]

7. The Kicker Conspiracy E5 6a 27m
An imposing route with much character: very bold at the start, then technical and strenuous, but with decent protection thereafter. From the large pinnacle, move up, and then traverse left along a slab. Move up into a scoop (just right of *Killerkranky*) and follow it past two pegs to finish.
[C Waddy, S Chesslett 08.87]

Glenda Huxter bridging up the final groove on **Killerkranky** E5 6a photo: Ray Wood

Clogwyn Gafr

Area: Llanberis Pass
Style: Trad (1-2 pitches)
Aspect: North-West
Rock type: Rhyolitic Tuff
Approach: 25 minutes
Altitude: 400m

The Nectarine Run	E5
Pulsar	E3
Sacred Idol	E3
Satsuma Special	E3
Diapasan	E1

An intense little crag situated at the head of the dramatic Llanberis Pass. This brilliant outcrop, which was once referred to as Craig Fach, has a fine clutch of action packed routes. It is also a good bet if you're looking for somewhere quiet on a busy day (assuming you can find somewhere to park!)

Conditions: The crag receives afternoon and evening sun, but does suffer from some persistent drainage streaks following rain.

Approach: From the Pen y Pass car park (current charges are £4 for a full day, or £2 for a half day) follow the PYG track leading up towards Crib Goch. About 500m after the path runs through a boulder field, turn down the hillside on the right and drop down onto the crag. Alternatively walk, hitch or catch a bus up from the Cromlech Boulders layby and approach the crag directly from the road.

Descent: Down easy slopes at either side of the crag.

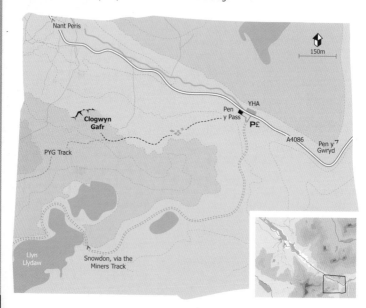

∧ Pete Robins facing an anxious moment on the upper section of **Satsuma Special** E3 5c photo: Jethro Kiernan

⬏ Welcome to Pen y Pass photo: Si Panton

Pete Robins keeping his cool on the headwall of
Nectarine Run E5 6b photo: Jethro Kiernan

1. Satsuma Special E3 5c 30m

An excellent pitch breaking out onto the pocketed headwall. Start up *Diapasan*, but move left above the roof, then reach up to a large pocket on the left. Continue up and left to a good spike, then finish up the rib. Take care with rope drag around the *Diapasan* roof.

[P A Targett, C Greatwich 23.06.92]

2. Diapasan E1 5c,5b 30m

A nifty route with contrasting pitches.

P1 5c 15m Start beneath the roof. Go up to the corner crack and follow it up to the roof. Shuffle rightwards in a cramped position, until it is possible to pull round onto a sloping ledge above. Belay on the right side of the ledge.

P2 5b 15m Ascend the steep crack (peg) and move up to a small pocket, before heading diagonally right to the steep arête. Go up the arête but, when 3m from the top, step round to the right to finish up a crack.

[T Panther, P Sorrell, J Fisher (3 pts) 23.08.64, FFA: D Pycroft, D Lancely 14.07.83]

3. The Nectarine Run E5 6b 37m

One of the best E5s in the valley! Start just left of the *Sacred Idol* corner. Go up the wall, clipping a RURP just beneath the short hanging groove. Ascend the groove with difficulty, then make a gripping traverse back down and right to a foothold just above the lip. More scary moves lead up the wall to easier ground. Be sure to get the good cam just above the flake, before finishing direct.

[J De Montjoye, H Sharp 25.06.86]

4. Sacred Idol E3 6a 30m

A well-protected, but fairly gruesome struggle up the obvious left-facing corner in the centre of the cliff.

[T Panther, R Stephens (VS/A3) 08.66/ Direct finish: T Panther, N Bradburn (VS/A2) 08.76, FFA: M E Crook, P Norton 09.05.84]

5. Pulsar E3 6a 30m

An outstanding pitch with the option of a fierce finish. Climb the crack a few metres right of *Sacred Idol* to a ledge at 20m. While the normal route traverses off right before finishing direct, the pegged headwall immediately above adds considerable spice, and is a must for those who were cruising on the lower section. Award yourself a sturdy E4 6a if you go for the *Red Giant Connection*.

[T Panther, P Warner, J Jiggins, S Mathewson (HVS/A3) 26.05.74, FFA: P Davidson, D Pycroft 20.07.83]

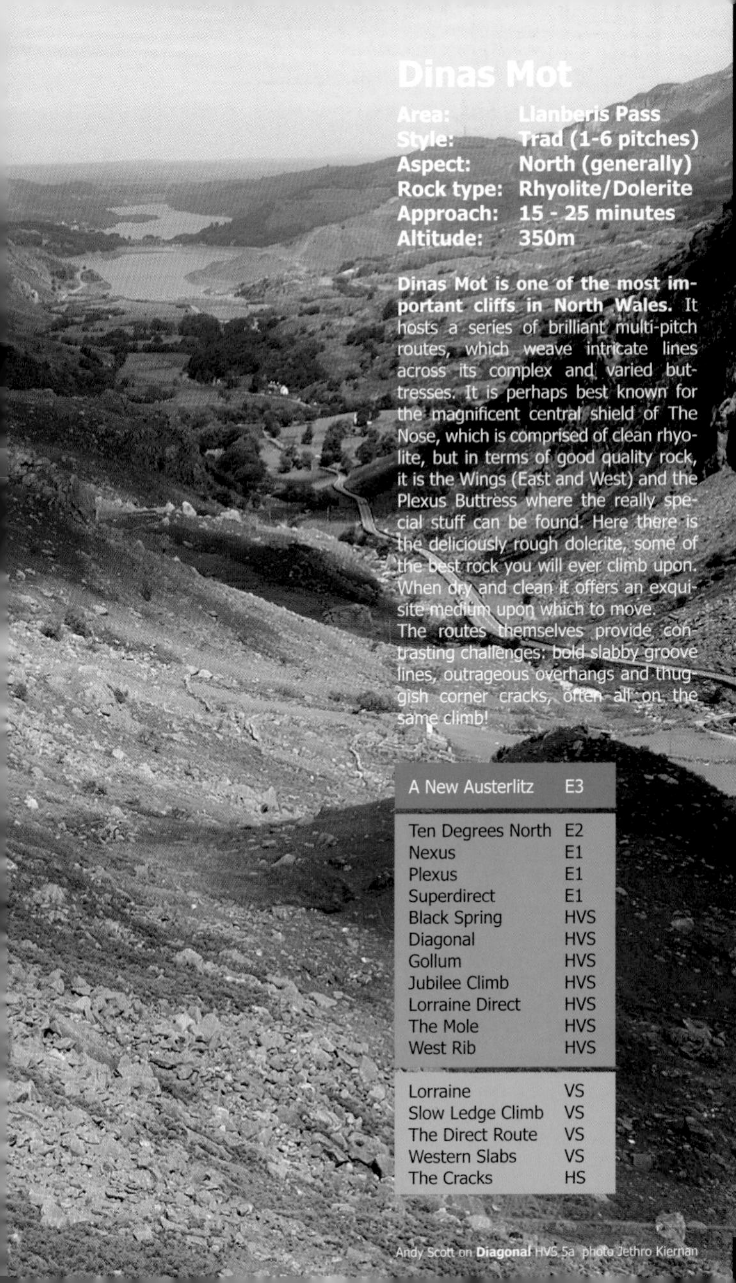

Dinas Mot

Area: Llanberis Pass
Style: Trad (1-6 pitches)
Aspect: North (generally)
Rock type: Rhyolite/Dolerite
Approach: 15 - 25 minutes
Altitude: 350m

Dinas Mot is one of the most important cliffs in North Wales. It hosts a series of brilliant multi-pitch routes, which weave intricate lines across its complex and varied buttresses. It is perhaps best known for the magnificent central shield of The Nose, which is comprised of clean rhyolite, but in terms of good quality rock, it is the Wings (East and West) and the Plexus Buttress where the really special stuff can be found. Here there is the deliciously rough dolerite, some of the best rock you will ever climb upon. When dry and clean it offers an exquisite medium upon which to move.

The routes themselves provide contrasting challenges: bold slabby groove lines, outrageous overhangs and thuggish corner cracks, often all on the same climb!

A New Austerlitz	E3

Ten Degrees North	E2
Nexus	E1
Plexus	E1
Superdirect	E1
Black Spring	HVS
Diagonal	HVS
Gollum	HVS
Jubilee Climb	HVS
Lorraine Direct	HVS
The Mole	HVS
West Rib	HVS

Lorraine	VS
Slow Ledge Climb	VS
The Direct Route	VS
Western Slabs	VS
The Cracks	HS

Andy Scott on **Diagonal** HVS 5a photo Jethro Kiernan

Dinas Mot

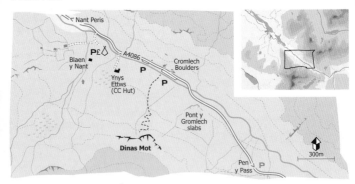

Conditions: The typically cool temperature of this shady crag is a bonus on hot summer days. However the cliff is arguably at its best when the morning sun hits the East Wing and The Nose, or later in the day when the western side of The Nose, The Western Wing and the Plexus Buttress are struck by gorgeously vivid light. The cliff does not dry as fast as the sunny northside crags situated just across the way. Even The Nose, which normally dries out first, is beset with persistent streaks of drainage in the cracks after rain.

Approach: From the Cromlech layby, cross the river (Afon Peris) directly, or via the road bridge if you are worried about getting your feet wet. Walk across to the last stile over the wall and reach the path zig zagging up the scree slope (passing the Barrel Boulder) to arrive at the base of The Nose. Traverse left or right to reach your chosen route.

Descent: See the individual crag sections for details.

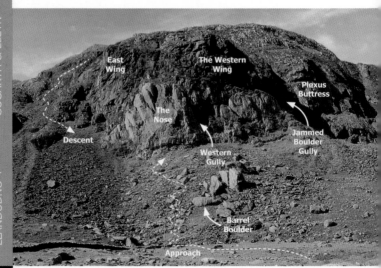

The final crux wall of **The Cracks** HS 5a photo: Al Williams >

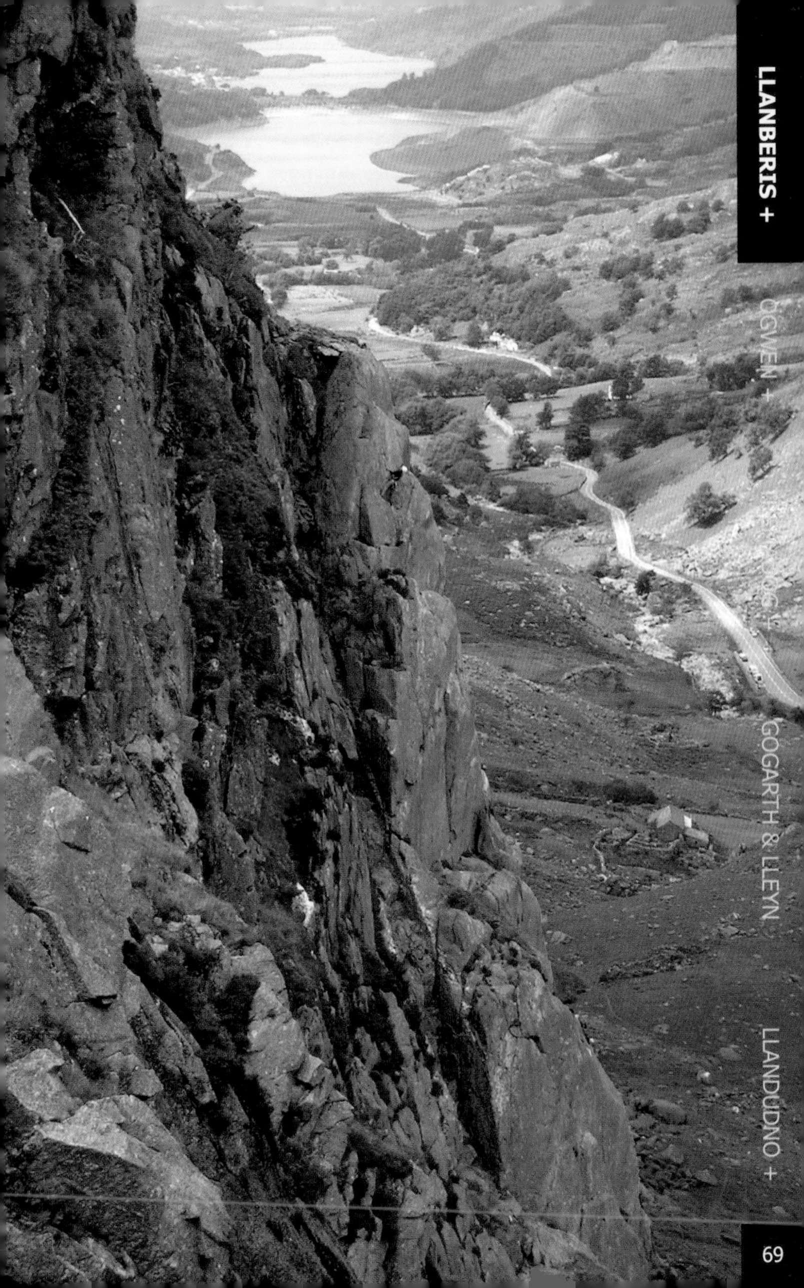

Dinas Mot • East Wing

LLANBERIS +

OGWEN +

TREMADOG +

GOGARTH & LLEYN

LLANDUDNO +

Both exotic and atmospheric, the East Wing feels like a crag from a lost world. To descend first scramble up the hillside then walk leftwards (facing in) over the top of the crag. Keep heading leftwards until it is possible to swing back down over scree paths in front of the crag.

1. The Mole HVS 5a 91m
A fantastic expedition through some challenging territory. Best saved for dry conditions.
P1 4a 27m Scramble up the gully to a position down and left of the prominent line of undercut slabs running up across the crag. Shuffle rightwards along/up the grassy rake, negotiating a clean slabby section of rock, before returning to the botanical theme, eventually gaining a comfortable belay ledge replete with lush vegetation.
P2 5a 34m Bridge up above, against what you now realize is a huge detached flake. Muscle on top and scuttle leftwards along the lip of the beast to gain a juggy flake. Difficult, 'locky' moves lead up and back right, easing with a delightful space walk across the lip. Continue diagonally rightwards up the hanging slab (thread runner up in the corner). Ignore the blank corner/roof above and move right to the slab's edge, following a diagonal crack, before moving up into a further corner. Pad rightwards on mossy smears below the overhang and pop up a short groove to a sloping ledge.
P3 4c 30m Traverse left across the slab, pulling steeply into the mossy groove and follow it for 7-8m until a series of ledges leads up and rightwards to heathery ground, and finally, cleaner, easier rock. (Or, much better, finish as for the top pitch of *Gollum*.)
[J Brown, E D G Langmuir 08.04.61]

2. Gollum HVS 5b 91m
A tremendous route with sustained interest and a wild, but well-protected overhang on P3.
P1 5a 30m Start from a grassy pedestal right of the gully. Trend diagonally right past a couple of ledges to tackle a tricky bulge leading onto a slab. Move up and follow a diagonal crack rightwards to gain a grassy ledge in the open groove (*A New Austerlitz* 1st belay). Layback up the generous flake above, exiting onto grassy ledges that lead back up right to a tree belay on the grassy rake.
P2 15m Walk leftwards along the grassy rake to reach a comfortable belay ledge with flake belays above (*The Mole* 1st belay).
P3 5b 34m Follow the diagonal slab rightwards for 10m to reach an obvious weakness in the capping overhang. Stitch it up with protection, turn on the turbo boosters and out you go...If successful, continue up leftwards, popping up a short groove to reach a sloping ledge and belay. (*The Mole* 2nd belay.)
P4 4b 27m Traverse across right to gain and climb an exposed rib to the top.
[B C Webb, A Harris, V Cowley (2 pts) 27.03.63, FFA: J Perrin 1966]

3. A New Austerlitz E3 5c 100m
A tremendous climb, similar in character to *The Mole* and *Gollum*, just harder.
P1 5c 21m Start beneath a large perched block at 15m height. Climb up to a niche just left of the large block. Teeter up its left side and make a brave pull over the bulge to gain a short slab. Belay at the small stance at the bottom of the open groove on *Gollum*.
P2 5b 18m Step rightwards around the arete onto the slabby wall. Follow this crack to its end, and continue directly up to the grassy ledges. Walk/scramble 12m left to belay on the right side of a flake.
P3 5c 34m Surmount the initial roof via a slim groove on the right to reach good holds. Move up to the next roof and head rightwards to a groove at the right side of the roof. Go up the groove to reach another roof (junction with *Gollum*). Move right and yard across the overhang on gratifyingly large holds. Climb up the slab, and short groove above, then traverse left to belay as for *The Mole* and *Gollum*.
P4 4b 27m *Gollum* P4.
[G Gibson, N Harvey 25.04.82]

Dinas Mot • The Nose

This prominent shield of rock has always been popular, since climbers first began to explore it in the 1930s. It is characterised by a bold slabby lower section and a range of stopper exit pitches that break through the steep upper lip.

Western Gully provides the easiest descent. If dry, it can be down climbed by the confident, although the last section is often wet and problematic. It is possible to abseil all the way to the ground with a pair of 60m ropes. With 50m ropes, a 2nd short abseil will be required.

If the crag is busy avoid hanging around or gearing up beneath *The Direct Route* and *The Cracks*. Any loose rocks knocked off from above will tend to funnel down and land in this area.

4. The Cracks HS 5a 90m

A classic and popular route, with a famously desperate, but entirely avoidable, crux on its final pitch. Start a few metres up and left from the toe of the buttress.

P1 12m Polished moves lead up onto a ledge. Continue up a leftwards-trending groove to reach a ledge. Move up to a further ledge 2m above.

P2 4a 18m Traverse across left for a metre or so, and follow the narrow left-facing corner, until a tricky crack allows access to a stance below the overhang. (It is common to link P1 and P2 together.)

P3 4a 14m Tiptoe rightwards beneath the overhang to gain a short chimney. Pop up this to a decent ledge.

P4 4b 14m Ascend the thin crack in the slab on the left to reach another good ledge (possible belay). Move up and walk across right to the large pinnacle.

P5 4a 18m Awkward moves lead right from the top of the pinnacle, onto a ledge. Take a moment to glance up right at the deathly thin sheet of blank rock that Leo Houlding's *Trauma* (E9 7a!) somehow manages to ascend, before continuing up the crack in the slabby left wall of the corner to reach a further ledge.

P6 5a 14m Trend up right to the base of a short, but very smooth wall. Heinous, and to be honest, partially height-dependant moves are required to gain a standing position on the sloping ledge above. If you make it in one piece, let out a suitable glory roar (only joking!) and continue to the top via the arête on the left. If you don't, well, console yourself with the fact that this crux obstacle is no more than an unjustified blot on an otherwise balanced and classic route. There's an easier way round on the left.

[B L Bathurst, H C H Bathurst 04.30]

5. Lorraine VS 5a 79m

An excellent series of parallel alternatives to *The Cracks*.

P1 12m *The Cracks* P1.

P2 4c 20m Move up and left over a bulge to gain a leftwards-slanting groove. Climb this past a tricky section, and step left to ascend the short chimney on *The Cracks*.

P3 4c 15m The slabby corner-crack is superb; continue up a further short corner to the large pinnacle on the right.

P4 4c 18m Awkward moves lead right from the top of the pinnacle, onto a ledge (possible belay). Scoot up the corner-crack.

P5 5a 14m P6 of *The Cracks*.

[J E Q Barford, N E Morin 07.09.41]

6. Lorraine Direct HVS 5a 37m

One of the best pitches on The Nose – well worth seeking out. Follow P2 of *Lorraine* for 8m, then move steeply across a bulge to gain a slab on the right. Delicate climbing leads up past a steepening, where you will be glad to find a decent runner. Keep going to a ledge in the centre of the shallow scoop above, then move down leftwards to the base of a crack in the arête. Follow this to the large pinnacle on the ledge of *The Cracks*.

[D E Alcock, C E Davies 07.06.65]

Trauma
E9 7a

Western
Gully

The Barrel

Dinas Mot • The Nose

7. The Direct Route VS 5b 74m

Another brilliant 'must-do' route with fine open climbing and a boulder problem crux.

P1 4a 15m From the toe of the buttress move up past a pair of short pinnacles and, after a further 10m, traverse left to first belay on *The Cracks*.

P2 4b 27m Head diagonally rightwards, past a blunt rib to the foot of the obvious open groove. Go left up a ramp, before moving delicately back into the groove; continue up to a large stance in a bay.

P3 4c 15m Large holds lead up right to a steep diagonal crack. Monkey along this for a couple of metres, then stride rightwards climbing easily to a long ledge. Belay on huge flakes.

P4 5b 17m Boulder out the smooth, polished corner on the left, and zoom up the flake cracks, finishing up a short corner.

[C F Kirkus, J B Dodd 22.06.30]

8. Superdirect E1 5b 75m

A fantastic climb, with contrasting pitches to suit the slab master or crack climbing thug.

P1 4b 21m From the toe of the buttress move up past a pair of short pinnacles, and then up to a spike. Go down right and follow the traverse line just above the rock scar, then climb up to a ledge 6m below a small overhang.

P2 5b 40m Ascend past the overhang to a good runner on *Diagonal*. Continue up for a few metres, until a delicate traverse leads left to a thin crack. Follow this with difficulty, past a flake on the right, until an easier crack leads up to the long ledge. Belay on huge flakes as for *The Direct Route*.

P3 5b 14m Ascend the pointed flake and continue up the short corner to the overhang. The overhanging corner-crack above provides a strenuous finale.

[R Evans, H Pasquill 28.06.74]

9. Diagonal HVS 5a 78m

A tremendous bold route swaggering across the slabby shield of The Nose, to face the inevitable strenuous crack finish.

P1 5a 24m From the toe of the buttress move up past a pair of short pinnacles and ascend the groove just left of the rock scar. Continue up the left side of a large perched flake. Step up from its top, then make a tricky traverse rightwards across the slab to a stance and nut belays under a small overhang.

P2 5a 12m Up to the right can be seen a large overhang, with a bottomless chimney on its right side. Gain the chimney by climbing up to a good runner on the left side of the overhang, and making a difficult traverse beneath it. Zip up the chimney to a small stance.

P3 5a 30m Make a thin traverse rightwards into a shallow scoop. Go up this and move right to make a nerve-racking mantel onto a small ledge. A decent pocket up right allows access to an easy crack, which in turn leads up to a stance below the steep corner-crack of P4.

P4 5a 12m The strenuous corner crack appears to respond best to an aggressive approach – give it all you've got and the top will soon be yours!

[A Birtwhistle, G F Parkinson 10.08.38]

10. West Rib HVS 5a 68m

This fine exposed route is a similar, if slightly more reasonable, proposition to its famous neighbour, *Diagonal*.

P1 4b 18m Wander up as if heading for the obvious overhanging chimney feature (*The Link*, an often damp E1 5c), then traverse right to a stance just left of the prominent rib.

P2 5a 32m Traverse out right onto the rib and follow it, past a good runner at 9m, continuing thinly with a slight trend to the left, then back to the right to gain a flake belay on *Western Slabs*.

P3 4c 18m Go around the arête on the left and ascend a thin crack, making careful use of some creaky flakes. Mantel onto the steep arête and trend delicately rightwards into the top of *Western Slabs*. A superb alternative exit, *The Chain* E1 5b, can be made up the attractive finger crack running up from the the large flake.

[C F Kirkus, I M Waller 13.09.31]

11. Western Slabs VS 4c 60m

A much-enjoyed excursion covering some delightful ground.

P1 4b 15m Start just left of the stile in the drystone wall. Gain the ledge above the quartzy block, and thereafter follow a rightward-slanting groove. At its top, go round the arête to a ledge.

P2 4b 27m Climb up past the ledge above and continue up on the right side of a small overlap to gain a small sharp spike. Traverse under another small overlap to reach and follow a groove leading up to a ledge. A further shallow groove leads rightwards to a ledge on the edge of *Western Gully*.

P3 4c 18m Move down left and follow the easy groove to a ledge by a large flake. Ascend the groove on the right which turns mean above the block. Finish easily up leftwards.

[J M Edwards, A R Edge, A M D'Aeth 06.08.31]

The Western Wing

This area of the cliff is oft overlooked in favour of the more obviously appealing routes on the Nose. However, there is a much to recommend here. The featured routes have a real sense of stepping into the unknown, and when the evening sunlight hits those upper pitches, there really is no finer place to be.

Descent is either by walking over the top and descending as for the East Wing, or by *Jammed Boulder Gully*. The latter can be tricky, especially if wet, and normally involves at least one abseil from the side of the jammed boulder itself. Do take care in the upper section of the gully, especially if other parties are below you as there is a lot of loose material.

Dinas Mot • The Western Wing

12. Slow Ledge Climb VS 4b 115m
A wonderful adventure and a logical continuation to *The Cracks* or *Western Slabs*.
P1 35m Start from the top of *Western Gully*. Scramble up the left side of the quartz rib immediately above, passing loose shattered rock to gain the shoulder, move up the rib for a few more metres, then break out right following the intersection between rock (above) and steep heather (below) for approximately 15m, when a muddy groove leads up to a flake belay (common with *Black Spring*) and just left of a detached block. Whilst techni-cally straightforward, this is a serious pitch requiring care. Remember that the *Western Gully* descent route lies directly below.
P2 4b 23m Tiptoe rightwards along the footledge and detached flake, before moving awkwardly up to a large flake. Pad up the rightwards-trending slab to gain and follow a horizontal rail of finger jugs, which lead somewhat anxiously on to the jutting 'Slow Ledge' (thus named because a person sitting on it would slowly slide off!). Continue right, and step up a small groove, to gain a strenuous hand traverse that deposits the leader on a finely positioned belay ledge, replete with its own wobbly finger stone.
P3 4b 24m Climb straight up into a groove, but quit this by shifting round the left rib to gain another cleaner groove, then zig zag the line of least resistance to a ledge with good nut belays.
P4 33m Scramble up slabs and wander up the grassy hillside to find a belay.
[J M Edwards, J Gask 30.3.34]

13. Black Spring HVS 5a 158m
An excellent route which gives delicate climbing up the steep black slabs right of *Western Gully*. The second pitch is unfortunately often wet.
P1 15m. Start 10m right of *Western Gully*. Ascend the wet wall to gain the terrace.
P2 5a 27m Go up the crack for 9m, before breaking out left for 3m. Thereafter climb directly up the pockety slab to a bulge. Pass this and move delicately left and up to reach a cave stance.
P3 5a 34m Overcome the overhang just right of the stance and move right onto a steep slab. Climb the shallow groove for a few moves, then head diagonally left to a quartz groove, which leads to the Great Terrace.
P4 4a 17m Scramble up over broken rocks, to a steep wall and large flake belay on Slow Ledge Climb.
P5 4c 37m Climb a crack on the left up to the large roof. Traverse easily rightwards to a belay where the roof runs out (also on *Slow Ledge Climb*).
P6 4a 28m Wonderful exposed climbing leads to the top.
[M Boysen, A Williams 03.04.65]

14. Jubilee Climb HVS 5b 105m
A splendid climb; a scrappy start is justified by the magnificent finish.
P1 4b 30m Start at the left side of a large flake. Ascend easy slabs for 18m, then climb tricky twin heather grooves to a niche (holly tree).
P2 30m Move left to a good flake and ascend easily to the terrace. Scarmble up to take a belay below a steep little wall.
P3 5b 24m Go up right around the corner of the wall and climb on spikes until a step back left leads onto the front wall. Nip up the crack to a good spike. The crack runs up a mossy slab to a large belay.
P3 5a 21m A leftwards rising traverse leads with difficulty up the slab to the central scoop. The crack line above the small overlap provides a glorious climax to the route.
[C J Mortlock, P M Hutchinson 23.04.59]

Alex Williams on P4 of **Ten Degrees North** E2 5c photo: Al Leary >

TREMADOG +

GOGARTH & LLEYN

LLANDUDNO +

Dinas Mot • Plexus Buttress

Just right of *Jammed Boulder Gully* lies the ominous looking *Black Cleft*. Right again is the intriguing Plexus Buttress. This slabby expanse of exquisite dolerite rock is cleaved at two-thirds height by an impressive line of overhangs.
The descent options are the same as for The Western Wing.

15. Plexus E1 5b 138m
A classic route, with immaculate rock, thrilling positions and delicate moves.
P1 21m Go up an easy groove to the large ledge and traverse easily left to a stance beneath the attractive shallow scoop running up to the large overhang.
P2 5a 42m Trend up left and climb the bold slabby groove until possible to traverse (or step out right onto the slab to a small thread, then back leftwards), to reach a layback crack that leads into the continuation groove. At the top of this, traverse diagonally left onto the arête, which leads past a couple of ledges to peg and nut belays below the huge overhang.
P3 5b 39m Traverse across the slab to a flake below a break in the overhang. Some forceful laybacking up the crack/groove thankfully gains good holds. Step left into a short groove and climb this for a few metres, then follow the delicate slab rightwards to a ledge by a detached block. Carefully move left past this, then make an awkward high step/mantleshelf back out right to the easier angled upper buttress which soon leads to a stance.
P4 4b 34m Race up shallow grooves and slabs to the top.
[B Ingle, P Crew (2 pts) 14.10.62]

16. Ten Degrees North E2 5c 127m
This stunning example of faith-in-friction style climbing is arguably the best route of its grade in the pass.
P1 21m *Plexus* P1.
P2 5b 15m Ascend a short wall and then move right (peg) and up to the groove. Step left and climb with difficulty to a belay on a slab. (Junction with *Plexus*)
P3 5c 27m Smear precariously up the open groove on the right. At the roof. step right and move up (peg), before stepping left and following the slab to a small overhang. Continue up rightwards to the large roof and swerve right to reach the *Nexus* flakes belay.
P4 5b 18m ascend the crack on the left side of the flake above to gain the *Nexus* traverse. Continue around the arête as for *Nexus*.
P5 4b 46m Surmount the large detached block on P3 of *Plexus,* and continue up P4 in one long pitch
[A Sharp, J J Zangwill 27.06.74]

17. Nexus E1 5b 129m
A companion route to *Plexus*, but slightly harder and better.
P1 9m Follow *Plexus* to the first ledge.
P2 5b 46m Ascend the slab on the right of the corner to the overhang. Traverse out left to the arête and layback the crack around the roof to reach the base of a narrow rightwards-slanting ramp. Pad up the ramp until it steepens; a hard move bars access to a sloping ledge on the right. Thereafter, ascend a short steep crack, and continue up a shallow groove to a stance and flake belays at the right side of the large overhang.
P3 5b 37m Ascend the slab on the right then move left onto a ledge. The traverse line leading out left to the arête proves to be hard. At its end swing blindly around the arête to an immediate easing of difficulty. Belay in the scoop.
P4 4b 46m Surmount the large detached block on P3 of *Plexus,* and continue up P4 in one long pitch.
[M Boysen, P Nunn (1 pt) 21.05.63]

Plexus Buttress • **Dinas Mot**

LLANBERIS +

OGWEN +

TREMADOG +

GOGARTH & LLEYN

LLANDUDNO +

Dinas Mot • Bouldering

There are some very worthwhile boulder problems in the vicinity of Dinas Mot. The most famous of these can be found on The Barrel, the conspicuous horizontal cigar-shaped boulder situated amongst the jumble of huge blocks below the right side of the Nose. Jerry Moffatt's classic traverse crosses the low break from right to left, before climbing up to reach the left side of the upper shelf. This goes at a burly V8+/Font 7b+, however more amenable lines exist. The end section of the traverse taken as a stand up problem is an excellent V3/Font 6a+, whilst in the middle of the traverse *The Minimum* V7/Font 7a+ breaks up from the undercuts to reach the shelf with the aid of a woeful crimp.

The nearby Pont y Gromlech slabs are often used by instruction groups, however on the right side there are some fine boulder problems. Most notable is *The Seam* V3/Font 6a+, which takes the centre of the obvious clean slabby wall. A classic problem with a good landing.

Pete Robbins eyeballing a small edge high on **The Seam** V3/Font 6a+ photo: Gav Foster ʌ

Diffwys Ddwr (Craig y Rhaeadr)

Area:	**Llanberis Pass**
Style:	**Trad (2 pitches)**
Aspect:	**North**
Rock type:	**Rhyolitic Tuff**
Approach:	**30 minutes**
Altitude:	**420m**

Ghosts	E3
The Wall	E1

A neglected, but atmospheric cliff. Slightly drowned out by the overwhelming presence of its larger neighbours, nonetheless, on closer inspection this proves to be an imposing and intimidating crag with a distinctly adventurous appeal. The central and most impressive section of the cliff is sprayed perma-wet by a 100m high waterfall/drainage line, which can freeze up in a most spectacular fashion during the winter months. Most other areas are heavily vegetated, however, on the left side a clean white wall rises up from a grassy ledge system. Here lie a couple of serious, but rewarding climbs, less travelled than the popular north side routes and all the better for it. The rock is very compact, yielding scant protection opportunities, but a steady, bold leader with a degree of route-finding savvy will be in his/her element. Best visited during a dry period of weather (unless of course you fancy a bash at *Cascade* (V) or *Central Icefall* (VI), which may or may not come into nick during a typical Welsh winter season).
Be sure to check out the excellent bouldering on the way back down.

Diffwys Ddwr
(Craig y Rhaeadr)

Diffwys Ddu
(Cyrn Las)

Utopia
Boulder

Grooves
Boulder

Wavelength
Boulder

Ynys Etws
CC hut

∧ Diffwys Ddwr, winter 2004 photo: Si Panton

Diffwys Ddwr • (Craig y Rhaeadr)

Approach: From the back of Ynys Ettws bear rightwards towards the large free-standing block (the Utopia Boulder). Stop for a quick boulder, or continue on up. The driest most pleasant route stays fairly close to the stream on the right. More sweet-looking boulders are passed on the way including the brilliant Wavelength block (see bouldering notes on page 85). Eventually a plateau is reached and the crag looms large above it. Pick your way through some boggy ground to reach the left side of the cliff. Scramble up ledges to the bottom of the white wall.

Conditions: The cliff doesn't receive much sun, although an evening visit in summer will see it lit up with sunshine. It is not particularly quick to dry, so it's probably wise to save it for one of those days when it's too hot to climb on the north side of the Pass.

Descent: Go down a grassy slope (with one small scrambling section) on the right side (looking in) of the cliff.

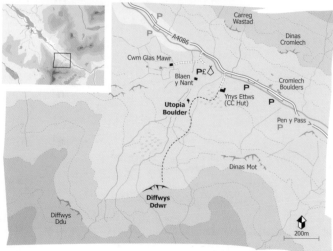

∧ Liam Desroy above the overhang on P1 of **Ghosts** E3 5c photo: Graham Desroy
↑ The Ynys Ettws bridge photo: Al Williams

Diffwys Ddwr • (Craig y Rhaeadr)

1. Ghosts E3 5c 95m

A fine but rather spooky wall climb. On P1 take care to both protect the second, and avoid rope drag.

P1 5c 40m Start at the left side of the white wall 6-7m up the grassy ramp leading up to the Cwm Glas Pinnacle. Climb up towards a small overhang at 11m. Avoid the overhang by moving left beneath it, then climb up for 5m, before traversing right for about 7m to gain the bottom of an obvious groove. Move up past loose broken blocks in the groove (the old stance!). Make a step right and trend diagonally leftwards, tracing a thin crack, then traverse leftwards above the overhangs to reach a shallow scoop. 3m above a semi-hanging stance on small spikes will be found.

P2 45m Climb easily up broken ground and take a belay close to the top of the crag. (If you have 60m ropes keep going.)

P3 10m Continue easily to the top.

[P Littlejohn, S Lewis 18.05.80]

2. The Wall E1 5a 93m

A lonely and atmospheric route, with some delightful open manoeuvres on extremely compact rock.

P1 5a 43m Start in the centre of the clean white wall at the left side of the crag (reached by scrambling up ledges). Zig diagonally rightwards until it is possible to zag back left-wards until tricky moves up and back right land you at the bottom of a striking shallow groove. Move up the right side of the groove taking advantage of useful holds out right before trending up rightwards to eventually gain a grassy belay ledge.

P2 4c 50m Traverse left for 5m and continue up leftwards until a series of shallow groove features lead up, slightly rightwards, past a small corner. Easier climbing leads directly to the top.

[J Brown, A C Cain, C T Jones (1 pt) 31.08.59]

(Craig y Rhaeadr) • **Diffwys Ddwr**

LLANBERIS + ⊕

OGWEN +

TREMADOG +

GOGARTH & LLEYN

LLANDUDNO +

The Wavelength Boulders

The boulders that you pass on the way up to the crag are arguably the best that North Wales has to offer. There are numerous classic problems throughout the grades.

The central flake line on the previously mentioned Utopia block is about VS. Just left is the fingery *Utopia Central* V4/Font 6b. *Utopia Groove* V2/Font 5+ is left again, exiting left at the top break, and *The Pebble* V6/Font 7a is the thin high wall right of the central flake. The wide crack leading into and out of an alcove is V1/Font 5, whilst the steep line to the right is a superb V5/Font 6c. Up the hill beyond a prominent low roof lies the Wavelength block, a beautiful and immaculately formed boulder bearing the trademark 'wavelength' rock feature. The left arête is V1/Font 5; manteling up onto the right side of the shelf is V4/Font 6b; pockets and a sidepull just right give a V2/Font 5+; *King of Drunks* V6/Font 7a starts sitting just right again, and *Wavelength* V9/Font 7c itself swerves up right from the same sitting start. Across the hillside to the left the large Grooves Boulder can be seen. *Boysen's Groove* V3/4/Font 6b takes the steep groove on the nearside facet.

Many other excellent boulder problems can be found dotted around the hillside and on the way up to the crag proper. It's entirely possible to get so distracted that you forget about the route that you set out to do!

∧ Chris Davies stretching for the break on **Utopia Groove** V2/Font 5+   photo: Ray Wood

Clogwyn y Ddysgl

Area:	**Llanberis Pass**
Style:	**Trad (3-6 pitches)**
Aspect:	**North-West**
Rock type:	**Rhyolite**
Approach:	**75/90 minutes**
Altitude:	**750m/850m**

Fallen Block Crack	VS
The Gambit Climb	S
Reade's Route	HVD
Rectory Chimneys	VD
The Parson's Nose	D

This splendid mountain crag nestles in a state of quiet serenity in Upper Cwm Glas, a world away from the bustling Pass below. Although a big cliff, it is sadly not as continuous as first appearances suggest. There is a distinct deterioration beyond the 50m height mark. The classic *Gambit Climb* does buck this trend by covering some fairly spectacular ground in its upper reaches, but in general most interest is concentrated in the lower pitches.

The splendidly positioned *Reade's Route*, high on the flank of the spectacular Crib Goch ridge, provides a wonderful finish to a day spent on the main crag.

Conditions: The crag does receive afternoon and evening sun, and is also relatively free of drainage problems. Although it dries fairly quickly after rain, it is still a mountain crag, so a general level of dampness can be expected outside of the summer months.

Approach: From the main road: cross the bridge over Afon Peris and continue past the Blaen y Nant field on the left and turn right over the second bridge. Turn left immediately and follow the path up towards Diffwys Ddu (Cyrn Las). To the left of the crag a steep stoney path continues up into Cwm Glas, where you will be greeted by the sudden and overwhelming view of the cliff, which dominates the right side of the cwm.

To reach *Reade's Route* bear left past Llyn Glas to reach the climb which is situated on the buttress left of the red-coloured col (Bwlch Coch) in a further 15 minutes. To reach the route from the top of Clogwyn y Ddysgl, continue up the ridge and head east along Crib y Ddysgl to Bwlch Coch. Descend the steep path down into the upper cwm and cut across the hillside to reach the Crazy Pinnacle Gully.

Descent: Scramble back down the *Clogwyn y Person Arête* and descend the straightforward Western Gully. Alternatively, if climbing with sacs, continue onto the Snowdon Horseshoe ridge, from which a number of fine walking/scrambling options are available.

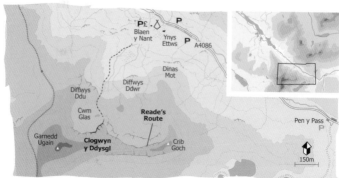

⋀ Ed Douglas stepping right from the pinnacle on P4 of **Gambit Climb** S 4a photo: Ray Wood
⋀ Looking towards Crib Goch from the entrance to Cwm Glas, below Clogwyn y Ddysgl photo: Graham Desroy

Clogwyn y Ddysgl

1. The Parson's Nose/Clogwyn y Person Arete D 75m/150m

An enjoyable and exposed combination of a fine route and a classic mountain scramble.

P1 24m Ascend easy-angled slabs from the lowest point of the nose.

P2 21m Continue up the slab, steeper now, but still blessed with good holds. Trend slightly rightwards towards, and take a stance at the foot of, a shallow groove.

P3 15m Follow a thin crack line rightwards to a large ledge overlooking Western Gully.

P4 15m Scramble easily up the side of the Nose to its apex. Descend Western Gully, or continue up and along the excellent ridge scramble of *Clogwyn y Person Arête*, and onto the Snowdon Horseshoe ridge. Interest can be added by pitching harder variants on the right side of the ridge.

[A H Stocker 1884/R Pendlebury 1879]

2. Gambit Climb S 83m

Arguably the best 'easy' route in North Wales. A classic and sustained trip up the best part of the crag.

P1 23m Start 60m right of West Gully, and 5m left of a pocketed wall. Ascend the crack with the hanging flake for a few metres, and then move left onto the shoulder. Step down and teeter across the slabby ramp on the left to reach a crack. Go up the crack to a ledge then continue up a further awkward crack to ledges.

P2 17m Trend rightwards, then follow a shallow chimney up to a grassy ledge (known as the Green Collar).

P3 14m Make a difficult traverse rightwards on dinky holds to gain a short broken chimney. Go up this to a good ledge.

P4 14m On the left is a chimney, climb it reaching the top of a pinnacle on its left side. Move right and scoot up the corner crack to a scree-covered ledges.

P5 4a 15m Climb up the rightward-sloping ledge to reach a right-angled corner. Boulder out this final tricky section and finish up broken ground.

[J M A Thompson, H O Jones, K J P Orton 09.10]

3. Fallen Block Crack VS 4c 81m

A splendid traditional route, which is arguably easier if done in mountain boots.

P1 4a 9m Start on the left side of the conspicuous Fallen Block. The initial crack leads, not without a tussle, to a chockstone belay.

P2 4c 26m The crack is steep and difficult from the start. At 9m a resting spot is reached. Catch your breath and continue up the crack, with the difficulties eventually easing off, to a large ledge.

P3 46m Go up the chimney on the left and continue up easy ground to the cliff top.

[I M Waller 11.09.27]

Clogwyn y Ddysgl • North Face of Crib Goch

4. Rectory Chimney VD 130m

An enjoyable and absorbing trip up and across the cliff.

P1 18m Start approximately 25m right of Fallen Block, up a narrow chimney, with a small flake leaning across at half height. Clamber up past the flake, and continue up a groove in the steep wall.

P2 21m Climb the short steep wall on the left, followed by a short crack, leading to a niche below a pinnacle. Avoid the difficulties of the crack above by a sneaky deviation to the left and enter the crack from behind, then continue up to a good stance.

P3 12m Move up in the corner and follow a narrow ledge leftwards to a large chimney. Climb up to a ledge.

P4 18m Climb up over broken ground to reach a rightwards-leading grassy rake.

P5 37m Follow the grassy rake rightwards, above a large crevasse, until a jumble of stacked blocks (The Vestry) is reached.

P6 24m Traverse right into the gully on the right and continue on easy, but loose ground to the top.

[M W Guiness, W McNaught, H R C Carr 27.08.25, The Vestry finish was first climbed by M W Guiness, H R C Carr 30.08.25]

North Face of Crib Goch

The final route is situated below the summit ridge of Crib Goch in the upper cwm. It is often done in combination with a route on the main cliff, but is a worthwhile trip on its own, especially if combined with a circuit of the Snowdon Horshoe.

5. Reade's Route HVD 66m

A classic, but rather shocking (given the relatively amenable grade) climb.

P1 30m Start by scrambling up broken ground left of the Crazy Pinnacle Gully, and belay where it steepens on a stance overlooking the gully. Go easily up the rib to a large platform beneath a steep wall.

P2 21m The wall proves to be a sturdy obstacle, with a very trying move up to the left. Ascend the pinnacle above and make a disturbing stride across to a crack in the wall (crux). Climb the crack to a stance at the top of another pinnacle.

P3 15m Climb the rib via the shallow groove to the top.

[W R Reade, G L Bartrum 08.08]

Sion Long feeling the exposure on P4 of **Main Wall** HS 4b photo: Steve Long

Diffwys Ddu (Cyrn Las)

Area:	**Llanberis Pass**
Style:	**Trad (3-6 pitches)**
Aspect:	**North-East**
Rock type:	**Rhyolite**
Approach:	**45 minutes**
Altitude:	**550m**

Long Kesh	E5
The Skull	E4
Lubyanka	E3
Overhanging Arête	E2
The Grooves	E1
Main Wall	HS

An impressive cliff hosting a range of spectacular routes. Diffwys Ddu, or Cyrn Las as it has been incorrectly known over the years, has a domineering presence. Its barrel chest is crowned by a band of intimidating overhangs that guard the cliff top. Unsurprisingly, all of the described climbs feature dramatic and exposed finales in their upper reaches. In spite of the well-travelled nature of these classic routes, the rock can be unpredictably snappy, and as such requires a considered approach. It is always worth placing that extra runner, even when moving on easy ground.

Conditions: If you make an early start it is possible to catch some morning sunshine during the summer months. Generally though, this is a cold and shady crag. Drainage lingers in the grooves and cracks for several days after rain, but a climb such as *Main Wall* will be feasible within a day or so of rain, as the more tricky sections tend to be on open sections of rock.

Approach: From the main road, cross the bridge over Afon Peris, continue past the Blaen y Nant field on the left and turn right over the second bridge. Turn left immediately and follow the path up towards the cwm. The routes are best approached by scrambling in from the left side.

Descent: Head well over to the left (facing in) and come down the main path from Upper Cwm Glas.

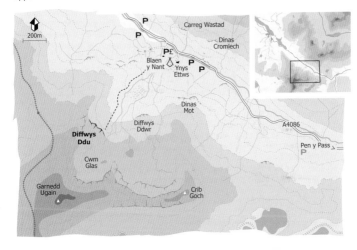

Diffwys Ddu (Cyrn Las)

1. Main Wall HS 4b 140m

A classic Welsh mountain route with enough exposure and general seriousness to demand respect from even the most experienced of teams.

P1 4a 21m From the scree 'fan' on the left side of the crag, scramble up rightwards to reach the start of the route at a point down and left of an obvious triangular overhang below a grassy terrace. Trend diagonally left up the boot-worn slab to reach a vegetated ledge at 9m. Go up a short corner for 3m, and then head right across a slab, move right around a rib, and then up to a pulpit stance.

P2 4b 24m Follow the rightward-sloping gangway with some difficulty to reach an oft-damp chimney. Ascend this for a few metres, then head back left along a ledge to a stance in a corner overlooking the gully. Peg belay.

P3 4a 14m Go up the arête above, and then trend diagonally right to a large triangular ledge in the corner.

P4 4b 27m Drop down slightly and move up to the tip of a flaky pinnacle on the left. Move onto the steep wall and then up into a niche. Traverse left around the corner and climb up a steep arête until a step across a chimney gains a short slab.

P5 4a 24m Move up to an overhang and head left across a broken chimney to the bottom of a large slab overlooking the gully on the left. Savouring the exposure, climb the left edge of the slab on generous holds to a good stance at the top.

P6 30m. Move up left to a ledge and climb a slab to the right. Scramble to the cliff top.

[P L Roberts, J K Cooke 27.07.35]

2. Lubyanka E3 5c 117m

A popular and absorbing climb, with sustained difficulties and a rather wild top pitch.

P1 4a 21m P1 of *Main Wall*.

P2 4b 24m Follow P2 of *Main Wall* into the chimney and climb it until it is possible to step out right at the top to reach a crevasse stance.

P3 5c 18m The groove above the stance proves to be a stubborn and sustained affair. Enter it from the left and follow it to a large stance.

P4 5b 15m Ascend the corner behind the belay, exiting right at its top to descend a slab to a spike belay.

P5 5c 21m Move directly up the slab, past the overlap, to enter and climb a short open corner. Make a difficult exit left at the top, and continue up a short slab to a small ledge.

P6 5c 21m Very out there! Hand traverse the quartz ledge for 3m to the first arête. A further metre along is a pocket where a cam can be placed. Step back and make a delicate step up onto the quartz ledge just right of the arête. The shattered rib up to the left is the source of dubious gear and good holds to its left. Teeter up these, or step up right in the groove onto a good foothold. Either way leads to the small final overhang. Pull through this with relief and ascend the slab above to nut and spike belays.

[E Cleasby, J Eastham, R Matheson 21.08.76]

3. Long Kesh E5 6b 130m

Another fine route with a magnificent and exposed top pitch.

P1 4c 27m P1 of *The Skull*.

P2 4c 30m P2 of *The Skull*.

P3 5c 18m P3 of *The Skull* to the belay, but continue for 3m to belay at the top of *Lubyanka* P3.

P4 5c 12m From the right side of the ledge, move up right onto the wall. Ascend a thin crack for 2m, and then move right to the arête, which leads up to the spike belay at the top of P4 on *Lubyanka*.

P5 6b 43m Move directly up the slab, past the overlap, to enter and climb a short open corner (as for *Lubyanka* P5). Step right, then climb up to a peg. Traverse right to an RP placement, and move up onto a slab on the right (crux). Climb up to the roof, clip 2 poor pegs, and head rightwards beneath the roof to the arête overlooking *The Skull*. Make a bold pull over the roof onto the slab above, and continue to the top. Belay on a flake at the top left corner of the easy-angled slabs.

[S Boyden, S Cardy 01.07.85]

∧ Jonny Garside climbing the corner feature on P4 of **Lubyanka** E3 5c photo: Steve Long

OGWEN +

TREMADOG +

GOGARTH & LLEYN

LLANDUDNO +

Scramble
Approach

4. The Skull E4 6a 127m

A stunning route with an exhilarating finale up the striking diagonal groove.

P1 4c 27m Start as for *Main Wall*. Ascend a steep slab, then a short strenuous chimney to reach the grassy terrace.

P2 4c 30m Go up a steep flake crack on the left of the arête. Drop down slightly and move right round the arête to gain a wall. Head leftwards to the bottom of the L-shaped Helter Skelter Chimney. Climb up the chimney to a stance level with the crevasse stance on *Lubyanka*.

P3 5c 15m Step down left, and move awkwardly left past a worrying flake to gain a thin crack. Follow the crack strenuously to a stance.

P4 6a 15m Gain the shallow groove in the overhanging arête on the right, and climb it with much difficulty. Continue up a slab to the spike belay at the top of P4 on *Lubyanka*.

P5 5c 40m Ascend the slab above the belay, heading right to the base of the prominent slanting groove. Make a hard step right and go up the right wall of the groove to a small ledge. Bridge onwards up the groove in a spectacular position until it eases and a slab runs up to a block belay. Easy scrambling leads to the top.

[M Boysen, A Williams, J Jordan (6 pts) 01.05.66, FFA: R Evans, H Pasquill]

5. The Grooves E1 5b 116m

A brilliant uncompromising route that is quite simply one of the finest E1s in Wales.

P1 5b 45m Climb up to the overhang and pull round it to make an entry into the striking groove line. The difficulties are often exacerbated by greasy holds. Continue up the groove until a large grassy bay is reached on the left. A short wall on the left leads to a large platform.

P2 5b 37m The groove line continues behind the belay. Follow it again with sustained but well protected difficulties until a ledge is reached. A short corner leads to a large platform on the right.

P3 5b 34m Move up right onto a sloping ledge and traverse across left to an overhanging groove. This provides a steep and spectacular climax to the route. Above, easier ground leads to the top.

[J Brown, D Cowans, E Price 13.09.53]

6. The Overhanging Arête E2 5b 37m

A breathtaking alternative finish to *The Grooves*.

Start at the bottom of the large open corner 6m right of the last stance of *The Grooves*. Climb the corner until an obvious hand rail leads out left. Follow this to a huge jug on the arête. The exposure is now sensational. Rapidly pull up to the 2nd jug and continue up and right to gain good holds before your strength fades. Easier ground leads to the top.

[H I Banner, J O'Neill (1pt) 15.06.58]

Jonny Garside heading out on the top pitch of **Long Kesh** E5 6b
photo: Steve Long

Cwm Glas Bach

Area: Llanberis Pass
Style: Trad (1-3 pitches)
Aspect: North-West
Rock type: Rhyolitic Tuff
Approach: 15 - 25 minutes
Altitude: 250 – 300m

Pretty Girls Make Graves	E6
Rimsky Korsakov	E5
Beasts of the Field	E4
Fear of Infection	E4
Weasels Rip My Flesh	E4
What a Difference a Day Makes	E4
El Guide Direct	E3
Rembrandt Pussyhorse	E3
Far from the Madding Throng	E2
The Stebbing	E2
Spitting Image	HVS

A wonderfully serene part of the Llanberis Pass with some excellent outcrop-style routes set above lush green grass. Cwm Glas Bach encompasses a network of crags spread across the hillside beyond the Cwm Glas Mawr Climbers' Club hut. Although only developed in relatively recent times, these intense, urgent climbs easily hold their own against the more famous routes found elsewhere in the valley. On hot summer days it provides a welcome alternative to the busy north side crags. The rock is invariably good quality and is rough and clean, except within some of the more persistent drainage streaks. In places its surface is pitted with delightful pockets where occasionally limestone-style thread runners can be found.

Conditions: Some late afternoon/evening sun can be expected in the summer months, but persistent drainage can be a problem on certain routes.

Approach: From the main road, cross the bridge over Afon Peris. Continue past the Blaen y Nant field on the left and turn right over the second bridge. A vague track runs along to the Climbers' Club Hut (Cwm Glas Mawr).

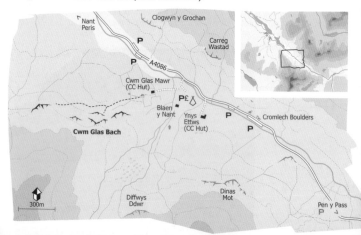

∧ Neil Dyer and 'the hand' on **Fear of Infection** E4 6a photo: Ray Wood

∧ Cwm Glas Bach with Crib Goch, Clogwyn y Ddysgl and the Gyrn Las ridge above photo: Graham Desroy

Cwm Glas Bach • Clogwyn Llo • The Gravestones

Grave
Diggers
Wall
E8 6c

Hidd
Wall

King of
Rumpy
E6 6a

Ring
My Bell
E6 6b

Moose's
Toothpaste
V5/Font 6c

Nick's Sexual Problem
V8/Font 7b

Moose's Toothpaste Font V5/Font 6c+, The Gravestones photo: Paul Houghough

Clogwyn Llo

This is the first major crag on the hillside up beyond the hut and is a large, tiered cliff dissected by horizontal, grassy ledges. Reach it by following a slight path from the back of the hut to a ruined building. Shortly after break off left and strike a line up to the base of the crag.

Descent is best made down grassy slopes over the back and down the left side (looking in) of the crag.

1. Far from the Madding Throng E2 5c 57m
A superb and aptly named outing from the old master himself; watch out though, the top pitch is pretty pushy for E2!
P1 5a 24m Start on the left side of a brown, rippled slab. Ascend the crack and continue up to grassy ledges. Belay beneath the obvious corner feature.
P2 5b 18m Climb the corner direct – a neat pitch.
P3 5c 15m The steep wall on the right has 2 shallow scoops at mid-height. Start from a block beneath the left-hand scoop. Climb up to a small overhang and move right, layback-ing up into the right-hand scoop. Head up left to a grassy stance; scrambling remains.
[J Brown, C E Davies 27.05.89]

The Gravestones

This area can be reached by continuing along the path from the back of the hut until it peters out after a second small ruin. The crag is situated on the left.

A hard crag with numerous desperate test piece routes. The featured route is by far the best, and probably the easiest of the bunch. There are also a couple of classic boulder problems with good landings.

2. Pretty Girls Make Graves E6 6b 18m
One of the best hard pitches in the Pass. Start down and left of the upper crack line. Yard up cracks to the overlap, then head right with difficulty to reach the base of the upper crack. Blast up this to the top.
[C Smith, I Jones 05.06.86]

Cwm Glas Bach • Hidden Wall

Rembrandt
Pussyhorse
30m

Hidden Wall

From The Gravestones skirt up the hillside on the right for about 100m until the crag comes into view on the left.

An impressive sweep of clean rock and a brilliant sideshow route, *Rembrandt Pussyhorse*. Descend via the gully (with a large chockstone at its top) on the left of the wall.

3. What a Difference a Day Makes E4 6a 21m
A tough route, which regularly halts cocky or careless leaders. Ascend the crack to the ramp, then go up left past a short wall and small slab to reach the dark groove. Nip up the groove to a wide crack (large cam), and layback up leftwards to finish.
[S Howe, I A Jones 06.07.87]

4. Rimsky Korsakov E5 6a 24m
A stunning route: sustained, pumpy, and just runout enough to keep the heart racing. Start in the middle of the wall. Climb up and follow the slanting crack line leftwards to a shallow groove. Continue up a line of flakes, then head straight up the wall to reach a wide crack. Quickly stuff some cams in (size 3 useful), and summon one final burst of energy to reach the large groove. Finish easily.
[J Dawes 05.87]

5. El Guide Direct E3 5c 30m
A fine open pitch. From a rock step move up to the diagonal crack and follow it for 2m, then move directly up to the snaking line of the crag girdle (*Wagner's Ring* E3 5b,6a). Head rightwards to the arête (size 1.5 cam slot), then ascend the wall directly with a tricky moment stepping onto the white slab. Finish up the wall to the right where easy scrambling remains.
[A Popp, G Hughes 1989]

6. Rembrandt Pussyhorse E3 6a 21m
A neat route with a fierce crux. Start down and left of the obvious cracked tower. Ascend cracks to a ledge and traverse rightwards to a peg, before heading up to the bottom of the crack. Breeze up the crack and bear down hard through the crux section above to reach the spike belay. Make a careful abseil descent from the spike.
[G Hughes, A Wells, A Amos 16.05.88]

Clogwyn Mawr

This is the large broken cliff on the hillside further right than The Gravestones/Hidden Wall area. It is easily identified by the striking crack line of the featured route *Fear of Infection* located about half way up the crag. Approach up the central slanting gully.

7. Fear of Infection E4 6a 15m
The compelling, eye-catching off width crack, situated about half way up the broken face of the crag. Attack the crack with a rack of large cams (sizes 4, 5 and 6) and a bag-load of enthusiasm. An essential part of the Yosemite training programme.
[G Smith, D O'Dowd 22.05.87]

Craig Cwm Glas Bach

At the point where the path from the back of the hut peters out, continue contouring rightwards across the hillside until the crag comes into view.

A fine crag, if you can catch it when it's dry. To descend, walk back from the cliff edge and head left (facing in) and go down a rift.

8. Weasels Rip My Flesh E4 6a 35m
This brilliant, bold excursion is the most popular route in the area. Go up to a good hold (peg), and make a tricky move right to gain a jug. Continue up and leftward to a thread. Sustained moves lead up the wall above. Luckily, as the fall potential increases, the difficulty of the climbing gradually drops away until easier ground and a crack are reached. Step up and right, and around the arete to reach a slim groove which leads to the top.
[S Howe, I A Jones 06.87]

9. Spitting Image HVS 5b 27m
The striking crack line provides a superb pitch, although the approach wall is often wet. Reach the base of the crack directly (or via a diagonal line coming in from the right), then swagger up it in fine style.
[P Trower, K Toms 17.06.84]

10. Beasts of the Field E4 6a 27m
A tasty route on wonderfully pocketed rock. Start down and left of the recessed wall. Climb up into the shallow niche hosting the sapling tree (thread runner above), then pull steeply out rightwards and climb up past a further thread. Continue up the slab and through the overhang to reach easier ground.
[S Howe, D Blenkinsop 10.04.88]

To the right lies a recessed wall. The left-hand line is *Noah's Ark* E5 6a, whilst the right-hand line is *Over the Beach* E7 6c. The right-hand corner is *Pan Alley* HVS 5b. Unfortunately it is often overrun with drainage water.

11. The Stebbing E2 5b 40m
A worthwhile pitch that is often the first to dry on this part of the crag. Climb up the slim groove, passing a small overlap at 12m to gain an area of ledges. A steep crack line leads up to a tower feature. Easier slabs above lead to the top.
[I A Jones, T Mitchell 06.89]

< Tim Emmett back on his old stomping ground: **El Guide Direct** E3 5c photo: Ray Wood

Clogwyn Du'r Arddu

Area:	Snowdon
Style:	Trad (1-7 pitches)
Aspect:	North
Rock type:	Rhyolitic Tuff
Approach:	90 minutes
Altitude:	700m

A Midsummer Night's Dream	E6
Womb Bits	E5
Great Wall	E4
Mordor	E4
The Axe	E4
The Boldest / Direct Finish	E4
Bloody Slab	E3
November	E3
Pinnacle Arete / The Hand Traverse	E3
West Buttress Eliminate	E3
Jelly Roll	E2
Scorpio	E2
Silhouette	E2
Shrike	E2
The Mostest	E2
The Troach	E2
White Slab	E2
Woubits	E2
Llithrig	E1
Octo	E1
The Boulder	E1
Vember	E1
Great / Bow Combination	HVS
Sheaf	HVS
The Corner	HVS
Curving Crack	VS
Longland's Climb	VS
Pigott's Climb	VS
Slab Climb Right-Hand	HS
Primitive Route	VD

An awe-inspiring mountain crag, hosting an impressive selection of classic routes, including some of the most famous rock climbs in Britain. Tucked out of sight from the tourist-ridden summit of Snowdon, it has a sombre, yet spiritual ambience. The dark shadow-cast form of the cliff, coupled with the still beauty of the adjacent Llyn Du'r Arddu, creates an air of peaceful serenity. Cloggy, as it is affectionately known, invokes a deep sense of attachment from its many devotees. A single visit is all it takes to fall under its supernatural spell. Before you know it you'll be planning return pilgrimages.

This immense brooding cliff is steeped in history and climbing folklore. Indeed some of the most important historical breakthroughs of the last century have occurred here, and many of the top climbers of the day have left their signature mark: Jack Longland, Colin Kirkus, Joe Brown, Pete Crew, John Redhead, Jerry Moffatt and latterly Johnny Dawes in 1986 with his headpoint ascent of the deathly serious *Indian Face*.

Away from the head-spinning difficulties of bold E9s, there are a plethora of atmospheric and adventurous mid-grade routes, particularly in the VS – E4 range. That said, the situations on the crag can be quite serious, and a level of multi-pitch competence is advisable for all members of the team. The rock is generally sound, however loose and creaky sections will be encountered in places. Helmets are advisable, especially on busy summer weekends.

Conditions: The altitude and aspect ensure that suitable climbing conditions are only likely between the months of May and September. During the middle of the day this cold northerly crag casts a chilling wraith-like shadow, however in the early morning and evening sections of it are transformed by a dramatic and enchanting light show. Watching the rock glow orange in the evening sun, shifting through ever-richer tones, is a spectacle not to be missed. The Far East Buttress (*Woubits* and *The Mostest*) receives early morning sun and the east face of The Pinnacle (*Shrike*, *Octo* etc.) catches rays until perhaps midday, depending on the time of year.

Llyn Du'r Arddu photo: Si Panton ∧

The Far West Buttress (*Primative Route* and *Slab Climb Right-Hand*) can get sun as early as 2.00pm in the afternoon, whilst East Buttress and the upper sections of West Buttress come into the sun around 7.00pm.

Cloggy has a reputation for being slow-drying, and this is certainly true for many of the routes, particularly the corners and cracks. However, several of the open face routes actually dry very quickly (eg. *Troach*, *Scorpio*, *Slab Climb Right-Hand*).

Approach: Park in Llanberis, and walk down Victoria Terrace (50m left of the Snowdon Mountain Railway station). Continue on the road as it narrows and winds up the hill, until a locked gate is reached. A little further along the road, the Snowdon summit path breaks off left. Follow this path for 2.5km to the Halfway House café, a welcome brew stop for those nursing a hangover! Continue along the path for a further km, and bear right, where the main path steepens, to follow the old miner's track, which contours around past the old copper mines to the base of the cliff. (1.5 hours)

The most pleasant approach for the Far West Buttress is to break off from the path leading into the crag and contour round the hillside on the Llanberis side of Llyn Du'r Arddu, then walk up to the foot of the buttress directly.

Descent: The Eastern Terrace provides both the best descent and arguably the most convenient way up to the top of the crag for climbers wishing to access routes on Far East Buttress or The Pinnacle from above. To reach the terrace scramble up right from the base of East buttress, over rock steps and grassy ledges. The terrace itself is littered with loose rock, so do take care not to dislodge any rocks whilst moving up or down it.

It is also possible (and preferable, for routes on the Far West Buttress) to descend to the right (looking in) of the crag. To do this walk downhill westwards to an inclined grassy area. There is a fence running down the ridge line; after a short distance cross the fence (small cairn) and follow a scree path down the hillside and back to the base of the crag. Neither East Gully, nor The Western Terrace are recommended as descents. Both are unstable and dangerous.

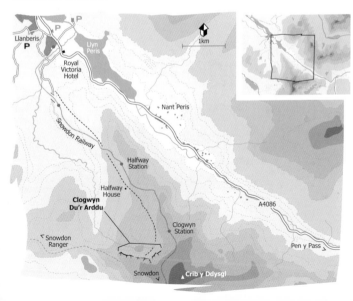

Clogwyn Du'r Arddu

East Gully

The Pinnacle

Eastern Terrace

The Boulder

West Buttress

Western Terrace

East Buttress

Far Eastern Buttress

Far West Buttress

This neglected section of the cliff is situated approximately 100m left of The Pinnacle. The described routes lie upon the exposed Upper Buttress and are approached from above, as if dropping into a big sea cliff. The crag top can be reached by contouring around from the railway line running up to the summit, or via Eastern Terrace. Reach the base of the routes by scrambling carefully down the Far Eastern Terrace, which terminates just beyond the start of *The Mostest*. (Abseiling the last tricky section of the approach makes it safer.)

1. Woubits E2 5b 80m
An atmospheric and somewhat daunting route.
P1 5b 36m Start from the terrace below short twin grooves just right of the overhangs. Surmount the bulge to gain the right-hand groove, taking care if the rock is damp. Go up the groove, or alternatively, drop down a touch and move into the left-hand groove. Either way, continue up the broken corner to a thin crack. Move right from its top to reach a stance on the arête below the overhanging wall.
P2 5b 44m Ascend the groove on the left, swinging out left past the small overhang at 12m to a good flake. Stand on it and mantel onto the ledge above before moving back rightwards into the groove (or alternatively move right from the flake and layback up). The groove leads more easily to the top of a slab; move left and squirm up a chimney in the corner. A final slabby groove runs to block belays.
[J Brown, D Whillans 30.08.55]

2. The Mostest E2 5c 96m
A splendid climb with fantastic situations. Save for a dry period, as the crux is often wet.
P1 4c 36m Start to the right of *Woubits* at a good belay just before the terrace drops away. Climb the grassy groove on the right, then a slab with twin cracks. A short chimney above leads to a grassy rake. Move left and go up a chimney-groove to reach a cave stance.
P2 5b 28m The crack on the left leads to the top of a pinnacle. Move right to a niche and make a bold move around the bulge onto the wall on the right. Move up a to a spike, then step back down and follow a rising traverseline (still tricky) to gain a foothold stance at the base of the bottomless groove.
P3 5c 19m Ascend the steep groove to the overhang. Move up left with difficulty; then make a hard move out into another groove on the left. Scoot up this and its left arête, and continue to a stance.
P4 13m The broken slab provides an easy finish.
[J Brown (4 pts) 09.04.57, FFA: E Jones 1968]

Scramble approach down Far Eastern Terrace

The Pinnacle

< The Llanberis Path photo: Si Panton

LLANBERIS +

OGWEN +

TREMADOG +

GOGARTH & LLEYN

LLANDUDNO +

Clogwyn Du'r Arddu • The Pinnacle

Perched up on the left shoulder of The East Buttress, The Pinnacle presents two distinct facets, one facing north, and one facing east. Approach to the routes can be made up the treacherous East Gully, however it is more common, and safer, to either abseil in from the top, or make a roped scramble round from the Green Gallery at the top of The East Buttress. Be careful to not dislodge loose debris from the base of The Pinnacle.

3. Shrike E2 5c 58m

A magnificent and thrilling route. Catch it in the early morning sun for a magical experience.
P1 5c 20m Start approximately 50m right of the east gully corner by the side of a pinnacle leaning against the wall. Ascend the crack on the left side of the pinnacle for 3m; reach left and continue for a few moves to better holds. Traverse left for 5m to a thin crack. Climb this with difficulty to jugs and traverse left for a few metres before moving up to belay below the groove.
P2 5b 38m Climb the groove to the overhang and jam strenuously round it to some good holds just left of a widening in the crack. Traverse left for a couple of metres to some ledges. Go up the crack; then follow a line of holds back right into the main crack. Continue up past a couple of spike runners to a small ledge. Head left to the arête and follow it for a few metres, before swerving back right to a narrow ledge beneath a final short wall. The difficulties of this last obstacle end with suitably glorious jugs.

[J Brown, H Smith, J Smith (4 pts) 25.10.58, FFA: J Perrin 09.06.68]

4. The Axe E4 6a 50m

A wild and exposed route scaling the dramatic hanging arête. Start a couple of metres right of the arête, beneath the overhangs. Climb the flake crack to the roof, taking care with some creaky rock. A crux pull round the roof gains a line of juggy holds leading leftwards to some large hollow flakes. Ascend a thin flake and the wall above it to reach the arête proper. Continue up the arete until a spike is reached on the right. Make a move up, and then return to the arête at a small overhang and follow it to the top of the tower in a sensational position.

[P Littlejohn, C King 06.07.79]

East Gully

East Gully

Roped scramble from the Green Gallery

5. Octo E1 5b 51m

The striking corner crack line provides a meaty, albeit well-protected, challenge. The start is gained by an unnerving and serious scramble out of East Gully, or (slightly easier) by traversing round from the base of *Pinnacle Arête*. It is probably advisable to rope up for either of these approaches.

P1 4b 18m There is a choice of cracks to start; climb up either to a stance in the chimney.

P2 5b 33m Move up to the overhang, muscle round it, and struggle into the crack above. Continue up the crack with sustained difficulties until relief arrives with an exit out right to easier ground. Wander up to the grassy platform on the right to belay. An easy scramble escape can be made up right.

[J Brown, M T Sorrell, D Belshaw 15.06.52]

6. Pinnacle Arête/The Hand-Traverse Connection E3 5c 82m

An exhilarating and dramatic excursion spiralling around the north and east facets of the Pinnacle.

P1 5b 40m Start below the groove capped by a roof (the line of *Taurus* E4 5c) just right of the arête. Scramble up loose spikes and go up the groove on poor rock (and poor protection) for 10m. Traverse out left on flakes, to reach a ledge by the arête. Move up to gain the arête itself and climb a tricky crack for 3m. Follow the obvious leftward traverse for 5m to the base of a groove. Scoot up this to a ledge.

P2 6m Move up to the higher ledge and take a belay at the top of *Octo*.

P3 5c 30m Step down and scurry boldly out across the incut traverse line for 6m, where a hard move up left leads into a thin crack. Go up the crack and corner above to a boulder-bridge.

P4 4a 6m Easy climbing leads to the top. (*Pinnacle Arete* can be climbed on its own at E2 5b. An easy scramble escape can be made up right as for *Octo*.)

[M Boysen, C J Mortlock (3 pts) 17.06.62, FFA: J Perrin 1968/H I Banner, C T Jones (1 pt) 7.5.60]

James McHaffie belaying Matthew Clifford up the top section of **The Axe** E4 6a photo: Phil Dowthwaite

Clogwyn Du'r Arddu • The East Buttress

The magnificent central showpiece of the cliff plays host to a high concentration of classic routes. In its centre lies the breathtaking sweep of Great Wall. This seemingly blank sheet of rock is breached by a collection of technical and bold routes, most famously the ineffably serious *Indian Face*. At either side, striking corner cracks and open faces soar upwards. Could this be the most impressive crag in Wales? Quite possibly.

7. Llithrig E1 5c 75m

A classic route, which can be done with a funky little pendulum at HVS.

P1 4a 13m Scramble up to the foot of *Sunset Crack*, and climb up to a belay stance a few metres up it.

P2 5c 22m Traverse right across the wall and go up a shallow groove to a small ledge on the arête. Move right beneath an overhang into a small corner. Climb through the overhang and follow the diagonal break up right to a good spike. Climb down and sketch across the thin slab (or apply the rope pendulum) to a good ledge and belay.

P3 4c 22m Traverse right; then follow the obvious weakness up to a stance at the base of a left-facing corner.

P4 4c 12m Go up the corner to a ledge at 5m. Move across the wall on the left to reach a crack. Climb up it, until better holds on the left wall lead up to a large grassy stance.

P5 4a 6m Nip up the wall behind to reach the Green Gallery.

[J Brown, J R Allen (1 pt) 14.06.52, FFA: C J Phillips 1967]

8. Pigott's Climb VS 5a 84m

An historic classic with much character.

P1 4b 22m Start by a mossy spring. Move up leftwards over grassy ledges for 12m then ascend a steep groove to a good ledge.

P2 5a 12m From the right side of the ledge, go up a steep rib, then move right to the '10-foot corner'. This desperate feature requires a determined push from the leader. Push hard enough and you will be rewarded with 'The Conservatory': a comfortable belay on a wide grassy ledge.

P3 4a 22m Easy climbing leads up the steep corner to a ledge on the right at 16m. Continue up the chimney above to the top of a massive pillar known as The Pinnacle. (Obviously not the same as the much larger Pinnacle home to *Shrike*, *Octo* etc.)

P4 5a 28m Strenuous corner cracks lead to the top.

[A S Pigott, M Wood, L Henshaw, J F Burton (3 pts) 01.05.27]

The attractive thin crack in the wall left of *Pigott's Climb* P4 is the brilliant *Capricorn*, a well protected E2 5c.

9. Great Wall E4 6a 72m

An outstanding route that easily lives up to the expectation of its grand name.

P1 6a 30m Start just right of the thin crack running up the left side of the wall. Go up diagonally left to a small overhang at 6m. Surmount this and continue up the crack and shallow groove. Thin bridging gains a thin crack above, which leads to a small stance.

P2 6a 42m Climb boldly up the shallow depression for 12m to reach a short, thin crack (good runners). The crack leads to a small left-facing corner. Move right on a sharp side-pull and stretch for a jug and a ledge. Traverse right along the ledge then head back left up easier ground to belay at the bottom of The Continuation Chimney. Take care to avoid dislodging loose stones with the rope.

[P Crew (6 pts) 27.05.62, FFA: J Allen, C Addy 28.06.75]

10. Womb Bits E5 6b 24m

If you found *Great Wall* easy, then try this harder direct version on for size. Start 6m right of *Great Wall*. Climb up for 8m to reach the thin vertical crackline. Continue up past the left side of the 'eye-lid' overlap to step left into the *Great Wall* stance.

[J Redhead, D Towse 23.07.84]

The Pinnacle

Roped scramble to Octo, Axe and Shrike

Roped scramble to Eastern Terrace descent

The Green Gallery

6

11

Capricorn
E2 5c

Indian Face
E9 6c

7

8

9

10

11

The Boulder

Eastern Terrace

Clogwyn Du'r Arddu • The East Buttress

11. A Midsummer Night's Dream E6 6a 75m

An elegant, but committing route. P1 gives a superb E5 6a in its own right.

P1 6a 25m Start half way across the base of the wall between *Great Wall* and the *Drainpipe Crack*. Head up leftwards to ledges (peg), then move up rightwards, before making sustained moves straight up to a wire loop on an old bolt. Move up and slightly left for 4/5m until it is possible to clip a peg hidden in a shallow flake corner on the left. Climb up and right, then back left until a hard move leads over a vague bulge. A line of holds runs diagonally left. Follow these until level with the *Great Wall* stance. To reach the stance, step down and traverse left.

P2 6a 22m Climb the groove of *Great Wall* for 12m, traverse left to an obvious 'mini-ledge' on the wall and ascend steeply on tiny holds until slightly easier moves lead left to the stance.

P3 6a 28m Move easily up leftwards over grassy ledges to the slab below the steep 'S' shaped arête. The first section of the arête is steep and strenuous so be sure to get the small horizontal wire placement round to the right. Above, the angle relents, and thankfully so does the difficulty. Continue to the top as cool as you can.

[P1: E Ward-Drummond (5 pts) 08.07.73, FFA: P Whillance, D Armstrong 28.07.77. P2 and P3: P Whillance, D Armstrong 28.05.78]

12. Jelly Roll E2 5b 94m

A tremendous route with a breathtaking top pitch.

P1 5a 32m *November* P1

P2 5a 22m Follow P2 of *November* until the crack closes; then move left and climb a hidden flake crack to The Green Gallery.

P3 5b 40m The steep groove is thankfully blessed with many surprising holds. Romp up it to a resting position at half height then continue up the groove for a few metres, before tracing a crack across the left wall and turning the final overhang by a crack on its left. Continue up to welcome finish jugs in the short chimney above.

[R Evans, C Rogers 17.09.71]

13. November E3 5c 112m

The sweeping crackline, arcing up the right side of The Great Wall yields a classic and uncompromising route. Start at the wide crack, just left of the *Curving Crack* pedestal.

P1 5a 32m Climb the unnerving *Drainpipe Crack*, which as the name suggests is often wet, until a ramp leads out right to a good belay. (A large cam takes some of the sting out of the initial bold section.)

P2 5c 44m Return to the base of the ramp, and continue up the crack to a ledge on the left, where the crack narrows. The crack now turns pushy and awkward; struggle on with a particularly taxing section just prior to the point where it widens into a shallow chimney. Move up past a grassy ledge just above the chimney, to a larger grassy ledge with a belay at the back.

P3 5a 36m Squirm up the awkward corner-crack to a large rock platform, and follow easier continuation cracks to the Eastern Terrace.

[J Brown, J Smith (8 pts) 03.05.57]

14. Vember E1 5b 92m

A genuine Cloggy classic – if you haven't done it, what are you waiting for?!

P1 5a 32m *November* P1.

P2 5b 36m Nip up the short cracked corner onto a small ledge to survey the crux, a shallow chimney. Dive in and tussle upwards to a small overhang. An open chimney above leads more easily up to a large grass ledge (junction with *November*) with a belay at the back.

P3 4b 24m Go up the right wall of the corner and follow cracks to the Eastern Terrace.

[J Brown, D Whillans 13.10.51]

15. Curving Crack VS 4c 66m

A good honest traditional route, taking a distinctive line up the deep crack curving behind the massive 60m high flake right of *Vember*.

P1 4c 12m Start at the right-hand side of 10m high pillar at the base of the huge flake. Sprint up the crack, jamming or laybacking, to reach the top of the pillar.

P2 4c 20m Traverse left into the main chimney/crack and follow it past an awkward bulge, to belay at a ledge on the left wall.

P3 4c 34m Fall back into the crack and follow it until the right wall drops back to a slabby angle. Move out onto the exposed arête and finish on good holds.

[M Linnell, C F Kirkus, A W Bridge, A B Hargreaves, W S Dyson 19.06.32]

16. The Troach E2 5b 66m

A superb, bold wall climb.

P1 4c 12m *Curving Crack* P1.

P2 5b 37m Move right past a shallow corner and stretch up to the quartz ledge above. Move up and slightly left into a shallow groove. Climb up it for 12m, before stepping right and continuing awkwardly to a small overlap. Move right again and overcome a thin section to grasp better holds. A short corner leads to a large flake belay.

P3 5a 17m Trend diagonally leftwards to the arête, and finish easily up it.

[H I Banner, R G Wilson 04.10.59, FFA: R Evans 1967]

17. Pedestal Crack HVS 5a 56m

A satisfying and energetic jamming exercise.

P1 5a 15m Reach the start by scrambling across from the base of *Curving Crack*. Swarm up the crack to reach a belay on top of The Pedestal.

P2 4c 10m Step back in and follow the crack to a stance in the corner.

P3 4b 31m The crack above remains steep, but is blessed with helpful holds. Belay in a grassy bay at the top. (An easier 4b variant climbs the rib to the right of the crack on P1 – this reduces the overall grade to VS.)

[C F Kirkus, G G Macphee 30.08.31]

18. Scorpio E2 5b 59m

An excellent route with a thrilling finish.

P1 5a 15m *Pedestal Crack* P1.

P2 5b 44m From the right side of the ledge, ascend the shallow groove to a hand-traverse line (thread runner) leading out right. Follow it for 6m then move up to a good ledge. Go up the shallow blank groove to a small overhang and continue up the thin crack on the left (peg), before traversing right to a blind flake crack. Surge up this to a good hold. The short wall above leads more easily to the Eastern Terrace.

[N J Soper, P Crew (2 pts) 27.04.61]

19. Silhouette E2 5c 64m

Another stunning route; the difficulties are sustained, but protection is plentiful (take a large rack!).

P1 4c 21m *The Corner* P1.

P2 5c 43m Ascend the tricky thin crack to the good ledge on *Scorpio*. Go up the shallow blank groove to a small overhang and continue up the thin crack on the left (peg). Ignore the line of *Scorpio* (which bears right at this point), and continue up the crack to a small roof. Reach through to a good hold and finish up the steady crack above.

[R Edwards, N Metcalf 23.05.75]

20. The Corner HVS 5b 53m

A truly classic climb, even when it's damp and pushing E1, which is most of the time! Strenuous and sustained, but eminently protectable.

P1 4c 21m Start directly beneath it, and scramble up grassy ledges to the base of a clean corner-crack. Trend diagonally left to more grassy ledges and onto a sloping platform at the bottom of the corner.

P2 5b 32m Take the corner more or less direct, save for a slight deviation left at 8m and the use of a crack on the right further up.

[J Brown, J R Allen, D Belsham 20.06.52]

21. Mordor E4 6a 47m

This fantastic pitch is bold and continuously difficult. Scramble up to belay at the base of the thin crack. Ascend the crack and continue up the slight groove above.

[C J Phillips, R Kirkwood (3 pts) 1969, FFA: A Sharp, S Humphries 1976]

26 27
24
25

Eastern
Terrace

22

Scramble from base
of East Buttress

23

Black
Cleft
E2 5c

24

25

26

East Buttress

29

Scramble appraoch
(to Western Terrace)

28

Far West Buttress

27

Clogwyn Du'r Arddu • The West Buttress

This vast tilted run of narrow overlapping slabs fans out across the right side of the cliff. The main routes up it are lengthy and involved affairs, which can easily eat up an entire day. Routes 22 – 25 are best reached by scrambling up right from the base of East Buttress, over rock steps and grassy ledges to the Eastern Terrace; then dropping down it's continuation which runs beneath The Boulder.

22. The Boulder E1 5a 117m

An intrepid and lonely lead. Although the climbing is steady the protection is very spaced making it a classic frightener!

P1 4c 12m Start up the left slanting groove just before the left arete, then pull rightwards through a bulge to a ledge (possible belay). Continue up for a few metres to a small slopey ledge with a rounded spike on the left and a thin crack and old peg on the right (micro wires are useful as a back up).

P2 5a 33m Climb up to an obvious undercut, then traverse quite steeply rightwards until a long reach gains the higher break line. Follow this past a hollow flake, and then continue along the easier angled delicate scoop to reach better holds on the left-hand side of a flake. Follow the holds to a small ledge immediately left of *The Black Cleft*.

P3 5a 12m Step into *The Black Cleft* and follow this to the overhang, then a swing up leftwards gains a ledge below a shattered overhanging crack. Surmount this via some fast bridging and laybacking, and then continue up the slab for a few metres to gain a ledge on the left. Belay at its left end at a flake crack.

P4 4a 60m Go up the slab above the belay, then trend rightwards to the base of the grassy gully. Scramble carefully up the gully passing another possible stance at a recess, then continue up to ledges (60m). The grass slope up and left soon leads to the top.

[J Brown 28.10.51]

23. The Boldest/Direct Finish E4 5c 83m

An outstanding yet ultimately harrowing climb.

P1 5c 45m Traverse into the obvious groove from the left and go up it to a large flake. Move right onto the arête and ascend to the level of the overhang and a spike runner. Move left beneath the overhang to a small ledge. Head up the wall above, trending slightly left to gain a faint depression. Step right and move up to a doubtful small flake. A hard move up gains an incut hold; move up and trace a line of handholds diagonally left to reach *The Boulder* traverse. Belay a few feet higher in a shallow niche.

P2 5c 38m Ascend the wall above, heading for the obvious left-facing groove. Climb this with some difficulty to the top; then scramble up over grass and loose rock for 15m to belay. Be careful to avoid dislodging loose rocks onto your second.

[P Crew, B Ingle 21.9.63/C J Phillips, P Minks 1969]

24. Longland's Climb VS 4c 126m

An elegant and exposed route, with a memorable sting in the tail.

P1 22m From the base of *The Black Cleft* go up the short gully in the corner and traverse right behind a large block to reach the bottom of the slender slab.

P2 4a 28m Climb up the slab and corner to reach a stance in the chimney where it widens.

P3 4b 12m Continue up, staying in the chimney at first, before moving out onto the slab and following an easier groove up to a stance on the right.

P4 36m Follow the slab up and move right onto a large crevassed ledge.

P5 4c 28m Exit from the right side of the ledge is blocked by overhanging rock. This final barrier responds best to an aggressive approach, so get stuck in and keep pulling! Just above is an optional belay, favoured by nervous, puny-armed seconds. To reach easy ground, move right and go up a short chimney. (It is possible to avoid the crux section by traversing right round the edge, then up and across the slab and back left, to finish up the short chimney. This is known as *The West Direct Finish* HS 4b.)

[J L Longland, A S Pigott, F S Smythe, W Eversden, M Wood 05.28]

25. Sheaf HVS 4c 162m

An elaborate route-finding wonder, with some fantastic transitional manoeuvres between the various interlocking grooves and slabs.

P1 4c 20m Scramble carefully down to the spike (often with tat) at the foot of the wet grassy terrace running down from *Longlands Climb*. From here, pull on and climb discontinuous vegetated grooves to a stance to the left of a flat shelf low on the edge of *White Slab*, which lies out of view around to the right. (It is possible to reach this point by climbing down from the large block on the P1 of *Longland's Climb*.)

P2 4c 15m Climb across and ever-so-slightly down to the flat shelf passing an obvious wobbly spike en-route. Surmount the shelf and shuffle around the arete before descending (Believe it or not, but this is Linnell's Leap!) the first few moves of P3 of *White Slab* to the large belay ledge.

P3 25m Traverse right around the edge to a broken slab. Climb up via grass steps to a ledge with a good block and continue up to a corner stance above cracked blocks.

P4 4b 22m Move out left, and ascend the steep slab to reach a small ledge on the arête. Move round into a shallow broken chimney and continue leftwards via a quartz band to join *White Slab* at a narrowing. Climb up a further 6m to belay in a slight recess.

P5 4c 20m This it, make or break time! Move right and climb the short awkward groove to good runners at the base of the evil looking *Walsh's Groove* on *West Buttress Eliminate*. *Sheaf* breaks out right through improbable steepness. Grit your teeth, stretch out and commit to the big swing out onto the hanging arête: a real heart in mouth moment! Go up the groove to the right to a small ledge, and belay in the groove above.

P6 4c 20m Make an eye-popping stretch out right for a good foothold on the arête and delicately pull round onto the slab (this is *Narrow Slab*). Move right for 5m; then trend up and left to good nut belays above a flake/block.

P7 40m Wander up grassy slabs, and up the right side of the pillar to a stance above it. Scramble off right to the cliff top.

[J Campbell, A D M Cox 17.10.45]

26. West Buttress Eliminate E3 5c 158m

A terrific climb with a bold start. Above interest is sustained, particularly in the notorious leg-pumping *Walsh's Groove* !

P1 5c 39m Start at the base of the red groove directly below the *White Slab*. Ascend the groove for 6m then move out right and ascend boldly on spaced but sizeable holds to grassy ledges. Move up to a large block and continue up the steep slabby groove just to the left. Move slightly left (crux) and go up to a short wall. Continue up to the right to belay at the bottom of *White Slab*. A serious pitch with some creaky holds.

P2 5b 34m Take the groove above direct, with a tricky section at 10m, then follow the diagonal crack up left to belay in a slight recess.

P3 5b 45m *Walsh's Groove*. Move right and climb the short awkward groove to the base of the main groove. The groove provides a sustained and gruesome battle; squirm up it, cursing the lack of conventional holds. At its top step left to belay, as for White Slab.

P4 4a 10m *White Slab* P6.

P5 5a 30m *Longland's Climb Direct Finish*. Step left and climb the superbly positioned (but poorly protected) slab. Finish up the loose chimney above.

[B Ingle, P Crew 03.06.62]

Clogwyn Du'r Arddu • The West Buttress

27. White Slab E2 5c 177m

A magnificent and sustained trip, reaching and following the attractive narrow slab right of *Longlands Climb*.

P1 5b 44m Start approximately 30m right of the point that the Eastern Terrace reaches the ground at a small shattered pinnacle just right of a wet grassy groove. Step off the pinnacle and make a tricky and bold traverse leftwards into a shallow groove. Continue traversing into the next damp groove, and climb up it to a large flake (possible stance). Remember to protect the second on the initial traverse section. Continue up the groove and crack behind the flake, to belay at the bottom of the main slab.

P2 5a 36m Move up for a few metres, then head diagonally left to the arête (Linnell's Leap in reverse). Climb the arête past a peg to a good spike at 20m. Make a delicate move right then go up the thin crack to a flake. Move left around the edge of the slab into *Gecko Groove* and climb up to a small stance.

P3 5c 21m Move back onto the arete and make bold moves rightwards into the groove. Alternatively lasso the infamous spike in the corner first. This does take the sting out of the situation, although it's not as easy as it sounds! Once you've got the spike, the choice is yours: swing across in a traditional style, or climb it free. Once in the groove, follow the diagonal crack up left to belay in a slight recess.

P4 5a 36m Follow the edge of the slab past a ledge at 20m to a stance at the top of the slab.

P5 4a 10m Traverse left and move up to the crevassed stance of *Longland's Climb*.

P6 5a 30m *Longland's Climb Direct Finish*. Step left and climb the superbly positioned (but poorly protected) slab. Finish up the loose chimney above.

[R Moseley, J Smith (1 pt) 19.04.56]

28. Great/Bow Combination HVS 166m

A popular and classic link, yielding a long and interesting climb.

P1 4c 40m Start approximately 50m up Western Terrace at an obvious break by a small pillar. Above is small slab capped by an overhang. Move up onto the slab and make a delicate traverse left into the base of the long narrow groove. Climb the groove to a large ledge and cave stance.

P2 4a 24m Step round to the right and climb up to a stance.

P3 5a 36m The crux traverse line leads out left. There are 2 possible methods: either traverse out for 3m and make a hard pull up onto the diagonal line or foot shuffle across at a higher level (easier but a little bolder). Once across, move up cracks past various ledges to a flake belay in the middle of the slab.

P4 4b 30m Continue up in the same line to a stance just above the final skyline of the slab.

P5 36m Escape from the recess on the left, move back right onto the rib and finish up the edge of the slab.

[C F Kirkus, G G Macphee 15.06.30/J M Edwards, J Cooper (1 pt) 20.09.41]

29. Bloody Slab E3 5b 90m

This splendid slab route is thin and sustained. The approach to the route is up the Western Terrace. There was a major rockfall here in 1986 and significant loose debris remains. Consequently it is not recommended as a descent and great care should be exercised when moving up it.

P1 5b 30m Scramble carefully up the Western Terrace to reach a good thread belay just above a rock step and below a prominent boulder. Move up then traverse left and continue up to a slot (runner) at 12m. Go up to the bulge and surmount it with difficulty. Step left and trace the flake crack to the triangular overhang. Turn the overhang on the left to reach a small sloping stance.

P2 5b 28m Traverse left and ascend to a small ledge. Continue leftwards, moving down slightly, to grass, before climbing up the grassy gully on the left.

P3 32m Go up the rib on the left and continue up over broken rocks to the top.

[J Streetly (1 pt) 10.06.52]

This slabby buttress is often overlooked in favour of the more obvious attractions elsewhere on the cliff. Nonetheless it provides some very good quality 'Idwal Slab-esque' climbing at an accessible grade.

30. Primitive Route VD 133m

This is a great opportunity to savour the Cloggy experience at a reasonable grade.

P1 28m Start just left of the foot of the buttress at a prominent ledge, below a short corner. Go up the corner to a jammed block. Step right for a metre or so and follow the leftward-slanting crack to a decent stance and belay.

P2 16m Move up broken rock, trending leftwards to a large grassy bay beneath twin grooves.

P3 32m Ascend the right-hand groove for 10m; then move left into and up the left-hand groove. Trend diagonally right to a ledge then continue to a higher ledge.

P4 8m Climb the short moss speckled corner leading to a flake belay.

P5 24m Ascend the corner above the belay (taking care with dubious blocks at the top) to steep rock. Traverse left past twin chimneys formed by a large block to nut belays at the left edge of the grassy ledge.

P6 25m The corner above is quite awkward and leads to a grassy recess. Trend up and right on scree then back left to blocks. The top is reached by a couple of rope lengths of scrambling, trending up right and gradually easing.

[H R C Carr, G A Lister 05.09.19]

31. Slab Climb Right-Hand HS 4b 152m

A delightful route. After a devious entry onto the slabby face, you are faced with open, delicate slab climbing on perfect rock, occasionally interspersed with grassy ledges.

P1 4b 36m Start just left of the foot of the buttress. Traverse rightwards for 6m across the sloping 'Giant's Causeway' to reach a corner. Ascend this; then trend diagonally right up the slab to belay on the blunt spike at the top of the grass furrow.

P2 24m Move easily up grass on the left until it a step up right gains the base of the large slab. Climb up to a ledge and a tricky belay.

P3 30m Trend diagonally right into the chimney, climb the edge of the slab for 10m and step back onto the slab proper. Climb up to belay on a ledge on the edge of the chimney.

P4 42m Move back left onto the slab and pick a line to reach easier ground above.

P5 22m Follow the easy prominent arête on the right to the far western terrace. The top is reached by a couple of rope lengths of gradually easing scrambling, trending right.

[G Milburn, D Gregory 27.10.73]

West Buttress

Lliwedd

Area: Snowdon
Style: Trad (5 - 12 pitches)
Aspect: North-East
Rock type: Rhyolitic Tuff
Approach: 60 minutes
Altitude: 650m

Terminator	E1

The Sword/Route 2	VS
Paradise/Black Arête	HS
Avalanche/Red Wall and Longland's Continuation	S
Jacob's Ladder/Via Media	S

Horned Crag Route	VD
Slanting Buttress Ridge Route	D

Lliwedd is the biggest of the Welsh mountain cliffs, and fittingly it offers some of the best adventure routes in the area. It is situated majestically above the deep blue water of Llyn Llydaw, its ridged back forming the southern arm of the dramatic Snowdon horsehoe. The views on a good day are unsurpassable, both en route and from the summit.

Although broken in nature the best lines link areas of excellent rock. Although the cliff is tilted at a generally slabby angle, protection is not overly abundant. Moreover there is a distinct lack of incut holds, often just where an anxious leader might need them most. These are points worth noting, if for any reason a retreat is being contemplated. The consequences of being caught out by the elements can quickly reach epic proportions. Experience, route-finding savvy and a general steadiness are prerequisites for the Lliwedd-bound team. If these elements are present, a grand day will be in order.

Conditions: The cliff does receive early morning sun, but then spends the rest of the day cast in shadow. Consequently it is best suited to bright sunny days. Excessive drainage is not normally a major problem (a day or so after rain, it should be dry), but the dearth of runners and typically non-positive nature of the holds means that wet ascents can't be recommended, save perhaps for *Slanting Buttress Ridge Route*.

Approach: Park at Pen y Pass (the car park is usually full by 8am on a weekend during the summer, in which case a park and ride scheme operates from Nant Peris). From Pen y Pass follow the Miners Track to the first big lake, Llyn Llydaw. The massive crag can be seen up and left dominating the skyline. Follow the path which runs up towards the ridge left of the cliff. After 300m the path dips down slightly. From this point it is possible to traverse across the slope to the base of the routes. Alternatively, traverse round to the left side of Llyn Llydaw and slog directly up to the cliff base.

It is feasible to mountain bike most of the way in, leaving the bikes at some point across the traverse (first approach method). This has the obvious advantage of being quicker and also enables great smugness to be achieved as you zip past all the exhausted walkers on the way out. In the summer months (1st May - 30th September) cycling is only allowed before 10am and after 5pm.

Descent: Most climbers will choose the option of climbing a single route per day, and then continue from the summit of Lliwedd, either on to Snowdon and perhaps round to Crib Goch (if they get a move on!), or to descend leftwards along the Snowdon Horseshoe path leading back to the approach route.

The true devotee, who made a suitably early start, may be hungry for a second route. In which case 2 descents are possible to the base of the crag. For all routes finishing from

Andy Bruce embracing the summit experience on top of Lliwedd photo: Al Leary ^

Lliwedd

LLANBERIS +

OGWEN +

TREMADOG +

GOGARTH & LLEYN

LLANDUDNO +

the East Buttress, descend leftwards (facing in) until a grassy col is reached. A steep grassy descent can be made down the gully and slopes, until the base of the crag can be reached. DO NOT attempt to descend East Gully. From the West Summit of Lliwedd, and for the routes on Slanting Buttress, a descent down a wide grassy gully can be made with care, to the right of Slanting Buttress (facing in). The initial steep ground quickly eases.

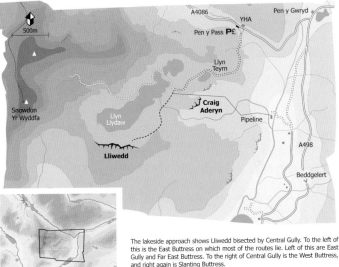

The lakeside approach shows Lliwedd bisected by Central Gully. To the left of this is the East Buttress on which most of the routes lie. Left of this are East Gully and Far East Buttress. To the right of Central Gully is the West Buttress, and right again is Slanting Buttress.

East
Gully

Great
Terrace

Green
Gallery

Shallow
Gully

Heather
Shelf

Central
Chimney

Birch Tree
Terrace

Routes from Heather Shelf (the Heather Shelf is the first grassy/heathery terrace system to the right of East Gully and is reached by an easy scramble up clean and quartzy rock).

▶ **1. Horned Crag Route VD** 255m

An excellent route up the left side of the East Buttress. Start at the left hand end of the Heather Shelf.

P1 18m Step down left and move left across one rib to a second rib, which is followed to a grassy ledge. Belay on the left of this below a steep corner.

P2 25m Climb the corner for 6m and step left onto the arête. Follow this on its right hand side to a large ledge.

P3 27m Continue up the right side of the broad rib to belay on another heathery ledge.

P4 30m Climb diagonally rightwards across a wall to reach a short V-chimney. Follow this and then move right along a quartz band to a good ledge.

P5 25m Scramble up the easy grassy rake to a stance below the Horned Crag.

P6 20m Climb the groove in the middle of the wall to a possible stance. From here climb the steeper groove until a tricky step right leads to good holds and the foot of the polished slab below the Horns.

P7 10m Polish the slab some more to reach the end of the difficulties.

P8/9 100m Scrambling remains until the summit is reached.

[J M A Thomson, O Eckenstein 09.05]

▶ **2. Paradise/Black Arête HS 4a** 270m

A great combination that requires a steady leader especially on the first pitch. Start at the rock spike at the left end of the Heather Shelf.

P1 4a 30m Climb directly up to the narrow overhang, then step right into the groove and follow this to a narrow ledge. From the right hand side of this ascend the vertical quartz band and belay below a grassy ledge.

P2 4a 22m Head leftwards up the slabs, climbing the short groove to the left of a dirty overhang. Continue in the same line to a ledge and belay below a smooth V-groove.

P3 4a 25m Traverse left to a wide groove. Climb the clean slabby rock on the left side of the groove to a good ledge on the right.

P4 30m (Start of *The Black Arete*.) Traverse 4m right to below a quartz wall. Climb this onto the arête and follow this to a stance on broken rocks with a large grassy ledge to the left.

P5 28m Climb the quartz veined arête to easier ground and a spike belay.

P6 35m Continue up the narrow quartz rib and follow easy ground to reach the arête on the right. This is *Terminal Arête*.

P7/8 100m Easy scrambling leads to the top.

[H O Jones, R F Backwell 23.09.09/J M A Thomson 09.07]

Lliwedd • East Buttress

Routes from below the Heather Shelf:

3. Avalanche/Red Wall and Longland's Continuation S 4b 286m

A deservedly popular classic. Start just to the left of the often-wet steep curving groove that runs up to the right-hand end of the Heather Shelf. Alternatively start at the right-hand end of the Heather Shelf to join the route at the start of P2.

P1 20m Traverse right into the groove and follow it to the Heather Shelf.

P2 30m Climb a gradually rising rightwards traverse, round two ribs, and to a belay 4m left of a large spike.

P3 15m Climb the slab above and belay to the left of a quartz band.

P4 25m Traverse to the right-hand end of the ledge and climb the short quartz band. Step left into a groove and follow this until it is possible to move right onto ledges. Move right round a rib and climb this for 5m to a good spike and nut belays.

P5 33m Climb up and rightwards to a grassy groove, which is followed to a large bollard at its top.

P6 30m Scramble rightwards to belay in the vicinity of a small jammed block at the bottom of some red slabs.

P7 4a 25m (Start of *Red Wall*.) Traverse right to a grassy groove. Move up and right gaining the well-worn rib. A tricky move onto this leads to good ledges. Belay about 6m below a large pinnacle.

P8 4a 28m Climb the slabby rib to the left of the pinnacle to a ledge. A hard move up the short wall brings you to the Green Gallery. Shallow Gully is to the right.

P9 10m Easy climbing leads to quartzy rocks, some 10m left of Shallow Gully.

P10 25m (Start of *Longland's Continuation*.) Start below a steep face with a distinct left edge. Climb the rib for 4m into a niche. Step right via a jammed block onto the slab and climb this for 6m. Trend up right past a groove and second slab to belay in a grassy rake.

P11 30m Move right onto the rib and follow this over various rock jumbles to a ledge below a steep slab.

P12 4b 15m You are now in full view of the assembled awe-struck walkers. The slab is not easy, whether direct, or by trending leftwards at half height. Scorch up the remaining summit rocks to tumultuous applause and flashbulbs.

[J M A Thomson, E S Reynolds 09.07/J L Longland and party Easter 1929]

Red Wall graffitti photo: Al Leary ∧
Andy Bruce on **Red Wall/Longland's Continuation** VD photo: Al Leary >

OGWEN +

TREMADOG +

GOGARTH & LLEYN

LLANDUDNO +

4. The Sword/Route 2 VS 4c/VD 154m

A great combination of routes. A long and bold VS pitch followed by a pleasant VD that leads up to the Great Terrace, where it is possible to follow *Red Wall/Longland's Continuation* or *Terminal Arête* all the way to the top. Scramble up to the base of the crag along the obvious quartz band until below an obvious rib, the route starts right of the rib below a corner with an overlap at 5m.

P1 4c 50m Climb up the corner to the overlap and step out left to the small ledge on the rib. Follow the rib up with sustained interest and some loose rock, until after an age (or so it seems) it eases. Belay on a quartz ledge at the top of the rib.

P2 20m Climb the easy and polished crack/groove directly behind the stance, to a spike belay on a ledge.

P3 12m From the top of the highest spike make a fantastic move out onto a polished foot hold and carry on up to reach the 'Thank God' holds, before traversing easily left to another ledge and belay below a groove.

P4 42m Climb the groove on good holds, after 12m there is a possible stance on the left, continue up an easy groove on the right for a further 30m to a small ledge and belays.

P5 30m Scramble easily upward to the Great Terrace and belay just below where the crag starts to steepen again. If you are continuing up *Red Wall/Longland's Continuation* belay 24m to the right of the obvious quartz blocks at the base of *Terminal Arête* (the obvious ridge at the left hand end of the terrace).

[J M Edwards, J H Buzzard, F A Champion 08.38/J M A Thomson, O Eckenstein]

5. Terminator E1 5b 172m

A truly great way to reach Terminal Arête. Start below Birch Tree Terrace and the corner of *Central Chimney*. Some 10m to the right is a left slanting rib.

P1 5a 30m Boldly follow the slanting rib on the left to eventually reach easier ground. Belay on Birch Tree Terrace at the base of a pinnacle underneath a steep inverted V-groove.

P2 5b 47m Climb onto the block at the foot of the right hand arête of the V-groove. Make a hard move onto the slab and follow this directly to belay below a steep wall by some quartz veins. A very fine and sustained pitch.

P3 5a 25m Climb through The Eaves above via an overhanging groove to easy ground. Follow this to belay below and to the left of a grassy groove.

P4 35m Follow the left side of the grassy groove to belay at a square block below a steep wall.

P5 5b 35m Climb the wall above the block, move right to a flat hold, and then back up left to another good hold. Trend left into the left hand groove, which is followed until a grassy ledge and a large block are reached after 20m. Climb onto the block a make a reachy move up the wall, which leads to the terrace and large quartz blocks below the start of *Terminal Arête*. Finish up *Terminal Arête*.

[First full ascent: J Hope, K Neal 13.05.90, P3: J M Edwards, A M Keith, G D Bryan 1938, P1: R Kay, J Toombs 08.89]

6. Terminal Arete D 120m

The classic finish from the Great Terrace.
Start by the large quartz blocks and follow the arête for 60m belaying at will. Scrambling leads to the top.

[J M A Thomson, O Eckenstein 24.04.03]

Lliwedd • Slanting Buttress

To the far right of the crag is Slanting Buttress, which is easily identifiable by the 2 prominent quartz chevrons visible from the approach.

7. Slanting Buttress Ridge Route D 250m

A truly great and exposed climb with the big mountain atmosphere. At the right-hand side of the West Buttress is the obvious gash of Slanting Gully. Start immediately to the left of the foot of the lower quartz chevron.

P1 45m Climb up the slabs to reach block belays at the top of the upper quartz chevron.

P2 30m Continue up easily in the same line to belay some 15m below the left hand of 2 obvious corner grooves.

P3 26m Climb up and left wards to belay in a recess at the foot of the left-hand corner groove.

P4 17m Climb the slab on the left to a ledge. Continue leftward up a broken slab to a fine exposed stance on the arête.

P5 20m Step left into the groove and follow this up and back right to a stance on the arête.

P6 20m Take the steep groove on the left for 3m. Head back right to the arête and follow it to block belays.

P7 20m Continue up the 5 star ridge, steeply at first, but then leveling out until belays are reached.

P8 22m Scramble up rightwards and climb the quartz rock up and right to the crest, until below a slabby groove.

P9 20m Climb the groove for 15m until above a large spike. Move right out of the groove and round the rib to belay on a ledge beneath overhangs.

P10 30m Climb leftwards up the slabs and step left round the rib to reach a corner. Follow this until the summit ridge is reached out to the right.

[G D Abraham, A P Abraham 04.04]

Streaky Desroy on **Slanting Buttress Ridge Route** D photo: Neil Dyer >

Lliwedd • Craig Aderyn

A surprising little crag, hidden at the back of Upper Cwm Dyli. It could be combined with a day on Lliwedd or just nabbed as a quick, accessible hit.

Approach: Walk along the Miners Track from Pen y Pass, as per Lliwedd. After about 15 minutes the track traverses above Llyn Teyrn. There are 2 obvious hummocks that lie on either side of the pipeline. Wander down to the pipeline and across to the furthest or most southerly hump. The crag is tucked in round the back of here. The slab is south-east facing and dries quickly after rain.

Descent: Traverse rightwards (facing in), drop down slightly to reach the top of a rib (after 12m) and go down this carefully. Follow it to the right before switching back left, underneath a short rock face, to a slabby step. From here a short grassy gully runs down to the bottom of the crag.

8. Jacob's Ladder/Via Media S 4a 50m

The attractive slab can be climbed anywhere at about VS, however the cleanest and by far the best line is almost straight up the middle to the highest point. The arete itself can be ascended at VD. Start 5m left of the right arete. Climb straight up to a quartzy hold at 14m, and continue up to a crack that leads diagonally left to the apex of the slab, climb this to the top.
[F Graham 07.10.24/F Graham, M W Guinness 24.08.25]

Bouldering

The Cwm Dyli Boulders situated on the open meadow in front of Craig Aderyn have numerous entertaining problems, with generally good landings.

Alex Williams ducking under the pipeline on the way to Craig Aderyn photo: Al Leary ∧
Alex Williams on **Jacob's Ladder/Via Media** S 4a photo: Al Leary >

LLANBERIS + B

OGWEN +

TREMADOG +

GOGARTH & LLEYN

LLANDUDNO +

133

Slate • Llanberis +

LLANBERIS +

OGWEN +

TREMADOG +

GOGARTH & LLEYN

LLANDUDNO +

The Dinorwig slate quarries provide an immense, surreal backdrop to the village of Llanberis. This vista is every bit as iconic as the classic Llanberis Pass, Snowdon and Cloggy postcard views. The history of the quarries defines the cultural base of Llanberis, and although closed since 1969, its impact upon the local community still resonates to this day.

During the 1980s a new generation of climbers set about developing this fascinating industrial wasteland into a premier climbing venue. The legacy of their efforts is a collection of exquisitely technical climbs, sometimes geared with the odd bolt, but typically run out. There are some proper clip-ups, but these tend to be in the harder grades. A recent re-equipping campaign and the prospect of a new definitive guide (produced by Ground Up) has seen a resurgence of interest in this remarkable collection of crags.

Unfortunately there is little in the way of easy routes. Climbers operating in the extreme grades will best appreciate the quarries. However the attraction of this bizarre, man-made landscape cuts right across the spectrum; one of the best rainy day activities in the Llanberis area is to spend a few hours wandering around these atmospheric holes in the ground.

Seasonal Conditions: The quarries provide opportunities for climbing throughout the year. The rock dries extremely quickly, making this a popular option in showery or changeable weather.

Getting There: Access to the quarries is made either from the Slate Museum car park (Gilfach Ddu) at the base of Vivian Quarry, or from the Bus Stop Quarry 'turning circle' on the outskirts of the village of Dinorwig. Dinorwig is reached either by driving up the Fachwen road, or across from Deiniolen, both of which are signposted from the Llanberis-Bangor road.

Access Restrictions: There is one area of Vivian Quarry subject to a climbing ban during the opening hours of the diving centre. See the Vivian Quarry pages for more details.

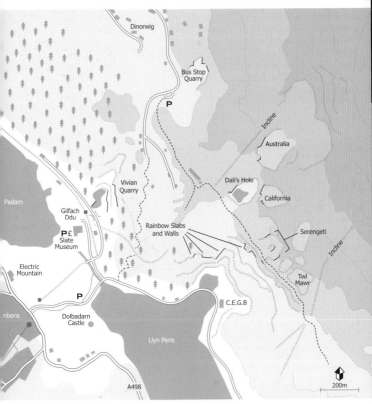

Dinorwig

Bus Stop
Quarry

P

Incline

Australia

Dali's Hole

California

Vivian
Quarry

Padarn

Gilfach
Ddu

P £
Slate
Museum

Rainbow Slabs
and Walls

Serengeti

Incline

Electric
Mountain

Twl
Mawr

P

nberis

C.E.G.B

Dolbadarn
Castle

Llyn Peris

A498

200m

Slate shot-hole or plant pot? photo: Rob Wilson ∧

The detritus of industrial times past, strewn across a surreal landscape - perfect for a Sunday morning stroll photo: Ray Wood ⅄

Vivian Quarry ®

Area:	Llanberis
Style:	Trad/Sport (single pitch)
Aspect:	Varied
Rock type:	Slate
Approach:	3 - 10 minutes
Altitude:	100m

Menstrual Gossip	F8a+
Manic Strain	F8a
Gin Palace	F7c

Dawes of Perception	E7

Flashdance/ Belldance combination	E5
Bathtime	E5
The Sweetest Taboo	E4
Soap on a Rope	E4
Comes The Dervish	E3

Is it a Crime?	E2
Never as Good as the First Time	E2
Last Tango in Paris	E2
Psychotherapy	E2
The Monster Kitten	E1
Mental Lentils	HVS

An atmospheric quarry with easy access and great diversity of climbing. This conspicuous gash in the hillside, with its multi-tiered quarry levels, sits within the wooded Padarn Country Park, on the opposite side of Llyn Padarn to the village of Llanberis. At the base of the quarry a dark and apparently fathomless pool adds a sense of otherworldliness to this already surreal place. The pool, which is actually 19m deep, is very popular with the diving fraternity. The spectacle of the divers and climbers often draws an audience of curious tourists, so please be on your best behaviour – no swearing when you fall off!

This is an excellent venue either for a quick route, or for a full day's cragging. Protection is varied and a selection of traditional gear should be carried on most routes. The selected routes are popular (*Dawes of Perception* excepted!) and as such loose holds are unlikely. However, this being slate, they are always a possibility.

There is a café in the Slate Museum for mandatory tea breaks and public toilets in the Gifach Ddu car park. There are also some very pleasant marked walks leading through the Padarn Country Park. Other alternative attractions include canoe hire, boat trips and the Electric Mountain (another café!) on the other side of Llyn Padarn.

Access restrictions: The quarry is a popular diving venue; for obvious reasons please don't climb on the Bathtime Wall whilst the Diving Centre is open. To check the opening hours call 01286 870889 or go to www.divevivian.com

Conditions: Most routes dry exceptionally quickly. You can easily keep tabs on this from Pete's Eats (yet another café in Llanberis!) with a pair of binoculars.

Rob Wilson slotting in a sinker wire on **Mental Lentils** HVS 5a photo: Jethro Kiernan

Vivian Quarry

GILFACH DDU

Approach: From the Snowdon Mountain Railway on the A4086 in Llanberis, take the road opposite towards the power station. At the first junction turn left and follow the road into the Gilfach Ddu pay and display car park. The car park is normally open from 9.00 am, however the gate closing time is seasonal (winter: 4.30pm, spring/autumn: 6.00pm, summer 7.00pm). Alternative parking is available in the Dolbadarn car park, which is passed on the road leading from Llanberis.

For the Mental Lentils Area, go through the archway next to the Diving Centre and walk past the side of the deep pool. The climbing begins after crossing the stile. For the Bathtime Wall, go up the ramp right of the archway to the first opening on the left. Go through this and turn left on to the road, After 100m, follow the steps on the right up a level, cross the fence and abseil down the right hand side of the prow to a ledge on the arete. For the Dervish Level, continue up the steps to the next level. Cross the stile over the fence and follow the path past a 'bad step' to the Dervish Slab and Nostromo Wall. The Conscience Slab is round to the right again past another awkward section.

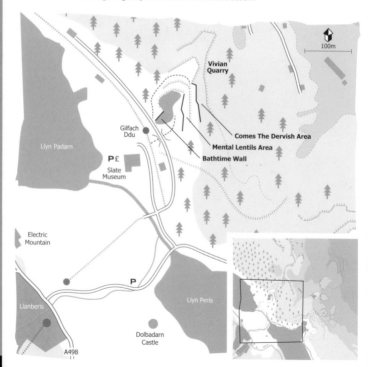

Mental Lentils Area • **The Pool Level, Vivian Quarry**

LLANBERIS +

OGWEN +

TREMADOG +

GOGARTH & LLEYN

LLANDUDNO +

Approach to
Psychotherapy

1. Mental Lentils HVS 5a 18m
A pleasant introduction to slate climbing. Start 5m after the stile. Follow the line of bolts and flakes up the right-hand side of the first slab. Take some medium wires. Lower off, or if you thought it was too easy, scramble over the top to belay at the base of the next route...
[P Barbier 28.10.86]

2. The Monster Kitten E1 5c 8m
A stark contrast to *Mental Lentils*, which, incidentally, forms the most agreeable approach. It is possible to scramble up the ramp to the start, but it is pretty unpleasant. This well named route follows the innocuous diagonal crack until a 'bad step' can be made right to a foot jug and the lower-off. It feels much pumpier than its length would suggest.
[S Andrews, S Britain 27.05.86]

3. Dawes of Perception E7 6c 25m
Tales of belayers diving into the lake to take in slack and near fatal top-roping accidents help ensure this hard route is not polished. A lonesome bolt on the slab 10m left of *Mental Lentils* gives the talented climber a target to aim for. The narrow niche and perched flake below it takes uninspiring gear and may protect a pre-bolt fall, but only if your belayer is brave enough to take the plunge...
With the bolt clipped, the technical crux awaits on the left. There's little let up after that, and even though there are some small wires in the diagonal cracks above, pulling on to the scree at the top will test even the bravest.
[J Dawes 23.10.85]

4. Psychotherapy E2 5c 25m
A good but unbalanced route with a hard, well-protected start and a run-out but easier top section. At the back left of The Pool Level is a narrow slab with a silver birch at the top. 2 bolts protect the hard lower section, but an awkward move high up may require a wire and a large friend. Lower off. Popular, and rightly so.
[A D Newton, P Pritchard 08.05.88]

Vivian Quarry, The Pool Level • Bathtime Wall

LLANBERIS +

OGWEN +

TREMADOG +

GOGARTH & LLEYN

LLANDUDNO +

Please don't climb on this wall whilst the diving centre is open.

5. Bathtime E5 6a 25m ®
A bold route, sometimes done as a deep water solo. From the bolt, climb the groove in the arete until it's possible to swing left onto a traverse line on the front face. This leads to a spike runner. From this, trend left to a crack. Follow this to a ledge and finish up the obvious left-leaning line above.
[P Pritchard 04.87]

6. Soap on a Rope E4 6a 22m ®
An easier, better-protected route starting from the same place as *Bathtime*. From the spike on *Bathtime*, head right and take the line of weaknesses just left of the arete passing 2 bolts en route.
[P Pritchard, P Johnstone 22.01.88]

Divers in the pool photo: Si Panton >

7. Menstrual Discharge (Kleinian Envy) F8a+ 18m
A sculpted route of an entirely desperate nature. A series of acutely difficult manoeuvres lead up the wall past 5 bolts to a lower-off. Don't confuse it with *Colditz* F7b+ which climbs the wall just right again.
[J Redhead 09.06.86]

8. Manic Strain F8a 18m
Another Redhead masterpiece with sculpted holds (just too far apart for some) and plenty of bolts. It climbs the bolt ladder above the Anarchist graffiti on the vertical wall left of the *'Dervish'* slab. The technical crux is near the bottom, but the redpoint crux is near the top.
[J Redhead 24.04.86]

9. Gin Palace F7c E6 6b (at least!) 18m
The massive flake groove right of *Manic Strain* is a real pumper, and the crack above the overlap is no easier. Bolts protect the lower section, but gear is needed for the top. To descend, either climb down to the *Manic Strain* lower off, or walk out on the level above and drop back down to join the original approach.
[C Smith 25.06.86]

LLANBERIS +

OGWEN +

TREMADOG +

GOGARTH & LLEYN

LLANDUDNO +

141

Vivian Quarry, Comes the Dervish Area • The Dervish Slab

10. Comes The Dervish E3 5c 40m
The most famous slate route! The line should be obvious as it can be seen from Llanberis High Street. However for those not in the know, it climbs the central crack on the big overlapped slab. The start is not to be underestimated as it requires commitment (the first good runner is a 1.5 cam at 8m), but once established in the crack proper, runners abound and excellent climbing leads eventually to the overlap. Pull through this with style and follow the crack to the top. Abseil station in situ. Well deserving of its classic status.
[S Haston 02.81]

11. Flashdance/Belldance Combination E5 6b 45m
2 great routes morphed into a sustained classic pitch. Start up the diagonal crack of *Last Tango in Paris*, then boldly follow the diagonal line of scoops and edges past some RPs to gain *Comes The Dervish* (*Flashdance*). Place a wire or 6 then traverse right to let round 2 begin (*Belldance*). Hard, fingery moves allow the overlap to be reached. Once over this, trend right and place some welcome gear. From here, head back left into the original crackline, which is followed to the top. Abseil off. (*Flashdance* itself is a superb E5 6a.)
[A Pollitt, T Freeman 08.83/J Redhead, D Towse 19.03.84]

12. Last Tango in Paris E2 5c 45m
Another good route curving up the right-hand side of the Dervish slab. Climb the diagonal cracks right of *Comes The Dervish* to the groove in the right arete of the slab. Get established on the ledge above and take stock. Pull leftwards onto the slab and follow the diagonal flake crack leftwards and so to the top. As with the other routes on the slab, the technicality eases after the overlap but care with the rock is still required. Abseil off.
[M Roberts, C Edwards 12.05.85]

< Breaking through the overlap
on **Comes The Dervish** E3 5c
photo: Ray Wood

Nostromo Wall

10

11

12

Approach to The
Conscience Slab

Vivian Quarry, Comes the Dervish Area • The Conscience Slab

LLANBERIS +

OGWEN +

TREMADOG +

GOGARTH & LLEYN

LLANDUDNO +

Approach from
The Dervish Slab

13. The Sweetest Taboo E4 6a 25m
The best route on this small slab forces a bold line up the centre, equiped with just
enough protection including a bolt and a wire. Lower off.
[M Raine, J Dawes 01.05.86]

14. Never as Good as the First Time E2 5c 23m
This is the easiest of these three routes.
From the right-hand side of the slab climb up and right until a tricky move back left gains
a bolt. (A wire can be placed below to ease the psychological commitment). Head left
then up to join *The Sweetest Taboo* at a large flake. Clip the bolt above, then follow the
crack rightwards to the belay. Lower off.
[M Raine, C Dale 10.05.86]

15. Is it a Crime? E2 5c 23m
Another alluring route with more good climbing that is slightly harder than its neighbour.
Start as for *Never as Good as the First Time* to the first bolt, then move up and right past
another bolt to a thin crack and a final bolt before the belay. Lower off.
[M Raine, C Dale 10.05.86]

PHOTO: ADAM LONG
BEN MOON
VOYAGER 8B
BURBAGE NORTH
moon
MOON
CLIMBING
CLOTHING/TRAINING/ACCESSORIES/MORE
VISIT: WWW.MOONCLIMBING.COM

Rainbow Slab Area

Area: Dinorwig Quarry
Style: Trad/Sport (1-2 pitches)
Aspect: Varied
Rock type: Slate
Approach: 30 mins +
Altitude: 100m

Bungle's Arete	F8b
Spong (is good for you)	F7c+
The Dark Destroyer	F7c+
The Dark Half	F7c+

True Clip	F7b+

The Rainbow of Recalcitrance	E6

Cystitis By Proxy	E5
Jack of Shadows	E5
Major Headstress	E5
Poetry Pink	E5
Splitstream	E5
Great Balls of Fire	E4
Ride the Wild Surf	E4
The Mau Mau	E4
Colossus	E3
Horse Latitudes (H.A. finish)	E3

German Schoolgirl	E2
Pull my Daisy	E2
Red and yellow...(R.O.Y. finish)	E2
Bella Lugosi is Dead	E1

A truly great climbing area featuring a wide selection of excellent routes, ranging right across the spectrum from bold trad lines to hard clip-ups, with a few hybrids in the middle. The magnificent Rainbow Slab is one of the most striking pieces of rock in the whole of North Wales. Even if you don't fancy trying the routes, be sure to go and see it at least once.

The approach is longer than for the other parts of the slate quarries, but the quality of the routes offsets this, and the area can still be used as an evening venue in the summer months. Please keep a low profile and remember that the Power Station staff may not wish to hear how upset you are after failing on the umpteenth redpoint.

As always on slate, it is worth carrying a small trad rack on the more sportingly protected 'sport' routes. The rock is almost all of excellent quality, but there are a few friable flakes in places.

Pull My Daisy E2 5c photo: Rob Wilson

Rainbow Slab Area

Conditions: As is typical of slate, the rock dries quickly after rain, with parts of the Colossus Wall being the exception. It may be wise to leave an extended drying period on the more committing routes, just in case you happen to encounter wet holds at the end of a run-out.

Approach: There are 2 main approaches depending on what time of day you envisage finishing, as the gates for the Slate Museum car park (Gilfach Ddu) will be locked at 7pm. If you are going to be back to the car by then, park at the Slate Museum and walk up 2 levels of inclines immediately right of the tunnel entrance into Vivian Quarry, to the second winding house. Follow the main path until it bends left, cross the fence (next to the warning sign) and carry on at the same level until you reach the old quarry buildings on the left. For the routes on the Rainbow Walls, continue along the main path until it bears up and left. Cross the fence and follow the descriptions for the separate areas below. This point can also be reached from the upper quarries by crossing the gate opposite Dali's Hole and following the main path downwards, but this means you have to walk back up at the end of the day.

For the Rainbow Slab area, drop down and right, opposite the quarry building. Follow a vague path on the right of the stream until it is possible to cross it. Continue down following a more distinctive path until you can cut back left on the Rainbow Level proper. The hulking Colossus Wall should be very obvious at this point, with the Bella Lugosi area just before it. The Rainbow slab is situated further along the level, just out of sight.

If you're not sure what time you'll be back, park in the Dolbadarn Castle car park on the left as you approach the power station from Llanberis. Carry on along the road to the main junction where an obvious footpath on the right (signposted) zigzags up and through the trees to a bridge, by the second winding house, and carry on as before. Either of the approaches can be reached from Llanberis by walking along the lakeside, adding about 15 minutes to the approach time.

Descent: For the Bella Lugosi Area head up and follow an obvious drainage line/rake that runs back down left (facing in). For the Colossus Area traverse (facing in) on a cliff top path to reach and follow the *Bella Lugosi* descent.

For the Rainbow Slab it is possible to abseil from the top of *Cystitis...*, although the scree approach to the abseil point is a little unnerving. Alternatively head across left (facing in) to reach the Colossus/Bella Lugosi area descent.

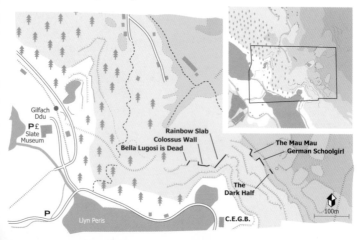

Colossus Wall

▶ **1. Horse Latitudes (The Horsin' Around Finish) E3 5c** 25m
A neglected route that deserves to be climbed more often, if only it wasn't so damned bold. Climb the dolerite dyke that forms the left hand arete of the *Bella Lugosi* slab with very little gear to the large ledge. Arrange protection, and then tussle up the final short wall on the right to finish as for *Bella Lugosi is Dead*.
[M E Crook, I A Jones, R Drury, D Jones 15.06.85/A Holmes, S Long 20.05.86]

▶ **2. Bella Lugosi is Dead E1 5b** 25m
A popular route on good rock with adequate gear. Climb the central crack with continuous interest until hard moves by the overlap gains the finishing ledges (medium-sized cam useful).
[M E Crook, N Walton 28.05.84]

3. Jack of Shadows E5 6a 40m

A good, varied route that will test both the nerve and technical prowess of most leaders. It climbs the obvious, continuous groove line on the left wall of the Colossus Buttress past numerous bolts.

P1 6a 22m Saunter up to the second bolt up and left. From here, step down and make contorted moves round the rib on the right (crux). Follow the sustained groove above to a perched flake and another awkward step right (trying not to weight the flake too much). One more hard move above gains a spacious belay ledge with 2 bolts.

P2 6a 18m Cross the ledges leftwards to a tapered, hanging slab with a trio of bolts on it. Climb past these with trepidation and swing leftwards to a juggy prow. Step back into the groove and follow it to the top (passing another suspect flake en route). Bolt belay.

[O Jones, R Whitwell 22.06.86]

4. Major Headstress E5 6a 45m

A well named route; bold, reachy climbing leads up the left side of the Colossus Wall, before a rightwards traverse is made to join *Ride*..... . Climb the crack, just in from the left arete, to a sloping niche. Clip the bolt above and climb the left arete of the V-groove to a long reach by the second clip. More sustained climbing gains the sanctuary of the third bolt. Pass this on layaways, then move right to good holds by the next bolt. Continue right to join *Ride*..... and do battle with its finishing groove and headwall.

[P Williams, C Gilchrist 06.05.86]

5. Ride the Wild Surf E4 6a 45m

'A most excellent route dude', that blasts up the flaked wall: engrossing climbing and airy situations. Start up the enticing flake line left of centre, clip the first bolt, then step up and right to clip the first bolt of *Great Balls*.... . Traverse back left with some deft footwork on 'chipedeedoodah' (the most obviously chipped hold in the quarries) and climb the small stepped corner to a small roof. A distant bolt above shows the way, so keep it steady, because when it's clipped, the headwall is a comparative path. Top out and hang ten.

[P Williams, D Jones 26.04.86]

6. Great Balls of Fire E4 6a 50m

Not as direct as the other routes on the wall, but nevertheless, a very worthwhile route that will 'shake the nerves' of most leaders. Start between the grooves of *Colossus* and *Ride*... . Pass the first bolt, aiming for double bolts above a small ledge. Make hard moves by these, and then continue directly up the groove until it's possible to step right into the base of the V-groove of *Colossus*. Keep going right into the obvious stepped groove system. This is awkward and bold, and leads eventually to a large ledge just below the top. Cruise onwards to glory.

[P Williams 12.04.86]

7. Colossus E3 5c 50m

A long, imposing route that, despite numerous bolts, feels run-out and committing. It climbs the groove on the right-hand side of the wall and stays wet for longer than the other routes on the wall. The first wall is tricky and leads into a ramped niche, with 2 bolts ridiculously close together. Continue up the groove system until a step left into a niche gives some respite. Step back right and climb the V-groove to the crux crack, exiting left onto a ledge. Continue up the small corners passing 2 more bolts to the top. Take a rack of wires.

[P Williams, A Holmes 27.03.86]

Bela
Lugosi
Wall

Rainbow
Slab

∧ High on the Colossus Wall, where **Major Headstress** meets **Ride the Wild Surf** photo: Rob Wilson

Rainbow Slab Area • Rainbow Slab

LLANBERIS +

OGWEN +

TREMADOG +

GOGARTH & LLEYN

LLANDUDNO +

8. Red and Yellow and Pink and Green, Orange and Purple and Blue (Richard of York finish) E2 5b 40m

A fine, but somewhat serious route that somehow manages to climb the entire length of the Rainbow Slab at a relatively amenable grade. From the lower left corner of the slab, wander upwards, heading right at first, then left on good holds to reach some much-needed protection by a ledge at around 25m. Step down, then climb the scoop to the right of the ledges, to finish direct.

[M Lynden solo 07.84]

9. Pull My Daisy E2 5c 40m

An excellent route that highlights all that is best in slate climbing. It is long, bold and technical and should delight all climbers operating at the grade. Towards the left-hand side of the slab is an obvious finger crack leading to a lonely metal pipe. Climb the crack, with no little interest, to the pipe. From here, climb direct at first (don't look down!), then trend leftwards to finish up easier ground. There is a good belay just below the top.

[M Lynden, J Silvester 07.84]

10. The Rainbow of Recalcitrance E6 6b 60m

A stunning visual line that traces the sweeping ripple feature up and across the slab. An extraordinary route, and one that is likely to test leaders and seconds alike.

P1 6b 35m Ascend the crack for 12m, then move right onto the ripple and follow it rightwards past stepped ledges (good nuts), then a scary clip of the bolt on *Raped by Affection* (an E7 which crosses the ripple). Continue on to belay on the optional *Cystitis by Proxy* stance.

P2 6a 25m Move out right and follow the obvious line (very bold) past a small ledge at 12m. Go up the lower of 2 black grooves to finish.

[J Silvester, M Lynden 07.84]

Trying not to think about the pendulum potential on P2 of **The Rainbow of Recalcitrance** E6 6b photo: Alex Messenger >

Rainbow Slab Area • Rainbow Slab • Manatese Level

11. Poetry Pink E5 6a 45m

This superb bottom end E5 climbs the slab right of the *Rainbow* 'ripple'. Double bolts at 10m are the first landmark, above this hard climbing leads to a mantel move below the next bolt. Once clipped, get established on the rainbow itself with difficulty. Ledgey climbing leads to a finger crack and a final tricky move gains the finishing groove right of the prow.

[J M Redhead, D Towse 07.84]

Johnny Dawes' masterpiece, *The Very Big and the Very Small* (F8b+) takes the line of bolts up the slab right of *Poetry Pink*.

12. Cystitis by Proxy E5 6b 45m

Another classic slate test piece, which is best done in a single pitch. The climbing is both bold and hard. Start by a sculpted rib directly below where the *Rainbow* 'ripple' peters out. Climb boldly up past shattered cracks to some small wire placements and a hard move leftwards (psychological crux). Gain the ledges on *The Rainbow*... directly and follow these rightwards to a small flake below a bolt (possible belay). Climb up and right of this bolt to clip a second bolt. A desperate step left above (technical crux) gains a right-ward trending line of holds up which the route finishes, via one more hard move.

[D Towse, J M Redhead 29.06.84]

13. Splitstream E5 6b 48m

A long pitch with spaced protection and involving sequences. Start 10m right of the rib of *Cystitis by Proxy* and follow small hidden holds up to the first gear at 10m. Continue up until it's possible to go left, then back right, passing more small wires to clip the solitary bolt with relief. Make hard moves past the bolt, then head left and up to join *Cystitis*... at the small flake. Clip the bolt above (as for *Cystitis...*), then make a hard traverse left for 4m. More fingery climbing gains the next bolt. Finish slightly leftwards.

[D Towse, J M Redhead 05.04.86/P2: D Towse, A Newton 26.04.86]

The following route starts from the hanging belay at the foot of the prow, gained by abseil or by starting up another route on the slab proper.

14. Bungle's Arete F8b 15m

A hard, dynamic route with balancey clips. Climb the right hand side of the prow directly above the belay with tenuous, fingery climbing and just enough bolts for it to feel like a sport route.

[S Myles 11.12.90]

Manatese Level

After crossing the second fence on the main approach, continue on that level until a steep two-tone wall comes into view. The pleasant tufty meadow below gives an ideal spot for 'chilling' between redpoint attempts.

15. The Dark Half F7c+ 18m

A good enough route on its own to warrant including the level in the book. Steep, technical and continually interesting. A wonderful sequence up the starting finger flake leads to a testing rockover then trend right to a bizarre pinch feature and the crux. The difficulties continue to the double bolt belay, albeit at a slightly easier level, thankfully.

[N Harms 27.11.90]

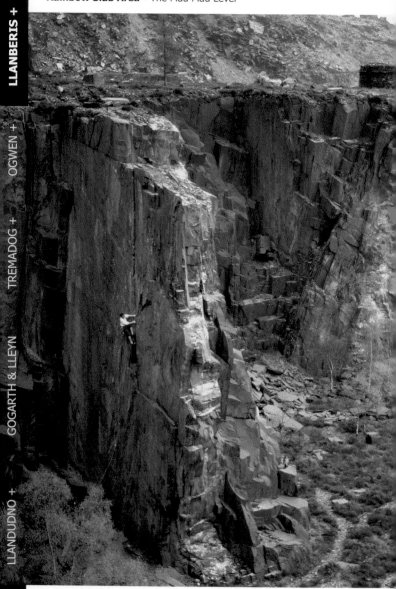

The otherworldly setting of **The Mau Mau** E4 6a photo: Al Leary

Cross the second fence as for the Manatese Level, then either abseil down *Terry's Wall* (just after the fence on the right by some rusty pipes) and walk along to the base of the pillar or abseil from the bolt at the top of *The Mau Mau* pillar itself (a little further along, just past the worrying rock crevasse).

▶ **16. The Dark Destroyer F7c+** 22m
This sport route left of *The Mau Mau* is strenuous and dynamic and surprisingly well bolted for a slate route. Double bolt lower-off.
[M Pretty 13.04.91]

▶ **17. The Mau Mau E4 6a** 22m
A must for anyone operating at the powerful end of the grade, although for some it feels more like a stamina test piece. Climb the left crack to the halfway ledge and relax for as long as your belayer will allow. The crack in the headwall above looks innocuous, but as the pump increases and technique falters.....holds on the left may be of use.
[P Williams 20.05.86]

German
Schoolgirl

Rainbow Slab Area • German Schoolgirl Area

On the other side of the promontory the last 3 routes can be found:

18. True Clip F7b+ 22m
A good, but mean route. Some people may feel a little short changed by the F7b+ grade, but that's all you get. There is a single bolt lower off, which can be backed up with a further bolt in the boulder on top.
[N Harms 19.09.88]

19. German Schoolgirl E2 5c 22m
A slate classic. Technical climbing up the well-protected corner. Enough said.
[M E Crook, N Walton 18.08.84]

20. Spong (is good for you) F7c+ 22m
The line of bolts right of *German Schoolgirl* yields to a dynamic, committed approach. A hard sport route, where the really strong will 'static' the crux moves, and cruise effortlessly to the top, whilst most will lay one on wildly and battle onwards to an uncertain and slightly gripping finish. Single bolt to lower off.
[N Dixon 04.89]

The Mau Mau

∧ Howard Jones on **German Schoolgirl** E2 5c photo: Al Leary

Bus Stop Quarry

Area: Dinorwig Quarry
Style: Trad/Sport (single pitch)
Aspect: Varied
Rock type: Slate
Approach: 5 minutes
Altitude: 350m

Forsinain Motspur	F7c
Geordie War Cry	F7a+
Scare City	E6
Scarlet Runner	E4
Scarlet Runner Direct	E3
Massambula	E2
Sterling Silver	E2
Fool's Gold	E1
Gnat Attack	E1
Solstice	HVS
Equinox	VS

A popular area for aspiring slateheads and a great venue for an evening's cragging, although there's enough here for a good day out too. The rock quality is generally good, but care should be taken with some of the flakes on the promontory. While most of the bolted routes sport the relatively new 'eco anchors', some of the old bolts still exist alongside them.

Conditions: The routes generally dry quickly, however the upper section of *Massambula* on the Rippled Slab can remain damp for longer than the others; the top slab on this route is a lonely place to be with wet holds. Climbing is possible throughout the year as all the routes get some sun, and shelter from the wind can usually be found. In the summer months, the setting sun catches the Rippled Slab, bathing it in gorgeous light and dramatically transforming its pallor.

Approach: The Bus Stop Quarry is the cirque of walls and slabs on the left of the Dinorwig road, just before you get to the Bus Stop roundabout, at the road end. Easily accessible by simply crossing the style and second fence at the left-hand side of the field and strolling to the routes.

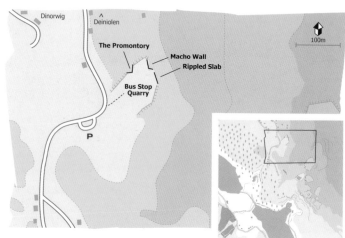

∧ Simon Melia on **Geordie War Cry** F7a+ photo: Ray Wood
↥ Simon Beal engrossed in the moment on the classic **Fool's Gold** E1 5c photo: Jethro Kiernan

Bus Stop Quarry • Fool's Gold Area

The promontory on the left as you enter the ampitheatre.

1. Fool's Gold E1 5c 20m
Good gear and varied climbing make this a popular first extreme. Climb the groove of what used to be *Wusty Woof* to a step right into the obvious crack in the slab on the right. Follow this, with interest, to the top. Bolt belay.
[P George, A George 24.06.85]

2. Scare City E6 6a 20m
A truly bold and nerve-wracking lead. Climb the thin flakes 3m right of *Fool's Gold* until stood on them (*1000 Tons of Chicken Shit* E5 6a sneaks off left from here to join *Fool's Gold*). Creep up the wall above with spaced gear and much trepidation.
[T Kay, P Pritchard 28.09.87]

3. Forsinain Motspur F7c 20m
The bolt ladder right again has a hard section low down and a sustained headwall leading to a double bolt belay.
[T Hodgson, S Jones 28.03.88]

4. Solstice HVS 5a 25m
An attractive line which unfortunately requires the use of some unnervingly hollow flakes. Start under the right-hand side of *Forsinian Motspur's* first overlap. Climb up and right to join the obvious curving line of hollow flakes trending right. On gaining the large flake (junction with *Equinox*) finish direct.
[A George, T Taylor 23.06.85]

5. Equinox VS 4c 25m
The easiest route on the promontory is also the most serious. This is a counter-diagonal to *Solstice* starting just left of *Sterling Silver*. Follow the flakes and ledges trending leftwards to the sanctuary of the big flake runner on *Solstice*. Follow the continuation line leftwards to finish.
[T Taylor, A George 24.06.85]

6. Sterling Silver E2 5c 25m
A surprisingly good route, which requires faith in some fragile flakes. Follow a series of flakes approximately 10m right of *Forsinain Motspur*, none of which seem to inspire confidence, to a hard move to gain the final flake and the top.
[J Banks, L Naylor, D Clark 04.07.86]

Fool's Gold Area/Macho Wall • **Bus Stop Quarry**

LLANBERIS +

OGWEN +

TREMADOG +

GOGARTH & LLEYN

LLANDUDNO +

The Macho Wall

The appropriately named back wall of the quarry.

7. Geordie War Cry F7a+ 25m

Strenuous and technical climbing up the bolt ladder(s) on the cleanest part of the back wall. A reachy crux past the in situ sling usually guarantees an in situ climber. The headwall is easier, but no picnic. Don't forget to let out a celebratory 'why aye man!' at the chains.

[B Wayman, D Kirton, M Barnicot 11.10.87]

Bus Stop Quarry • Rippled Slab

The attractive white slab on the right has spaced bolts, with delicate and insecure climbing. In short, an excellent slate apprenticeship with a smooth grade increase from E1 to E4. Described from right to left.

8. Gnat Attack E1 5b 20m
A popular excursion, and rightly so. Climb carefully up left of the diagonal break to the 1st bolt on the slab. Shorties can now show off their technical prowess, whilst giants can casually span to the good holds and so reach the 2nd bolt. Pleasant, and thankfully easier, climbing leads a long way up to a bolt belay.
[A D Newton, R A Newton 31.07.85/direct start: J Pitts, S Jones, D Jones 04.04.86]

9. Massambula E2 5b 22m
A more sustained alternative to *Gnat Attack*, with a trickier move to reach the 1st bolt, but the crux is no harder. Climbs the middle clean streak of the slab with 2 bolts to mark the way. The upper section is bold, but steady. (Do not attempt if the top section looks at all wet!)
[P Williams, W Wayman 03.07.85]

10. Scarlet Runner E4 5c 25m
Probably the best route on the slab, the climbing is sustained and technical. The technical crux is well-protected, but an insecure rock up to gain the first bolt will test most leaders. Climb the centre of the 3rd clean streak with 5 bolts to aim for.
[W Wayman, P Williams 28.06.85]

11. Scarlet Runner Direct E3 6a 25m
More like a harder, left-hand start than a direct, but with better protection than the original, it is becoming the more popular of the two.
[F Haden, M Davies 22.07.94]

Evening light on **Gnat Attack** E1 5b photo: Jethro Kiernan >

Dali's Hole Area

Area: **Dinorwig Quarry**
Style: **Traditional (some bolts)**
Aspect: **Various**
Rock type: **Slate**
Approach: **10 - 20 minutes**
Altitude: **350m**

Central Sadness	E5
Waves of Inspiration	E5
Goose Creature	E3
The Burning	E3
Holy, Holy, Holy	E2
California Arete	E1
Looning the Tube	E1
The Launching Pad	E1
Zambezi	VS

A dramatic and awe-inducing part of the quarry landscape with a variety of classic routes. Some are short and well-protected while others are long, drawn out affairs sure to test the nerves of all but the most experienced slate head. Each of the different crags is situated within truly astounding surroundings. Dali's Hole, with its dead tree pool, suggests a ghostly surreality, whilst the sheer vastness of Australia (or Garret as it was known by the quarrymen) threatens to overwhelm any sense of scale that you might hope to place upon it. The enclosed California, isolated by a double tunnel approach, feels otherworldly. Its main wall is a decidedly impressive sheet of rock. The sparse bolts on the chosen routes are good. Traditional gear should be taken on most routes.

Conditions: Good rock that dries quickly.

Approach: Follow the main path through the quarries until the dip past the old working buildings. At the bottom of the dip, cross the gate on the left into Dali's Hole. Holy, Holy, Holy Wall is on the left, and the tunnel through to California is visible up on the right. Go through the tunnel and another to emerge in California itself. California Arete is on the left and the magnificent main wall should be obvious enough from there.
For the Australia routes, walk round above the Holy, Holy Wall and go up 2 levels of steps to a tunnel on a promontory. *The Burning* is on the right and the main slab is through the tunnel on the left.

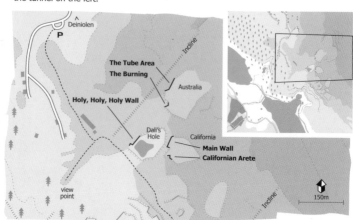

166

∧ Jon Ratcliffe pulling the chain on **Looning the Tube** E1 5b photo: Jethro Kiernan

↥ Tunnel entrance to Australia photo: Jethro Kiernan

LLANBERIS +

OGWEN +

TREMADOG +

GOGARTH & LLEYN

LLANDUDNO +

Dali's Hole • The Holy, Holy, Holy Wall

1. Zambesi VS 4c 15m
A pleasant route up the leaning corner on the left. Take some large gear and save some energy for the strenuous finish!
[T Taylor 05.06.86]

2. Launching Pad E1 5b 15m
A good little route if a little naive in conception (it had been climbed without the bolts). Climb the left-hand side of the slab left of *Holy, Holy, Holy* with an awkward move to reach the 1st bolt and good climbing above.
[1988]

3. Holy, Holy, Holy E2 5c 15m
The obvious corner looks about the same grade as *Zambezi*, but is a completely different proposition (and the crack is often damp).
[C J Phillips 28.05.84]

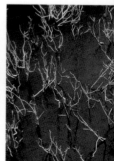

4. The Burning E3 5c 15m
The steep and awkward groove line 5m right of the tunnel entrance. Plenty of bolts for protection. Lower off.
[M Turner, C Stephenson 08.08.91]

5. Goose Creature E3 6a 15m
A technical slab route just right of the left arete of the slab through the tunnel. A bolt on the route on the right (*Menai Vice* E4 6b/c) protects the moves up to the first bolt proper. Hard moves above this lead up to a lower-off.
[A Swann and party 20.04.86]

6. Looning the Tube E1 5b 20m
A popular route that feels more serious than it really is. Traverse right from the end of the ledge, bolt, to reach a hanging chain at the bottom of a crack (this can be lassoed if required). Climb the crack, bolt on the left, to the top. Good climbing, but slightly unnerving. To descend, walk off and drop back down to the entrance tunnel. (A medium cam will be a useful addition to your rack.)
[C J Phillips 19.06.84]

Approach

5   6

<< Australia, with its vast scree glacier photo: Ray Wood

< Ghost trees in Dali's Hole photo: Ray Wood

Dali's Hole • California

LLANBERIS +

OGWEN +

TREMADOG +

GOGARTH & LLEYN

LLANDUDNO +

Abseil
descent
50m

Espirit de
Corpse
E4 6b

9

Californian
Arete

8

7. Californian Arete E1 4c 45m
The classic route of its grade in the quarries. Straightforward climbing, with no real protection, gives a virtual solo proposition. Climb the sculpted arete left (looking out) of the
2nd tunnel exit. Scramble off leftwards with care to find the exit tunnel.
[C J Phillips 16.06.84]

8. Central Sadness E5 6a 66m
One of the best of the grade in the area with 2 equally good, but contrasting pitches. The
first requires a steady approach due to the somewhat serious nature, whereas the second
is well-protected but seems to go on forever.
P1 6a 30m Start at the obvious diagonal crack about 10m right of the hanging chain.
Climb the crack with some difficulty and continue up on insecure ground to a good spike
runner. Climb the bold wall above to the ledge and bolt belay.
P2 6a 36m Step left and trend up and right to join the long, sustained crack. Follow this
to an easier hand crack on the right to finish.
[J Silvester, C Dale 05.05.86]

9. Waves of Inspiration E5 6a 50m
Although somewhat overshadowed by some of its neighbours, this wandering slab climb is
still a classic. Although a handful of bolts protect, it doesn't feel like a sport route and a traditional rack of gear is essential. Start by scrambling up to a bolt belay on ledges up and right
of Central Sadness. From 3m left of the belay, climb the diagonal crack then trend up up a
curving crack to the crack proper passing 2 bolts. Traverse left and climb a flake to good holds
and clip the next bolt. Traverse back right for 3m and head up passing another bolt en route.
Follow a line of good flat holds and a thin crack to the top, clipping a peg on the left.
[C Parkin, P Hawkins, G Smith 04.08.86]

Descent from *Central Sadness* and *Waves of Inspiration* can be made, either by making
a 50m abseil from chains at the top of *Espirit de Corpse* (see topo), or by scrambling up
the hillside to reach a line of steps running down leftwards on the edge of the Australia
Quarry, then heading back round to reach Dali's Hole.

Serengeti

Area:	Dinorwig Quarry
Style:	Trad/Sport (single pitch)
Aspect:	South-East
Rock type:	Slate
Approach:	15 minutes
Altitude:	350m

The Medium	F8a
The Carbon Stage	F6c
Heading the Shot	E5
Never Never Land	E5
Tentative Decisions	E5
Kubla Khan	E4
Short Stories	E4
Slug Club Special	E4
Slippery People	E2
Seams the Same	E1
Seamstress	VS

A popular area with a handful of slate's classic routes. If you like company, this is the place to come to as you'll seldom be alone. Some routes are getting polished, but this is not detrimental to the climbing. The rock is sound, and there are quite a few pieces of un-usual in situ protection.

Conditions: All the routes are quick-drying.

Approach: Cross the fence on the left just after the dip in the track by Dali's Hole (if you get to the circular air vent, you've gone too far). Follow the well-worn path up and right past a shelter to the pleasant slab on the left (Seamstress Slab). To get to the Yellow Wall, scramble up and right, with care, from behind *Heading the Shot*. On the same level as the main approach track (the level below the Seamstress Slab) lies The Never Never Land Area. This is the clean, open slab tucked round left from the circular air duct (past another shelter).

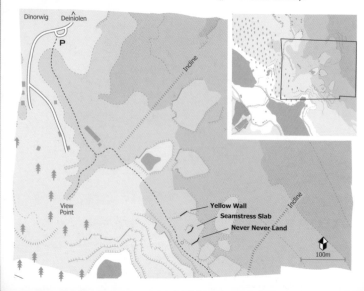

∧ Jon Ratcliffe on the ultra thin **Heading the Shot** E5 6b photo: Jethro Kiernan
⋏ Quarry building photo: Rob Wilson

LLANBERIS +

OGWEN +

TREMADOG +

GOGARTH & LLEYN

LLANDUDNO +

To Yellow W

1. Slug Club Special E4 6a 20m
A superb pitch. Climb the polished, insecure slab left of the cracks to an obvious spike. Clip this with relief, step left with commitment and make tricky moves up past a bolt and a peg to the top. (*Stack of Nudebooks meets the Stickman* E4 6a wanders over to finish up *Seamstress* from the spike) If the spike is lassoed from below, subtract an E grade and if lassoed from the ground, subtract two.
[P Hawkins, R Caves 08.08.85]

2. Seamstress VS 4c 20m
Your first slate lead? The left-hand of the two central cracks is nicely sustained with gear placements shaped to the exact profile of your rack. Popular and polished but still good.
[S Haston 06.83]

3. Seams the Same E1 5b 20m
Another excellent line. The right-hand crack is harder and more sustained than the left; the placements are obvious, but not as frequent.
[S Haston 06.83]

4. The Medium F8a 23m
The best hard slab on slate? The route climbs the slab left of *Heading the Shot* past 3 bolts. An easy start (only 6b) lands you at the 3rd bolt where the interest begins. A desperate rockover and a ridiculous dynamic move on 'cornflakes' gains *Heading the Shot* (by the peg at the end of its traverse). Finish up this.
[J Dawes 24.07.86]

5. Heading The Shot E5 6b 23m
This infamous test piece takes a line of weakness just left of the right arete of the slab. The line of old rusty bolt hangers show the line and this is a good thing as not many of the tiny holds are visible from the ground! Take extra-thin-nosed quickdraws to clip the bolts. After the 3rd bolt traverse left to the peg and finish direct.
[S Haston, N Walton 08.84]

6. Slippery People E2 5c 18m
An interesting and well-protected route. The obvious groove on the left of the wall features a move that definitely punishes the shorter climbers out there.
[P Hawkins, D J Cuthbertson, J Silvester 11.04.86]

7. Tentative Decisions E5 6a 18m
A well-named route requiring commitment above gear. The climbing is involved and rewarding, but never too desperate. Start up the first few metres of *Slippery People*, then break out right and climb the wall trending slightly rightwards.
[C Davies, P Targett 23.12.89]

James Lillie on **Seams the Same** E1 5b >
photo: Jethro Kiernan

LLANBERIS +

OGWEN +

TREMADOG +

GOGARTH & LLEYN

LLANDUDNO +

Serengeti • Never Never Land

8. Never Never Land E5 6a 43m
A bold route with some indifferent, flaky rock. An iron spike protects the crux, but only if you can put the repercussions of slipping onto it out of your mind. Start below the staggered overlaps in the centre of the wall and battle up and round them to gain the spike. The crux section above leads via a sustained finger flake to a rest and a wire. Continue up trending slightly left to an easing near the arete. The bolts on the route to the right can be clipped for comfort, but it was originally done without. The belay is way back, so a pre-placed rope may be prudent.
[M E Crook, N Walton, A D Newton 02.84]

9. Kubla Khan E4 6b 27m
An interesting, varied route with a desperate well-protected crux and a runout groove above. Climb the slab between the overlaps of *Never Never Land* and the bolts of *Short Stories*. The move above the bolt is hard, but can be circumnavigated on the left, although probably just as difficult; lassoing the iron spike can protect the upper reaches of the groove above. Finish on the ledge on the right at 2/3 height.
[M E Crook, A D Newton 03.85]

10. Short Stories E4 6a 27m
A fine route marked by the line of spaced bolts starting on the right of the slab before curving leftwards and upwards to the obvious ledge; more sustained but less 'cruxy' than *Kubla Khan*. The top bolt is hard to clip for shorter climbers.
[S Howe, S Harland 02.04.87]

11. The Carbon Stage F6c 20m
30m right of the *Never Never Land* slab is a well-bolted sports route with good climbing. 4 bolts lead to a double bolt belay.
[M Jones 19.08.94]

Lasso metal spike

Seamstress Slab

To The Carbon Stage

Kubla Khan E4 6b >
photo: Ray Wood

176

The Ogwen Valley is an enduringly popular destination, particularly for climbers operating in the lower grades. Famous crags such as the Idwal Slabs or the East face of Tryfan; a dramatic peak of if ever there was, provide fantastic multi-pitch routes with a strong mountaineering slant. Indeed, in the Idwal area, there is much potential for extended link-ups, echoing the Alpine experience. Elsewhere in the valley there are a multitude of smaller cliffs offering varying degrees of an adventurous and physical nature.

To the north is the vast expanse of the Carneddau mountain range. Hidden away amongst its many secluded cwms lie a number of high and remote crags. If you wish to escape the hustle and bustle of the Idwal circus, then this is the place to come to. Up here peace and solitude can be found, not to mention classic climbs of unquestionable pedigree.

As with the Llanberis area, the climbing is predominantly traditional multi-pitch.

Seasonal conditions: It is possible to climb in this area all year round, but realistically only on the easier routes, and assuming you don't mind a bit of dampness. The higher cliffs (Glyder Fach, Clogwyn Du, Llech Ddu and Craig yr Ysfa) are best saved for the summer months when they will present a more hospitable front.

Getting there: On summer weekends the parking opportunities around the Ogwen Cottage are soon overwhelmed. However, further down the valley towards Tryfan, space can normally be found in one of the large lay-bys. The main crags are also accessible via the Sherpa bus service, which runs up and down the valley from Capel Curig to Bethesda.

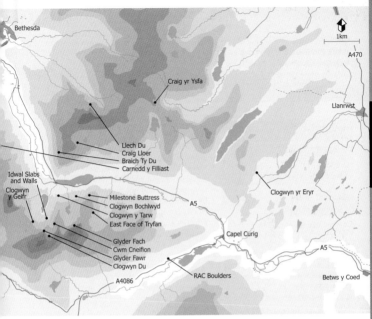

First Pinnacle Rib VD/S, East Face of Tryfan photo: Steve Long ∧
Looking across Llyn Ogwen to Tryfan and Glyder Fach photo: Al Leary <

East Face of Tryfan

Area:	**Ogwen Valley**
Style:	**Trad (2 – 8 pitches)**
Aspect	**East**
Rock Type:	**Rhyolite**
Approach:	**45 minutes**
Altitude:	**750m**

Munich Climb	HVS
Belle Vue Bastion	VS
Pinnacle Rib Route	VD/S
Overlapping Ridge Route	VD/S
Grooved Arête	HVD
Gashed Crag	VD

A traditional mountain crag, home to a rack of splendid multi-pitch routes. The striking East Face of Tryfan dominates the south side of the Ogwen Valley as you travel up from Capel Curig. The climbs on its steep ridges and buttresses have a classic mountaineering feel, with the additional bonus of topping out on a peak that provides un-paralleled views of the valley. Close proximity to the road and the abundance of easier grade routes ensures the enduring popularity of this big cliff, especially at weekends, when you are more than likely to find queues on routes such as *Grooved Arête*.

The East Face consists of 3 main buttresses: the North Buttress, Central Buttress and South Buttress. The face is split by two major gullies: North Gully and South Gully. Other smaller buttresses and gullies can make locating your position at the bottom of the cliff baffling at times. At the base of the buttresses is Heather Terrace, an obvious wide terrace that slants upwards from right to left, which affords access to the routes.

Conditions: Although arguably best savoured on a bright sunny day, much atmospheric fun can be had in less clement weather (when you may have the crag to yourself). In fact the easier routes provide a good day out even in the wet.

Approach: The usual access points are from the A5, either parking in the car parks below the North Ridge or at Gwern Gôf Uchaf farm to the east. From either access point the obvious Heather Terrace that runs along the base of the routes can be gained. From Gwern Gof Uchaf follow the obvious path up and rightwards passing below the gentle slabs of Tryfan Bach (Little Tryfan), until a fence is reached. Follow this rightwards until a final gully leads up onto the shoulder of the North Ridge. This point can be reached from the car park below the North Ridge by taking the steep path to the left of the wall. This path then heads up leftwards (do not go too high on this path on the shoulder as it leads up the North Ridge itself) to reach a junction with the previous route at the top of the gully. A path now leads up and left of the gully until the Heather Terrace is reached. Follow this to pass some slabs capped by roofs, where 30m later the first deep gully of Barstow Gully is encountered. A further 75m leads to Nor Nor Gully identifiable by the obvious jammed block known as the Tombstone seen lying 30m up the bed of the gully. 75m beyond this are more slabs capped with roofs and the grassy gully of Green Gully. Just to the left, and above a pinnacle below Heather Terrace, is the start of *Grooved Arête*.

Descent: The simplest way down off the mountain is to follow the South Ridge down to the col and then drop down the left side if heading back to Gwern Gof Uchaf farm or the right side if aiming for the car parks below the North Ridge. For those wishing to return to the base of the cliff then North Gully provides a suitable descent although it is necessary to branch off rightwards halfway down to pick up Little Gully. The top of Heather Terrace can also be reached from the col on the South Ridge. South Gully is not recommended as an easy descent, as 2 abseils are involved in the upper reaches.

East Face of Tryfan

LLANBERIS +

OGWEN +

TREMADOG +

GOGARTH & LLEYN

LLANDUDNO +

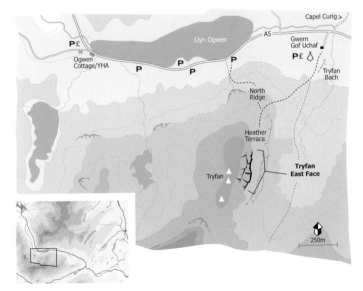

∧ Mark Reeves contemplating the pendulum potential on the crux of **Munich Climb** HVS 5a photo: Graham Desroy

↟ The Pinnacle on Central Buttress photo: Graham Desroy

East Face of Tryfan

1. Grooved Arête HVD 233m
A classic expedition up the North Buttress. Queuing for quality is de rigeur.
P1 30m Start below the well-polished slabby corner to the left of Green Gully, where the letters 'GA' are scratched on the rock (a practice not to be encouraged). Skate up the corner for 12m. Step right and then move left up the slab to the rib which is followed to a large spike belay.
P2 30m Move left and climb the rib and groove to a good stance below a corner capped with a small roof.
P3 50m Climb the right side of the corner, passing the small roof to its right. Move left and scramble easily up to a grassy path.
P4 20m Amble right and belay under the rib, where it reaches the path.
P5 35m From the right side of the rib climb up and leftwards to enter the main groove. Climb this mainly on the right until another steeper groove to the left is gained. Follow this and exit left thankfully onto The Haven - a block belay is set well back.
P6 18m From behind the belay climb up the crack to reach the checkerboard-cracked slab: The Knight's Move Slab. Make a Knight's move or even a Bishop's one to exit at the top right-hand corner, where a step right round the arête reveals a stance.
P7 20m Continue up the corner to reach a good platform belay.
P8 30m Pawns can now wander off rightwards. Royalty must crown their achievement by moving right up the steep rough rock, which quickly eases. Follow the crest to the top.
[E W Steeple, A G Woodhead, G Barlow, H E Bowron, A H Doughty 04.11]

P1 of **Belle Vue Bastion** VS 4c photo: Graham Desroy V

East Face of Tryfan

LLANBERIS +

OGWEN +

TREMADOG +

GOGARTH & LLEYN

LLANDUDNO +

Heather Terrace continues from Green Gully underneath the North Buttress until North Gully is reached. This is characterised by the block forming a cave below it some 30m up the gully. Beyond this the path passes either side of a large boulder. The next subsidiary gully is Little Gully. The next route starts high up on the North Buttress from the Terrace. The Terrace is reached by scrambling up Little Gully, which leads into North Gully. The Terrace is the grassy ledges below Tryfan's summit walls on the right side of the upper reaches of North Gully. The Terrace can also be reached by descending into North Gully.

2. Belle Vue Bastion VS 4c 65m
A classic exposed climb on perfect rock.
P1 4c 25m Start at the right-hand end of the terrace below *Terrace Wall*. Climb easily up and step right round the arête. Follow the crack and groove past a small niche. Step left onto a slab and follow the faint groove. Move left to the arête to belay below the obvious undercut nose (The Groove of Bollards). A harder version is to step left onto the arête as soon as the slab is reached.
P2 4b 40m Exposed climbing rightwards on the edge of the nose enables a step right round it to be made. Move up and left until easier climbing leads to the top.
[I M Waller, C H S R Palmer 07.06.27]

Back on Heather Terrace and 50m to the left of Little Gully is a grassy bay that is set into the Central Buttress.

3. Pinnacle Rib Route (Second Pinnacle Rib) VD/S 175m
Good and continuous climbing up the Central Buttress. Confusingly this is the first of the two Pinnacle Ribs reached when ascending Heather Terrace. To the right of a grassy bay is a rib. Unfortunately the graffiti artists have scratched 'FPR' on the rock, which is also scratched below the real *First Pinnacle Rib* some 50m further to the left!
P1 25m Climb the groove to the right of the rib on a long flake.
P2 30m Follow the steep thin rib into a small V-groove. Belay above this on the crest of the ridge.
P3 30m Continue up the crest to a large stance below a steep wall.
P4 30m Continue up until a traverse left leads to a belay some 15m directly above the base of the pinnacle (the Pinnacle of *First Pinnacle Rib* is to the left).
P5 35m Climb the curved cracked ribs on the left until easy ground leads to belays below the final steep walls.
P6 25m Above lies *Thomson's Chimney* (Severe); walk the 20m to its base and set up a further belay. Ascend the initial chimney, move right and struggle up the final chimney. Those who do not wish to accept the challenge can scuttle off rightwards to a more ignominious finish up the path.
[J M A Thomson, H Hughes October 1894]

4. Overlapping Ridge Route (First Pinnacle Rib) VD/S 185m
A very popular route taking a direct line up the mountain. The Yellow Slab on P4 is 4b and Severe, but can be avoided.
P1 30m Start 20m to the left of the grassy bay and to the right of the scree gully that extends down from Heather Terrace and forms the bottom of South Gully at a slab. 'FPR' is also scratched on the rock. Climb the slab and exit right at the overhang. Then take the cracked groove to the right, which soon leads back onto the slabby ridge. Follow this to belay below where the ridge steepens.
P2/3 80m Follow the ridge belaying at will, until the Pinnacle is reached. Belay below the Yellow Slab, behind the Pinnacle.
P4 15m The Yellow Slab is polished but must be ascended somehow for 3m until a groove on the right is reached and followed to a stance. If must becomes can't, then an easy escape to the right of the Pinnacle up easier ground will lead to the start of P5.
P5 35m As for *Pinnacle Rib Route* P5.
P6 25m As for *Pinnacle Rib Route* P6.
[E W Steeple, G Barlow, A H Doughty 09.14]

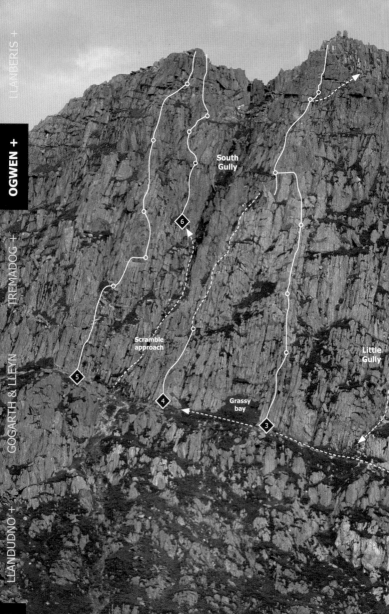

South Gully

6

Scramble approach

5

4

Grassy bay

3

Little Gully

Scramble descent

Terrace Wall

2

North Gully

Green Gully

Nor Nor Gully

Heather Terrace

1

East Face of Tryfan

5. Gashed Crag VD 170m

A very fine route, which follows the ridge with an obvious horizontal 'V' notch, The Gash, some 60m up.

P1 45m Start some 20m left of South Gully where the path steepens and meets the first buttress. Start below the small groove on the right. Climb this to a small roof at 8m. Step right round the rib and continue up to the right. Climb the crack and groove on the right side of the crest. Walk rightwards and belay below the main ridge and The Gash.

P2 15m Climb up the ribs and into The Gash. At the roof of The Gash step right to a belay below a chimney.

P3 20m The chimney is rarely climbed with style. Scramble above until a wall leads to the crest of the ridge.

P4 35m Climb the broad ridge where it narrows and steepens.

P5 40m Great climbing up the ridge eventually leads to two grooves which are followed to a belay below the final wall.

P6 15m A final effort up the groove and chimney leads to the South Summit.

[H B Buckle, G Barlow 09.02]

6. Munich Climb HVS 5a 96m

A spicy climb with some exciting positions for both leader and second.

P1 4c 28m Start half way up South Gully just below the level of the obvious pinnacle on its right-hand rib (*First Pinnacle Rib*). A grassy scramble up the left wall of the gully leads to a grassy platform with a large detached block. To the right are three grooves of varying quality. Climb the right-hand groove for maximum satisfaction. This leads to a slab split by a flake crack. Follow this and make a hard move to reached perched blocks on the right edge. One of these rocks alarmingly, so belay with care!

P2 5a 18m Stand on the right block and make an unnerving move up and left onto the nose. Teeter leftwards to reach the sanctuary of the wide crack, *Teufel's Crack*. Slither up this to a belay on a grassy rake.

P3 15m Scramble up the rake and make a belay beyond the large block.

P4 4b 35m Climb the groove to the right of the block until a move left leads into a crack. Follow this to a rocky ledge. The steep crack to the right quickly eases and enables the top to be reached.

[H Teufel, H Sedlmayr, J R Jenkins (2 pts) 01.07.36]

Graham Desroy out there on P2 of **Belle Vue Bastion** VS 4c photo: Mark Reeves >

Jon Ratcliffe dropping in a wire on P3 of **Super Direct** HVS 5a photo: Si Panton ∧
Direct Route VD photo: Alex Messenger ◢↑

Milestone Buttress

Area: Ogwen Valley
Style: Trad (1 - 5 pitches)
Aspect: North-West
Rock type: Rhyolitic Tuff
Approach: 15 minutes
Altitude: 375m

Super Direct	HVS
Boot Crack	HVS
Soapgut	HS
Direct Route	VD
Pulpit Route	VD
Rowan Route	D

This popular roadside crag has a fine selection of absorbing multi-pitch routes, all on immaculately clean rock. The one minor drawback is the ubiquitous polish. Only the nearby Idwal Slabs bare similarly striking scars of sustained and heavy traffic. A century's worth of relentless footfall has irredeemably left its mark. The older, easier routes are buffed to the point of gleaming and to some extent it is possible to navigate by tracing the deeply worn holds! In spite of this polished sheen the routes still radiate enough character and charm to maintain their ongoing popularity.

Conditions: The crag dries quickly (apart from *Soapgut* which takes drainage) and receives afternoon/evening sun, except during the winter months.

Approach: From the layby, follow the diagonal path that runs up to, then parallel with the stone wall running down from the crag.

Descent: Via Little Gully (normally wet) over on the right side (facing in) of the crag.

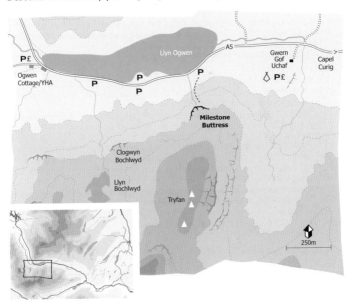

189

Milestone Buttress

1. Boot Crack HVS 5a 25m
The eye-catching crack line offers sustained difficulties following an awkward start. A fine pitch. Abseil descent.
[A J J Moulam, G D Roberts 19.07.66]

2. Wall Climb/Soapgut/Chimney Route HS 4b 79m
This disjointed connection yields a surprisingly classic route.
P1 20m Start 10m right of the stone wall. Trend rightwards up the wall to reach a scoop, step right and climb up to reach ledges.
P2 15m Traverse left to the base of the large curving corner *(Soap Gut)*.
P3 4b 29m Waltz up the corner, easy at first, until a tricky mantelshelf lands you on a ledge on the left (possible belay). Step out right to gain a ramp, then move up into the Narrows. This awkward section leads to good ledges. To reach the base of the corner on *Chimney Route* traverse across to the rib on the right and descend rightwards.
P4 4a 15m Start in the corner and move to gain the crack in the right wall. This proves to be disappointingly smooth. Stay calm and focus on the solution, as the difficulties do soon ease.
[W R Reade, R P Bloor, C W Marshall 17.09.27/J M Edwards, C W F Noyce 04.09.36/E W Steeple, G Barlow 08.13]

3. Super Direct HVS 5a 90m
A classic and varied route, building to a shocking finale on the upper wall.
P1 4c 30m Start below an inverted scoop at the base of the central ridge. Follow the layback flake, taking care with the extremely polished footholds, up right into the easier slabby groove. Continue up the hand crack in the ridge to a ledge.
P2 4c 40m From the left side of the ledge climb up and leftward beneath the overhang to an impasse at a steepening in the arête. Make bold moves up to gain jugs (honest!) and continue up the slabby arête, past a ledge to the Bi-valve block/flake. Continue up left to belay by the jutting Central Block.
P3 5a 20m The final test awaits! Rock up awkwardly onto the ledge by the arête and traverse somewhat anxiously out left towards a thin juggy flake. Swing round left to the sanctuary of a secluded bay and pile up a steep crack (or alternatively the right arête). Easy climbing leads to the top.
[G Barlow, H Priestly-Smith 1910/P4 – J M Edwards 1941]

4. Direct Route VD 85m
An exceptionally polished route, but still a classic fun trip. The final chimney is a beast; some folk have been known to mutter 'Severe' as they emerge puffing and panting at the top. Of course they are wrong. It's just a bit traditional, that's all!
P1 30m. Start at the slab to the right of the central ridge. Follow the polished diagonal crack to a scoop, and swing up into a groove and follow slabby ground to reach a pinnacle belay.
P2 27m. Behind the pinnacle lies a smooth left-hand corner, follow this past a leg jamming section to a niche (possible belay). Continue up the steep crack until a large flake block (the Bi-valve) stalls progress. Hand traverse leftwards beneath this block, and move delicately round its back to belay (thread belays low down).
P3 10m Scramble up left to reach the back corner of the large ledge.
P4 9m. The infamous Corner Chimney is actually not so bad if you face right initially, then exit leftwards.
P5 9m. The short slabby wall leads to the top.
[G Barlow, H Priestly-Smith 1910]

Milestone Buttress

LLANBERIS +

OGWEN +

TREMADOG +

GOGARTH & LLEYN

LLANDUDNO +

5. Rowan Route D 88m

A fine route, blessed with good ledges and belays.

P1 21m. Start at the base of the long slabby rib 10m right of *Direct Route*. Follow the edge of the rib, to the terrace.

P2 15m. Take the open groove up to the ledge on the right, passing the bi-valve feature (a different one to the *Direct Route*), then a rib to the next ledge.

P3 15m. Above is a small shallow chimney; approach this from the slabs on the right and climb up it.

P4 37m. Scramble up over easy slabs, and finish up the little wall at the top or the chimney over to the right.

[H O Jones K J P Orton Mrs Orton 01.10]

6. Pulpit Route VD 87m

A great climb with an entertaining finish up the Ivy Chimney.

P1 27m Climb up the slabby rib on jugs and continue up the slim slab on the right to reach a large block (the Pulpit).

P2 24m The steep slab on the left leads to an easier slab. Go up through the small trench in the wall to reach ledges.

P3 12m Scramble up and wander across to the Ivy Chimney (which overlooks the descent gully).

P4 15m Make a steep entry into the chimney, then an airy exit through a hole on the right.

P5 9m Finish up the slab on the right, with a leftwards step at the top.

[G Barlow, E M Barlow 07.11]

Streaky Desroy on **The Wrack** E2 5b photo: Liam Desroy ∧
View back down to Llyn Ogwen from the walk in photo: Si Panton ⩔

Clogwyn Bochlwyd

Area: Ogwen Valley
Style: Trad (1 - 3 pitches)
Aspect: North-West
Rock type: Rhyolitic Tuff
Approach: 20 minutes
Altitude: 450m

The Wrack	E2
Bochlwyd Eliminate	HVS
Marble Slab	HS
Wall Climb	HS
Chimney Climb	S
Arête and Slab	D

A neat little crag, ideal for an evening visit, or alternatively, in combination with one of its neighbours (Milestone Buttress or Clogwyn y Tarw) have a notable intensity, typical of outcrop style climbing. The rock is good quality, although the hanging block on *The Wrack* should be treated with respect.

Conditions: The crag dries reasonably quickly, although dampness will persist in cracks after rain. It receives evening sun, except during the winter months.

Approach: From the Ogwen Cottage car park, follow the path that runs up left from the slate cutting. After a few hundred metres the main path kinks back right towards Llyn Idwal. Continue diagonally leftwards on the Cwm Bochlwyd path, before traversing across left to reach the crag base. More direct approaches are possible from further along the A5 towards Milestone Buttress.

Descent: Come down the hill slope to the right (looking in) of the crag.

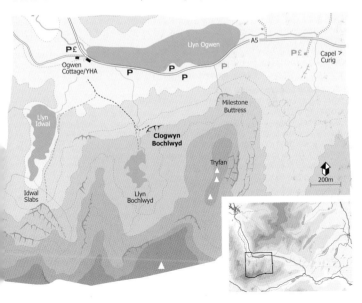

1. Wall Climb HS 4b 46m
A fine open route and quite hard for the grade.
P1 4b 26m Move onto the upper of the 2 sloping gangways and make an awkward step, from its top, across to a sharp flake on the left. Climb up past a tricky mantelshelf, and continue directly to a comfortable heather ledge.
P2 4b 20m Climb onto the exposed nose on the right. Continue up the steep wall, passing a heather ledge on the left, to reach an easier upper section.
[F E Hicks, C V A Cooper, W E Woosnam Jones 26.09.29]

2. Bochlwyd Eliminate HVS 5a 37m
A great little climb with care needed to avoid rope drag.
Start just to the left of the foot of the buttress. Climb up the easy quartz slab to gain the upper gangway on *Wall Climb*. Use the crack above to step up and right to a sloping ledge. Make a move up to gain the hand traverse ledge. Follow this rightwards for 4m until it is possible to move up and stand on the ledge. Climb up and slightly rightwards on holds that keep on appearing until the angle relents and the top is reached. A more direct line is possible at much the same grade, but protection is more sparse.
[R James, R Barbier 06.62]

3. The Wrack E2 5b 30m
A fine and stiff climb up the steep groove left of *Chimney Climb*. Start just right of *Wall Climb* and move easily up the slab for 7m. Step right into the corner groove and climb it with a tricky move to gain undercut jams on the hollow hanging block. Take this on the right until it is possible to reach the good holds left of the arête. Move back right and follow the crack, which leads through a small overlap; easier ground leads to the top.
[T F Allen, W Hurford 28.08.63]

4. Chimney Climb S 34m

An energetic and entertaining climb.
P1 12m Start up the right-hand chimney and move out onto the face to reach a sloping ledge. Take a belay at its left end.
P2 22m Enter the main chimney, and squirm up it passing an overhang with a long reach. Continue more easily to the top.
[F C Aldous, A C Adams, O Thorneycroft 08.09]

5. Marble Slab HS 4b 30m

A delightful climb, forming a direct start to *Arete and Slab*.
Start a few metres left of the bollard near the right side of the buttress. Go up parallel cracks to the overlap. A high runner protects the transition to the upper slab. Continue with interest to join and finish up *Arete and Slab*.
[C F Kirkus, C Brennand 21.07.35]

6. Arête and Slab D 34m

An agreeable route taking the right arête and upper slab of the buttress.
P1 18m Climb the steep crack in the arête, and continue more easily up to a ledge.
P2 5m Good holds lead up the steep wall on the left to a sloping ledge.
P3 11m Make an awkward move out left onto the exposed slab, then continue to the top in a more straightforward fashion.
[C H S R Palmer, D G MacDonald 27.03.27]

Orion boulder

An excellent boulder can be found 100m left of the crag in a slight hollow, close to the path leading up the west face of Tryfan. The groove feature on the front face is the superb *Seren* V4/Font 6b+, whilst the right arête is *Attack Ships* V3/Font 6a+. Other lesser problems exist.

∧ Dave Norton on **Seren** V4/Font 6b+ photo: Si Panton

Liam Desroy out on the edge of **Hawk's Nest Arete** VS 4c photo: Graham Desroy ∧
Wrestling with the Vertical Vice on **Chasm Route** VD photo: Rob Greenwood ⌐∧

Glyder Fach Main Cliff

Area:	**Ogwen Valley**
Style:	**Trad (1 - 5 pitches)**
Aspect:	**North-West**
Rock type:	**Rhyolite/Rhyolitic Breccias**
Approach:	**60 minutes**
Altitude:	**800m**

LLANBERIS +

OGWEN +

TREMADOG +

GOGARTH & LLEYN

LLANDUDNO +

Kaya	E7
Glyder Crack	E6
Hyndsight	E4
Get Close	HVS
Lot's Groove	HVS
Hawk's Nest Arete	VS
Direct Route	HS
Gamma	S
Chasm Route	VD

A fine mountain crag hosting a number of fêted classics and a handful of harder test pieces. The cliff is positioned high above Llyn Bochlwyd on the steep slopes running up to the Glyder Fach plateau.

The cliff presents a pillar-like structure, forming a series of soaring arêtes and corner cracks. The rock is clean and rough, of excellent quality and a real joy to move on. In fact, on a sunny summer's day, there are few finer places to climb in the whole of North Wales.

Conditions: Best visited during the summer months when a few days of dry weather should see dampness and seepage restricted to the odd wet patch. The cliff receives the sun from the late afternoon onwards.

Of course, *Chasm Route* can be 'enjoyed' in all weathers by hardy mountaineering types.

Approach: From the Ogwen Cottage car park, follow the path that runs up left from the bottom of the slate cutting. After a few hundred metres the main path kinks back right towards Llyn Idwal. Continue diagonally leftwards on the Cwm Bochlwyd path. (More direct approaches are possible to this point from further along the A5 towards Milestone Buttress.) Follow the path steeply up to reach Llyn Bochlwyd, where a swim on a hot day is most tempting. Continue on the left side of the lake towards Bwlch Tryfan, before cutting back right across the hillside to reach the base of the cliff.

Descent: For routes on the East Buttress it is best to come down the Main Gully, which bounds the cliff on its right side (facing in). For routes on the Gable Buttress and Hawk's Nest Buttress, head left (facing in) and come down East Gully to the base of the routes.

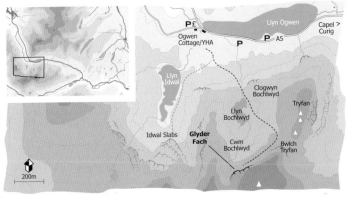

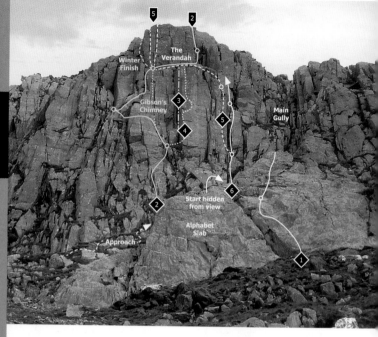

1. Gamma S 44m

This delicate slabby route is perhaps a suitable aperitif for one of the main routes above.
P1 24m Start just right of the slanting break. Move onto the slab, zig zagging first right, then left up a shallow scoop. Move left to a thin crack, and continue up and right to a belay.
P2 20m Ascend easier ground to a steepening and an awkward finish up the little wall.
[C F Kirkus, G G Macphee 31.05.36]

2. Direct Route HS 4c 91m

This famous route provides a superb and continuously interesting jaunt.
P1 4a 36m Start just behind the prominent 3m high block (The Capstan) on the terrace below the main face. Climb easily to the left of the obvious rib to gain a ledge and 'arrowhead' belay beneath a V-shaped chimney. Continue steeply up positive holds, until it is possible to move right onto the face. Trend up and rightwards and climb up to a comfortable bay.
P2 4a 15m Go up the sometimes greasy scoop to a ledge on the left at 6m. *Gibson's Chimney*, a fine VS 4c pitch leads directly up from here to The Verandah. If you don't fancy that, fear not, as The Rectangular Excursion provides a less stressful alternative: Traverse left across the narrow ledge, and continue around to the fallen spike spanning *Arch Chimney*. Belay over on the left.
P3 4b 23m Climb the corner on the right to reach the infamous Hand Traverse. The best tactic is to work rightwards with your trailing left leg stuffed in the crack. If you make it in one piece, the wide crack above leads more easily up to The Veranda.

P4 8m *The Winter Finish* (VD 24m) gives a comparatively straightforward, but still very worthwhile finish: traverse left along a broad flake and climb the corner crack to the top. However, those who found the Hand Traverse a doddle, or perhaps arrived via *Gibson's Chimney,* should press on across to the right end of The Veranda and nip up a slanting chimney and crack to a small platform.

P5 4c 9m The Final Crack sits in a narrow vertical corner. The thin crack in the left wall will prove most useful, especially if you can jam.

[K M Ward, H B Gibson 1907/The Winter Finish: J M Edwards, A R 'Sandy' Edge]

3. Glyder Crack E6 6b 18m

A brilliant, but extremely intense pitch tackling the eye-catching thin crack left of the *Kaya* arête. Start from the huge block above the start of *Kaya*. Gain the long pod and swerve rightwards into the crack. A tricky and precise sequence leads past 2 pegs, and up to some ledges. Finish up the short groove above.

[G Smith, D Kendal 05.92]

4. Kaya E6/7 6b 24m

A stunning pitch up the impressive left arête of the central pillar. (Clipping both 1st and 5th pegs as well).

Start on the left-hand side of the arête from the ledge at the top of P1 on *Direct Route*. Climb up rightwards past an awkward RP placement to a nerve-wracking and reachy clip of the 1st peg runner. Continue up the arête, switching onto the left side. At the break, make a rightwards deviation, and move up to another troublesome clip. A hard move now gains the flake up left. Continue up the arête and wall to reach The Verandah in a state of exaltation.

[N Craine 1988/direct finish added by J Dawes]

5. Lot's Groove HVS 5a 84m

A fantastic route with a brilliant main pitch, and a choice of brutal cracks to finish.

P1 27m P1 of *Chasm Route.*

P2 5a 27m Ascend the groove, with increasing difficulty, moving onto the right wall at 12m for a couple of moves before stepping back left and bridging up the groove to the overhang. Move up past the overhang awkwardly, then continue up to a stance.

P3 15m Follow the slanting crack on the right up to The Verandah. Walk across left to belay at the far side.

P4 5a/5b 15m A suitable finale can be chosen from the 2 striking crack lines above. The *Left-Hand Crack*, at VS 5a, is the easier option, but *The Right-Hand Crack* HVS 5b will be irresistible to connoisseurs of the art of aggressive jamming and laybacking.

[C F Kirkus, F E Hicks 25.06.29]

6. Chasm Route VD 85m

A classic traditional route of much character.

P1 27m Start 10m right of the prominent 3m high block (The Capstan) at the base of a flat rib leading up towards the Chasm feature (a steep smooth-sided chimney). Ascend the front of the rib, then follow a jamming crack to gain the ledge on the left. Move round to the right to the bottom of the Chasm.

P2 21m Climb up the Chasm to a rightwards exit from the upper section. Move over blocks to belay in a corner on the left.

P3 22m Ascend the crack in the steep left wall and follow juggy holds out to the left. Return to the gully bed via the narrow gangway. Go under the fallen splinter of rock and move up a corner to the chimney on the left.

P4 15m Wriggle through the chimney and continue up the Vertical Vice, typically with a considerable expenditure of energy. Finish up a difficult crack on the right.

[J M A Thomson, H O Jones, L Noon 1910]

The following routes can be reached by traversing right along the terrace above the Alphabet Slabs or from below and to the right.

7. Get Close HVS 5a 24m
A superb climb, well worth seeking out. Start below the crack line. Climb the crack in the left wall of the pillar until it is possible to make a move rightwards into the groove in the right arête of the wall. Continue up the groove to the top.
[L Hardy, C Parkin 06.89]

8. Hyndsight E4 6a 26m
An excellent 'monkey-up-a-stick' route taking the front face of the thin pillar.
The initial section runs steadily up to a small spike on the right arête. Move left to place some gear in the groove of *Get Close*. Return to the front face, and squeeze your way to the top.
[C Parkin, L Hardy 06.89]

9. Hawk's Nest Arête VS 4c 40m
An exhilarating excursion and a true classic.
P1 4c 27m Climb up the edge of the buttress to a perched flake at 12m, and then continue on steeper ground, on the right-hand side of the arete until good holds lead rightwards to a small ledge. Step onto the ledge and move right along it, then go up an open little chimney to reach a flake, which leads back leftwards to the arete. The belay is quickly reached.
P2 12m Follow the crack to the top.
[P W W Nock, H Harrison 22.07.40]

< James McHaffie onsighting the awesome **Kaya** E6/7 6b photo: Graham Desroy

Clogwyn y Tarw

Area:	Ogwen Valley
Style:	Trad (1 - 4 pitches)
Aspect:	North
Rock type:	Rhyolitic Tuff
Approach:	20 minutes
Altitude:	450m

Trouble with Lichen	E2
Diadem	HVS
Herford's Crack	HVS
Yob Route	HVS
Flake Crack	VS
Llyn	VS
Rocking Chair	VS
Zig Zag Climb	HS
Monolith Crack	S
Slab Climb	D

This popular outcrop style crag, referred to as Griben Facet in the past, is easily accessed from the Ogwen Cottage – Llyn Idwal path. Characterised by deceptively difficult routes, which pack a considerable amount of action into their relatively diminutive form.

Conditions: The crag dries reasonably quickly, although dampness will persist in cracks after rain. It receives evening sun, except during the winter months.

Approach: From the Ogwen Cottage car park, follow the path that runs up left from the slate cutting. After a few hundred metres it kinks back right towards Llyn Idwal. The crag comes into view, and is best approached by following a faint path, which breaks off left from the main path approximately 100m before Llyn Idwal is reached.

Descent: Scramble down grassy ledges between East Buttress and Central Buttress, heading right (facing out) in the lower section. The last part is quite awkward. For routes on West Buttress walk over the top and descend on the Llyn Idwal side of the crag.

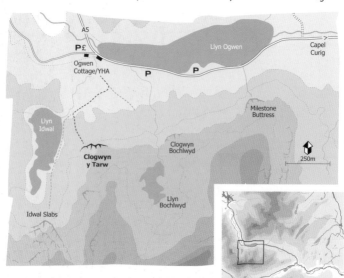

∧ Alex Williams in the V-groove on P1 of **Zig Zag Climb** HS 4b, Clogwyn y Tarw photo: Jethro Kiernan

Clogwyn y Tarw • East Buttress

LLANBERIS +

OGWEN +

TREMADOG +

GOGARTH & LLEYN

LLANDUDNO +

1. Yob Route HVS 5a 57m
A steep and sustained route, saving its crux enigmatic layback 'til the end.
P1 5a 45m Follow the ramp up left into the narrowing groove. Step out left and move up into the slim square-cut groove and continue in the same line, switching onto the slab on the right to reach a pair of twin cracks. Plug in some protection and commit to a difficult layback to reach good holds. Climb up to belay on *Slab Climb*.
P2 12m Follow the polished holds to the top.
[K R C Britton, R Beasley (3 pts) 21.08.57, modern finish: M G T Plant, P E Wright 25.07.67]

2. Llyn VS 4c 64m
A classic struggle, thankfully well protected.
P1 4c 38m From the start of *Yob Route* follow the ramp system up right into the steep crack which leads, not without a few moments of desperation, into the upper chimney. Continue up to belay on *Slab Climb*.
P2 26m Follow the polished holds to the top.
[C H S R Palmer, J M Edwards C H S R Palmer, J M Edwards 13.07.31]

3. Diadem HVS 5a 53m
A superb climb; just a shame it isn't longer.
P1 5a 27m Start 6m right of *Llyn*, and trend up right to reach a ledge beneath the thin crack running directly up the wall. Flounce up the crack, laybacking and jamming as you see fit.
P2 26m Follow the polished holds to the top.
[M Crook, D Farrant 1979]

Clogwyn y Tarw

LLANBERIS +

OGWEN +

TREMADOG +

GOGARTH & LLEYN

LLANDUDNO +

Central
Buttress

West
Buttress

Flake Crack
and
Herford's Crack

The fierce looking crack to the right is *Sweet Sorrow* HVS 5a.

4. Slab Climb D 52m
A polished, but enjoyable romp. The steep face below adds a pleasing element of exposure.
P1 15m. Ascend for a metre or so on the right side of the slab, before tracing an easy but bold traverse line leftwards to reach a sandy corner on the left. A harder, but arguably better alternative start, up P1 of *Slab Intermediate Route* VD is possible: gain the sandy corner directly by the groove situated 9m left of the normal start.
P2 11m Follow the slab on the left to a crevasse stance.
P3 14m Continue up the slab to a stance below the quartzy veins below the top.
P4 12m Stay on the left edge slab, and move up over blocks to the top.
[J Laycock, S W Herford 05.12]

5. Rocking Chair VS 4c 30m
An old style classic tackling the obvious V-groove. Reach the bottom of the groove from the right side of the slab. Ascend the groove to a ledge on the right, and continue somewhat precariously up the smooth chimney/groove to reach easier climbing as the angle eases.
[R L Roberts, E Birch 14.11.58]

6. Trouble with Lichen E2 5b 36m

A punchy and intense little route.

P1 5b 18m Start at a short wall directly below the hanging arête left of *Monolith Crack*. Move up the wall with difficulty and head left over a heathery ledge and across to belay beneath a finger crack. (This point can be reached by scrambling up on the left.)

P2 5b 18m Go up the tricky crack to reach the fault line. Follow this right and fight up the prominent crack to a ledge. Steadier climbing leads to the top.

[J C Peart, J Holt (1 pt) 02.07.76, FFA: R Fawcett 1979]

7. Monolith Crack S 40m

This notorious, but utterly classic route will delight the cavers in the party, but appal the claustrophobic wimps!

P1 9m Start on the right side of the Monolith block, and squirm up through a cave beneath it.

P2 9m Ascend the difficult chimney, or its harder twin on the left.

P3 12m Slide into the chimney facing right and wriggle upwards with conviction, passing through a hole behind the chockstone to reach with relief, daylight and the quartz slab. *De Selincourt's Variation* is the dishonourable cop out: from the pedestal step onto the edge of the wall and move up right followed by a tricky mantelshelf which lands you on the quartz slab. A further option for leaders who baulk at the evil cleft, is to adopt some combined tactics on its outer edge. Either way, the family name will be muddied forever.

P4 9m The quartz slab leads up to the final chimney; scoot up it to the top.

[G D Abraham, A P Abraham 05.05]

8. Zig Zag Climb HS 4b 42m

An engaging route, with a tricky and polished groove.

P1 4b 21m Start on a rock step just right of the Monolith. Ascend the corner and crack, then head right along a sloping ledge to reach a smooth V-groove. Climb up the groove with no little difficulty to reach a quartz slab and a belay higher up.

P2 21m Continue up the slab to a pair of cracks. The strenuous right-hand crack leads to the top.

[S W Herford, J Laycock, W G Milligan, R Hodgkinson 05.12]

9. Flake Crack VS 4c 26m

An amusing and varied climb featuring the infamous wobbly flake! Climb up *Herford's Crack*, passing a small ledge on the right, and continuing up to a footledge seam. Make a tenuous transfer into the left-hand crack via some polished footholds. The reward is a big spiky block. Enter the cleft above and 'back and foot' up (don't push too hard!) to gain a ledge. Bridge up and make an airy and anxious stride from the tip of the 'torpedo' onto the wall. A delicate step-up precedes the final easier section. Belay just below the cliff top on flake belays.

[O Thorneycroft 04.09]

10. Herford's Crack HVS 5a 25m

A fantastic jamming pitch up the arrow-straight crack right of *Flake Crack*. The difficulties are sustained, but a selection of size 2.5 to 3.5 cams and a few chunky hexes will ease any worries of a downward plummet.

[S W Herford, J Laycock 05.12]

Cwm Cneifion

Area: Cwm Cneifion
Style: Trad (4-5 pitches)
Aspect: West
Rock: Rhyolite
Approach: 35/50 minutes
Altitude: 550/750m

Sub-Cneifion Rib	VD
Cneifion Arete	D

A pair of excellent ridge climbs that can easily be linked together, or taken individually, depending on the inclination of the party. Cwm Cneifion is the conspicuous glaciated bowl perched high above Cwm Idwal. *Sub-Cneifion Rib* is not strictly speaking in the cwm itself, but it does sit adjacent to the traditional approach line. *Cneifion Arête* has a more legitimate claim, standing as it does at the entrance to the cwm proper, on the west-facing flank of Y Gribin, and it forms the prominent ridge that runs down to eventually meet the top of Clogwyn y Tarw.

Conditions: The sunny and open aspect of both ridges means that they are quick to dry. *Sub-Cneifion Rib* is quite rounded and compact, and as such would be very tricky in the wet, whereas *Cneifion Arête* is an entirely feasible option on a wet day (possibly as a link up with the similarly difficult *Ordinary Route* on the Idwal Slabs), as long as care is taken on the tricky lower section.

Approach: From the Ogwen Cottage car park, follow the path that runs up left from the slate cutting. After a few hundred metres it kinks back right towards Llyn Idwal. Follow the path along the left side of the lake, until the *Sub Cneifion Rib* can be seen above. Strike a line-up the steep grassy hillside to its base. If you just wish to climb *Cneifion Arête*, then follow the diagonal path running rightwards up the hillside into the base of the upper cwm. *Cneifion Arete* looms up on the left at this point, marking the right edge of a large broken crag, stretching leftwards across the western face of Y Gribin.

Descent: For *Sub Cneifion Rib*, simply drop back down the hillside on the right side of the rib. From the top of *Cneifion Arête* it is best to head left and follow the path down past Llyn Bochlwyd and then back towards Idwal Cottage. Alternatively, and weather permitting, the day could be extended with a refreshing romp across the Glyderau.

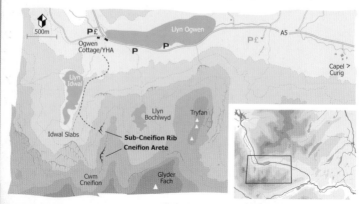

Cwm Cneifion

LLANBERIS +

OGWEN +

TREMADOG +

GOGARTH & LLEYN

LLANDUDNO +

1. Sub-Cneifion Rib VD 125m

A delightful route on wonderfully clean rock.

P1 30m Start at the bottom of the main rib from behind a pointed block. Pad up cracks and grooves on the apex of the ridge, passing a bulge on the left. Continue up a crack running up the front of the rib to reach a belay stance.

P2 35m. Scramble up leftwards over grassy ledges and climb the rib on the left.

P3 27m Scramble right across the rib and drop down to a grassy ledge. Traverse across right and move up a few metres to belay below a steep nose.

P4 34m. Gain the shelf on the nose and tip toe delicately right around to a shallow groove. Follow this back up onto the front of the rib, where a crack cutting the crest leads to the top.

[J M Edwards 12.07.31]

Cneifion Arête

Idwal Slabs

↑ Al Leary padding up P1 of **Sub Cneifion Rib** VD photo: Graham Desroy

Cwm Cneifion

2. Cneifion Arête D 135m

A pleasurable and exposed climb with a tricky lower section followed by a pinnacled alpine-esque ridge.

P1 25m Start just right of the base of the ridge from the arête at a shallow groove. Ascend steeply for 10m, then swerve right, before heading back left towards the crest of the ridge. Move up to belay below a chimney.

P2 10m Tussle up the chimney to easier ground.

P3-5 100m Continue by scrambling up the airy ridge, belaying as you see fit.

[G Barlow, E M Barlow 1905]

Distant view of Clogwyn Du (hidden in the shadow at the top of Cwm Cneifion) photo: Al Leary

Clogwyn Du

Area:	Cwm Cneifion
Style:	Trad (2 - 4 pitches)
Aspect:	North-East
Rock type:	Basalt
Approach:	90 minutes
Altitude:	900m

Stratosphere	E3
Hebenwi	E2
Manx Wall	HS

A dark mountain crag perched high on the lip of Cwm Cneifion. Clogwyn Du is a small, but decidedly atmospheric cliff. It attracts only a fraction of the attention visited upon the bustling Idwal slabs below, and is all the better for it. The routes themselves have an unexpected big crag character that belies their relatively modest length.

During the colder months of the year it provides some of the best and the most reliable winter climbing in North Wales.

Conditions: The high altitude and northerly aspect ensure that this is a crag for balmy summer days. After rain expect drainage and dampness to linger for several days. Even then the lack of traffic will mean that dirty rock will still be encountered. The good news for early birds is that during the summer months the crag receives a warming blanket of morning sun. Come the afternoon though, it'll be cool and shady once again.

Approach: From the Ogwen Cottage car park, follow the path that runs up left from the slate cutting. After a few hundred metres it kinks back right towards Llyn Idwal. Follow the path along the left side of the lake, until the *Sub Cneifion Rib* can be seen above. Strike a diagonal line up and across the hillside, keeping to the right of *Sub Cneifion Rib*, until the base of the upper cwm is reached (*Cneifion Arete* looms up on the left at this point). From here a vague path leads up to the base of the crag.

Descent: Come back down the steep slope left (facing in) of the crag.

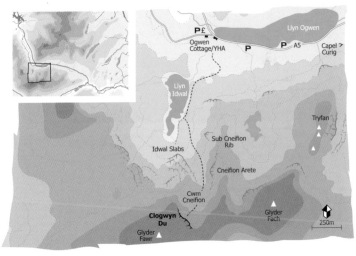

Clogwyn Du

1. Stratosphere E3 5c 92m

A splendid route that is both exposed and fairly serious.

P1 5a 15m As for *Hebenwi* P1.

P2 5c 20m Follow the undercut diagonal ramp leftwards with escalating difficulty, until a committing stride gains a foothold on the lip of the overhang. Ascend the wall above, until it is possible to traverse left to gain a sentry box stance.

P3 5b 33m Traverse out right to a ledge on the arête. Climb up the open groove above, and then go up the steep wall to a grass ledge.

P4 4c 24m As for *Hebenwi* P4.

[S Boyden, S Cardy 05.06.82]

Streaky Desroy on P1 of **Manx Wall** HS 4b photo: Al Leary ∧

2. Hebenwi E2 5b 76m

An exhilarating route, covering some impressive ground.

P1 5a 15m Start by scrambling up the grassy rake. Stop and belay below the steeper chimney section. Climb up leftwards to reach a narrow grass ledge beneath the bulge guarding access to the main face above and belay on the right.

P2 5b 24m Move right to some good holds beneath the steep wall. Climb up boldly to gain a rest, then follow a thin crack above and traverse a few metres right to reach a grassy bay.

P3 5a 13m Go up the shallow groove, passing the block and making a tricky exit onto the slab on the left. Trend up left to belay beneath the steep arête.

P4 4c 24m Ascend the arête, passing the overhang on the left. Finish up the easy chimney to the top.

[D Alcock, M A Boysen 11.10.69]

3. Manx Wall HS 4b 55m

A brilliant route, cutting an audacious line through some intimidating territory. Often done as a finale to a day of link-ups around Cwm Idwal.

P1 4b 35m Start by scrambling up the grassy rake (one awkward chimney section) to reach a belay at the foot of the obvious pillar. Climb the leftward-slanting groove to a small ledge beneath a little groove. Move right into another groove and follow this up to a ledge. Step left to a corner and climb this with interest to a narrow grass ledge which leads horizontally left to a thread and nut belay in a highly exposed position.

P2 4b 20m Climb the corner/crack of the slab to the overhang. Step around the arete and shuffle leftwards along a shelf for a few moves until possible to pull into the spectacular crack splitting the roof. Follow this in a fantastic position to the cliff top.

[A J Lowe, W K J Pearson, J G Pearson, P Russell 1942]

Idwal Slabs and Walls

Area: Cwm Idwal
Style: Trad (1-7 pitches)
Aspect: Generally North
Rock: Rhyolitic Tuff/Breccias
Approach: 25 minutes
Altitude: 450m

Mur y Meirwon	E5
Penal Servitude	E4
Capital Punishment	E3
Demetreus	E3
Homicide Wall	E3

Rowan Tree Slabs	E2
Suicide Wall Route 1	E2
Suicide Wall Route 2	E2
Javelin Blade	E1
Rampart Corner	E1
Continuation Cracks	HVS

East Wall Girdle	VS
Heather Wall	VS
Javelin Buttress	VS
Original Route	VS
Tennis Shoe	HS
Faith West Finish	S
Groove Above	S
Lazarus	S

Faith	VD
Hope	VD
Ordinary Route	D

A classic traditional crag situated in the beautiful mountain setting of Cwm Idwal. The Idwal Slabs, or Rhiwiau Caws (translated literally as Cheese Slabs), hold a special place in the hearts of British climbers. It is here that many of us took our early, tentative steps into the world of rock climbing. However, regardless of its traditional apprenticeship role, it should be borne in mind that this sizeable cliff is far from suitable for total novices. The slab is exposed and not overly featured with belay ledges. In places, the rock is exceptionally polished, and the descent route has a certain, and justified notoriety. In short, there are probably better places to learn the art of multi-pitch climbing.

The main slab is a dramatic sweep of rock. Although home to a collection of elegant low-grade classics the appeal of the crag runs right across the spectrum, as the steeper surrounding walls offer more challenging pitches. Many of these are accessed from the main slab, and link ups and connections are popular, often continuing up the mountainside to the upper crags (e.g. Grey Slab, Cneifion Arete, or Clogwyn Du).

On the left side of the slabs, at the top of the East Wall sits the ominously titled Suicide Wall; a most atmospheric section of crag, and one that is criss-crossed by a series of sustained and intricate climbs. The route names suit its sombre brooding presence, their dark nomenclature adding further resonance to the spooky ambience.

The rock is good quality rhyolite, delightfully featured, especially on the East Wall and Suicide Wall where a rough, pocketed texture is found.

Conditions: The main slab receives afternoon sunshine in the summer, and dries very quickly after rain, but drainage streaks will linger in corners and overlaps. The shady north-east-facing East Wall and Suicide Wall suffer badly from drainage problems and will take several days to dry out after wet weather.

Approach: From the Ogwen Cottage car park, follow the path that runs up left from the bottom of the slate cutting. After a few hundred metres it kinks back right towards Llyn Idwal. Follow the path along the left side of the lake to reach the base of the main slab.

Descent: The best descent from climbs on the Idwal Slabs is known as the Easy Way Off. Ironically this is not entirely obvious to the first time visitor and it does require some care. From the left side of the quartz seamed terrace beneath Holly Tree Wall, head left and zig zag up easy rock steps and broken ground. A quartzy ramp running leftwards is a memorable feature to spot, before going back right up more rock steps.

The Idwal Gate photo: Al Leary ∧

Idwal Slabs and Walls

Above the last rock step is a grassy area and a short brown slab. Go up the slab to a rounded ledge with short walls on the right. Descend a polished groove and drop down steeper rock to reach easier ground. Care should be exercised on this section: if in doubt rope up, as accidents have happened here before. The path then runs out onto the hillside before dropping down via a little gully to return back to the base of the slabs.

From the top of the East Wall and Suicide Wall the Easy Way Off can be accessed, either directly or via *Tennis Shoe*.

From the top of both Holly Tree Wall and Continuation Wall, the Easy Way Off can easily be reached by heading leftwards (facing in).

For routes on the West Wall see descent details in the introducton to the routes.

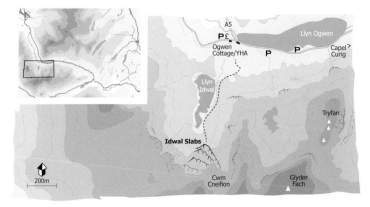

LLANBERIS +

OGWEN +

TREMADOG +

GOGARTH & LLEYN

LLANDUDNO +

215

Idwal Slabs and Walls • East Wall • Suicide Wall

The East Wall is the slabby, ramped wall on the left flank of the main slab.

1. East Wall Girdle VS 4b 170m/215m
A long and charming excursion across the East Wall. Although the climbing is not too difficult, there are some relatively serious situations, demanding steadiness from both leader and second.
P1 4a 30m P1 of *Tennis Shoe* (page 219).
P2 4b 50m Climb the quartz slab, moving onto the left edge at 30m where it narrows and steepens. Continue up to the shared stance at the top of slab on P1 of *Heather Wall*.
P3 4b 20m Move across left past the rounded arête, and continue leftwards, dropping down slightly to gain a grassy ledge.
P4 4b 45m Traverse diagonally left above the steep slab, and continue to a small ledge (possible belay on poor spikes on the right). Move round to the left, and ascend a narrow slab to reach a grassy area.
P5 4b 25m Move up to a flake in the centre of the slabby wall above, then head left into the long shallow groove. This leads to the grassy terrace. It is possible to reach the descent route from here, but there is a worthwhile continuation pitch for the keen:
P6 4b 45m Ascend the slab and steep groove on the left.
[J M Edwards, C H S R Palmer 13.07.31]

2. Heather Wall VS 4c 55m
A splendid route, with 2 fine pitches.
P1 4b 30m Start up the gangway, then head leftwards up the slab to reach a small stance at its top, and a junction with *East Wall Girdle*.
P2 4c 25m Move across left below the 3 short grooves to reach a rounded arête. Go up the arête, passing a small bulge on the left via some good holds, leading to more good holds. An easier groove trends up right to join *Tennis Shoe*.
[F E Hicks, A B Hargreaves, E A Stewardson 30.08.29]

Suicide Wall is the dark wall at the top of the East Wall.

3. Suicide Wall Route 2 E2 5b 43m
An excellent route with some funky rock features.
Gain the crescent-shaped recess from the left and head right around a blunt rib to access a line of rightward-leading flakes. Follow these with some difficulty to a ledge. Ascend the groove on the right for 10m, and then continue up the right arête to finish.
[P Crew, B Ingle 22.09.63]

4. Penal Servitude E4 5c 46m
A serious lead, with some excellent, relatively steep climbing.
The slight ramp leads boldly up leftwards to the crescent-shaped recess on *Suicide Wall Route 2*. From the right side of the recess, wander up leftwards initially, aiming for a thread in the wall. The girdle ramp is soon reached where an awkward thread gives some protection. Shuffle right to reach the edge of the slab and follow a thin crack to the top.
[B Wayman, T Jepson 08.77]

5. Capital Punishment E3 5c 49m
A magnificent, intricate pitch sweeping up the wall.
Gain the crescent-shaped recess on *Suicide Wall Route 2*, then move up to a triangular slab which leads to the base of a shallow groove. Continue up the groove with difficulty, passing a good thread, and following good holds above to reach the girdle ledge. Continue up the steep ramp to a joint finish with *Suicide Wall Route 1*.
[M A Boysen, D E Alcock (1 pt) 11.09.71, FFA: M Berzins, R Berzins, C Hamper 07.76]

John Coefield on **Suicide Wall Route 1** E2 5c photo: Coefield collection >

6. Mur y Meirwon E5 6b 34m

A superb climb. Initially desperate, then running into some classic open wall climbing.
A thin crack runs up the bulging wall to the ledge on *Suicide Wall Route 1*. Awkward moves
up the crack prelude an easy ride to the ledge. From its right-hand end climb up, then trend
left across the steep red rock, passing a pair of stacked pegs, to fondle an undercut. The
upper wall is bold but better holds are within reach and lead rightwards to the top.
[R Fawcett, C Gibb 30.06.79]

7. Suicide Wall Route 1 E2 5c 30m

An extraordinarily bold lead for its day. It marked a significant leap in standard for wall
climbing and still remains a serious proposition. Start at a slight weakness below and left
of the obvious grass ledge at 13m. Climb straight up the wall making a hard move to pass
a tiny spike, recessed in a pocket. The difficulties ease quickly towards the ledge. From the
right end of the ledge, climb up and right to a difficult scoop. Continue rightwards, following
improving holds, to meet the rib and a ledge. Follow the ramp leftwards to the top.
[C Preston, R G Morsley, J Haines 07.10.45]

Rhiwiau Caws is the magnificent main slab.

8. Tennis Shoe HS 4a 155m

A wonderfully open and entirely classic route following the left edge of the main slab.

P1 4a 30m to the left of the main slab is a narrow subsidiary slab, climb it to a ledge, taking care on the extremely polished holds.

P2 15m Move round to the right, and follow a groove up into a crack near the edge of the main slab. Soon after a ledge is reached.

P3 18m Continue up on the edge of the main slab to a large flake.

P4 37m Cross the gully on the left and follow the exposed rib and quartz slab to a good rock stance.

P5 30m Continue easily up the slab to a grassy terrace.

P6 10m Walk across left and take a belay beneath the final tower.

P7 4a 15m Ascend the steep face of the tower to reach a scoop with a tricky move. Continue delicately on to the slab above and finish by surmounting the perched block.

[N E Odell 08.19]

9. The Ordinary Route D 140m

The original and easiest route on the slabs ploughs up a series of polished furrows and cracks. The suggested belays are just that; feel free to break the route up into smaller pitches if you want to stay in closer contact with an inexperienced second.

P1 46m Follow the polished trough to a comfy niche belay.

P2 46m Climb the crack that leads right, before making a switch back left into a polished scoop. Easier climbing leads up the polished scoop trending rightwards. At its top move up onto the slab above and continue up to a spike belay.

P3 24m Climb the polished crack above, stepping right from the top of it onto the slab; good holds lead to a large ledge on the right.

P4 24m Trend easily up left, before switching back right to reach the terrace. A harder direct pitch (VD) is possible for the tiger in the party.

[T K Rose, C C B Moss 23.08.1897]

10. Hope VD 136m

A brilliant climb featuring clean rock, elegant climbing and sustained interest.

P1 46m. Start about 25m right of *The Ordinary Route*. Take your pick from the quartz slab, rib or the groove, on the left, to reach the long rock ledge at 10m. Head up slightly right then trend back left to the inverted V-slot cutting through the overlap on the left. Pad up the quartz-veneered slab above to a spacious platform.

P2 30m. The infamous Twin Cracks are both polished and unnervingly difficult. Luckily a thank god jug arrives just when you need it most. Trend up the slab leftwards, then continue directly, before heading slightly right to meet the diagonal overlap. Move up again to a small stance in the corner/groove.

P3 35m Move up, turning a steep section of the overlap/groove to the left. Follow the groove up right and out onto a quartz area.

P4 25m Trend up leftwards on quartzy rock to the terrace.

[E H Daniels, I A Richards, T J Roxborough, R B Henderson 14.08.15]

Holly Tree Wall is the steep wall perched at the top of the main slab.

11. Rampart Corner E1 5c 45m

This excellent pitch is technical, but well protected.

Start as for *Original Route*, but traverse left beneath the small overhang, then striking a direct line through its left side to reach the corner crack. Continue up the line with difficulty, passing a rest position and eventually gaining easier ground.

[H I Banner, R Wilson 13.09.77]

12. Original Route VS 5a 40m

Another superb, but rather tough proposition.

P1 5a 27m Just above the large boulder on the terrace lies a polished diagonal scoop. Enter the bottomless groove with a bit of a tussle, then continue rightwards up the gangway (The Crescent Slab) and step into the chimney on the right. Thrash up this to a rock bay above.

P2 4c 13m The obvious continuation crack leads, with further interest, to the top.

(A more dignified and stylish variation exists at the same grade: climb the wall above the quartz-topped flake right of the normal start, to gain the gangway. Follow it initially up to the right, and then traverse out left along a narrow ledge. From its left end move up delicately and make a mantelshelf move to reach better holds leading to the rock bay.)

[I A Richards, C F Holland, D E Piley 22.05.18]

13. Lazarus S 4a 43m

As the easiest line on the wall, this is a popular option for teams arriving at the top of the main slab, eager for more challenges. It is, however, no pushover.

P1 17m Go up the stepped gully on the right and belay where it opens out into a bay.

P2 4a 26m Traverse delicately out across the wall, heading for a rock nose over on the left side. Continue up via a slabby groove just to the right. A steep little wall provides the crux; continue up past a niche, trending right to reach the top.

(First ascent unknown, circa 1922)

14. Javelin Blade E1 5b 40m

A fine bold lead, and all the more incredible when you consider the first ascent date! Ascend the groove of *Javelin Buttress* to the thread runner, then step down and go across the slab to the left edge of the buttress. Above a narrow rib forms a corner groove. Teeter up the groove and make a disconcerting and committing swing out right. Gladly the difficulties soon ease after that.

[J Longland, C Williams Easter 1930]

15. Javelin Buttress VS 4c 40m

The striking diagonal line provides a cracking pitch on immaculate rock.

Start at a groove about 5m down and right of the start of *Lazarus*. Follow the groove line (past a thread runner on the left) to its end, and carry on up the line of the continuation crack line, eventually reaching easier ground.

[F Graham, C E Jerram 11.04.25]

LLANBERIS +

OGWEN +

TREMADOG +

GOGARTH & LLEYN

LLANDUDNO +

Continuation Wall is the final tier right at the top of the crag.

16. The Arête VD 24m
A great pitch to top all that has gone on below.
Ascend the corner for a metre or so, then traverse left across the slab and follow the arête to the top.
[F E Hicks, C B M Warren, A L Spence 23.06.29]

17. Continuation Crack HVS 5b 18m
A sparkling climb of the utmost quality. Trace the thin crack, using holds on the left when it suits.
[First ascent unknown]

18. Groove Above S 4b 24m
Entry into the V-groove is frankly, desperate. Above, where the difficulties relent considerably, finish rightwards beneath the steepening.
[T S Knowles, H Poole 11.12.26]

The West Wall is in fact a series of walls situated above the right side of the main slab (see topo on page 220). The best descent for the next routes is to pop over the top of Idwal Buttress and follow a faint path leading down into an obvious furrow. Scramble down this to the scree, then cut back to the base of the crag.

19. Demetreus E3 6a 24m
This stunning and intense pitch is well worth the trot up *Hope* to gain its base.
An incipient crack/seam forms a central weakness on the wall. Reach it from the right and follow it, finishing directly with haste when it peters out.
[D Beetlestone, G Gibson 08.79]

Kim Pearson just above the crux entry to the **Groove Above** S 4b photo: Ray Wood **>**

Idwal Slabs and Walls • West Wall • Idwal Buttress

LLANBERIS +

OGWEN +

TREMADOG +

GOGARTH & LLEYN

LLANDUDNO +

P2

Terrace above P1

Idwal
Staircase

20. Rowan Tree Slabs E2 5c 48m
A very fine route, if a little thin and bold.
P1 37m Start below the right-most section of the main slabs. Climb a line holds leading leftwards, then a crack running up the centre of the slab to the terrace (This is P1 of *Subwall Climb* S).
P2 5c 34m Climb easily up to a niche at the left corner of the slab, and head right onto the slab, moving up on small holds. Trend up leftwards, with escalating difficulty, until a final thin move, past a strange pocket, leads up to a ledge.
P3 5b 14m Go up the steep groove in the arête, on the left, to reach a ledge. Finish in a splendid position back on the arête.
[F E Hicks, C V A Cooper, W E Woosnam Jones 1929, modern version: J O'Neill 1963, finish added by M A Boysen, D little 1969]

Idwal Buttress

The prominent undercut buttress at the bottom right side of the main slab.

21. Homicide Wall E3 5b 38m
A thrilling route tracing the line of huge pockets running diagonally up the wall above the Idwal Staircase.
P1 4c 24m From the toe of the buttress follow pockets up to a quartz gangway, and then head left and slightly down around a blunt rib to gain a stance.
P2 5b 14m Move up left onto a small slab. Make a bold swing up to a strange horizontal spike in a pocket and continue steeply leftwards to gain an obvious jug. Finish more easily.
[D G Peers, J Whittle (2pts) 1971, FFA: L McGinley, Strappo Hughes 05.77]

∧ Looking down on Llyn Idwal and Nant Ffrancon from Suicide Wall photo: John Coefield

LLANBERIS +

OGWEN +

TREMADOG +

GOGARTH & LLEYN

LLANDUDNO +

225

Glyder Fawr

Area: Cwm Idwal
Style: Trad (2-7 pitches)
Aspect: North-West
Rock: Rhyolitic Tuff
Approach: 80 minutes
Altitude: 800m

Grey Arete	HVS
Grey Slab / Lost Boot Climb	VS
Central Arete	VD

A fine pair of classic slab routes and a grand alpine-esque ridge (yes another one!), all situated rather magnificently at the top of Cwm Idwal, below the summit of Glyder Fawr. Although these climbs provide a traditional extension to the routes on the Idwal Slabs, they are well worth seeking out on the basis of their own considerable merit. The lofty position adds a degree of magic to the cliff, especially when it is bathed in glorious evening light, and the rock in the Grey Slab area is simply superb, although it can feel rather bold in places.

Conditions: *Grey Slab* suffers from a drainage problem (it would be rare to find it completely dry), whilst *Grey Arete* and *Central Arête* dry quickly after wet weather. The routes all catch the evening sun.

Approach: From the Ogwen Cottage car park, follow the path that runs up left from the bottom of the slate cutting. After a few hundred metres it kinks back right towards Llyn Idwal. Follow the path along the left side of the lake to reach the base of the Idwal Slabs. It is traditional to approach the Upper Cliff after having completed a route (or a series of routes) on the Idwal Slabs and Walls. A traverse is then made rightwards across the hillside (see topo). If time is short then thrash directly up the screes to the right of Idwal Buttress.

Descent: From the top of *Grey Slab* area of the Upper Cliff, traverse the ledge back left, and then follow a grassy cleft/furrow to the crest of the ridge. From here a gently descending terrace leads into Cwm Cneifion. Alternatively, continue the day's adventures by linking in with a route on Clogwyn Du.

After topping out on *Central Arete* the summit of Glyder Fawr beckons the hardy mountaineer. From there, continue round the top of Cwm Cneifion and descend the Gribin Ridge. Alternatively come down the path on the north west slope of Glyder Fawr to Llyn y Cwn, then follow a path north-east and drop down past the Devil's Kitchen via the heavily scratched diagonal rake.

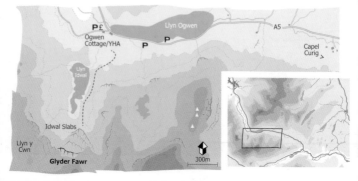

∧ Kim Pearson on the bold start to P2 of **Grey Arete** HVS 5a photo: Ray Wood

↖ Evening sun on Glyder Fawr Upper Cliff photo: Al Leary

Glyder Fawr • Grey Slab Area

Start the first 2 routes by scrambling up to a ledge at the base of the corner.

1. Grey Slab/Lost Boot Climb VS 4b 85m

A classic bold slab climb, which unfortunately does suffer from a drainage problem.

P1 4a 35m Ascend the corner for 15m, then head leftwards across the slab on pockets, moving up a slight rib to good belays (including a size 3/3.5 cam) under the bulge, and just left of the water streak. Having clipped the gear, it is worth stepping back down for a few metres to a more comfortable stance.

P2 4b 50m Pull over the bulge (taking care with a loose hold) and move steadily up the faint rib on the left. Pock-marks lead up, first right, then left to the left-hand end of the overlap. Surmount the overlap via a shallow groove on the left. The upper slab provides a final test: work up between the oft-present water streaks to gain a ledge with a block and nut belay.

[A S Bullough, C V A Cooper, J Marchington 02.07.32]

2. Grey Arête HVS 5a 83m

Another exquisite slab climb, harder, but not as bold as *Grey Slab*.

P1 4c 37m Ascend the scoop in the arête until it is possible to gain the slab on the right. Wander up in a more casual fashion to the long ledge; belay on the right.

P2 5a 46m The pock-marked wall is both delicate and bold; it leads quickly to a ledge on the left arête. A fine crack leads upwards, before kinking awkwardly to the right. Follow it to its end and continue to the top with a scramble up to reach the descent ledge.

[R James, P Benson 16.08.59]

Glyder
Fawr

Clogwyn
Du

Cwm
Cneifion

Grey
Slab
Area

The
Upper
Cliff

Continuation
Wall

Holly Tree
Wall

Descent

Idwal
Buttress

Idwal
Slabs

3

3. Central Arête VD 200m

A splendid mountaineering excursion, with a thin and difficult lower section followed by an easier finish on a spiky ridge.

P1 46m Start beneath the large buttress right of the narrow grassy rake running up the crag. Slabby rocks lead to a good grassy platform.

P2 34m Climb the delicate slab on the right edge of the arête, and belay in a groove.

P3 15m Move back left and continue up the arete.

P4-6 105m Continue again on the edge, passing over an assortment of pinnacles and spikes.

[G Barlow, H B Buckle 1909]

Clogwyn y Geifr

Area: Cwm Idwal
Style: Trad (1 - 3 pitches)
Aspect: North-East
Rock type: Bedded Pyroclastics
Approach: 50 minutes
Altitude: 700m

Devil's Nordwand	E1
Devil's Staircase	S
Devil's Kitchen Route	VD

A vast and heavily vegetated crag that appears at first glance to offer little in the way of conventional rock climbs. On closer inspection this proves to be largely true. Nonetheless this immense rotting synclinal arc of volcanic tuff does provide a few routes of tremendous, albeit unconventional, character.

During the cold snap of the winter months Clogwyn y Geifr is oft transformed by plummeting temperatures into an ice climber's (frozen) wet dream. Yet for the best part of the year it just sits at the back of the cwm; moody, dank and foreboding.

These cliffs, and in particular the boulders that sit beneath them, provide a vital habitat for several species of rare flora. Please respect their presence, and do not disturb their delicate existence.

Conditions: *The Devil's Kitchen Route* will always be a somewhat damp experience, but then that is part of the fun. *The Devil's Staircase* rarely dries out entirely (again, the wetness is a feature to be cherished), whilst the *Devil's Nordwand* is more conventional. This should be in climbable nick a day or so after rain.

Approach: From the Ogwen Cottage car park, follow the path that runs up left from the bottom of the slate cutting. After a few hundred metres it kinks back right towards Llyn Idwal. The crag can be reached by circumnavigating the lake on either side, until the steeper stepped paths converge below the ominous gash of Twll Du (The Black Pit), or The Devil's Kitchen as it is known in English.

Descent: For the first 2 routes walk over the top, heading south east (leftwards, facing in), before turning back down and returning to the base of the Kitchen via the heavily scratched (winter crampons) diagonal rake. For *Devil's Nordwand* carefully descend the ramp that runs down left (facing in) from the top of the route.

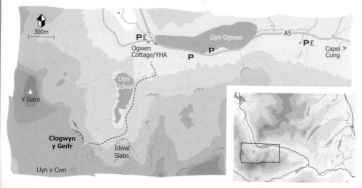

∧ Streaky Desroy on P1 of **Devil's Nordwand** E1 5b photo: Al Leary

⋏ Clogwyn y Geifr photo: Al Leary

Clogwyn y Geifr

1. Devil's Kitchen Route VD 24m

The dark, sepulchral cavern that plunges deep into the heart of the cliff - scoured out by the rushing torrent that descends from Llyn y Cwn - hosts an unforgettable Hobbit's adventure. An atmospheric right of passage that is sure to burn itself into the memory of all who answer its calling.

Start by scrambling up and around a series of cascades, pools and rock steps until a large boulder blocks the gully floor. This is known as the Waterfall Pitch. It can be tackled on the right (easiest), underneath, or by its left corner (hardest, but driest). Beyond lies the darker innards of this hellish place, barely illuminated by a feeble slash of sky that peaks in from above. Tiptoe onwards, in awe. A huge pinnacle leans against the right wall and a waterfall gushes over the capstone, which overhangs the gully. The escape pitch scales slanting cracks in the left wall until level with the capstone, then an awkward move onto the spiky block on the right is made before a long traverse right leads to the top of the capstone.

[W R Reade, W P McCulloch 1898]

2. Devil's Staircase S 89m

Like a turbo-charged version of *Lockwood's Chimney*, the striking slender fissure that splits the edge of the cliff to the right of the Kitchen is both fascinating and repellant – an absolute must for those with a penchant for claustrophobic thrutching.

P1 26m The difficulty of the initial smooth section soon relents with the arrival of good holds. Continue up past a ledge on the right to belay on a further ledge.

P2 33m Steeper and looser rock leads to the base of a cave on the left. Advance up the damp confines of the chimney to reach the capstone, then make a surprising exit up the wall on the left. Scramble up the gully bed and ready yourself below the final daunting challenge.

Clogwyn y Geifr

LLANBERIS +

OGWEN +

TREMADOG +

GOGARTH & LLEYN

LLANDUDNO +

Descent

3

P3 30m The normal route takes the right-hand crack (the left exit offers a desperate wet tussle). Climb up the wall and rib to reach 'The Drainpipe'. Pretend you have been born again as a hungry rat and wriggle and squirm up inside past a chockstone to regain glorious daylight and soon after, the top of the cliff.
[O G Jones G D Abraham 1899]

3. Devil's Nordwand E1 5b 100m
A superb excursion up the centre of the North Cliff.
P1 5b 25m From a small spike belay, trend up leftwards on the cleanest section of slab to the base of the steep wall. Climb this, stepping left at a bulge, then continue until level with the square niche; an awkward traverse rightwards gains the base of this. The belay requires a bit of cunning to construct; there is a useful small thread in the right hand corner.
P2 5b 40m Pull out of the notch via the top left hand corner and climb up to a ledge with a small sapling. Move up leftwards, then make a high step back right over a bulge to gain the crack/groove. Follow this to a slanting ledge on the right, and then trend up left to the large ledge.
P3 4c 35m Climb straight up, until it is possible to trend diagonally leftwards to a spike on the arete. Follow the stepped rib to the heather terrace. Belay at a well-featured short band of rock 10m back from the edge.
[R James, J V Anthoine 02.10.59]

Carnedd y Filiast

Area: Ogwen Valley
Style: Trad (2 - 5 pitches)
Aspect: North-East
Rock type: Sandstone
Approach: 45/60 minutes
Altitude: 550/650m

| Central Route | S |
| Left Edge | VD |

A pair of delightful slab climbs situated above Nant Ffrancon in a quiet corner of the Ogwen Valley. An ideal retreat from the Idwal crowds on a busy weekend. Make sure you check out the remarkable Waved Slab left of *Left Edge*.

Conditions: Open slabs that are fairly quick to dry.

Approach: From the Ogwen Cottage car park, walk along the old Nant Ffrancon road and follow the wall from the Tai-newyddion farm up the hillside into the cwm.

Descent: It is possible to descend the hillside areas adjacent to the routes, but from the top of *Left Edge*, the day can be extended with a fine circuit round the tops. Go over Mynydd Perfydd and follow the ridge past Y Garn and down to the Clogwyn y Geifr (Devil's Kitchen) descent to reach Cwm Idwal.

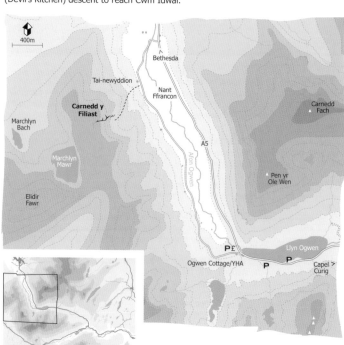

Carnedd y Filiiast

LLANBERIS +

OGWEN +

TREMADOG +

GOGARTH & LLEYN

LLANDUDNO +

The Red Slab

The eye-catching slab on the right side of the cwm has excellent rock, but protection is scarce.

1. Central Route S 86m
An excellent slab route; the climbing is reasonable, but it does require a steady lead.
P1 36m Start just left of *Underlap* (a VD taking the obvious rightwards-leading diagonal line, then finishing direct up the corner feature), and trace the quartz seam past good pockets to a small niche.
P2 50m Keep on trucking for the top in the same line, staying cool through a bold section, to reach improving holds.
[F Graham 08.10.24]

The Central Slabs

The featured route lies on the right side of the main sweep of slabs, right of the huge V-shaped gully.

2. Left Edge VD 183m
A splendidly situated excursion up the rim of white slab overlooking the Waved Slab – an amazing undulating sheet of rock.
P1 40m Trace the edge of the slab to reach a small ledge and spike belay.
P2 45m The zig zagging ridge leads up to a belay at a series of crevasses. This is the point where the edge of the slab is closest to the heathery slab below.
P3 30m Go up to the last ledge before the next big zig zag left (spike belay).
P4 48m Continue up to a small grass ledge at a narrowing of the slab.
P5 20m Scramble on until the rock fades into the hillside. Exit right onto easy vegetated ground.
[first ascent unknown]

The Waved Slab

This can be climbed at Moderate standard. The climbing is very straightforward, but there is a dearth of belays.

↖ Sam Leary on the upper section of **Left Edge** VD photo: Al Leary

Craig Lloer

Area: Carneddau
Style: Trad (4 pitches)
Aspect: North
Rock type: Rhyolitic Tuff
Approach: 60 mins
Altitude: 700m

Kirkus's Route VS

A peaceful crag, tucked away in a secluded and picturesque cwm. No crowds, no polish, and solitude guaranteed. In fact the perfect antidote to the Idwal circus across the way.

Approach: From the eastern end of Llyn Ogwen walk past Glen Dena and follow the path right of the farm, over the A-frame stile and up the hill side. The path follows the approximate line of Afon Lloer up into Cwm Lloer. Once in the cwm, keep left of the lake and stay quite high up. Follow the intermittent, and at times, boggy path round to the crag base.

Conditions: The crag gets morning sun and, being an exposed rib line, the featured route is reasonably fast drying.

Descent: Come down the gully to the left of the main buttress.

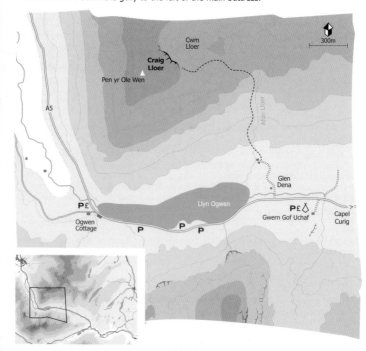

∧ Streaky Desroy eyeing the offwidth groove on P2 of **Kirkus's Route** VS 5a photo: Chris Rowlands
⬏ Chris Rowlands enjoying the crux offwidth on P2 of **Kirkus's Route** VS 5a photo: Graham Desroy

Craig Lloer

1. Kirkus's Route VS 5a 102m

An historic route. Classic yet unjustifiably neglected. It takes the obvious and cleanest rib line to the right of a very small grassy amphitheatre on the left side of the main buttress.

P1 4a 25m Start 6m left of the lowest point of the buttress. A short grassy chimney leads to a platform on the right. Step right to a groove, then back left to edge of slab. Climb up to a flat grassy ledge on the left. Protection is a bit sparse on this pitch.

P2 5a 20m Climb the rib above and mantel onto a sloping ledge. The obvious offwidth crack can be climbed in style but mostly it is not. There are a couple of chockstones, sporting old threads and bits of rope. This is the only real hope of protection unless you're carrying some large cams (Remember that Kirkus soloed this on the first ascent!). Belay at the top of the crack to arrange a grandstand view of your second's struggle.

P3 4a 27m Move easily up onto a heather shelf and traverse right out to the rib (a bit delicate). Ascend the rib and a little groove, then move left and bridge up above the square cut groove. Go up the slab to a large spike belay.

P4 30m Easy scrambling leads to the top of the buttress.

[C F Kirkus 11.07.28]

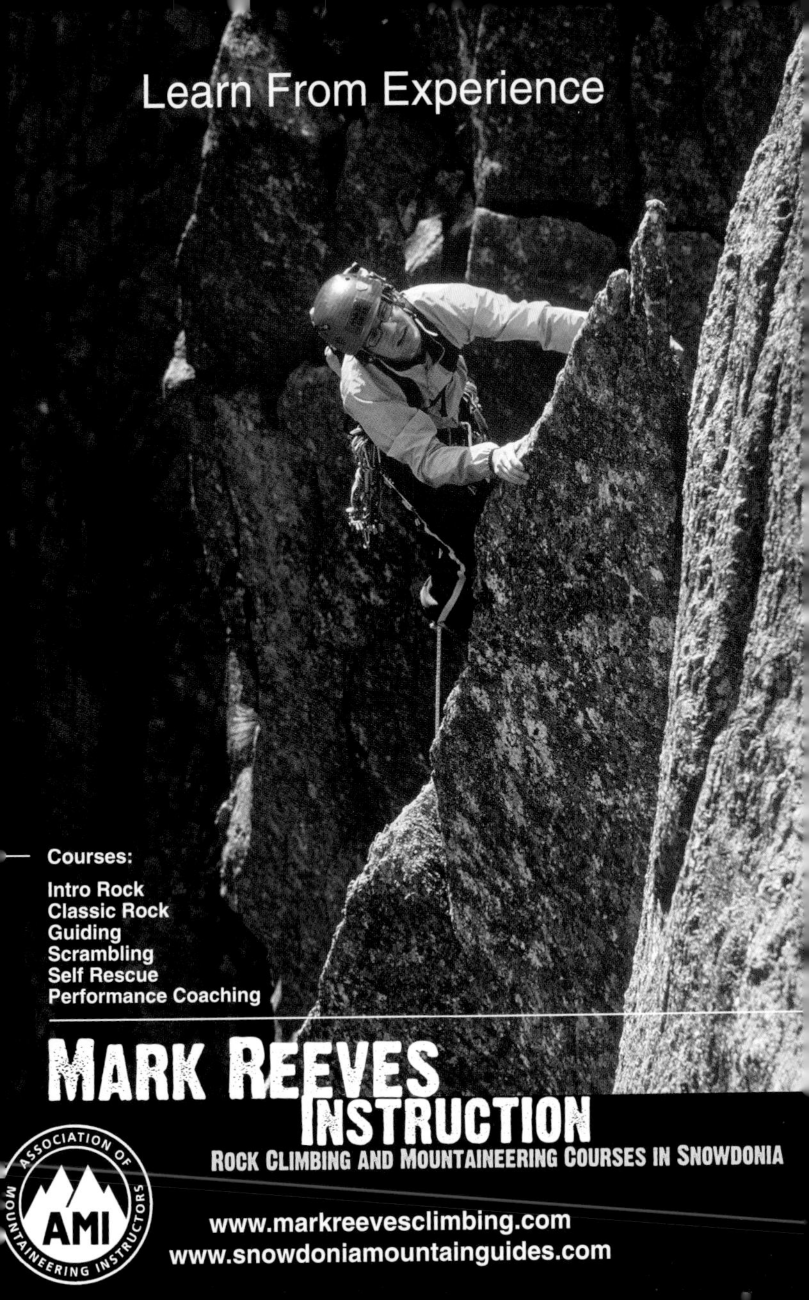

Learn From Experience
Courses:
Intro Rock
Classic Rock
Guiding
Scrambling
Self Rescue
Performance Coaching
MARK REEVES
INSTRUCTION
ROCK CLIMBING AND MOUNTAINEERING COURSES IN SNOWDONIA
ASSOCIATION OF MOUNTAINEERING INSTRUCTORS
AMI
www.markreevesclimbing.com
www.snowdoniamountainguides.com

Braich Ty Du

Area:	**Carneddau**
Style:	**Trad (4 pitches)**
Aspect:	**West**
Rock type:	**Rhyolitic Ash Flow**
Approach:	**25 minutes**
Altitude:	**400m**

YR YMDDIRIEDOLAETH GENEDLAETHOL

THE NATIONAL TRUST
CARNEDDAU

Pinnacle Ridge Route	VD

An accessible mountain route on the steep, complex slopes of Pen yr Ole Wen, overlooking the Nant Ffrancon end of the Ogwen Valley. Suitable for a quick hit, or an escape from the Idwal crowds.

Conditions: The westerly aspect and exposed position ensure that the ridge dries quickly after rain.

Approach: Historically, this cliff has been approached via the 'Alfred Embleton' stile on the A5, then by tracing the faint path up leftwards until it is possible to contour round to the route base. Although perfectly feasible, the best line across the rather loose hillside is not particularly easy to follow, so an alternatve approach is offered. From Ogwen Cottage, walk down the A5 towards Bethesda for approx 2/3km, until just before the start of the rockfall barrier fence on the right-hand side of the road (useful landmarks are the square drainage wall imediately before the fence, and the prominent tree growing between 2 large embedded blocks over to the right). Head up the hillside to the lowest rocks of the buttress, then traverse right below a large square block, with a band of roofs at half height, to gain the steep scree path which runs up right of the crag. Follow this until a short distance below the dry stone wall in the gully, where a grass ledge runs out left and descends slightly to the start of the route.

Descent: Continue up to a grassy col, and then head right (facing in) to descend an open grassy gully.

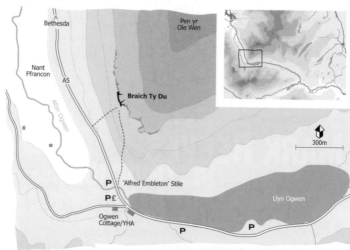

Braich Ty Du

LLANBERIS +

OGWEN +

TREMADOG +

GOGARTH & LLEYN

LLANDUDNO +

1. Pinnacle Ridge Route VD 100m
A splendid traditional route, which stays true to its very apt name.
P1 40m Start at the base of the right hand slabby rib at the foot of the ridge. Climb the rib to a large block at 18m. A high step up right leads into a groove, continue up to a heather terrace.
P2 15m Scramble up easier ground to reach a sloping heather ledge and a spike belay.
P3 22m Traverse right and ascend the ridge to reach a stance on its right side.
P4 23m Move steeply onto the crest of the ridge and negotiate an exciting section of pinnacles to reach the top.
[K U Ingold, P J Fearon, J M Ball 1950]

⚐ Sign by the Alfred Embleton stile photo: Al Leary

Llech Ddu

Area: Carneddau
Style: Trad (2 - 6 pitches)
Aspect: North
Rock type: Rhyolite
Approach: 75 minutes
Altitude: 600m

The Great Arête	E5
The Great Corner	E2
Elliw	E1
The Groove	E1
Central Route / Scarface finish	HVS

A magnificent mountain crag, deceptively big and decidedly intimidating. The cliff has an adventurous feel. Wet holds, vegetation and some loose rock will most likely be encountered. Nonetheless, the quality and character of the routes shines through. These are unquestionably some of North Wales' finest rock climbs, and the 'grand' nomenclature (*The 'Great' Corner, The 'Great' Arête*) seems entirely appropriate. The Pillar is a remarkable feature in itself; a huge plinth of rock entirely detached from the main crag. Wait 'til you get to the top of P5 on *The Groove* and peer into the vast *Pillar Chimney!*

Conditions: A shadowy cold cliff that is slow to dry. Save it for a warm day in a dry period. That said, *Elliw* does catch the summer sun by late afternoon.

Approach: From the kinked Mynydd Llandegai crossroads at the Capel Curig end of Bethesda turn right up the Braichmelyn road towards Gerlan. Follow the road over the river and up a steep hill to a junction, turn right and go past a shop on the left. Parking spaces in Gerlan are limited so please park sensibly, and with consideration for local residents.

Continue along the road by foot crossing Afon Caseg, then take a right fork to cross a bridge over Afon Llafar. The first stile encountered (just to the right of the entrance to the water treatment plant) allows you to skirt the treatment plant, by walking through the field, to the next stile at the top left corner. Hop over this, turn right & follow the path that trends rightwards past some old ruined buildings that have a couple of big trees growing out of them. Cross a small stone bridge, turn immediately right onto another path, which soon leads to a drystone wall & stile. Continue along the now boggy path (some footpath marker posts) until you reach a fence line and the final stile. After a further marshy area, a better-defined track running parallel to Afon Llafar rises gently into Cwm Pen Llafar.

From the final bend in the main track (after the crag has made its rather dramatic appearance), follow a faint path up towards the furthest right of the biggest boulders scattered beneath the cliff. Skirt round the right side of the boulders, then follow the diagonal track up leftwards to arrive at the crag approx below the prominent chimney of *Central Route*.

(The large vegetated cliff in the cwm beyond is Ysgolion Duon (Black Ladders), the famous winter climbing crag.)

Descent: Scramble up to open hillside and head across rightwards (facing in) to descend a scree slope in a zig zag fashion, skirting back rightwards (looking downhill) to regain the crag base.

Wild Carneddau horses photo: Al Leary ∧
Sam Leary following P2 on **Central Route/Scarface** HVS 4c photo: Al Leary >

Llech Ddu

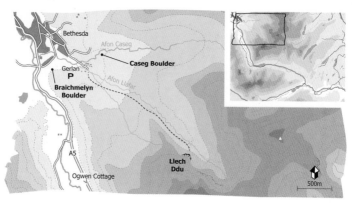

Bethesda

Afon Caseg

Caseg Boulder

Gerlan

P

Braichmelyn Boulder

Afon Llafar

A5

Ogwen Cottage

Llech Ddu

500m

1. Central Route/Scarface Finish HVS 4c 151m

A big atmospheric trip with some superb situations.

P1 4c 34m Climb up the V-chimney until the wall above overhangs; follow a rib diagonally rightwards to a bulge. Make a big stride left and swing into the slanting groove. Go up this to a small flake and continue up for 6m to nut belays in the base of the main corner/groove.

P2 4c 30m Follow the corner line up to the roof then step right onto a spectacular narrow ledge, climb the wall just to the right of a block, then delicately traverse up and right across the short slab to nut belays at the base of a flake.

P3 4c 24m The *Scarface* flake traverse. This pitch involves exposure of near Dolomitic proportions! Follow the diagonal crack up rightwards; after the initial traverse, there is quite a delicate step across a smooth section to regain the continuation of the flake, which then leads into the shallow groove. From a very welcome flake hold at the top of the pitch, step down a few metres to the nut belays at the top of P4 of *The Groove*.

P4 4b 18m Ascend the wall on the right to reach a grassy bay; belay in the chimney beyond.

P5 4b 45m Climb boldly up the slabby rib on the left and continue up easy ground to belay at a large block.

[G Dwyer, R G Morsley 22.04.46/L E Holliwell, L R Holliwell 17.06.67]

2. The Great Corner E2 5b 164m

This classic feature provides a route of great character.

P1 4c 34m P1 of *Central Route*.

P2 4b 30m P1 of *Central Route*.

P3 4a 30m Nip up the flake crack and head left across the grassy terrace to the base of the main corner.

P4 5a 40m Ascend the corner with escalating difficulty. Move up into a niche and gain a stance above under the roof, right of a large detached flake.

P5 5b 30m Good holds lead leftwards across the wall to the arête; drop down for a metre or so and step left into the right-hand of the twin grooves. The groove turns hard at a steepening; continue up past a small roof. The groove above leads to the top.

[J H Clements, D Potts 08.65]

3. The Groove E1 5b 156m

A tremendous route; the climbing is exciting and difficulties are suitably sustained. One of the best routes of its grade in the area.

P1 5a 24m The narrow groove leads past a cruxy section at 2/3rds height to a grassy terrace.

P2 5b 18m The groove line above appears to lean back, but is in fact quite steep. Climb up it, turning the bulge on the right wall; then step back left to a small stance (there is a good nut higher up).

P3 5a 21m Make a tricky traverse slightly down and leftwards to gain the main groove line on the left. Ascend the groove for 9m to another poor stance.

P4 5a 30m Follow the groove line up to a ledge (junction with *Central Route/Scarface*). A magnificent pitch!

P5 4b 18m P4 of *Central Route/Scarface*.

P6 4b 45m P5 of *Central Route/Scarface*.

[J V Anthoine, I F Campbell (much aid used during epic cleaning stints) 10.61]

4. The Great Arête E5 6a 151m

A wild and exposed route, taking the sensational groove line in the towering arête.

P1 5a 24m P1 of *The Groove*.

P2 5a 18m P2 of *The Groove*.

P3 6a 37m Head left and up to a poor rest below a small deep hole. Make precarious and sustained moves up the hanging groove to reach the first overhang. Have a quick breather; then pass the overhang using a crack on the right to gain another groove on the right of a second overhang. Continue up the groove as it narrows until it is possible to swing right on positive holds as the angle eases. Trend rightwards for 8m to a belay on the slab.

Llech Ddu

P4 4c 27m The fantastically positioned left arête leads in a steady but rather bold fashion to the top of *The Pillar*.
P5 4b 45m P5 of *Central Route/Scarface*.
[B Campbell-Kelly, E Drummond (4 pts) 01.09.69, FFA: P Livesey, S Foster 06.75]

5. Elliw E1 5b 151m
A splendid climb on fine clean rock.
P1 30m Walk across to the right side of the cliff and cut back up onto the grassy terrace. Follow this leftwards until it steepens below the large groove of the Y Chimney. Belay in this vicinity down and right of the large groove of Y Chimney and scramble up the chimney groove, then head diagonally left up the rake to a worn area below the open groove of the route. Belay next to a prominent jammed block.
P2 5b 43m Carefully climb the shattered crack and traverse diagonally rightwards to gain the light coloured open groove. Follow this, curving leftwards under a steep wall, then continue directly to a small overhang. Traverse left for a couple of metres to a hanging stance at a thin crack.
P3 4c 48m Traverse diagonally right to gain a slim groove, which leads to a low fault line on the right. The original finish followed this feature out rightwards on increasingly vegetated ground, until scrambling led to the cliff top. However to maintain interest, and the aesthetic line of the lower section, bridge delicately up the continuation groove to a grass ledge. Easier climbing on either side of a wide crack leads to a grassy alcove, down and right of the large roof.
P4 30m Gain the right edge, then an easy right-trending slab, to arrive at the cliff top just below the prominent quartz bands.
[A A Bell, J H Clements 30.05.65/direct finish Al Leary, Catrin Thomas 2006]

∧ Naomi Fisher seconding P2 on **Elliw** E1 5b photo: Al Leary
⌁ Paul Barker on the V0/Font 4 groove, Caseg Boulder photo: Si Panton

The village of Bethesda is blessed with a couple of small but excellent bouldering venues that are some of the best in the whole area. The Caseg and Braichmelyn Boulders both have superb problems with good landings. They are also both located in delightfully tranquil settings. Any team members not keen on the big crag adventure that Llech Ddu promises are provided with the perfect excuse to slope off and try their hand at a range of fine problems - or failing that, a spot of peaceful sunbathing.

The Braichmelyn Boulder

The main face of the left hand boulder is clean and laden with small holds. The obvious ramp line is a classic V2/Font 5+, whilst the superb *Central Wall* (V5/Font 6c+) scales the wall, moving left to reach the end of the ramp. The right arête is a splendid V1/Font 5 from standing, or a desperate V6/Font 7a from sitting. Other harder lines exist and the there are a few good easier problems on the block to the right.

Approach: From the kinked Mynydd Llandegai crossroads at the Capel Curig end of Bethesda turn up towards Gerlan. After 300m park sensibly (probably best close to the bridge over the river where the road widens) and turn back down Nant Graen (a small road leading off the main road). Follow the narrow road until it ends (100m), then walk down the right side of the house (as suggested by the footpath sign) and around the back of the house. Walk up the vague path through the woodland, bearing right towards the boulder (which is slightly hidden) after about 100m.

The Caseg Boulders

There are 2 excellent boulders sitting on the banks of the charming Afon Caseg. Most attention is focussed upon the exquisite lower boulder. The river side of the boulder hosts the magnificent *Caseg Groove* V5/Font 6c+ and various harder test pieces. On the land side there are more fine problems, but at a more manageable grade. The second boulder situated approximately 100m up stream is worth a look, particularly for the easy slab problems and the steep V5/Font 6c traverse on the sheep pen side.

Approach: Just as you are leaving Gerlan, towards the end of the road and near the access route to Llech Ddu, take the left-hand turning (Ciltwllan), parking sensibly by the last buildings on the road. Follow the track for approximately 100m to a left-hand bend. At the apex of the bend go through the gate on the right and follow the wall for 50m along the side of the field to another gate. Drop down to the river and choose a crossing point. The lower boulder lies 50m upstream.

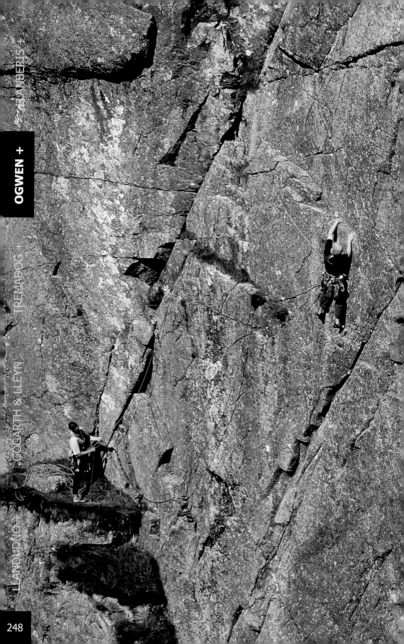

Craig yr Ysfa

Area: Carneddau
Style: Trad (2 - 11 pitches)
Aspect: North-East (South-East)
Rock type: Rhyolitic Tuff
Approach: 1 hour 30 minutes
Altitude: 600m

Aura/Pinnaclissima	E2
Mur y Niwl/Pinnacle Wall	HVS
The Grimmett	VS
Great Gully	VD
Ampitheatre Buttress	VD

A superb mountain crag, with all the atmosphere and adventure that such a description implies. Here you will find challenging routes, both thrilling and magnificent in execution. Hidden away at the head of Cwm Eigiau in the depths of the rolling mass of the peaceful Carneddau hills, Craig yr Ysfa sits in a state of secluded serenity. The crag as a whole presents an initially disappointing vegetated northern front. This rambling mess of heathery ledges is bisected by two major gullies and the real action is located within their confines. The right-hand gully provides the line of the epic *Great Gully* – as fine an example of the genre as exists. The left-hand gully (The Amphitheatre) is a broad scree-filled expanse. The left edge of the gully is defined by the attractive 'alpine-esque' ridge of *Amphitheatre Buttress*, whilst the south-east wall of the gully forms an impressive sweep of steep rock hosting a number of fantastic routes.

Conditions: The main Amphitheatre face catches the afternoon sun in the summer months. The routes are reasonably quick to dry, but crack lines will retain drainage for a few days after rain. *Amphitheatre Buttress* is quick drying, but unpleasant if wet. *Great Gully* is slow to dry and fills quickly with hand numbing 'run off' in wet weather.

< Stepping out on the intimidating crux traverse on P2 of
Mur y Niwl/ Pinnacle Wall HVS 5a photo: Ray Wood

Craig yr Ysfa

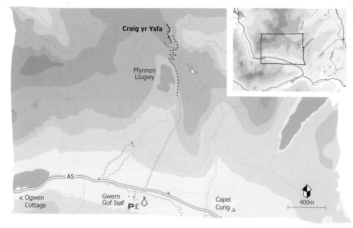

Approach: Park at the Gwern Gof Isaf farm/campsite (parking fee £1), walk along the road back towards Capel Curig and turn up the access road to Ffynnon Llugwy. The road climbs steadily in a long and laborious fashion to reach the lake. Leave the road as it turns left towards the lake and follow a path that skirts round the right side of the reservoir. This then zigzags steeply up to the col between Craig yr Ysfa (on the left) and Pen yr Helgi Du (on the right). To reach the base of the crag, descend diagonally from the col, contouring leftwards (facing out) via a small trail. *The Grimmett, Mur y Niwl/Pinnacle Wall* and *Aura/Pinnaclissima* can also be reached by walking over the top of Craig yr Ysfa and dropping in from above. The choice here is either to brave the steep loose gully, keeping to the left (looking out), or abseil from the top of *Pinnacle Wall* to Bilberry Ledge (the mid-height terrace), then abseil again to land at the base of the wall. The abseil belay kit left on Bilberry Ledge can be retrieved on the way back up.

If you choose to leave your rucsac at the base of the crag then descent is down the main amphitheatre.

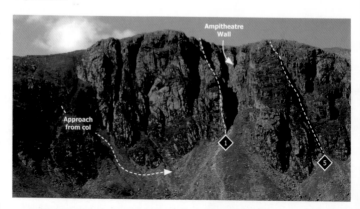

Mark Reeves and Ed Douglas on the glorious top pitch of **Mur y Niwl/Pinnacle Wall** HVS 5a   photo: Ray Wood >

Craig yr Ysfa

1. Ampitheatre Buttress VD 287m
A classic alpine ridge offering entertaining climbing and some airy positions.

P1 30m Friendly slabs and easy climbing/scrambling to a good stance.

P2 37m More easy slabs lead to a groove, the first significant obstacle.

P3 and **4** 55m Easy climbing leads to a large platform beneath a steep wall.

P5 20m The polished corner on the right leads with difficulty to a large detached block. Move up again to finish on rounded holds. (Well done, you've just done the crux pitch!)

P6 and **7** 60m Scramble onwards along vegetated paths.

P8 30m Traverse the apex of the ridge, passing a gap, a couple of gendarmes and a narrow knife edge which can be ridden a-cheval if you so please.

P9 and **10** 55m The ridge on the right leads to the top.

[G D Abraham, A P Abraham, D Leighton, J W Puttrell, May 1905]

2. The Grimmett VS 4c 50m
A superb route breaking through some steep ground.

P1 4c 35m Climb the corner groove to reach a cave. Exit this leftwards to gain another corner which is followed until it pushes you leftwards into a narrow groove. Bridge up past the overhang then go more easily to reach some grass and a belay up right.

P2 4b 15m Traverse left around an arête and ascend a steep rough wall, stepping left to gain a wide crack which is followed to the top.

[A D M Cox, R L Beaumont 24.07.38]

3. Aura/Pinnaclissima E2 5c 111m
An amazing connection of contrasting pitches yielding an immaculate and sustained route.

P1 5b 46m Start just right of a damp step in the gully floor below a triangular overlap at 10m. Climb up to the overlap, then move up left before heading back right to reach a rightwards-slanting crack which is followed to the belay ledge.

P2 20m Scramble to the terrace, walk left and belay under the left end of the Quartz gangway.

P3 5b 15m The left-facing corner leads strenuously to the Quartz gangway. Traveres right to belay at the base of the prominent corner.

P4 5c 30m An initial thin section is followed by an alarming wide crack which leads to the horizontal break just below the apex of the pinnacle. Swing out left and finish as for *Pinnacle Wall*.

[R Carrington, A Rouse, B Hall 05.75/C T Jones, R F Jones (2pts) August 1969]

4. Mur y Niwl/Pinnacle Wall HVS 5a 150m
Another stunning connection, linking a series of challenging lower pitches into a quirky and magnificent finish on the Pinnacle headwall.

P1 4c 13m Start beneath the left side of a narrow ledge leading rightwards to the base of a large open groove. Boulder up the wall and rock out right on to the ledge. Walk right along the ledge to belay beneath the groove.

P2 5a 30m Move up past a small niche and move right and up to reach a parallel set of horizontal ledges leading rightwards away from the large V-groove. Fix some runners, take a deep breath and launch rightwards with conviction; hands on the top ledge and feet on the lower ledge (which soon disappears). A fingery step-down manoeuvre leads with some anxiety to the sanctuary of a diagonal, rising 'staircase'. Take a semi-hanging belay at its top.

P3 4c 18m Drop down the right side of the 'perch', then move right with exposure snapping at your heels and make powerful moves up and right on sharp holds to reach a ledge. Move back left and continue up past a ledge and arête to gain a belay ledge.

P4 4c 20m Nip up the groove, then follow the ramp up left to finish up a tough little crack. Belay a little further back, on a patch of rock.

P5 39m Shift the belay to the base of the obvious diagonal rampline. Amble rightwards up the ramp, then gain and follow the sloping quartz gangway all the way back left. A final awkward step gains a belay at the base of a large open corner.

P6 4b 30m From the corner, after 10m, head out diagonally right to gain a wide crack leading up to the apex of the Pinnacle. Step left onto the slab and head for the top. (*Pinnacle Wall*, the upper half of the link, provides a good outing on its own at HS 4b.)

[A J J Moulam, J B Churchill 26.04.52/C F Kirkus (solo!) 21.06.31]

Craig yr Ysfa

5. Great Gully VD 267m

A route of tremendous character, old fashioned in every way and all the better for it. Do not be fooled by the grade, this is a beast in all but the driest conditions.

To reach the start cross the central scree slope below the Ampitheatre and ignore the decoy line of Vanishing Gully, situated close to the lowest point of the buttress, and continue up right to reach a cavernous gully entrance.

P1 Scramble up the gully bed for 45m, passing the first mossy step on the right.

P2 27m Overcome the chockstone on the left and continue up easily to belay beneath a further chockstone.

P3 37m Skirt the chockstone again on the left and continue up to belay beneath:

P4 18m 'The Door Jam' is a short steep groove on the right which provides a way around the impasse. Pass a ledge on the left, to a larger ledge, then walk back left into the gully bed.

P5 11m Ascend a 12m chimney and a crack on the right, moving back left in to gully bed near its top.

P6 14m 'The Chimney' An awkward obstacle best climbed facing right to gain a platform on the right. (This can be avoided 6m below by following a flake in the right wall, then a muddy path leading right then back left.)

P7 34m Climb the groove on the right, then continue up scree to reach:

P8 and **P9** 61m Ascend the narrow sloping chimney right of the rib (or tackle the 2 mossy chockstones on the left). After 18m of scrambling surmount a large jammed block to reach another.

P10 5m The awkward undercut chimney on the right of the stone. (Alternatives exist either side.)

P11 15m 'The Great Cave Pitch' - a fitting climax to a splendid route! Climb the left wall of the cave with difficulty, then traverse left to gain the outer of 2 chockstones. Scrambling remains.

[J M A Thomson, R I Simey, W G Clay April 1900]

Mike Jones enjoying prime conditions in **Great Gully** VD photo: Al Leary ∨

Clogwyn yr Eryr

Area:	Crafnant Valley
Style:	Trad (1 -2 pitches)
Aspect:	South-East
Rock:	Rhyolitic Ash Flow Tuff
Approach:	25 minutes
Altitude:	350m

Connie's Crack	E5
Astoroth Direct	E4
Clonus	E4
Clonus Left Hand	E4
Snowdrop	E4
Oriole	E3
Astoroth	E2
Phoenix	E2

A great but often forgotten crag, tucked away in the quiet Crafnant Valley on the eastern side of the Carneddau. It offers the extreme leader a superb collection of steep wall climbs situated in a quite idyllic location. For many years the crag was subject to almost mythical status. Detailed information was hard to find and the occasional glowing, third-hand report only added to its kudos. This situation has gradually changed, but the combination of the grades on offer and the crag's isolated nature will always ensure that climbing here is a tranquil affair.

The climbing is mainly vertical although the starts are often steeply undercut and the routes reward a decisive and powerful approach. In the higher reaches of the crag the climbing becomes more technical and good footwork pays dividends. The rock is well featured and normally allows plentiful amounts of gear to be placed. The blanker areas often have peg protection, although a lot of this is now old and of dubious quality. It is worth saving a medium cam and a long sling for the belays at the top of the crag.

Conditions: Although generally south-facing and sunny, the cliff is quite exposed to the elements. Typically bad weather will stop short of the Crafnant Valley, hovering over Capel Curig and the Ogwen Valley instead. Because this is a quick-drying crag there are no real seepage problems, and climbing is possible in showery conditions.

Approach: The easiest approach is via the village of Trefiw in the Conwy Valley. Access the B5106 from Betws Y Coed, Llanwrst or Conwy and head towards Trefriw. At the south end of the village near the Woollen Mill is the Fairy Falls pub. Take the steep road that runs up the hill opposite the pub towards Llyn Crafnant. Ignore all the spurs and stay on this road to the far end of the lake. As you reach the end of the lake there is a metal gate blocking the road. Park just beyond the gate on the right-hand side.

Take the vehicle track that runs rightwards around the lake and follow it past some houses towards Hendre Bach. The vehicle track ends at the gate to Hendre Bach. Cross the small stream on the right via a small bridge and follow the Forestry Commission Green/Yellow posts uphill. Go past a stile and 20m later turn left onto another Forestry Commission track, almost immediately crossing a concrete bridge. Clogwyn yr Eryr is the obvious buttress directly ahead on the skyline. Continue on this track for 250m until the first hairpin bend. At the exit of the hairpin a small track (cairn) leads off leftward. Follow this for 20m to the fence, cross it and then follow the fence directly uphill.

After 90m the fence ends at a small buttress. Turn left on a faint track and contour along the hillside towards the crag. The path initially follows the buttress closely, but after 40m it veers slightly left to stay 20-30m from the buttress until the Main Wall of the crag is reached in 220m.

Descent: There is a fixed abseil point with threads just right (looking out) of the finish of *Oriole*. It is also possible to come down steep and bramble-infested terrain to the left (looking out) of the crag.

Clogwyn yr Eryr

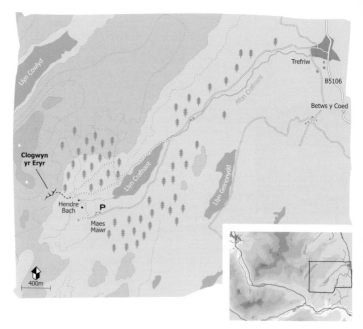

The first two routes start 2m right of the only mature tree close to the cliff base and share the same start. This is a long shallow corner that leads to a long overlap at 20m.

1. Oriole E3 5c 48m

A fine, steep first pitch that although never desperate is quite sustained and maintains interest throughout.

P1 5c 36m Start 2m right of the tree and climb into the undercut fangs from the left. Awkwardly place gear and smear into the corner with difficulty. Follow the corner itself more easily until 1m before the overlap and then step slightly left in order to pull around the overlap (peg). Continue up and very slightly leftwards on surprisingly good holds to reach some spikes. Traverse delicately right and up to a fine, exposed belay.

P2 5a 12m Climb up rightwards on good holds to join the arête and the top.

[J Grieve, M A Reeves 05.11.67 HVS/A1, FFA: P Gomersall, P Livesey 20.04.80]

2. Phoenix E2 5c 48m

This would be a classic route on any crag and is totally involving. It is not easy for the grade and may be considered E3 by many, although the protection is very good.

P1 5c 35m Start as for *Oriole* with the same difficult start. Climb up the corner to the overlap and then make an awkward rightward traverse to the arête. It is possible, even logical, to belay here. This belay also balances out the two pitches but the original route continues up the arête until the groove on the right can be reached. Climb this until a very cramped mantelshelf allows access to a small belay ledge in the corner.

P2 5b 13m Bridge upwards and move left under the roof to gain another groove. Romp up this to the top.

[J Ball, M A Reeves 14.05.66 HVS/A2, FFA: P Livesey, P Gomersall 20.04.80]

Clogwyn yr Eryr

LLANBERIS +

OGWEN +

TREMADOG +

GOGARTH & LLEYN

LLANDUDNO +

3. Clonus Left-Hand E4 6a 48m

A great route; initially steep and bold, then technical and finally steady. The route was initially done in two pitches, but can be done in one. The peg that protected the hard starting moves is in a very poor state but a large cam in a pocket offers some hope.

P1 6a 35m Start 8m right of the tree below the major V-groove on the front face. Pull gymnastically through the bulge with conviction to gain good pockets and then move into the groove itself more easily. Climb the groove and as it closes up move left to a crack. Climb this with difficulty to gain an area of downward-pointing spikes and continue up and leftwards to gain the line of *Phoenix* and its belay.

P2 5b 13m *Phoenix* P2.

[P Livesey , P Gomersall 20.04.80]

4. Clonus E4 6a 47m

An equally good partner to the previous route that goes through some steep territory and is quite intimidating. Harder than the Left-Hand version.

P1 6a 35m Start as for *Clonus Left Hand* and follow it to the area of downward pointing spikes. Fight back rightwards around the bulges to regain the main groove line. Follow this, stepping right to belay on the good ledge below the final perfect V-groove.

P2 5b 12m Climb the overhanging groove on surprisingly good holds.

[M A Reeves, R Hornby VS/A2, FFA: R Edwards 1970s]

Clogwyn yr Eryr

5. Connie's Crack E5 6b 47m

A brutal start gives access to a variety of finishes. The original route veered off leftwards after the initial roofs, but it is more fitting and balanced to do either the *Carousel Waltz* Variation or finish up *Snowdrop*. The *Connie's Crack/Snowdrop* link is awesome.

P1 6b 35m Start 5m right of *Clonus* in a square-cut recess under the steepest part of the cliff. Follow the rotting line of pegs leftwards through the overhangs until the vertical groove is almost within reach (thread up right, that can be backed up). Pull very awkwardly into the groove to gain a welcome rest. Traverse left along a break line to the arête and climb the groove until harder moves allow the crack on the right to be gained. Follow this to the *Clonus* belay on the large ledge below the steep V-groove.

P2 5b 12m *Clonus* P2.

[R James, J R Lees HVS/A2 08.61, FFA: R Fawcett, S Foster 07.78]

5a. Carousel Waltz Variation E5 6b 47m

P1 6b 35m Follow *Connie's Crack* to the rest in the groove above the overhangs. Then continue straight up the groove via some very technical bridging (peg). Pull up delicately and pull right onto a slab. Cross back left into the final crack of the original route and climb this to the ledge belay.

P2 5b 12m *Clonus* P2.

[A Pollitt, P Bailey 17.07.82]

5b. Connie's Crack/Snowdrop link E5 6b 47m

Follow *Connie's Crack* to the rest in the groove above the overhangs. Then continue straight up the groove via some very technical bridging (peg). Pull up delicately and pull right onto a slab. Fire straight into the upper section of *Snowdrop*.

6. Snowdrop E4 6a 50m

A brilliant route with a stunning finale up the overhanging headwall.

P1 5c 20m Start 5m right of the square cut niche of *Connie's Crack* at a vertical groove line. Climb the groove past a slight bulge and move up until below the continuation groove of *Astoroth*. Make a delicate traverse slightly down and left around the nose to the arête. Take a hanging belay here making sure to back up the pegs.

P2 6a 30m Climb leftwards into the groove and pull up right onto a slab. Climb the crack system in the headwall straight above. Initially this is quite hard, but as the angle gets steeper the holds get bigger.

[P D Boardman, M Wragg 1 pt 24.06.70, FFA: P Gomersall, P Livesey 10.06.78]

7. Astoroth E2 5c 45m

A satisfying route that combines good climbing with plenty of exposure.

P1 5c 25m Start in the same groove system as *Snowdrop* and follow it past the bulge to where *Snowdrop* steps left. Continue straight up into the perfect V-groove and climb this with more difficulty. As it closes move right onto the wall and pull onto the arête. Move up to a large block and a belay.

P2 5b 20m Move up into a flake crack and follow this. Finish leftwards as the climbing eases.

[B Ingle, P J Nunn 3 pts 01.61]

8. Astoroth Direct E4 6a/b 42m

A stunning finale on the dramatic headwall.

P1 5c 25m *Astoroth* P1.

P2 6a/b 17m Leave the belay on the left and move up until it is possible to pull leftwards on good holds into the steep groove. Climb the groove with increasing difficulty until the cracks close up and a reasonable rest can be gained using a wide bridge. The hard pull into the continuation crack is the start of a difficult and sustained sequence with easier ground only arriving just below the top.

[P Livesey, P Gomersall 19.04.80]

RAC Boulders

Area:	**Mymbyr Valley**
Style:	**Bouldering**
Aspect:	**South**
Rock type:	**Rhyolitic Ash**
Approach:	**2 minutes**
Altitude:	**200m**

The RAC Boulders are a popular choice both for the weekend visitor and the time-pressed local wanting a quick stretch on a familiar circuit. These boulders have a lot going for them; easy access, a sunny aspect, friendly landings and a diverse collection of problems throughout the low to mid-grade range, with endless variants to play upon.

Conditions: Year round climbing is possible. Even in the depths of winter the front sides of the boulders soak up enough sunshine to guarantee agreeable climbing conditions. The boulders dry quickly after rain, although there is one section of marshy ground beneath the lower boulder, which normally requires a pad to keep your feet dry.

Approach: The boulders are clearly visible from the A4086 Pen y Gwryd – Capel Curig road, approximately 2km west of Plas y Brenin (and about 200m from the entrance to Garth Farm at the end of Llynnau Mymbyr). Park in the layby, but do not block the gate.

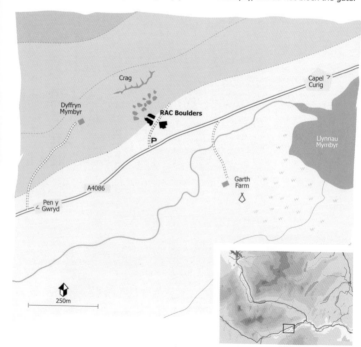

∧ Emma Flaherty laybacking up a superb V0+ Font 4+, The RAC Boulders photo: John Coefield

↖ Chris Davies wrapped up in the technicalities of the **On One** traverse, V8/9 Font 7b/c, RAC Boulders photos: Si Panton

The superb Tremadog crags remain an attractive option for both visiting and local climbers. Little wonder when you consider the high concentration of top quality routes throughout the grade spectrum. Other factors such as the ease of access, the wonderful frictional qualities of the fast-drying dolerite rock, and last but not least, the perfectly positioned Eric's Cafe, all contribute to this popularity.

This section of the guide also covers a selection of outlying crags situated throughout the southern part of the region. These cliffs vary in scale and style from big mountain crags like Craig yr Ogof in Cwm Silyn to more accessible roadside venues such as the radical Carreg Hylldrem and the delightful Moelwyn crags.

Throughout the area the climbing style is traditional, and typically multi-pitch.

Seasonal Conditions: The Tremadog and Moelwyn cliffs are well known as alternative options to rain-blighted mountain crags (year-round climbing is also possible in both areas). The Tremadog crags in particular will dry very quickly after rain with a decent breeze. The higher mountain crags are, of course, best approached tactically during dry summer periods.

During torrential or persistent rain the bouldering wall at Carreg Hylldrem provides a dry retreat, albeit a rather steep and desperately physical one.

Getting There: The main Tremadog and Moelwyn cliffs are conveniently bunched together in two clusters. However the rest of the crags are dispersed across a broad geographical expanse. Consequently getting around the area is not as easy as it is in the Llanberis Pass and the Ogwen Valley. The bus services are less useful for climbers, and it seems traditional to get stuck behind a tourist coach traffic jam on the Nant Gwynant hill at least once during a weekend visit.

Access Restrictions: To prevent disturbance to roosting birds there is a night-time restriction on Y Garn, which runs from 1 hour before sunset, until sunrise during the August to November (inclusive) period.

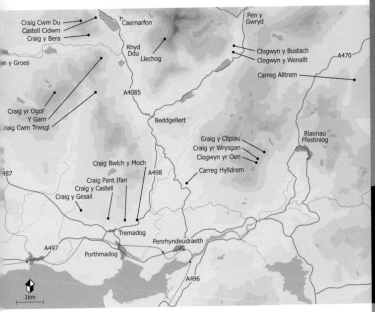

Craig Cwm Du
Castell Cidwm
Craig y Bera

Caernarfon

Pen y
Gwryd

Rhyd
Ddu
Llechog

Clogwyn y Bustach
Clogwyn y Wenallt

A470

Carreg Alltrem

n y Groes

Craig yr Ogof
Y Garn
Craig Cwm Trwsgl

A4085

Beddgellert

Blaenau
Ffestiniog

Craig y Clipiau
Craig yr Wrysgan
Clogwyn yr Oen

Craig Bwlch y Moch

A498

Carreg Hylldrem

487

Craig Pant Ifan
Craig y Castell
Craig y Gesail

Tremadog

Penrhyndeudraeth

A497

Porthmadog

A496

1km

Craig Bwlch y Moch from Eric's Cafe   photo: Si Panton   ∧
Clogwyn y Bustach in Nant Gwynant   photo: Si Panton   <

Craig Bwlch y Moch

Area:	**Tremadog**
Style:	**Trad (2 - 4 pitches)**
Aspect:	**South**
Rock type:	**Dolerite**
Approach:	**5 minutes**
Altitude:	**50m**

Strawberries	E6
Bananas	E5
Cream	E4
The Atomic Finger	
Flake/Void	E4
Vulture	E4
Zukator	E4
Geireagle	E3
Neb Direct	E3

Daddy Cool/The Sting	E2
Extraction	E2
The Grasper	E2
Nimbus/The Snake	E2
The Weaver	E2
Valor	E2
Vector	E2
First Slip	E1
Grim Wall Direct	E1
Leg Slip	E1
The Plum	E1
Merlin/Direct Finish	HVS
Meshach	HVS
The Fang	HVS

Grim Wall	VS
One Step in the Clouds	VS
Shadrach	VS
Striptease	VS
Christmas Curry/Micah Eliminate	HS
Valerie's Rib	HS

Classic routes, perfect rock and roadside convenience ensure the enduring popularity of this fine crag. The magnificent Vector Buttress is one of the finest pieces of rock in Wales. The only downside is the polished gleam evident on some of the higher profile routes; such is the price of fame.

The adjacent café, campsite and bunkhouse have long provided a traditional base for visiting climbers. Interestingly, the crag has been owned and managed by the BMC since 1979.

Conditions: The crag dries very quickly after rain and has a mostly sunny southern aspect, aside from the *Vector* headwall, which only gets the sun in the morning. *Striptease* is fairly sheltered, and is always worth a look on a showery day.

Approach: The crag looms prominently over the A498 Tremadog – Beddgelert road between Eric's café and the sharp bend at Portreuddyn castle. Convenient parking is available at Eric's Café. Short-stay parking is free but there is a £1 charge for long-stay parking. There are a few top tips that will make any visit to the cliff run a little smoother:

1. Cafés are important. Life is always easier if you take time out for a brew and a cake.

2. Finding the base of a route at Bwlch y Moch is sometimes harder than climbing it. Read (and follow) the approach notes carefully. The ground at the bottom of the crag is steep and broken and densely populated by trees. This can make locating the start of your intended route somewhat tricky, particularly if the leaves are in full bloom, and especially if this is your first visit to the crag. Ignore the blasé locals and nonchalant regulars, and follow this method: from a position by the roadside, match the appropriate topo with the crag extending above the tree line, then follow the approach instructions which will guide you through the labyrinth of paths weaving up through the trees.

3. Getting lost at the top of a crag is not much fun and may cause problems with adjacent landowners. If you want to avoid such a fate, then be sure to follow the descent details given below.

4. And finally, if you see a local cruising up a route, don't be impressed, they've probably done it loads of times before. These routes are so good they get done over and over again (hence the polish!).

Descent: There are two descent paths leading down from the cliff top:

1. Main path descent for the left-hand side of crag: (Described from the top of *Grim Wall/Meshach* area.) Walk in the direction of the cafe, squeezing between a boulder and the fence (a popular gear-snagging/clothes-ripping spot), until the path drops down away from the main fence line and back towards the cliff. After a short distance, the path trends right above another fence, until a style is reached at the far end of a flat area. Climb over this, and follow the well-worn track downhill. A smooth section just below a white lichen spotted rock needs a bit of care. Near the base, outflank the buildings by traversing leftwards (facing out) over some boulders, then continue directly down to the road - 10 mins max.

2. Main path descent for the right-hand side of crag: From the flat area at the top of *Merlin Direct*, head directly away from the cliff and follow the path leftwards to a stile. Climb over this, and immediately walk downhill for a few metres, until a series of awkward rock shelves on the right lead into the gully. Clamber over and around various boulders until the gully opens out, then zigzag down to a wooden ladder. Below this, the path leads to a well-worn traverse on the right (facing out), fortunately well garnished with an excellent root handhold. A final short slither down some small blocks leads to easier ground and the crag base on the left - 10 mins max.

In addition, from the top of the Slips Area, it is possible to follow the fence down towards Merlin Buttress. However, a smooth slatey series of steps just above the very top of Belshazzar Gully (currently fenced off) are quite awkward in descent. At the base of the steps hop over a stile, then follow the path down to the stile previously described.

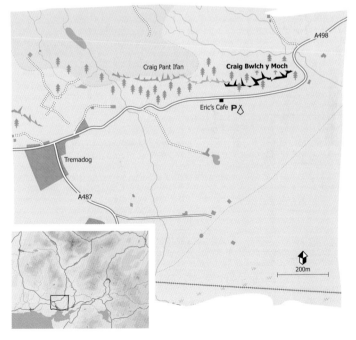

⚲ The Eric Jones cafe, perfect for endless festering and prevarication photo: Si Panton

Craig Bwlch y Moch • Grasper Area

Approach for routes 1 and 2: the access for this area is described as one walks from the cafe towards the BMC signpost located beneath the *Vector* Buttress.

Gain a path that starts from the right-hand end of the tarmac area extending from the very last building on the crag side of the road. From the top of the big flat boulder, zigzag first right then back leftwards until the track levels out. A big moss-covered detached flake a few metres above is a good landmark for the start of *Valor*. Drop down a touch, then follow the path up left (squeezing between the twin-stemmed tree and the slab), until level with the jutting prow on the skyline. Carefully traverse across the mossy slab, which leads to the tree belays at the start of *Valerie's Rib*.

A slightly more direct alternative is to negotiate the smooth little slab, which is just up and left of the flat boulder (some handy tree roots), before traversing rightwards to join the above footpath.

1. Valerie's Rib HS 71m

A delightful open route. P2 requires poise and a steady head (small wires will help).

P1 10m Climb up at first, then head diagonally right to a ledge on the rib.

P2 34m Ascend to the base of a groove, then step right and continue up, keeping right of the slabby rib where possible, until a ledge and nose of rock is gained. Climb the crack on the right to reach a large grassy ledge.

P3 27m Scramble up right to a ledge and tree above the rock scar. Follow the crack above to a further tree and continue left, then up a broken crack to the top.

[P Vaughan, W Smith, J Cunningham 12.07.51]

2. Valor E2 5c 79m

A fine route with an exposed and technical finish.

P1 5b 18m From the start of *Valerie's Rib* move up the slabs, passing a small overlap to reach the roof. Move right, then over the right side of the roof to gain the stance on *Valerie's Rib*.

P2 5a 27m Climb up and rightwards to gain and climb a short groove capped by a small overhang. Turn the overhang and continue up a short ramp. Move diagonally right, then traverse left for 6m to a tree belay (which is shared with *Valerie's Rib*).

P3 10m Scramble up and right to another tree belay on the left edge of the main cliff.

P4 5c 24m Move rightwards across the rockfall area to gain a layback crack. Ascend this, then continue up the smooth slab on the right to reach a small ledge in an airy position. A steep wall guards entrance to the slanting groove which leads quickly to a good ledge and belay. (To finish, climb the easy wall on the left.)

[D Yates, D H Jones (3 pts) 1964/first complete ascent: F Cannings, D Peers 1967]

Approach for routes 3 – 5: from the BMC notice board, retrace your steps back towards the cafe for just over 50m (passing an initial set of road drains), until you arrive at a footpath immediately in front of a second batch of drains (a metal cover and a small flat rock covering what was probably the original old drain are useful landmarks). Follow the path over a 3m long, low rock and the smaller boulders directly above, until approx 25m below the obvious blocky chimney (P1 of *Christmas Curry*). The path splits here, so take the track branching off leftwards directly below a large vegetated boulder. The path, which steepens considerably, leads to another split; this is directly below the deep gully/groove of *Kestrel Cracks* (*Neb Direct* starts up the wall just to the right). Continue horizontally left to a slightly unstable and awkward chimney, which requires a bit of care, then stepped ledges and a short slab soon lead to the base of *The Grasper*. Due to the restricted nature of stances at the base of all routes in this area, it is worth leaving sacs or extra gear in the vicinity of the path split below *Neb Direct*.

3. The Grasper E2 5c 45m

A classic and notorious bridging test piece. A real hamstring stretcher!

P1 5c 24m Start on a clean, sloping ledge at the base of the steep wall right of *Valerie's Rib*. Ascend a shallow groove to a thin ledge, then move left past a rib into an overhanging niche. Move left again on to a further rib and go up a groove on the left to a small roof.

Layback round the roof to gain a good ledge on the right, then move left to a thin crack which leads to a large spike just right of *Valerie's Rib*. Traverse right to a stance beneath the final groove.

P2 5c 21m Ascend the short steep wall and bridge up the groove to the overhang. A fierce pull is required to surmount this obstacle; thereafter, move out left and follow a sharp rib to the top.

[J Brown, D Thomas bach (5 pts) 02.06.61]

4. Zukator E4 6b 54m

A brilliant climb, with a hideously technical groove on P2 which, in contrast to *The Grasper*, seems to favour the shorter climber.

P1 5c 27m Start 6m right of *The Grasper* beneath a corner (*Clapton's Crack* VS). Go up left into a niche, then move left from this around the arête to a little ledge. Ascend with some difficulty to a square-cut ledge in the centre of the wall. Move up and rightwards to some overhangs, before traversing left to *The Grasper* stance.

P2 6b 27m Ascend the short steep wall into the groove (as per *The Grasper* P2), but make tricky moves down and right to gain a small ledge at the base of the infamous groove. Squirm up the perplexing groove in a state of boggle-eyed desperation. Exit right at the top.

[P Crew, A Harris (7pts) 10.64/Neb Direct first aided possibly by B Brewster in the 60s, FFA: P Livesey, J Sheard 1976]

5. Neb Direct E3 6a 63m

A superb and intense route that will delight the crack technician.

P1 5b 27m Ascend the wall right of the corner, heading up right to a small ledge, before climbing directly up the arête to a stance.

P2 15m Climb a rib on the right and traverse right to reach the foot of a thin overhanging crack in a grassy bay.

P3 5c 6m The crack is fierce, but thankfully short lived.

P4 6a 15m A similarly desperate steep crack leads up to a slab beneath a roof (the E2 version scoots off right from here, and finishes up a short groove). The continuation crack splitting the roof provides a fearsome finale.

[The Neb: J Brown, D Thomas bach 06.61/Neb Direct first aided possibly by B Brewster in the 60s, FFA: H Barber P1: M Lewis, H Davies 1968]

Craig Bwlch y Moch • Plum Area

Approach for routes 6 and 7: follow the *Grasper/Neb Direct* approach until the first split in the path below the blocky chimney, which forms P1 of *Christmas Curry*.

To gain the start of *The Plum*, follow the left branch around the corner (the stepped slope immediately above can be followed to a good ledge just left of the first tree belay of *Christmas Curry*); however this is often very slippery so continue across left for a short distance until the path turns uphill. After 10m or so the path splits, follow the righthand branch, which leads past some useful tree roots to the ledge. The diagonal crack starting on the right leads with care to the start of *The Plum*, which is just out of sight around the corner. (The line of *Christmas Curry* can easily be regained from this ledge, thus avoiding the initial chimney.)

6. Christmas Curry/Micah Eliminate HS 4b 76m

A celebrated Tremadog classic with a bold and exposed finish.

P1 12m Climb the chimney to a tree belay.

P2 27m Go diagonally left to sloping ledges, then continue up the steep wall to reach a recess. Climb up right on good holds before stepping back left on to the slab where a crack leads to a ledge.

P3 4b 37m Move right from the stance and climb a short groove, then go up a further groove to gain a ledge. Ascend the thin crack then traverse right to join the final arête of *The Plum*.

[A J J Moulam, J M Barr 25.12.53/M J Harris 1954]

▶ **7. The Plum E1 5b** 42m
A variety of challenging obstacles await the leader on this stunning route, which tackles the prominent arête right of *Christmas Curry*.
Start up an awkward corner crack at the base of the arête (or avoid it by traversing in from above and right) and step left on to the rib, which leads with difficulty to a small ledge. Tiptoe up the V-groove above to a ledge (possible belay if you suspect rope drag is likely). The wide flake crack above leads to a small ledge. Step right and ascend the arete past one particularly unnerving move. Have faith in your high tech rock shoes!
[R James, D Yates (2 pts) 12.61]

< Andy Newton topping out on **Christmas Curry/Micah Eliminate** HS 4b
photo: Ray Wood

Approach for routes 8 – 10: Follow the approach for routes 6 and 7 towards the blocky chimney (*Christmas Curry*), but head right and take the path up the gully to the right. This leads to the base of the routes. The last section of this is quite awkward, especially in descent, and requires a bit of care.

8. The Fang HVS 5a 61m
A route of two halves: at first strenuous, then delicate and bold.
P1 5a 24m Start at the base of the *Striptease* gully. Ascend the leaning pinnacle just left of the gully, then move left into a short steep groove. Go up this to a ledge and step right and follow a crack up to a small stance.
P2 5a 37m Climb up onto the wall and make an intricate and bold traverse out left and slightly down to a sloping ledge on the arête. Traverse again left for a metre or so, then move up and back right into the centre of the upper slab and follow it to the top.
[J Brown, C E Davies 04.06.61]

9. Extraction E2 5c 48m
Another thrill-packed route with contrasting pitches.
P1 5c 18m Start just right of *The Fang* and climb the strenuous thin crack direct to the first stance on *The Fang*.
P2 5c 30m Go across the wall on the right, making bold moves to gain a ledge on the arête. Go up to an overhung niche where a crux section leads out left (where is that hidden finger jug?) to reach the upper slab on *The Fang*. Follow the right side to the top.
[C J Phillips, M Crook 16.06.75]

10. Striptease VS 5a 49m
This sheltered gully feature provides an absorbing and strenuous route. It also stays 'relatively' dry in all but the most persistent of rainstorms.
P1 5a 37m Swarm up the deep V-groove, surmounting the first overhang on the right and continue up the groove. Move right again at a 2nd overhang and climb up to a tree belay.
P2 4b 12m The arête on the left leads to the top.
[J Brown, C E Davies 03.04.61]

Approach for routes 11 – 22: From the BMC signpost beneath Vector Buttress, clamber up the slippery steps through a short gully that is formed by a couple of large boulders. Trend slightly leftwards then straight up to a small worn flat area on the path; *One Step in the Clouds*, *Vector,* etc start just on the left. Continuing up rightwards, taking care while passing a smooth little boulder that blocks the path (the scene of many a tumble, especially in descent), soon leads to the right-hand section of the crag; *Grim Wall Direct* starts from where the path levels out, just before a rock step with a prominent tree at 3m. For *Grim Wall/Meshach/Shadrach,* etc, step up onto the slab below the tree for a move, then follow the path rightwards to a tree-filled alcove directly below the prominent chimney of *Shadrach.*

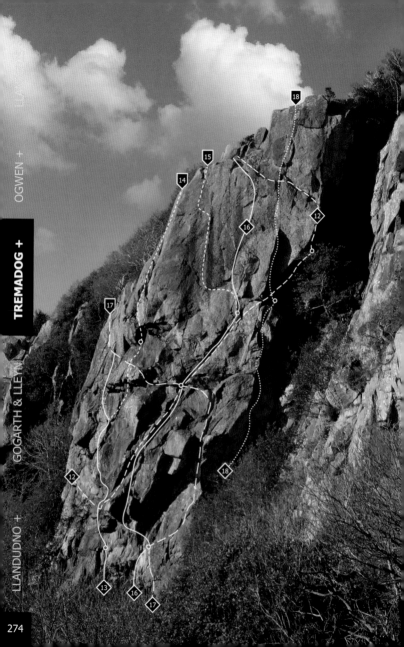

11. One Step in the Clouds VS 4c 69m

An exposed classic that tiptoes up the slabby left shoulder of the mighty *Vector* Buttress.

P1 4b 27m Start at the foot of the buttress. Climb up left over blocks and around the back of a large tree. Continue up the wall to gain a V groove split by a hand crack. Jam up this to reach a large flake belay.

P2 4c 27m Step up left and follow a crack for a few metres before traversing right to the lip of the overhangs. Delicate and sustained climbing leads up and rightwards before a final interesting move gains a well-positioned stance.

P3 4b 15m Move right and climb a short slab to reach a rightwards trending flake. Follow this with a final thin step up to a stance.

[C.T. Jones, R. Moseley 11.05.58]

12. Nimbus/Snake Connection E2 6a 92m

The longest route on the crag yields a wild and satisfying trip, cutting through some impressive territory on the *Vector* headwall.

P1 4b 27m As for P1 of *One Step in the Clouds*.

P2 5c 27m Traverse right past the old tree, dropping down and across the lip of the stepped overhangs. Move steeply up (as for *The Weaver*) and step right to gain a right-wards-trending groove system. Follow this past a testing steep section to eventually gain the *Vector* 'cave stance'.

P3 4c 18m Pull out right from the cramped belay and follow the diagonal ramp line rightwards to a large sloping ledge beneath the groove of *Void*. Continue up rightwards to gain a nifty belay just right of the *Snake* pod.

P4 6a 20m Entry to the hanging pod is less than straightforward; if you make it, squirm up to better holds and exit onto the edge of the hallowed ground of the *Vector* headwall. Relishing every delicious moment, traverse diagonally leftwards across the void (quite literally!).

[J Brown, C Goodey (1pt) 06.61/A Sharp, C Dale 01.06.75]

13. The Weaver E2 5c 64m

A splendid route snaking upwards through steep ground to meet the finish of *Vector*.

P1 5b 12m From the foot of the buttress climb straight up the faint groove, then move right and overcome a short wall to gain the first *Vector* stance.

P2 5c 37m Make a move up, then traverse left for 3m. Ascend the steep wall to the stepped overhangs on the *Nimbus* traverse. Step right and go up a groove before making blind moves back left (good footholds, but what do you do with your hands?). Continue up a short crack and a hanging flake. From the large thread up on the right, step left and climb up a groove (junction with *Vector*), with tenuous moves to reach the final layback exit, to easier ground and the 'well-positioned stance' on *One Step in the Clouds*.

P3 4b 15m P3 of *One Step in the Clouds*.

[P Williams, C Shorter 02.80]

14. Bananas E5 6b 66m

A wild and aggressive route in an outstanding position.

P1 5b 12m P1 of *The Weaver*.

P2 5c 30m Follow *The Weaver* to the 'large thread', then move right and pull over the roof to gain a hanging stance beneath a wide crack (*The Croaker* E2 5c).

P3 6b 24m Ascend the crack then head up and right to the flake-arete. Shake out on a knee-lock then blast up the flake crack to an excruciating mantel. Easy ground remains.

[J Redhead, K Robertson 30.03.80]

15. Strawberries E6 6b 18m

An impressive, historic route featuring immaculate and sustained climbing.

Start from a belay on the spike on P4 of *Cream*. Traverse left as for *Cream* but continue out leftwards to gain the next thin crack. An intense sequence leads up to its top; swing out left to a further crack which leads with more difficulty to decent holds and shortly the top.

[R Fawcett 03.80]

Craig Bwlch y Moch • Vector Buttress

16. Cream E4 6a 61m

A tremendous route muscling up through the lower overhangs to a spellbinding crescendo on the final pitch.

P1 4c 12m Start just right of *The Weaver* at the foot of the buttress. Scoot up the groove to a spike belay on the right (*Vector* belay).

P2 5c 24m Ascend to cracked blocks; step around and down to the left to climb a short wide groove (junction with *Nimbus*). Follow the rightwards-trending groove system to eventually gain the *Vector* 'cave stance'.

P3 4c 10m Pull out right from the cramped belay and follow the diagonal ramp-line rightwards and across to a spike belay below the top crack.

P4 6a 15m Climb up on to a detached flake and fire up the thin crack until a line of good holds leads diagonally leftwards to the top. A dazzling pitch!

[P Livesey, R Fawcett 01.05.76]

17. Vector E2 5c 75m

A polished, but utterly classic route.

P1 5a 18m Start at the base of the buttress just right of *The Weaver* by a large flake. Go up a short groove and step right on to a slab. Pad up leftwards and climb a short groove to a spike belay.

P2 5c 24m The infamous Ochre Slab pitch is a highly polished, hanging blade of rock waiting to chop the technically inept! Make a tricky move rightwards into a diagonal crack which leads to a large spike. Step left from the top of the spike and make precarious moves to gain the start of the Ochre Slab itself. Locals can be seen affecting a sense of cool on the following section, but first-timers can be forgiven for jittering and flummoxing their way up. Move over a bulge at the top and step left into a groove, which leads to a large roof. Traverse left to a cave belay.

P3 5b 18m Traverse left out of the cave and pull over a small overhang. Continue leftwards with a tricky section to reach the final layback exit to easier ground and the 'well-positioned stance' on *One Step in the Clouds*.

P4 4b 15m P3 of *One Step in the Clouds*.

[J Brown, C E Davies (2 pts) 26.03.60]

18. The Atomic Finger Flake/Void connection E4 6b 63m

A dramatic combination. A radically steep start leads up to a grand finale on the majestic headwall.

P1 5b 15m Climb the sustained groove right of *Vector* to reach a stance directly under the Ochre Slab.

P2 6b 27m A shallow technical groove on the right leads up to a vegetated ledge. Move up to a bulge and swerve left, undercutting aggressively across the fiercely overhanging wall to gain a steep corner crack. Race up this frantically to a ledge on the left. Make an awkward move over the bulge on the right into a groove that leads to a large sloping ledge belay stance.

P3 6a 21m Climb up into the hanging pod on the left. Exit left at its top to a finger jug and blast up the thin crack above; initially desperate, but easing towards the top.

[J Redhead, P Williams, C Shorter, K Robertson 02.03.80/R Edwards, I Pomfret (1 pt) 1975]

19. Grim Wall Direct E1 5b 54m

An enjoyable eliminate line; sustained, interesting and with a bold feeling on P1.

P1 5b 30m Start at the base of a slabby wall just right of the vegetated gully marking the right side of the *Vector* Buttress. Ascend the indefinite crack line and move diagonally left to surmount a bulge. Continue up the slab with difficulty to a large ledge.

P2 5b 24m Climb up directly behind the top tree on the ledge, making a steep pull through a bulge. Step across to join the shallow groove system on the right. Pull round a small overlap and follow the groove to a rightwards exit at its top.

[unknown]

Noel Craine getting stuck into the top pitch of **Cream** E4 6a photo: Ray Wood >

Craig Bwlch y Moch • Grim Wall

20. Grim Wall VS 4c 54m

A good route with a steep and memorable finish.

P1 4b 30m From the base of the *Shadrach* chimney, go up and left to a scoop. Move left and hand traverse a flake to gain a corner on the left. Climb this and the rib on the left to the large ledge.

P2 4c 24m Go up diagonally right, then pull leftwards through an overlap to a narrow ledge. Traverse left to a rib and climb this to the top.

[C T Jones, H Fox, H Smith 03.57]

21. Meshach HVS 5a 58m

An extremely popular route, with a superb P2 that easily justifies all the fuss.

P1 4c 34m From the base of the *Shadrach* chimney, follow the slabby rake up left to a ledge. Gain a scoop above then go up a shallow groove, stepping out right to a good ledge. Move up the wall for a brief junction with *Shadrach*, before stepping down left into a small niche. The wall on the left leads to a good spike; traverse left from here and go up a corner to the large ledge.

P2 5a 24m Go up diagonally right, then pull leftwards through an overlap to a narrow ledge (as per *Grim Wall*). Step right above the overlap climb the wall heading rightwards beneath a peg (crux). Climb up to the left side of a long, narrow ledge. Traverse this rightwards, stepping up and moving right to finish.

[R James, A Earnshaw, M Petrovsky (1pt) 07.62]

22. Shadrach VS 4c 52m

A popular and polished line: initially serious and strenuous, then tricky, but safe.

P1 4c 34m Move up to the base of the intimidating offwidth crack snaking skywards; either lose your helmet and squirm desperately inside, or make a bold and unnerving ascent of its outer edge (feels like HVS this way!). At its top, step left and ascend the slabby wall to reach a small belay stance beneath a large pillar. If you don't fancy either of the first options then try *The Brothers* start (VS 4b) which sneaks up the wide crack right of the chimney.

P2 4c 18m Climb up onto the top of the pillar, then stride back leftwards onto the wall and make a further tricky move to gain the groove. Pop up this and trend rightwards to the top.

[A J J Moulam, G W S Pigott, D Thomas 13.05.51]

Approach for routes 23 and 24: From the BMC signpost, follow the path rightwards, parallel to the stream and road, for 50m, until an old and rather dilapidated bridge across the drainage channel is reached. Backtrack for a few metres, then follow a path into the trees and over some mossy blocks before trending leftwards to a slab (several trees growing out of the left-hand corner are a good landmark). The right edge of the slab - up a series of short steps with various handily placed trees - leads to a small ledge just to the right of the routes.

23. Leg Slip E1 5b 58m

A sustained and absorbing outing.

P1 5a 15m Start beneath an obvious groove capped by a roof. Climb up the groove, which is initially difficult, until a leftwards exit is possible to gain the top right end of a sloping ramp. Belay at the small stance under the roof.

P2 5b 28m Surmount the overhang on the right and move in to the obvious groove. Bridge up this and make a committing swing out on to a flat hold on the right arête. Move back into the groove and head up to an overhang. Move left (tricky) to gain easy ground and a tree belay.

P3 15m Scramble up to a grassy ledge and continue up a slab to the top.

[J Brown, C E Davies 13.03.60]

24. First Slip E1 5c 64m

An intense and precarious route – the epitome of Tremadog technicality.

P1 5c 34m Climb up the groove (as per *Leg Slip*), continuing up to the roof where an insecure traverse leads rightwards to a ledge at the base of a smooth groove. Squeak your boots and bridge upwards to reach a delightful belay ledge.

P2 4b 15m Romp up the flake above, then a series of ribs to a ledge.

P3 15m Scramble up an arête and slabs to finish.

[J Brown, C E Davies (1 pt) 13.03.60]

V Louise Thomas on the top pitch of **Meshach** HVS 5a photo: Ray Wood

Craig Bwlch y Moch • Merlin Buttress

Approach for routes 25 - 28: From the BMC signpost follow the path rightwards, next to the stream that runs parallel to the road, for approximately 150m (passing the dilapidated bridge) until a more substantial bridge is reached where the cliff almost reaches the path. The footpath directly opposite the bridge leads to the start of *Daddy Cool*. For *Merlin Direct*, keep going for a further 10m, then follow the track which soon kinks to the right around some boulders, before quickly leading to the base of the big slab climbed by the first pitch of *Oberon*; *Merlin Direct*, *Geireagle*, etc start just to the left.

25. Daddy Cool/The Sting E2 5c 63m

An elaborate and interesting excursion on the steep wall left of the Merlin Buttress.

P1 4c 12m Start just left of the open groove. Climb up the rib on the left and continue up the ramp to reach the tree in the 2nd groove on the steep side-wall. (This is the start of *Salamanda* HVS.)

P2 5c 20m Go up the ramp for a metre or so and step back left onto a pedestal beneath the diagonal crack. Move up past the crack and surmount the overhang. Move back left to a large stance.

P3 5a 11m Climb up and right onto the steep wall where an obvious traverse line leads into the corner.

P4 5c 10m Ascend the superb clean cut yellow corner. A real calf pumper!

[D Roberts, P Williams, R Edwards 15.01.78/R Edwards, P Williams 05.01.78]

26. Merlin Direct HVS 5a 50m

A delightful route building to a memorable finish on the clean headwall. Perhaps your first HVS?

P1 4c 24m Start just left of the pedestal. Climb up for 6m, then make a hard diagonal traverse rightwards into the V-groove. (A slightly easier line can be followed just above.) Follow the V-groove up left to pop out on the slab. Belay immediately.

P2 5a 26m Move up the slab to reach the prominent layback crack. At its top continue directly up for a few metres before moving left to gain a thin rightward-slanting crack that leads to the top. A fitting finale to another Tremadog classic.

[A.J.J. Moulam, B.A. Gillot 1956]

27. Vulture E4 6a 36m

A strenuous beast! If you fancy a bit of well-protected, fiercely-sustained, barndoor-lay-backing, then step this way.

P1 6a 30m Start up *Merlin* to reach the base of the *Geireagle* ramp (or take the direct start up the groove at 6a). Step onto the ramp and attack the diagonal layback flake above. After much huffing and puffing a triangular niche is passed and a junction with *Geireagle* is reached. Head up left to the arête (long reach), and surmount the overlap onto a slab below a corner.

P2 4a 6m Nip up the corner to finish.

[A Sharp, C Dale 05.05.75]

28. Geireagle E3 5c 40m

A stunning route following the precarious/strenuous diagonal ramp line beneath *Vulture*. Hard for the tall.

P1 5c 34m Start up *Merlin* to reach the base of the ramp (or take the direct start up the groove at 6a). Balance up the ramp to its end and overcome an unfathomable section to reach a good ledge. Follow shelves back left to the arête (long reach), and surmount the overlap onto a slab below a corner.

P2 4a 6m Nip up the corner to finish.

[R Edwards, J Edwards (2 pts) 27.02.66]

Craig Pant Ifan

Area: Tremadog
Style: Trad (1 - 5 pitches)
Aspect: South
Rock type: Dolerite
Approach: 20 minutes
Altitude: 100m

Cardiac Arête	E4
Fingerlicker	E4
Sexual Salami	E4
Silly Arete	E3
Vulcan	E3
Pincushion	E2
Plastic Nerve	E2
Barbarian	E1
Falcon	E1
Helsinki Wall	E1
Scratch Arete	HVS
Strapiombo	HVS
Stromboli	HVS
Scratch	VS
Borchgrevinck /	
Poor Man's Peuterey	S

One of the finest crags in the area and home to numerous well-established classics. The rock is the usual immaculate Tremadog dolerite formed into bold and striking features. The close proximity of Eric's Café and of course, Craig Bwlch y Moch, ensures a regular flow of keen climbers.

Conditions: Generally this south-facing crag dries very quickly after rain. Some lingering dampness may be found on lower pitches and in corners and crack lines.

Approach: The crag is situated above the A498 Tremadog – Beddgelert road west of Eric's Café and Craig Bwlch y Moch. Convenient parking is available at Eric's Café. Short stay parking is free, but there is a £1 charge for long stay parking.

From Eric's Café walk along the road towards Tremadog until you reach a rock plinth bearing a Snowdonia National Park sign (on the Tremadog side). 30m further on hop over the fence, then follow the easiest line up through the boulders, until a prominent large block gets in the way. Outflank this on the left, before trending up leftwards until level with a 'large slabby-topped block on the left, with trees at its base'.

To reach the *Vulcan/Falcon* section of the crag, head up and slightly rightwards following a narrow track upwards through vegetation to a T-junction. Turn right past a big block just above the path and lying against the hillside, and follow the path as it descends, then runs across a level section before ascending quite steeply to the base of the cliff. (Turning left at the T-junction would lead up to the Scratch Arete area.)

To reach the *Scratch Arete/Barbarian* area continue on the diagonal, leftward leading path running up into the trees from the aforementioned 'large slabby-topped block on the left, with trees at its base'. The path leads up past a a short zig zag to the base of the cliff beneath the obvious large corner of *Barbarian*. To gain *Scratch Arete* ascend the wooden ladder on the right, before descending a short distance to the start of the route: 'SA' is chiselled into the rock. From the base of *Barbarian* the path rises leftwards until levelling out at a lower subsidiary section of the cliff - a good reference point is the tree with a huge root that drops down towards the base of the main crag (the start of *Pincushion*). Continuing up left soon leads to a level area below a big gully/groove with a twin stemmed tree growing out of its right edge (approximately 6m up). The continuation of the track, that leads around leftwards, is actually the final section of the main descent path from Porkers Gully.

   Rachael Barlow just above the lip of the overlap on **Scratch Arete** HVS 5a photo: Jethro Kiernan ∧

Craig Pant Ifan

Stromboli Buttress is probably best approached from the Tremadog itself. Park sensibly in Tremadog and walk back in the direction of Eric's Café. Take the left turn on the opposite side of the road to the garage and follow this small road for 150m to a sharp left turn next to a gated entrance. From just beyond the apex of the bend a public footpath leads up through fields and woods. The path levels out at a gate; further on it reaches a small compact crag (the Upper Tier). Stromboli Buttress lies directly below. Descent to the crag base is possible via Helsinki Gully, which lies on the left where a path and some steps lead over a stone wall. It is also common to abseil directly in and avoid the poor quality lower section of the crag.

Access issues: Although access to the crag has in the past been the subject of some controversy, the situation has changed. In 2006 the BMC formed a management partnership with the owners of Craig Pant Ifan, permitting a continuation of access for climbers and protecting conservation interests.

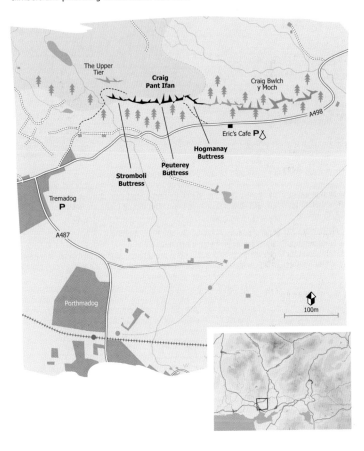

Craig Pant Ifan • Hogmanay Buttress

LLANBERIS +

OGWEN +

TREMADOG +

GOGARTH & LLEYN

LLANDUDNO +

The immaculate upper section of the cliff is guarded by a lower band of shaly, friable rock. Descent is normally made by abseil, however it is possible to walk off and descend via Porker's Gully to the left (looking in) of Peuterey Buttress. Initially head rightwards and up, then turn left and follow vague paths to the top of Peuterey Buttress where the clifftop path is more obvious.

1. Falcon E1 5b 54m
An entertaining and continuously interesting route.
P1 18m Start by scrambling up to a slab in the vegetation beneath and right of the obvious corner of *Vulcan*. Ascend the slab, then move right and go up a short groove to reach a tree. Trend up left to take a belay below the overhangs.
P2 5b 36m Ascend the steep crack, surmounting a bulge to reach a short smooth groove, as for *Vulcan*. Bridge up thinly to gain a small ledge on the right below the overhang. Swing out blindly rightwards onto the face. Savour the exposed position for a moment, before turning your gaze upwards. The crack above weaves towards the crag top; follow it with gusto past a few more mini-cruxes.
[R James, M Petrovsky (9 pts) 10.62, FFA: J Clements 1964]

2. Vulcan E3 6a 54m
A stunning line with tremendous climbing; sustained and technical and quite possibly E4!
P1 18m P1 of *Falcon*.
P2 6a 36m Ascend the steep crack, surmounting a bulge to reach a short smooth groove. Bridge up until it is possible to step left into the main corner. The corner proves to be fairly relentless, at least until you've passed the overhang. Above it still keeps coming, albeit in a slightly friendlier manner.
[B Wright, C Goodey (15 pts) 20.04.62, FFA: R Fawcett spring 1977]

∧ Pete Robins variously embroiled in the technicalities of **Vulcan** E3 6a photos: Jethro Kiernan

285

Craig Pant Ifan • Peuterey Buttress

A brilliant section of the crag with a stunning array of classic routes. Descent is best made down Porker's Gully on the left (looking in) of the buttress.

3. Scratch Arete HVS 5a 60m
A popular classic with a committing crux pulling through a stubborn overlap.
P1 4c 30m A rib and a shallow groove lead to a ledge at the base of a crack. Shoot up the crack, moving right at the top, with a tricky move surmounting the bulge. Tree belay.
P2 5a 30m Wander up the slab, heading left at first, then back right to the arête just below the overlap, passing wires and a peg on the right. Step up left and pull quickly through the overlap on the front side. Continue up the edge of the slab to join the top of *Scratch*.
[B Ingle, R F Jones (1 pt) 24.03.62]

4. Scratch VS 4b 50m
A fine route with a tremendous corner crack on P2.
P1 4b 20m Start at the base of *Barbarian*. Ascend the slabby wall on the right for a metre or so, then follow an intricate and gently rising traverse rightwards to reach a tree belay at the base of the corner crack.
P2 4b 30m Bomb up the corner crack, throwing in jams and layback manoeuvres as you see fit, until a rising traverse leads rightwards to a crack. Follow the crack to the top.
[A J J Moulam, W R Craster 19.12.53]

5. Barbarian E1 5b 48m
The striking corner line provides a Tremadog classic.
P1 4a 15m Ascend the wall just right of the main corner, then move left into the corner and go up it to a stance beneath the overlaps.
P2 5b 27m Pull round the overlap and continue up the corner until cracks on the right can be reached. Go up these to a niche below the 2nd overlap. Pull through strenuously and move up to a ledge on the left.
P3 4c 6m Move right and finish up the shallow groove.
[C T Jones, C E Davies, E Millington, M King (A2) 16.08.58, FFA: J Brown circa 1960]

6. Fingerlicker E4 6a 39m
A brilliant crack-climbing testpiece.
P1 5c 19m From the foot of the *Barbarian* corner move across left into the overhanging chimney. Wriggle upwards and pull out into the crack. Plug in the jams and keep on trucking up to the roof, then follow the corner above to a ledge. Traverse right to the Barbarian belay.
P2 6a 20m Follow *Barbarian* through the 1st overlap, then head diagonally leftwards across the steep wall, via an initially baffling sequence, and pull around the arête on to the slab. Finish up the top section of *Silly Arete*.
[P Livesey, J Lawrence 11.05.75]

7. Silly Arete E3 5c 39m
This magnificent, celebrated route is bold, dramatic, and in places, outrageously thin.
Start at the tree below the *Pincushion* chimney. Step onto the slab and gain the arête on the right, which leads somewhat seriously up to the overlap. Reach disappointingly poor crystal holds above the overlap directly above the chimney and somehow pull round onto the upper slab. Move up then right to the arête, and follow this to the top in an exhilarating position.
[J Pasquill, J Nuttall, R Evans 18.04.71]

8. Pincushion E2 6a 45m
A classic teaser, which sees many failures. If you're going well, give it a go.
Start at the tree below the obvious chimney. Scoot up the chimney to the overlap, then make desperate moves leftwards and pull over onto the upper slab. Follow a thin crack up the slab, until 3m below the next overlap, then move right into another crack, which is followed to the 3rd overlap. Traverse right gain and finish up a short crack.
[D P Davies, M J Harris, R R E Chorley (16 pts) 06.10.56, FFA: H Barber 1973]

9. Borchgrevinck/Poor Man's Peuterey S 76m

A popular and varied excursion, with some interesting climbing and delightful positions.
P1 12m Start just left of the break leading up to the *Strapiombo* chimney. Ascend the groove for a metre or so, then move right onto the rib, which leads up to a tree belay.
P2 12m The damp cracks leads to a further tree belay.
P3 14m Traverse right to a stance on the edge of the slab.
P4 30m Move up on the right, then step right in an airy position onto the nose. Climb up to a small ledge, and continue up cracks in the slab, before making a big stride rightwards and moving up to a decent stance.
P5 6m Move over a block and nip up a short chimney to finish.
[G J Sutton, J Gaukroger 20.12.53]

10. Strapiombo HVS 5a 42m

A classic feature and one for the chimney specialist, if such a thing exists nowadays.
P1 24m Move directly up to the tree at the base of the deep chimney.
P2 5a 18m Struggle up the flared chimney in a state of physical exhaustion and abject horror - you didn't expect runners did you?! Old school gnarlers will wonder what all the fuss is about.
[D Whillans, G J Sutton 21.05.55]

LLANBERIS +

OGWEN +

TREMADOG +

GOGARTH & LLEYN

LLANDUDNO +

Craig Pant Ifan • Stromboli Buttress

A stunning piece of rock, slightly spoilt by the lower band of slippery shale and vegetation. Access to and from the crag top can be made via Helsinki Gully on the left (looking in) of the buttress. It is also common practice to abseil in from the top of the buttress, and thus avoid the vegetated lower section of the crag.

11. Cardiac Arête E4 6a 18m
Immaculate rock and superb technical climbing.
Start from the tree belay beneath a small groove. Climb the groove until it is possible to move left and go up to the 1st overlap. Step right and gain a ledge on the arête. Surmount the overhang on the right and swing left onto the upper arête, which leads to the top.
[J De Montjoye, V Thomas 07.12.80]

12. Sexual Salami E4 6b 18m
Another stunning pitch, alternating between balancey sections and fierce pulling.
Follow *Cardiac Arête* to the 1st overlap, then make difficult moves leftwards past the overlap to gain a slab and a 2nd overlap. Hard moves through the overlap guard access to the final easier finishing groove.
[J Redhead, K Robertson, C Shorter 15.03.80]

13. Stromboli HVS 5a 56m

A thrilling and surprisingly affable route.

P1 4c 36m Start at the bottom left side of the buttress, below a groove capped by a roof. Move right along ledges, then climb up past 2 small overhangs to vegetated ground. Scramble rightwards and up to reach a tree belay beneath the central weakness in the buttress.

P2 5a 20m Move up towards the capped chimney for 5m, then traverse left beneath the overhang and pull up onto the slab. Go up over the 2nd overhang and into the V-chimney. Pull over onto the upper slab beneath the final roof. Difficult moves up and right lead to the top.

[H Smith, C T Jones 07.08.56]

14. Plastic Nerve E2 5c 55m

A rewarding climb, if a little on the reachy side.

P1 4c 36m P1 of *Stromboli*.

P2 5c 19m Move diagonally left across the slab to gain ledges beneath a thin crack. Go up the crack to the right side of the large roof. Make an on-off move past a peg and stretch for a crack, which lands you at the bottom of the large corner. Go up the corner and layback round the overhang. All that remains is the final offwidth.

[G Gibson, S Keeling 04.80]

15. Helsinki Wall E1 5b 43m

A pleasant and absorbing route.

P1 5a 18m From Helsinki Gully traverse rightwards across the yellow slab to a ledge. Move back left and up to a niche, then step out right and follow a diagonal crack to a stance.

P2 8m Traverse left beneath a small overhang, and move up past the break, then left to a stance below the upper wall.

P3 5b 17m Ascend the wall and groove to the overhang. A hard move left leads up to a steep crack; finish with a step to the right.

[J H Longland, B E H Maden (1 pt) 27.09.55]

elsinki
Gully

Helsinki
Wall

< Neil Dyer on **Plastic Nerve** E2 5c photo: Ray Wood

Gav Foster perched on the nose on P2 of **Creagh Dhu Wall** HS 4b photo: Si Panton ∧
Gav Foster balancing across the slab on P1 of **Creagh Dhu Wall** HS 4b photo: Si Panton ⌐

Craig y Castell

Area:	**Tremadog**
Style:	**Trad (2 - 3 pitches)**
Aspect:	**South-West**
Rock type:	**Dolerite**
Approach:	**15 minutes**
Altitude:	**150m**

Tensor	E2
The Wasp	E2
One Step in the Crowds	E1
Tantalus	E1

Creagh Dhu Wall Direct	VS
Creagh Dhu Wall	HS

This is a fantastic crag, with an open aspect and several outstanding routes, all on delectable Tremadog dolerite rock. It is also, generally, a good deal quieter than nearby Bwlch y Moch or Pant Ifan. The climbing itself is wonderfully varied and continuously interesting.

Conditions: A very sunny and quick-drying cliff.

Approach: If approaching by car, park in Tremadog village square and walk westward along the A487 Caernarfon road. Just before you reach the junction with the A498 there is a short lane bearing off right. Follow this in front of the school and then along the continuation path, for a further 50m until it is possible to turn right along a path leading across the fields (by the side of the new hospital). Go over the 'A' frame at the far side and turn right along a narrow path through the bushes. After 10-20m scramble through boulders on the left and head diagonally rightwards up the scree slope to the base of the crag.

Descent: Via a steep path on the right side of the crag (looking in).

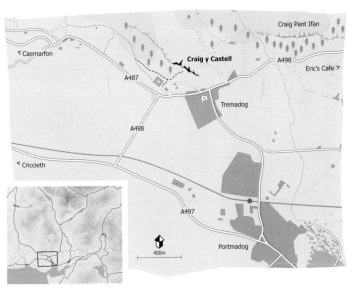

Craig y Castell

1. One Step in the Crowds E1 5b 52m

A pleasant and varied route.

P1 5b 15m Start as for *Creag Dhu Wall* up the corner, but move left into a steep groove. Go the groove to an overhang, then step right on to a rib. Tricky moves lead up to a sloping ledge (possible belay). The diagonal quartzy crack in the overhang leads to a protruding rib on the left. Pull up to another crack and trace around the roof to gain better holds on the right. A shallow groove on the left leads to small ledge.

P2 5b 37m Continue up the groove/crack to the overhang. Surmount this on the right, the step around the arête on the left. The thin slabby wall provides a spicy finale.

[A Evans, S Tansey, S Beresford 01.06.79]

2. Creagh Dhu Wall HS 4b 63m

A much hyped, but ultimately essential, route.

P1 4b 27m Climb up into the open corner that leads up to the right side of the overhangs. At the top of a wide diagonal quartzy crack, swing rightwards around the arête and tiptoe along a footledge (no handholds!) to reach a second corner system. Nip up this to reach a large tree belay on a comfortable ledge.

P2 4b 36m It is possible to traverse out left along the higher break, but it is more fun to drop back down and yard leftwards along the lower flake to reach the arête. From here climb directly up the slabby wall to a step left from a hollow block (and once-upon-a-time popular belay position) to gain the base of a very polished sloping groove: the final test.

[J Cunningham, W Smith, P Vaughan 12.07.51]

3. Creagh Dhu Wall Direct VS 5a 44m

A harder direct variant yields another classic outing.

P1 5a 34m Start as for *Creag Dhu Wall* up the corner, continuing up to a bulge, where a tricky move left across the steep wall leads to a diagonal crack. The crack leads up to a junction with the parent route on the slabby nose. Climb up to a stance at the hollow block.

P2 4c 10m Climb directly up the bold slabby groove.

[A Beanland, C T Jones 11.57 / D T Roscoe, A J J Moulam 02.06.57]

4. The Wasp E2 5c 51m

A superb climb, with a pronounced shift in character between its two pitches. Start beneath the large corner at the left side of the *Tensor/Tantalus* slab.

P1 5c 27m The physical crack. Climb up the corner for 10m, then move left to reach a pinnacle below a crack in the overhanging sidewall. The crack leads up, somewhat strenuously, to the spacious belay ledge.

P2 5c 24m The technical groove. From the left side of the ledge a prominent V-groove points skyward. Follow it with sustained interest, and without deviation, until a leftward exit presents itself at the top.

[J Brown, C E Davies (5 pts) 09.60]

5. Tensor E2 6a 67m

An excellent route forcing an impressive line through the overhangs.

P1 4b 27m Wander up the centre of the slab, moving right into a short groove, which leads to a small ledge.

P2 6a 30m Step down and traverse left across the hanging slab then move up to the overhang. Traverse left just under the overhang and layback up into the hanging groove. Climb up the groove to a niche, then step right with difficulty and move up to the roof. Reachy/desperate moves lead through the roof to a groove, which is followed to a stance.

P3 10m The groove above provides an easy finish.

[J Brown, C E Davies (2 pts) 07.03.64]

6. Tantalus E1 5b 67m

A fine route. Exposed and difficult.

P1 4b 27m P1 of *Tensor*.

P2 5b 30m Ascend a series of ribs and grooves on the right, until it is possible to traverse across the wall on the left. The arête is reached by a hard move, and followed by thin moves, trending left, across the slab to gain better holds and the *Tensor* stance.

P3 10m P3 of *Tensor*.

[H I Banner, J Neill 03.07.55/P2: D Yates, G Simpkin (1 pt) 1964]

Simon Panton just about to turn the arete on P1 >
of **Creagh Dhu Wall** HS 4b photo: Gav Foster

Craig y Gesail

Area:	Tremadog
Style:	Trad (1 - 3 pitches)
Aspect:	South-West
Rock type:	Dolerite
Approach:	15 minutes
Altitude:	150m

Javelin	HVS
Clutch	VS
Plumbline	VS
Princess	VS
Touch and Go	VS
Bramble Buttress	VD

The least frequented of the Tremadog cliffs, and arguably the least important. Nonetheless Craig y Gesail provides a welcome break from the hustle and bustle of its neighbours. The routes are good, if a little vegetated in places. The rock, where free of the creeping tendrils of greenery, is the usual immaculate dolerite that we all know and love.

Conditions: The crag has a sunny, open aspect and is fairly quick to dry.

Approach: The crag is approached from Penmorfa on the A487 Caernarfon road, west of Tremadog. At the top end of the village make a right turn onto Yr Hen Lon, a small lane, that leads in a km or so to the gate of Tyddyn Deucwm Isaf. Park just inside the gate, but do not block access to the fields. If parking space is limited either choose another crag, or find a sensible place to park in Penmorfa and walk back up the lane. A way marked path leads up to the left of the farm and on up to the crag.

Descent: Descent is possible at both ends of the cliff, but the most used is the path that follows the cliff top westwards (on the left side of the crag when facing in). It does involve a bit of a hike though. From just beyond Bramble Buttress/Castle area, follow a narrow section of path close to the cliff edge, slither through a smooth 'V' alcove, and keep going until the mountains to the north come into view (weather permitting, of course). Turn downhill and head into the wide boggy grassy gully, which leads to a stile over the fence. Continue down until the path leads back round to the cliff base (12-15 mins).

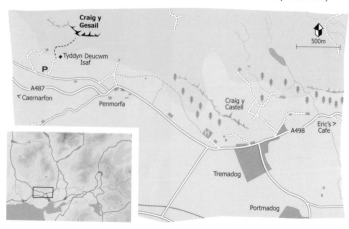

∧ Libby Peter on the top pitch of **Bramble Buttress** VD photo: Ray Wood

↖ Winter sunshine on the crag photo: Si Panton

Craig y Gesail

Bramble Buttress

Javelin Buttress

Princess Buttress

Midas Buttress
(Touch and Go)

1. Bramble Buttress VD 56m

A classic excursion up the striking rib line, which builds to a splendid, and rather photogenic finale.

P1 20m Go up a series of short walls just left of the rib to reach a small corner at 10m. Climb up the corner then move right on to the rib itself and continue up to the top of a pinnacle. Take a belay in the gap behind the pinnacle.

P2 18m Head left into a groove, then move back right to ascend the arête. Continue up through trees to reach the bottom of the final wall.

P3 18m Start on the left and trend up leftwards, stopping only to strike the odd front cover pose.

[M J Harris, J Neill 13.12.53]

The next 2 routes are best approached by abseil to belay stances just above the vegetation. Useful landmarks at the top of the cliff are as follows: a big block near the cliff edge, with a pyramid shaped block just up to the right; there is also a stacked boulder slightly further leftwards up the hillside, which has a useful thread.

2. Clutch VS 4c 27m

A pleasurable pitch up the central grooveline.

Start as for *Plumbline*, or from a better ledge and flake belay up to the left. A step right, then back left gains the base of the groove. Follow this via steep sustained climbing until a few metres below the top of the groove, where moves out rightwards round the arete leads into *Plumbline*. Follow this to the top of the flake, then up the short wall to the top.

[A J J Moulam, W R Craster, J F Mawe (4 pts) 20.12.53]

3. Plumbline VS 4c 30m

A fine steep route.

Start from a semi-hanging nut belay immediately above the vegetation band and just down and left of a sloping ledge. A delicate step up right gains the ledge, bridge/back-and-foot up the cleft until a crack leads out leftwards onto the front face. Climb up, until it is possible to step back right across the top of the cleft to gain a ragged crack. Follow this to gain the top of a spike (junction with *Clutch*). Finish up the short wall.

[C E Davies, G Holmes 07.04.65]

Craig y Gesail

LLANBERIS +

OGWEN +

TREMADOG +

GOGARTH & LLEYN

LLANDUDNO +

4. Javelin HVS 5a 64m

A popular, but bold climb.

P1 5a 30m Start just left of *Princess* slab from a ledge above a small tree. Go up the slabs left of a small overlap, heading left to gain a large block beneath an overhang. From the top of the block, step onto the wall and climb up to a sharp rib. Move boldly up the rib and traverse along the horizontal edge. Belay at the bottom of a small wall behind.

P2 4c 34m Go up the wall, then follow a grassy line up left to a ledge beneath the final wall. The left-hand groove and a short wall leads to a finish up a corner crack.

[D P Davis, D Thomas, J Neill, M J Harris 16.09.56, P2: D Yates, G Simpkin 1964]

5. Princess VS 4b 69m

A good and varied outing which is mostly S/HS, but with one harder section.

P1 4a 33m Start from the toe of the right-hand side of the big slab at a rib peeking through the vegetation. There is a big ivy-covered block approx 6m further right. An initial slatey lower section gains the rib; follow this to a ledge with a small tree on the right. A traverse up rightwards on the lip of the overhang leads into the white-speckled groove. Climb this, and then traverse up leftwards under steeper rock to gain a small, restricted stance in an alcove.

P2 4b 36m Negotiate the vegetation to gain the arete on the left, and continue to a ledge on the edge of the buttress below some blocks. Step off the blocks and climb the steep crack (crux) to a ledge, then continue up another crack to a vegetated ledge. Step off the block and follow the curving groove/crack to gain the right edge a short distance below the top.

[M J Harris, J Neill 19.12.53]

6. Touch and Go VS 4c 35m

An excellent route with some lively manoeuvres on P2. It can be found on the Midas Buttress at the right side of the crag.

P1 4c 20m Climb the groove in the centre of the buttress. At the overhang make a a delicate traverse left to a good ledge. Continue up to belay on a further ledge 3m above.

P2 4c 15m up and right lies a short groove; pull into it with some difficulty and climb it to reach the top of the flake. Finish up the steep wall above.

[R James, P Benson 11.57]

Craig Cwm Trwsgl

Area: Cwm Pennant
Style: Trad (1 - 2 pitches)
Aspect: West
Rock: Dolerite
Approach: 45 minutes
Altitude: 350m

The Exterminating Angel	E3
Day of Reckoning	E3
Efnisien	E1

An isolated slabby crag at the head of the Cwm Pennant Valley, a place to find solitude and some of the best rock North Wales has to offer (similar to that found on the Plexus Buttress in the Llanberis Pass).

Conditions: The crag does need a good dry spell to be climbable. To a certain extent the rock will always be slightly dirty, however the quality of the climbing more than makes up for this.

Approach: From Dolbenmaen on the A487 Caernarfon - Porthmadog road there is a turning signed Cwm Pennant. Follow this small road along the valley, travelling through a few gates on the way. At one there is a charge of £2 to park, as well as some great free range organic eggs. Drive on to the end of the road where it is possible to park in a small field just off the road. Follow the way-marked path up towards the mine workings, then head left up toward a dam. From here the crag can be clearly seen. Scramble up to its base from the far side of the lake.

Descent: Scramble up and head well over to the left (facing in) before descending. On the left of the crag there is a very large slabby boulder, which is a useful landmark.

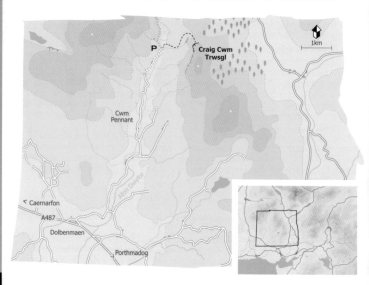

1. Efnisien E1 5b 37m
The crack line running up the left side of the main slab gives a great pitch.
[J Perrin 09.74]

2. The Exterminating Angel (with The Iconoclastic Exit) E3 5c 43m
This excellent route takes a reasonably direct line up the steep slab above and to the right of the slabby boulder.
P1 5c 18m Start below a downward-pointing tongue of rock and below the tree some 20m above. Climb up the short V-groove to the right of the tongue of rock. Step up left onto it and climb diagonally up and left to a small and delicate spike (hard move for short climbers!). Step down and left to arrange better gear, then move up and left over the overlap before heading rightwards across the slab to reach the holly-infested ledge.
P2 5b 25m *The Iconoclastic Exit*. Climb onto a flake above the belay ledge; then step left onto the slab to reach the slanting shelf. Climb straight up the slab to reach a small diamond-shaped niche. Move out of this into a shallow scoop, step right and follow the seam to the ledge. Another cracking pitch.
[J Perrin, D C O'Brien 09.74/A Phizacklea, D Lampard 31.07.87]

3. Day of Reckoning E3 5c 55m
Fine steep slab climbing on the P2 makes this a well worthwhile trip.
P1 5b 21m Start some 30m right of *The Exterminating Angel* at a blunt rib which leads up to the bottom right-hand end of the grassy ramp which forms the base of the steep upper slab. Climb the rib with a tricky move at its top to gain the grassy ramp. Wander up this to belay beneath the right-hand crack of the upper slab.
P2 5c 34m Climb the rightwards-trending crack until good holds lead leftwards to the centre of the slab. Follow the crack above to a small niche. Make a tricky move out right followed by thin moves back left and up into a shallow groove. This quickly leads to the top.
[D Lampard, A Phizacklea 31.07.87]

↑ Dave Simpson seconding P2 of **Day of Reckoning** E3 5c photo: Graham Desroy

Craig yr Ogof

Area: Cwm Silyn
Style: Trad (2 - 6 pitches)
Aspect: South-West
Rock type: Rhyolitic Tuff
Approach: 45 minutes
Altitude: 600m

Jabberwocky	E2
Crucible	E1
Kirkus Direct	HVS
Kirkus's Route	VS
Outside Edge Route	VD
Ordinary Route	D

A classic mountain crag hosting a number of celebrated routes. Nestled in the north-west flank of the Nantlle ridge this impressive cliff feels wonderfully isolated. That said, you might be surprised how many other climbers turn up on a sunny summer weekend. The popularity is easy to understand. Here we have a fine collection of authentic mountain routes on an attractive cliff, invariably blessed with sunshine, and all surrounded by the beautiful upland setting of Cwm Silyn.

The rock is quite compact, and largely sound. However, in places it does leave little option for runners.

Conditions: The south-west aspect guarantees that the crag soaks up any sunshine that is available. The Great Slab dries quickly, although the upper sections of *Outside Edge Route* and *Ordinary Route* can remain greasy for a few days after rain. Seepage should also be expected in the cracks and grooves following any wet weather.

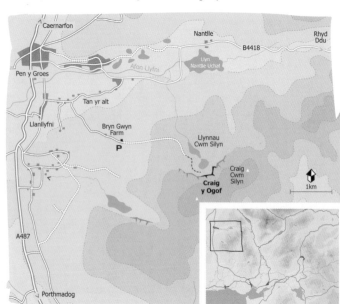

Craig yr Ogof

Approach: From the A487 Porthmadog – Caernarfon road turn off at Pen y Groes and head for Llanllyfni. Once there, take the signposted road to Tan yr Allt. After approximately 1km turn right and follow the narrow road for 2km to Bryn Gwyn Farm. Just beyond the farm a gate marks the end of the metalled surface. Park immediately in the field on the other side of the gate, taking care not to block the track. (Thieves have targeted this parking spot in the past, consequently it would be foolish to leave any valuables in your car, especially on a weekend.) Walk along the grassy track passing three locked gates to reach some old mine ruins by the 2 lakes (Llynnau Cwm Silyn). Follow the path rightwards as it contours above the lakes, and slog up the scree slope to the base of the crag.

Descent: If you have carried your sack up one of the easier routes, then trace the top of the cwm rightwards to descend a grassy shoulder leading back down to the approach path. To return to the base of the crag it is best to go down the Great Stone Shoot. This lies approximately 200m right of the exit from the summit ridge. An old fence identifies its top; avoid awkward steps in the gully by keeping to the left (looking out).

Descent from *Crucible* and *Jabberwocky* can be made down *Ordinary Route*, although this is best avoided if there are any teams on the lower pitches. If that is the case, then why not go for the summit experience and continue up either *Ordinary Route* or *Outside Edge Route ?*

∧ High up above Llynnau Cwm Silyn on **Outside Edge Route** VD photo: Ray Wood

⌐ Craig yr Ogof, Cwm Silyn photo: Matt Tuck

Craig yr Ogof

1. Crucible E1 5b 91m
An established classic which requires a steady approach from both leader and second.
P1 4c 30m Start on right side of a depression below twin grooves (12m left of the Great Slab). Go up the left-hand of the twin grooves, stepping right at a small overhang to climb another groove. Move left to reach a triangular overhang at 18m. Climb up left into a further groove, after a few moves step back right above the overhang and trend diagonally rightwards to a stance.
P2 5b 24m Traverse leftwards and slightly down onto a large block, and ascend the corner above it passing an overhang with difficulty. Continue boldly out leftwards to gain a sloping ledge. Move left into a groove, then go down and left to reach a sloping gangway. The gangway leads left to the base of the large corner. Move up to a small stance next to a large block.
P3 5a 37m Step left from the top of the large block and climb a groove and rib until it is possible to move back into the main corner. Go up past a bulge to gain a small ledge, then traverse right across a slab to make thin moves up to the big roof. Escape rightwards into a niche, then right again into a slabby groove leading up to Sunset Ledge.
[B Ingle, R G Wilson 01.06.63]

2. Jabberwocky E2 5c 64m
A superb and thrilling climb, covering some airy ground.
P1 5a 30m Start in a grassy groove 6m left of the Great Slab. Go up the groove to a grassy ledge and move up left onto the arête. Follow the right edge of the arête by the easiest line to gain a sloping stance.
P2 5c 34m Step left from the small roof, then up to gain a spike. Climb up right into the main groove and follow it with some difficulty until a move out left allows access to a hanging ramp. Go up the ramp leftwards, then right across a slab, and past an arête, back into the groove proper. Climb up the groove to Sunset Ledge.
[R Evans, J Yates, C E M Yates 18.05.70]

3. Outside Edge Route VD 136m
A classic mountaineering route of much character.
P1 21m Start 6m right of the edge of the Great Slab. Follow a rightwards-trending groove up to gain the top of the large semi-detached block from its right side.
P2 24m Make steep moves up onto the next ledge. Follow a rising traverse line leftwards to the arête, and up to ledges.
P3 12m Climb up for 6m to gain Sunset Ledge. Walk leftwards for 6m to take a belay at its left side.
P4 15m Make a delicate and airy traverse leftwards around a couple of ribs into a groove. Ascend the groove to a grassy ledge in a splendid position.
P5 24m Move up and left to make a difficult entry into a wide corner crack. Soon enough it is possible to step out left onto the rib, which leads up onto the crest of the ridge.
P6 30m Ascend easily, before crossing a step in the ridge to gain large spikes. Scramble onwards up the summit ridge.
[J M Edwards, C H S R Palmer 14.07.31]

4. Ordinary Route D 109m
Another fine and popular excursion.
P1 27m Start 12m left of the corner marking the right edge of the slab. Ascend the short polished wall above on the right, then head up leftwards along a series of ledges to belay beneath a broken groove.
P2 21m Continue trending up left to the edge of the slab, then go up to reach Sunset Ledge. Belay below an open groove 5m along the ledge.
P3 24m Ascend the groove to reach a short slab at 12m. Make delicate moves up the slab and continue up the exposed rib to reach a ledge where the angle of the crag falls back.
P4 37m Move round to the left (junction with *Outside Edge Route*) and ascend easily, before crossing a step in the ridge to gain large spikes. Scramble onwards up the summit ridge.
[D R Pye, W R Reade, C A Elliot, N E Odell 04.04.26]

The Geat Stone Shoot
Approx 200m

Great
Slab

Sunset
Ledge

Ogof
Terrace

5

6

4

3

2

1

5. Kirkus's Route VS 4c 94m

A graceful and sustained climb, featuring some delightfull pocketed slabs.

P1 4c 34m Start as for *Ordinary Route* up the short polished wall to ledges. Move up and climb a forked diagonal crack, following the right branch round into a niche. Ascend steeper ground to a stance on blocks.

P2 4b 21m Move right and climb a shallow scoop leading up right, then step left into a groove leading back left to the mid-height break.

P3 4c 15m A vague weakness in the centre of the smooth slab leads up past a series of small overlaps to a stance.

P4 4c 24m Head diagonally leftwards past a protruding block to reach good holds beneath a nose of rock. Move rightwards, then follow holds above the overlap up leftwards to the summit ridge.

[C F Kirkus, G G MacPhee 31.05.31]

6. Kirkus Direct HVS 5b 94m

A thrilling route with some thin and taxing sections.

P1 5a 27m Start 5m left of the corner marking the right edge of the slab. Ascend the slab (normally wet) to an overhang. Go round this to gain a shallow groove, which leads up right to a sentry box at its top. Traverse left and step down to the *Kirkus's Route* stance.

P2 4c 24m Easy ground leads up left to a small corner at the end of 2 rakes which run up from the left. Ascend the corner for 3m then step right onto the rib. Follow the thin crack above until it is possible to move left into a rightwards-leading groove. Follow the groove up to the mid-height break.

P3 5b 43m Head right into the corner at the right side of the slab and follow it to a small overhang. A crack on the left leads to a mossy area; step left and climb directly up the slab (3m left of the corner) to gain the upper break in the slab. The slim groove in the final slab leads to the top.

[V Ridgeway and party 1951]

The eye-catching boulder that you pass on the way up to the crag provides a pleasant diversion once the main business of the day is done with. It has enough interesting problems to keep the casual boulderer amused for at least an hour or so. Indeed, the main arête, known as *Inside Edge* is one of the best problems of its grade (V3/Font 6a) in North Wales.

Henry Griffiths on the V3/Font 6a+ traverse >
photo: Andy Godber

< Matt Tuck wearing big boots for a big route **Ordinary Route** D photo: Tuck collection

Y Garn ®

Area: Gwellyn
Style: Trad (5 - 7 pitches)
Aspect: North
Rock type: Micro Granite
Approach: 90 minutes
Altitude: 450m

| Mallory's Ridge | VS |
| Eastern Arete | VD |

A traditional mountain crag presenting an inspiring profile that is clearly seen from a distance. Included here are a fine pair of mountaineering objectives; namely the two compelling ridges leading to the summit of Y Garn. Some loose rock will be encountered, but nothing too unconventional.

Conditions: As might be expected, this north-facing mountain crag requires a day or two to dry out after heavy rain.

Approach: Park in the National Park car park in Rhyd Ddu, then follow the footpath running west from the other side of the road. This quickly leads to a junction with the prominent bend in the adjacent Rhyd Ddu – Nantlle road. Turn immediately left and take the footpath heading south-west. After 300m/400m an area of open ground is reached and the path giving access to the Nantlle ridge breaks off to the right.
Follow this path up over a stile halfway up the hillside. Continue up the path, which eventually trends rightwards. Where it starts to head back left, a 1m high pale 'finger stone' is visible to the right. Heading rightwards after the finger stone you are quickly confronted with a dilemma: either head high over a steep knoll and follow a sheep track that runs across the steep heathery ground between the broken crags and scree below (not recommended if vegetation is wet), or head lower past a boggy section and skirt below the screes until you meet the dry stone wall, which can be followed up to the crag. Neither are pleasant but both infinitely better than traversing across the unstable screes.

Access Restrictions: To prevent disturbance to roosting birds there is a night-time restriction on the crag, which runs from 1 hour before sunset, until sunrise during the August to November (inclusive) period.

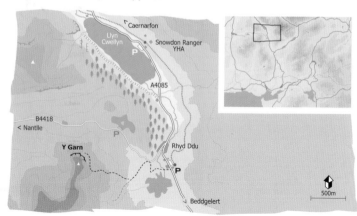

∧ Rachael Barlow on **Eastern Arete** VD photo: Graham Desroy
↖ Looking back down to the Rhyd Ddu - Nantlle road photo: Graham Desroy

Y Garn

Eastern Arete is the left-hand ridge and starts some 50m right of where the wall meets the crag.

1. Eastern Arete VD 146m ®

A great traditional route, which provides a fitting access to the Nantlle Ridge.
Start a few metres up the right-hand side of the ridge at some flakes.
P1 30m Climb up the gully for 3m to the crest of the ridge. Take the grassy groove to the left and either follow it to its end, or break out onto the ridge after a few metres, which is followed through a short corner of loose rock. Easy climbing leads to below a steeper nose of rock.
P2 9m Ascend the nose and rib to finish on a slabby ledge.
P3 24m Climb the easy corner to behind a pinnacle. Ascend the slabby wall and head rightwards to a large ledge below where the ridge steepens again.
P4 10m Step right round the rib and airily climb the cracks to a belay below an easy slab.
P5 20m Follow the slab and ridge more easily until below a steep stepped groove.
P6 45m Climb the groove and follow the ridge until below the final steep groove.
P7 8m The final groove provides a tricky finish. Easy scrambling remains.
[W P Haskett Smith 1905]

Y Garn

LLANBERIS +

OGWEN +

TREMADOG +

GOGARTH & LLEYN

LLANDUDNO +

Mallory's Ridge is the next prominent ridge to the right of Eastern Arete.

2. Mallory's Ridge VS 4c 115m ®

The striking ridge on the skyline offers a superb mountaineering excursion.

P1 4b 40m From about 6m up to the right of the base of the ridge beneath a small Rowan tree, climb a rib to the right side of a wide heather ledge (optional belay). Trace ledges up and rightwards via spikes to gain and follow the groove nearest the edge of the steep slab. Ascend to a small overhang and swing steeply back left to a fine perch on the front of the arête.

P2 4b 20m Move up for a couple of metres then trend right to gain the arête above the steep slab. Follow the arête and groove above to a spacious ledge.

P3 4c 20m Skirt round the arête on the right and traverse right again for a metre or so until it is possible to head up and slightly rightwards past a flake-covered ledge to reach a terrace.

P4 4a 15m Climb the groove/crack in the wall above to memorable stance amongst tottering pinnacles.

P5 20m Continue up the wobbly alpine-esque ridge to an emotional moment on the summit cairn.

[H E L Porter, G H L Mallory 09.11]

∧ The 1m high finger stone photo: Graham Desroy

Craig y Bera

Area: Gwellyn
Style Trad (5 pitches)
Aspect: South
Rock type: Micro Granite
Approach: 40 minutes
Altitude: 400m

Angel Pavement	HS

A striking mountain crag perched on the northern side of the valley through which the Rhyd Ddu – Nantlle road passes. The central broad-based Pinnacle Ridge dominates this cliff, which is broken into a series of ridges, and it is here that the featured classic route lies. Although *Angel Pavement* is a well-travelled line from which most loose material has long since departed, the rock on the crag is known for its unpredictable nature. A degree of care is best applied, especially when you consider the run-out nature of the route.

Conditions: This is a quick-drying cliff with a sunny aspect.

Approach: There is space for a couple of cars at the entrance to the Planwydd campsite/farm 1km north of Rhyd Ddu, but do park considerately (don't block any gates). If there is no room here, it is also possible to park at a wider section of the main road 1km back towards Caernarfon, or opposite the Snowdon Ranger Youth Hostel.
From the first gate follow a footpath across the field on the left and continue in the same direction through the woods until open land is gained again. Follow the path tracing the edge of the woodland until you reach the highest point of the trees on the hillside. From here it is possible to contour leftwards around to the base of the crag. A conspicuous drystone wall runs up to meet the base of Pinnacle Ridge.

Descent: From the top of the pinnacle head left (facing in) and come down via an exposed path and gully.

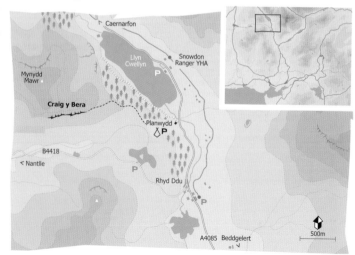

Craig y Bera

LLANBERIS +

OGWEN +

TREMADOG +

GOGARTH & LLEYN

LLANDUDNO +

1. Angel Pavement HS 4b 183m

An intriguing and atmospheric mountain route, with an air of seriousness accentuated by the long pitches, less than abundant protection and suspicious rock quality.

P1 46m Start 30m left of the drystone wall that runs up to meet the base of the buttress. Climb boldly up the slab to the large grassy terrace, and find the thread belay at its right end.

P2 46m Trend diagonally left across the steep slab on decent holds then move directly up to a grassy ledge and a belay below the overhang, in a crack on the right.

P3 4b 30m Left of the overhang is a narrow rib, ascend this with some difficulty, and continue up broken ground to a small ledge.

P4 46m Ascend the rib on the left and move up to a grassy area. Go into a corner and head across left below steep walls to gain some good ledges.

P5 15m Scramble up over broken rock and easy but loose ground to the top.

[C P Brown, A J J Moulam 05.07.46]

⚲ Craig y Bera photo: Si Panton

Craig Cwm Du

Area: Gwellyn
Style Trad (4 pitches)
Aspect: North
Rock type: Micro Granite
Approach: 60 minutes
Altitude: 500m

Adam Rib	HS

A quiet, neglected cliff composed of a series of rambling and confusing buttresses. Earlier generations revelled in its alpinesque challenges but these days you are unlikely to see another soul. Despite its lapsed popularity, the described route gives a fine mountaineering experience, with stunning views of the Nantlle Ridge and all the way down to the Menai Straits and Anglesey beyond.

Conditions: The northerly aspect and relatively high altitude ensure that this is a crag best left for a sunny summer day. The complexity of the approach should also preclude any mooted visits on a misty or gloomy day. Unless of course you are keen for an epic!

Approach: The crag is best approached from Fron, which can be reached from a number of directions (Rhosgadfan, Pen y Groes, from the A487). Once there, follow the main road through the village, and take the left fork up into the quarry. Park at the old quarry buildings by the cattle grid or if you're lucky continue down the road until it turns into a track and park on the right. Follow the track, which bears rightwards after 1km to reach a saddle, and starts to ascend the well-worn path up Mynydd Mawr. From this saddle, head left through the heather to the edge of the Cwm. The rambling buttresses of Craig Cwm Du are seen across to the right. *Adam Rib* is on the far left-hand side of the crag. The dilemma is how to get there. Either descend diagonally rightwards and traverse just below the buttresses on steep heather and scree, or descend to the bottom of the cwm and ascend up the scree and heather on the other side. Neither is likely to avoid much cursing. Persevere as the effort is worth it. As you get closer the landmark of the undercut square-ish *Crazy Pinnacle*, which seems to defy gravity, will become visible high on left. The slender Eden Buttress is the first major one some 300m to its right and is bounded on its right by a narrow and very lush gully (Eden Gully). *Adam Rib* starts below and follows the right-hand rib of the buttress. Climbing with the sacs is vital to avoid yet another descent into the cwm.

Descent: Via the footpath descending from Mynydd Mawr.

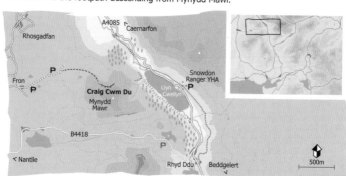

Crazy Pinnacle

Adam Rib

1. Adam Rib HS 4b 120m

P1 45m Scramble easily upwards to reach the foot of the rib proper.

P2 4a 27m Traverse left into the wide groove and climb it on the left side to gain the rib on the left. Ascend this until it is possible to take the obvious foot ledge rightwards across the groove to reach the main rib and a grassy stance.

P3 4a 27m Climb the cracks on the left of the rib to a small ledge. Move left and up to a large spike belay in a delightfully airy situation.

P4 4b 21m The dramatically exposed rib above is tackled initially from the right. Follow it 'quietly' to the top.

[J M A Thomson and party, Easter 1911]

Eden Gully

On the walk-in to Craig Cwm Du photo: Graham Desroy

Castell Cidwm

Area: Gwellyn
Style: Trad (2 – 3 pitches)
Aspect: South-East
Rock type: Micro Granite
Approach: 30 minutes
Altitude: 200m

Potency	E6
Heading for Heights	E5
Central Wall	E3
Dwm	E1/3
The Curver	HVS
Vertigo	HVS

Far from the bustling crowds, this quietly adventurous cliff awaits those who appreciate their day's climbing spiced with a touch of uncertainty. There is something vaguely supernatural about this ugly, yet compelling crag. The rock is compact and largely devoid of major visual lines (*Dwm* and *Curver* excepted), and whilst not overtly loose, it is not above suspicion. Just bang a few of those blocks and hear that unnerving, shuddering boom! The routes themselves weave wild and occasionally devious passages through steep and uncompromising territory; this is not a place for the timid or inexperienced.

Conditions: The crag has a sunny aspect, and thus dries quickly, but sections of it (such as the *Dwm* roof) are often wet.

Approach: There is space for a couple of cars at the entrance to the Planwydd campsite/farm, but do park considerately (don't block any gates). If there is no room here, it is also possible to park at a wider section of the main road 1km back towards Caernarfon, or opposite the Snowdon Ranger Youth Hostel. Follow the forestry track past the campsite and beyond until a disused quarry is reached on the left. Just after the quarry cross the fence (taking care not to damage it) and follow a small stream up through dense trees (a bit awkward) to pop out at the base of the crag.

Descent: Scramble carefully down the ramp that slants back down beneath *Dwm*, or walk over to a gully on the far left side of the crag.

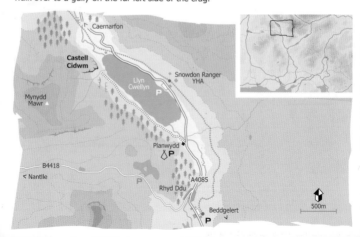

∧ Ian Parnell on P1 of **Central Wall** E3 6a photo: Graham Desroy
↑ By the side of Llyn Cwellyn photo: Jethro Kiernan

Castell Cidwm

The first 5 routes start from the grassy terrace below the main part of the cliff. This is best accessed from the top left side.

1. The Curver HVS 4c 55m
The obvious rising gangway starting at the left side of the crag provides a good natural line with exciting situations for both leader and second.
P1 4c 18m Start in the corner below the start of the gangway and follow it rightwards to belay in a niche.
P2 4c 37m Keep traversing rightwards, passing a steep section. Continue on friendly holds with mounting exposure, until a tricky move leads into a small corner. Finish up this. (Take care with rope drag on this pitch.)
[J Brown, C T Jones 26.09.60]

2. Potency E6 6b 57m
An action packed and thrilling route of the highest quality.
P1 6b 27m Start a few metres left of *Central Wall* at the right side of a low roof. Climb the slabby rib and short wall above, then traverse left along a break and round a mini rib into a niche below a roof (rest). Gain the spike above the lip with difficulty and trend left to better holds and a peg (which can be backed up). Climb straight up above to a small stance 4m below the roof.
P2 6b 30m A fantastic pitch. Move right and up to the roof. Take a deep breath and make some wild layback moves around the lip; follow the finger crack up to a break. Either traverse left and up a shallow groove (*The Erg* finish), or step right and boldly climb the middle of the face to good finishing holds (*The Potency* finish).
[P Littlejohn, J de Montjoye 10.05.88]

Castell Cidwm

LLANBERIS +

OGWEN +

TREMADOG +

GOGARTH & LLEYN

LLANDUDNO +

3. Central Wall E3 6a 54m
This fine route makes a direct assault upon the central defences of the cliff. The wild finish is particularly memorable.
P1 6a 24m Climb up to the obvious clean cut V-groove and follow it to a difficult leftwards exit at its top to reach a block. Move up the awkward wall above, then climb leftwards through the overhang to reach a belay ledge.
P2 5c 30m Move left a few metres, then climb diagonally rightwards and pull through a roof on good holds. Continue up the ramp to its top then make alarming moves leftwards through the capping roof to finish.
[A Bell, J Clements (2 pts) 03.10.64/ FFA: W Wayman, T Jepson 05.77]

4. Heading for Heights E5 6b 48m
A brilliant climb with a powerful crux.
P1 6b 27m From the start of *Vertigo* climb straight up the flaked cracks, then head rightwards up a ramp to rejoin *Vertigo* for its crux section moving around the left side of the long overhang. Once past this, move up leftwards and climb a smooth open groove, then follow a diagonal crack up leftwards to a bulge. Move onto the left side of the bulge to place some runners, then undercut the crack and make a long blind reach rightwards onto the wall above. Continue up to better holds in a groove, which leads up and left to a belay position below a steep white wall.
P2 5c 21m Move out onto the wall and trace the left arête up to reach less steep territory. Bear rightwards to the top.
[P Littlejohn, J de Montjoye 27.05.88]

5. Vertigo HVS 5a 39m
A superb route, with a fairly serious P1 and an exposed P2.
P1 5a 18m Start 6m right of *Central Wall* below and left of black slabs leading up to a scoop. Climb diagonally right for 6m, then swerve around the left side of the long overhang before moving back right into the scoop. Exit right from the top of the scoop to reach a belay stance.
P2 4c 21m Move rightwards around the arête to gain a flaky crack, which leads steeply to some final bulges. Traverse right to finish, revelling in the considerable exposure.
[J Brown, B D Wright 26.06.60]

6. Dwm E1 5b/A1 (E3 6a free) 54m
A classic historic route taking the most striking line on the crag. There are numerous degrading in situ pegs distributed across the route – trust them at your peril!
P1 5a 18m From a few metres up the ramp traverse diagonally left across a steep wall to gain a good flake hold in the hanging groove. Continue up the right-trending crack/groove taking care with the occasional hollow hold, until a short vertical section leads to a sloping ledge belay up on the left.
P2 5b 18m Step out left and sidle up the stepped groove to reach a ledge. Tricky, blind moves lead diagonally up rightwards (back above the lip of the roof shielding the previous belay) to better holds. Continue in the same line (still tricky), moving a few moves up a short groove before striding right to reach a belay in the large corner on the right.
P3 5a/A1 (6a free) 18m Climb up the dirty, damp, wet corner and follow the undercut roof/slab 'juncture' towards a hidden chimney, switching to aid manoeuvres when it all gets too much. Pop out rightwards from the chimney to gain the top.
[J Brown, H Smith 27.03.60]

Alex Williams on P2 of **Zarquon/Resurrection/Erection** E2 5c photo: Al Leary ∧
Rhyd Ddu train station sign photo: Al Leary ↑

Llechog

Area: Snowdon
Style: Trad (4 pitches)
Aspect: North-East
Rock type: Rhyolitic Tuff
Approach: 90 minutes
Altitude: 650m

| Zarquon/Resurrection/Erection | E2 |

A peaceful and largely neglected mountain crag nestled high up in Cwm Clogwyn on the western side of Snowdon. As the name suggests, this is a slabby crag with mostly excellent compact rock.

Conditions: Although this is definitely a 'mountain crag', both in its altitude and position, Llechog is a bit more approachable than its larger neighbours, Cloggy and Lliwedd. During the summer months it receives plenty of sunshine in the morning and early afternoon and there are also no significant drainage problems to contend with.

Approach: Start from the car park next to the Rhyd Ddu station, which is located just east of the village, on the Welsh Highland Railway. Follow the Rhyd Ddu Snowdon footpath to the ruins of Rhos Boeth. This takes approximately 35 minutes. Strike off left from the main track on a gradually ascending faint track that leads through a boulder field to a stone wall running up the hill. Hop over this and contour round the hillside - passing above a large lone boulder with an adjoining ruined circular stone wall - until you reach Llyn Nadroedd in the lower reaches of Cwm Clogwyn. Continuing up into the Cwm to reach the base of the cliff.
It is also possible to reach Cwm Clogwyn via the Snowdon Ranger path, which runs up from the Youth Hostel further up the valley. This is a more gentle approach but longer and most likely boggy in places.

Descent: Walk carefully down the big, steep convex grass ramp towards the lower end of the cliff. The easiest line down through the array of craglets that pepper the hillside is not that easy to follow and involves a fair bit of zigzagging about. Keep an eye out for a faint track towards the left side (looking down the slope). Once you are down at the base of the cliff, contour back round to collect your rucsacs.

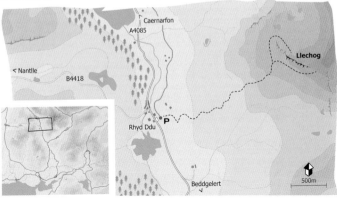

Llechog

1. Zarquon/Resurrection/Erection E2 5c 114m

This combination of mix-and-match pitches yields a classic mountain route with a stunning top pitch finale.

P1 5a 18m To reach the start walk up rightwards from the grassy gully at the lowest point of the buttress to belay left of a prominent bollard that leans against the cliff. Go up into the groove, then make awkward moves right into a crack, which leads to grassy ledge with a block; good wires in the crack above on the right.

P2 5a/b 36m Perform a thin, delicate traverse above the bulge, then follow a faint groove in the arete to a ledge. The slanting groove leads leftwards to a ledge below a steep corner. Go up the corner, and then step right onto a delicate slab, which leads to a grassy ledge. Scramble around left (watch out for rope drag here) to small flake and nut belays at the base of a rib below the big slab.

P3 4c 30m Climb up the rib, then cross some vegetation to gain a short right-facing corner, which leads to a ledge on the left. Go up the groove, which then opens out into a scoop. At the top of this, carefully drop down the back of the slab for 6m to nut belays.

P4 5c 30m The one you've been waiting for! Ascend the crack in the middle of the smooth slab, and then follow a thin diagonal crack leftwards to gain a footledge on the arête. The striking crackline above beckons. With a distinct lack of footholds, tramline up between the crack and the arete until it becomes necessary to fully commit to the crack. Some urgent finger locking leads to a very welcome ledge. Flake belays can be found 6m above. Scramble up to the plateau to finish.

[H.I.Banner, C.E.M.Yates 14.08.82/J.Perrin, N.J.Escourt, C.E.M.Yates 15.08.70/H.I.Banner, C.E.M.Yates 24.07.82]

The idyllic Nant Gwynant photo: Si Panton

Clogwyn y Bustach

Area:	**Gwynant Valley**
Style:	**Trad (2 - 4 pitches)**
Aspect:	**East**
Rock type:	**Rhyolite**
Approach:	**15/25 minutes**
Altitude:	**225m**

Gallop Step	HVS
Lockwood's Chimney	D

A quiet backwater crag nestling in a state of peaceful obscurity on the sylvan flanks of the beautiful Nant Gwynant valley. The appeal of this largely broken, vegetated cliff is boosted by the curious attractions of a peculiar pair of routes. Also, a trip to the crag can easily be combined with the nearby Clogwyn y Wenallt.

Conditions: The crag receives morning sun and is fairly quick to dry, although some drainage streaks do tend to linger.

Approach: From the back corner of the Nant Gwynant campsite cross the footbridge over the river and turn right to follow a path which eventually runs parallel to the river and reaches a huge and radically overhanging boulder on the left. This is the Homage Boulder, which you may be interested to note has a good and pumpy V6/Font 7a traverse that runs right-to-left across the main face. Putting the temptation of a nifty bouldering session aside, press on along the path and skirt up the right side of the wooded boulder field to arrive at North Buttress up on the right. The start of *Lockwood's Chimney* can be reached by weaving a diagonal line through the wooded boulder field to reach the streaked wall up to your left.

There is normally a £3 charge for parking on the campsite or there is limited free parking by the main road where it runs close to the lake. From here follow the lakeside path back round to the campsite.

Descent: Come down the left (facing in) side of the cliff.

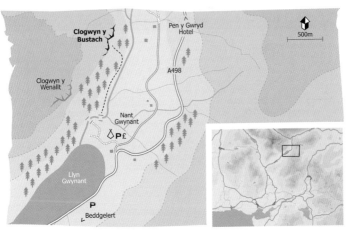

Clogwyn y Bustach

LLANBERIS +

OGWEN +

TREMADOG + B

GOGARTH & LLEYN

LLANDUDNO +

Lockwood's Chimney

North Buttress

Streaked Wall

Homage Boulder

Approach

1. Lockwood's Chimney D 70m

An entertaining and entirely traditional classic, often done on a wet day by rowdy teams in search of fun. The route lies on the extensive, and extensively vegetated buttress left of North Buttress.

P1 18m Start right of a steep streaked wall on the left side of the buttress at an archway (The Marble Arch). Drop down a metre and trace ledges rightwards to a short crack.

P2 10m Ascend the crack, which proves to be tricky, moving out left to ledges. Go right to a belay beneath the chimney. (This pitch can be bypassed by an easier alternative 6m to the left – a useful option in wet conditions.)

P3 30m Enter the chimney, either via the crack above, or by skirting around the rib to the right and climb 6m towards the chockstone. Squirm along the bottom of the cleft (tricky for the more rotund members of the party) and move up at the end to an abrupt exit onto ledges.

P4 12m Follow polished holds to the top.

[A Lockwood 1908]

Clogwyn y Bustach

LLANBERIS +

OGWEN +

TREMADOG + ₿

GOGARTH & LLEYN

LLANDUDNO +

The obvious buttress on the right, characterised by a broad overhanging band arching across the crag.

2. Gallop Step HVS 5a 50m
A quirky, but very worthwhile traverse line starting and finishing on the ground.
P1 5a 20m Start at the obvious block below the left end of the large overhang. Move up to the fault line and follow it rightwards beneath the overhang. At 15m make strenuous moves around an arête and reach a belay position in a niche.
P2 4c 30m Continue along the traverse line, past a vegetated section until you reach the base of the crag again.
[J I Disley, D Morin 08.01.56]

∧ Andy Townsend on P2 of **Gallop Step** HVS 5a photo: Ray Wood

Clogwyn y Wenallt

Area: **Gwynant Valley**
Style: **Trad (2 pitches)**
Aspect: **South-East**
Rock type: **Bedded Pyroclastics**
Approach: **10/20 minutes**
Altitude: **225m**

Poacher	E5
Ferdinand	E2
The Death Wisher	E2
Torero	E2
Oxine	VS

A beautifully situated crag with a neat cluster of intense routes. Clogwyn y Wenallt nestles on the wooded hillside above the idyllic Llyn Gwynant. The sunny aspect and laid back feel of the Gwynant valley is likely to instill a sense of calm in the mind of the bedraggled visitor. It certainly offers a pleasingly serene alternative to the busy Tremadog cliffs or the nearby Llanberis Pass. Be warned though, these routes can turn stroppy and awkward if treated with contempt. In fact, anything less than a concerted effort is likely to end in weighted runners and bruised egos!

This is a deceptively steep crag, albeit one blessed with good quality rock, and featured with an array of positive flakey holds. Expect to get pumped, and you'll be fine.

That being said, if it all feels too much like hard work, then why not give yourself a break. Go dip your toes in the river, or hire a canoe from the campsite and head out for a relaxing paddle on the lake.

Conditions: The crag gets morning sun and the rock dries quickly. On summer evenings it can be particularly midgey.

Approach: From the back corner of the Nant Gwynant campsite cross the footbridge over the river and turn left along the path, before breaking steeply up the hillside to reach the crag base. There is limited parking by the main road where it runs close to the lake, or parking on the campsite (there is normally a £3 charge).

Descent: Via the obvious path running down the left (facing in) side of the cliff.

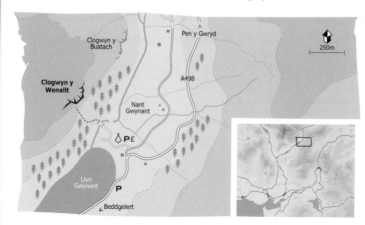

∧ Graham Frost surging up the uber classic **Ferdinand** E2 5b photo: Ray Wood

↳ Clogwyn y Wenallt poking out of the trees photo: Si Panton

Clogwyn y Wenallt

1. Ferdinand E2 5b 25m

One of the best crack climbs in the area. As brutal and uncompromising as you would expect from a 'Rock and Ice' era classic. To reach it walk up left and follow the terrace, back right, to a lovely belay spot beneath the soaring crack. Ascend the corner for 6m, then pull into the steep crack in the right wall, closing the 'barndoor' behind you! The crack is not as pure as, say *Grond* (Dinas Cromlech in the Llanberis Pass). It is quite featured, especially for the feet. Nonetheless this is still the stuff of nightmares for your average crimp-happy wall climber. Turn the top overhang on the left and finish up another crack. Great stuff!

[J Brown, C T Jones 07.02.59]

2. Torero E2 5b 45m

An exciting and difficult route, with a forceful and scary start to P2.

P1 5b 15m Bridge up the prominent corner until a small ledge signals the start of a rising traverse line leading up right across a short wall to reach the grassy terrace.

P2 5b 30m Stand on the flake and pull into the scoop. Go up, then step back right onto a flake and up to the *Poacher* belay. Step left and finish up the corner.

[J Brown, D D Whillans (1 pt) 05.59]

Clogwyn y Wenallt

LLANBERIS +

OGWEN +

TREMADOG +

GOGARTH & LLEYN

LLANDUDNO +

3. Poacher E5 6b 50m

A hard test piece, originally freed by a Yorkshire raider.

P1 5c 22m Pull over the bulge and climb directly through the *Oxine* traverse. Climb boldly up the wall left of the obvious corner (P1 of *Bovine* HVS 5a) to a ledge. A shallow groove leads to the grassy terrace.

P2 5c 14m Move right into a sentry box/groove feature. Climb up it and make a hard pull to exit on to a sloping ledge, which provides an awkward belay stance beneath the final groove.

P3 6b 14m Boulder up the fingery leaning wall past a poor peg (small wires can be fiddled in, assuming one is fit/strong enough) and gain the groove. Further contortions, past a peg, lead to the top.

[P Burke, G Kent (1 pt) 04.78, FFA: R Fawcett 1980]

4. Oxine VS 4c 57m

A justifiably popular combination of *Oxo* and *Bovine* allowing easy access to the amazing top pitch of the latter.

P1 4b 30m Start by a black recess 10m left of the stone wall which abuts the crag. Move up and traverse right to a black ledge, then past a detached pinnacle to a small wall. Climb this then go up and follow a gangway rightwards to the grassy ledge.

P2 4c 27m Ascend the groove for a metre or two, then make a hard swing out right. Race on up the steep, pumpy wall on gloriously positive flakes.

[J R Lees, G D Roberts, W A Trench 12.04.53/C E Davies, B D Wright, D McKelvey 19.05.57]

5. The Death Wisher E2 5b 57m

Another exciting steep route.

P1 4b 30m P1 of *Oxine*.

P2 5b 27m Start up *Oxine*, but swing out left from its crux into a steep flake crack. Follow the crack past a barndoory move to the top.

[M E Crook, S McCartney 06.77]

Carreg Hylldrem

Area: Nantmor
Style: Trad (2 - 4 pitches)
Aspect: South-East
Rock type: Felsite
Approach: 2 minutes
Altitude: 50m

Wildebeest	E4
King Kong/	
Troubador Connection	E3
Samurai Groove	E3
Hardd	E2
The Burner	E2
The Hylldrem Girdle	HVS

A radical cliff with a series of impressive routes working up through some bewilderingly steep ground. The smooth compact rock, cleaved into alternating slabby and overhanging facets, is initially confusing. Routes can flit from ultra-strenuous to strange and balancey in the space of a single move.

Conditions: Hylldrem is always worth a look if the weather closes in elsewhere. The crag receives plenty of sunshine and is quite sheltered. It is possible to climb the girdle in rain, although parts of it might be wet. The crag dries quickly after rain, and the bouldering wall stays dry, even in torrential downpours.

Approach: The crag leans conspicuously over the A4085 Aberglaslyn – Penhyndeudraeth road 1.5km north of Garreg and approximately 4kms from the junction of the A4085 and the A498 Beddgelert – Tremadog road. The road takes a sharp turn over a bridge; park in the small layby opposite the crag just along from the bridge. A steep path leads up to the right side of the crag where the bouldering wall is over the fence on the right, and further paths traverse across the hillside leading to *Samurai Groove* and *King Kong*.

Descent: The best way down is over on the right side (looking in) of the crag.

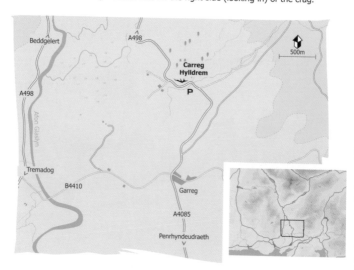

∧ Graham Desroy fiddling kit post-crux on **Hardd** E2 5c photo: Jethro Kiernan
↖ View of cliff from the Carreg road photo: Si Panton

Carreg Hylldrem

1. Hardd E2 5c 48m
A classic climb, which demands an equally competent team. Scramble up the ramp behind the large oak tree to belay on a ledge.

P1 5c 24m Head left across the steep wall to reach a short crack. Follow this over a bulge and traverse delicately to a resting position. Move onto the smooth slab on the left and continue over bulges to gain a petite and exposed stance.

P2 4b 12m Descend the steep groove below the stance and escape left on good holds to easier ground. Move up to a stance.

P3 12m Broken rocks lead easily to the top.

(P2 of *Wildebeest* can be substituted for P2 and P3 of *Hardd*, giving an overall grade of E3.)
[J Brown, G D Roberts, N Drasdo (1pt) Easter 1960]

2. Wildebeest E4 6a 45m
A brilliant, uncompromising route. Scramble up to take a belay at the bottom of the ramp behind the large oak tree.

P1 6a 30m Swing out onto the steep arête and make powerful moves up into cracks, and continue up leftwards to the overlap. Pull over the overlap rightwards to a junction with *Hardd* at the base of its short crack. Follow *Hardd* to its exposed stance.

P2 5c 15m Move right into a short groove (peg), and step right again onto short smooth wall. A hard move allows an awkward position to be gained on the left side of a steep groove. Ascend directly on overhanging rock to a niche below an overhang. Exit left to easier ground, and the top.
[S Haston, G Tinning 01.81]

3. The Hylldrem Girdle HVS 5a 67m
The reliable all-weather classic provides an interesting and wacky excursion. Be warned though, in places it is probably more harrowing to second than lead!

P1 5a 20m Start at the large oak tree. Traverse leftwards along the break to a short groove. Go up this and make a tricky move out left onto the slabby rib. Belay immediately.

P2 4c 11m Make awkward moves left across the short slab to gain another rib. Climb down the groove on the far side for 6m to a stance.

P3 4b 12m Traverse the slab on the left and descend the broken groove to a ledge below the final slab.

P4 4c 24m Ascend the slab to a tree belay.
[J Brown, G D Verity 27.03.60]

4. Samurai Groove E3 5c 54m
A spectacular and intimidating route.

P1 5a 18m P1 of *The Burner*.

P2 5c 24m Go up the short groove above the stance, then follow a traverse line rightwards beneath the overhangs to a 'saddle' underneath an overhanging chimney (*Raging Bull* E5 6b). Move right with difficulty and fumble blindly around the steep nose for a hidden jug. Make a wild swing round into a steep groove. Follow the groove in an outrageous position to an overhung niche. Escape leftwards to easier ground and the *Hardd* belay.

P3 12m P3 of *Hardd*.
[B Wyvill, D Mossman (2 pts) 25.04.71, FFA: P Thomas 1979]

5. The Burner E2 5b 47m
Another wild space-walking trip.

P1 5a 18m Start below twin grooves approximately 10m left of the large oak tree. Ascend the right-hand groove to a traverse line leading leftwards to a stance on the rib.

P2 5c 20m Ascend the rib on the left to a small platform. Launch out across the steep wall to reach a big spike. Move up into a small niche and go left around the arête to a stance.

P3 4c 9m Climb up above the spike on the left and move left to finish.
[R Evans, I R Esplin 21.08.66]

6. King Kong/Troubador Connection E3 5c 41m

A thug's delight, linking together impressive roof pitches.

P1 5c 9m The obvious overhanging flake crack on the left side of the crag leads to a stance on the slab.

P2 5b 8m Move left along the hanging slab (one tricky move), to belay below the detached flake in the roof.

P3 5c 12m Ascend the flake and chimney to a poor stance.

P4 4b 12m The groove leads to easy slabs and the top.

[R Evans, H Pasquill 06.07.74/J Perrin, D Britt 25.03.73]

The Bouldering Wall

Aside from being a good place to warm up, this perma-chalked steep wall also stays dry in even the most tropical of rainstorms. The landings are good, although some might appreciate a mat. The four main independent up lines (all of which are superb) rate approximately V4/Font 6bish. The low-level traverse is of a similar grade, once you've sussed all the tricks out. After that, and assuming that it is still raining, I suggest you start inventing eliminates. The possibilities are, thankfully, endless.

Streaky Desroy looks on (in awe?) as his son Liam powers up the V4/Font 6b ramp, on the right side of the Hylldrem bouldering wall photo: Jethro Kiernan

Carreg Alltrem

Area: Lledr Valley
Style: Trad (2 pitches)
Aspect: West
Rock type: Rhyolite
Approach: 15 minutes
Altitude: 225m

Penamnen Groove	E1
Fratricide Wall	HVS

Lavaredo	VS
Lightning Visit	VS

A pleasantly situated crag with a fine collection of mid-grade routes. The rock is good quality and the described climbs distinctive in character. Cwm Penamnen is a peaceful backwater place; sure, *Laverado* has a certain amount of crowd-pulling fame, but the chances are you'll have the cliff to yourself.

Conditions: This quick-drying crag receives plenty of sunshine.

Approach: From the main road running through Dolwyddelan (A470), turn south towards the railway station. Cross the river and railway bridges, then turn immediately left. After 50m a track on the right leads into the forest. Park, if there is space, in the area adjacent to the gate. Walk along the track into the forest, taking the left fork at the first junction. The crag can be seen up on the left.

Descent: Via Pinnacle Gully located on the far right side of the crag. It is also possible to descend at the left side of the crag.

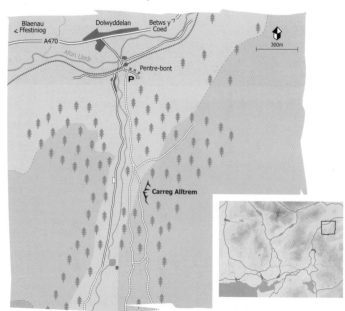

∧ Martin Crook setting off to do battle with **Penamnen Groove** E1 5b photo: Ray Wood

⋏ View of the crag photo Ray Wood

Carreg Alltrem

1. Fratricide Wall HVS 5a 44m
A splendid route that is steep, technical and absorbing.
P1 5a 21m Climb up the short groove leading to the right side of the grassy ledge. Ascend the wall directly above, continuing up a smooth groove. Step round a bulge to the right, then double back left. Keep going left more easily to a decent stance below the steep wall.
P2 5a 23m Ascend the short thin crack to a sloping ledge. Traverse delicately rightwards along it, around a nose, then move up to a ledge below a steep corner. Climb up the corner until wild moves lead out right to the arête. Finish up the arête in a superb position.
[C T Jones, A S Jones, A Daffern (1pt) 23.04.60]

2. Lightning Visit VS 4c 40m
A delightful climb tackling the attractive groove line.
P1 4a 17m Start up the first groove left of the *Penamnen Groove* corner, and continue up the wall to reach a block belay.
P2 4c 23m Move up to a ledge and step right to a pinnacle. Entry to the V-groove proves to be slightly baffling at first. Perseverance will deliver you to its pleasant upper reaches.
[R James, C T Jones 06.59]

3. Penamnen Groove E1 5b 37m
The striking corner crack provides a strenuous struggle.
P1 4c 14m Climb the left wall of the corner with a stretch at the top, or go direct up the corner itself if dry. Wander up right to a pinnacle belay.
P2 5b 23m Thrutch up the corner to the roof and surmount it on the left with as much grace as you can muster.
[R D Downes, J E M Clark 18.09.56]

4. Lavaredo VS 5a 42m
An exhilarating, popular route and quite hard for the grade.
P1 4b 21m Start up a groove just right of a detached pillar. The groove leads to a flake on the right at 9m. Move up onto a ledge and follow a rib up right to the ledge. Block belay.
P2 5a 21m The steep wall above the block is no pushover. Reachy, powerful moves lead up past spikes to good holds. Move up steeply and swerve left into a groove to finish.
[R James, K Forder, I F Campbell 20.03.61]

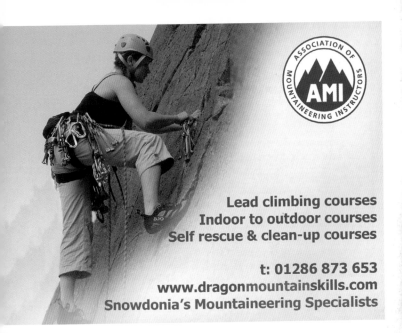
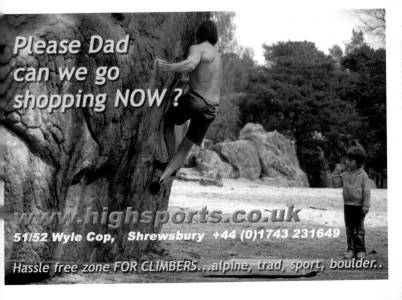

Craig y Clipiau

Area:	Y Moelwynion
Style:	Trad (1-3 pitches)
Aspect:	South
Rock type:	Rhyolite
Approach:	20 minutes
Altitude:	400m

Crimson Cruiser	E5
Non Dairy Creamer	E4
Great Feat/Mean Feat	E1
Mean Feat	HVS
Eagle Finish	VS
Asahel	S
Africa Rib	VD

A proud little crag, perched in a surreal position high above Blaenau and tucked in amongst the spoils of bygone industry. The rock is rough and pocketed and a real delight to climb on. The routes are fantastic. In fact as good as anything in Snowdonia.

Conditions: A sunny and quick-drying venue, even worth a look on a bright winter's day.

Approach: From the A496 road running from/to Blaenau Ffestiniog turn off to the small village of Tan y Grisiau. Follow the road up to a tight crossroads then a narrow and very steep lane leads up the hill and underneath the narrow gauge railway. Continue up the road until it changes into a track at a small parking area beneath a quarry tip.

An alternative route avoids the steep hill. Just after turning off the A496, take the left turn towards the power station and follow the road round, past the head of the lake and back right, to reach a locked gate (blocking access to the Stwlan Dam service road). Just before this point turn right, then left onto the road running up to the Cwm Orthin parking spot. Warning: do not leave anything of value in your car. There is a history of theft from cars parked in this area.

To reach the crag, walk up the Cwm Orthin track, then turn right from the broken down buildings on the first level. Follow a vague path rightwards towards the right side of the slate tips. Another path then heads steeply up to the crag.

Descent: Via a grassy gully on the left (looking in) side of the crag.

John Maskell facing steep ground on **Crimson Cruiser** E5 6a photo: Rory Shaw

Craig y Clipiau

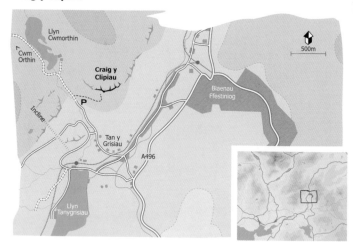

1. Africa Rib VD 37m
A delightful excursion up the left edge of the White Slab.

P1 12m Start at the left side of the slab beneath a block pinnacle. Take your pick from 3 choices: the front face of the pinnacle or the chimneys on either side of it. All options lead to a ledge with a rowan tree.

P2 20m Step left, and head up the left edge of the White Slab onto a large block. Continue up, eventually moving right to a large stance.

P3 5m The corner-groove on the right leads to the top.

[R Buckland, J Neill 16.08.53]

2. Asahel S 43m
A dainty route tackling the White Slab feature.

P1 4a 23m Ascend the slab, staying close to the corner. A good quartzy thread is passed before a small stance is reached.

P2 4a 15m Move delicately up the slab to the overhang, traverse left and climb a rib to a large stance above the overhangs. (*The Eagle Finish* VS 4b is a sensational alternative finish: break out right from beneath the top overhang, step out right onto a block - the Eagle - and reach a hanging slab. Go up a few moves then climb rightwards across the exposed nose.)

P3 5m. P3 of *Africa Rib*.

[R James, R L Roberts 07.55]

3. Great Feat/Mean Feat E1 5b 40m
A stunning combination; one of the best of its grade in the area. Start 6m right of *Asahel* in a grassy bay. Pull strenuously, slightly rightwards, past the nose. Then trend leftwards past quartz bands to a groove. Step left and climb up to join *Mean Feat* at its V-groove.

4. Crimson Cruiser E5 6a 40m
A fantastic pitch: steep, strenuous and as wild as they come. Climb *Great Feet* until above the quartz holds. Move right and ascend directly to the ledge below the steep groove. Move up to the green ledge just right of the groove, and step left and make hard moves up the groove. Near the top of the groove hard, blind moves left gain easier ground and a rest. Move back right and up to the ledge on *Mean Feat*. Step right and finish up the overhanging prow in an outrageous position.

[R Fawcett, P Williams 12.80]

5. Mean Feat HVS 5a 33m

A classic route with a well protected, but obstinate crux in the V-groove.

P1 4b 15m Start below a vegetated corner at the right side of the slab. Scramble up and follow the rising juggy traverse leftwards across the top of the slab to reach a stance at the base of the V-groove.

P2 5a 18m Climb the V-groove, which quickly turns tricky; from the good ledge at its top, step up right to another ledge. The final short wall provides an awkward exit.

[R James, P Vaughan 07.57]

6. Non Dairy Creamer (with the Non Creaming Dairy Start) E4 5c 33m

An outstanding and rather bold route. From the first spike on the traverse of *Mean Feat* ascend the steep shallow groove and wall above trending rightwards, until a traverse line leads out left along ledges. Take a breather at a resting-place below the steep pocketed wall, then move directly up past a good flake hold to reach a crack, and shortly after, the top.

[R Fawcett, P Williams 1980/M Griffiths, E Jones 06.81]

7. Double Criss VS 5a 33m

A pleasant rib is topped by a brutal, but mercifully short corner crack.

P1 4b 27m Climb up the slabby wall, heading left onto the rib. Continue up to reach a belay below the final corner.

P2 5a 6m The savage corner crack rears over head. It looks steep and unforgiving, particularly for those lacking in brawn or good technique. Your only option is to get stuck in and find out if it really is a beast (it is).

[C J S Bonington, C W Brasher 06.09.53]

Craig yr Wrysgan

Area:	Y Moelwynion
Style:	Trad (1-3 pitches)
Aspect:	South-East
Rock type:	Rhyolitic Tuff
Approach:	15 minutes
Altitude:	400m

Nosferatu	E4
The Green Wall	E3
Condor	E1
Space Below My Feet	HVS
The White Streak / Honeysuckle Corner	HS
Y Gelynen	VD

A fine crag featuring a diverse range of pitches. The bold ribs and slabs, well-protected groove lines and steep walls are all on wonderfully rough, gas-pocketed rock. The slightly surreal juxtaposition with the remnants of the quarry workings adds a quirky element to the crag ambience – check out the descent tunnel!

Conditions: This exposed and relatively sunny aspect ensures that most routes are quick to dry after rain.

Approach: On the A496 road, from/to Blaenau Ffestiniog, turn off for the small village of Tan y Grisiau. Follow the road up to a tight crossroads then follow the narrow and very steep lane up the hill, underneath the narrow gauge railway. Continue up the road until it changes into a track at a small parking area beneath a quarry tip. An alternative route avoids the steep hill: just after turning off the A496, take the left turn towards the power station; follow the road round past the head of the lake and back right to reach a locked gate blocking access to the Stwlan Dam service road. Just before this point turn right, then left onto the road running up to the Cwm Orthin parking spot.

Warning: do not leave anything of value in your car; there is a history of thefts from cars parked in this area. Follow a path breaking off left from the Cwm Orthin track, cross the footbridge over the stream and continue over to join the private service road for Llyn Stwlan which runs across the hillside beneath the crag. At the left side of the crag a prominent incline runs down the hill and across the service road; from this point head diagonally right up to the crag.

Descent: Walk over the back and return to the base of the crag via the rather conveniently positioned incline and tunnel on the left (facing in).

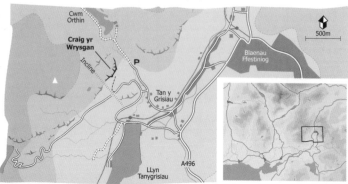

∧ Dafydd Davis on the top pitch of **The White Streak/Honeysuckle Corner** HS 4b photo: Si Panton
∟ Dafydd Davis at the top of the descent tunnel photo: Si Panton

Craig yr Wrysgan

Y Borfa

1. The White Streak/Honeysuckle Corner HS 4b 53m

A route of considerable character: a stunning and bold slab pitch contrasts markedly with a steep and classic corner pitch.

P1 4a 35m A lonely, yet 'steady' pitch up the big white slab, which is thankfully pocked with a steady supply of positive gas-pocket holds. Start beneath the undercut slab in a grassy recess (reached from the left by scrambling up ledges). Follow a slabby ramp up left to a ledge before making a bold diagonal traverse back right on to the main slab. An optional belay ledge presents itself out right, but it is probably best to press on up the upper slab to reach the comforts of Y Borfa (the Pasture).

P2 4b 18m The steep corner on the left provides a cracking pitch.

[G Dwyer, R L Roberts 05.07.58/J R Lees, G Moffatt 01.04.61]

2. Y Gelynen VD 70m

A delicate and bold climb on immaculate rock.

P1 37m Start just left of the central V-groove (*Dorcon* VS); reach this point by an easy scramble. Trend leftwards onto the blunt rib and climb up, stepping left past a small holly tree. The rib leads to a flake belay below a steep little wall.

P2 15m Move left and up to the overlap; go over this and follow the slab up to Y Borfa.

P3 18m Head diagonally rightwards up the wall past a steep corner on the left (which gives a superior optional finish at S).

[R Davies, G Williams 27.07.53]

3. Condor E1 5b 70m
The attractive crack line yields a sweet pitch.
P1 37m Start just left of the central V-groove (*Dorcon* VS). Make tricky moves up the wall to gain the crack. Scoot up the crack and continue up the rib above to the *Y Gelynen* flake belay.
P2 and **P3** As for *Y Gelynen*.
[M Crook, M Griffiths 05.78]

4. The Green Wall E3 5c 26m
A stunning and rather pumpy pitch up the leaning wall, with a bold first half.
Scramble up to the ramp below a short leftwards-facing corner. Ascend the short corner, moving with trepidation up the wall beyond to reach a scoop. Climb the thin crack above with a couple of long moves on good holds. Trend left over ever steepening territory on fortunately ever improving holds. Take plenty of slings for spike runners.
[J Perrin, A Cornwall (1 pt) 14.08.72]

5. Nosferatu E4 6a 26m
Another brilliant and strenuous pitch.
Start up the shallow groove just right of The Green Wall start. Continue directly up to reach and follow the obvious crack line with sustained, steep climbing on good holds.
[M Griffiths 11.80]

6. Space Below My Feet HVS 5a 30m
A delightful climb, taking the prominent rib right of the large dirty corner (*Gethsemane* HVS). Climb up the steep groove above the boulder to gain a ledge. Move up the wall and left to the arête. Follow the arête in a fine position until it leans back and leads to a slabby finish.
[J R Lees, D W Walker (some aid) 09.06.61]

Cath Wilson keeping it together on **Flake Wall HVS 5a,** on Clogwyn y Bustach photo: Al Leary ∧

Looking down the incline to Llyn Tanygrisiau photo: Si Panton ↑

Clogwyn yr Oen

Area: Y Moelwynion
Style: Trad (3-4 pitches)
Aspect: South-East
Rock type: Rhyolite/Dolerite
Approach: 20 minutes
Altitude: 400m

Flake Wall	HVS
Pinky	VS
Kirkus's Climb Direct	S
Slack	S

A superb crag with some classic low-grade routes.
This is the largest of the Moelwyns crags, and although it lacks the more distinctive features of its neighbours, the climbing is varied and always interesting. *Flake Wall* on the adjacent Clogwyn y Bustach provides a tasty excursion for those who were cruising on *Pinky*.

Conditions: This is a sunny and exposed crag. Consequently it dries fairly quickly after rain. That said, the lichen on the rock means that it can be excessively slippy in the wet, should you be considering a wet ascent of any of the routes.

Approach: From the A496 road running from/to Blaenau Ffestiniog turn off to the small village of Tan y Grisiau. Follow the road up to a tight crossroads, then follow the narrow and very steep lane up the hill and underneath the narrow gauge railway. Continue up the road until it changes into a track at a small parking area beneath a quarry tip.
An alternative route avoids the steep hill: just after turning off the A496, take the left turn towards the power station; follow the road round past the head of the lake and back right to reach a locked gate blocking access to the Stwlan Dam service road. Just before this point turn right, then left onto the road running up to the Cwm Orthin parking spot.
Warning: do not leave anything of value in your car. There is a history of theft from cars parked in this area. Follow a path breaking off left from the Cwm Orthin track, cross the footbridge over the stream and continue over to join the private service road for Llyn Stwlan which runs across the hillside beneath Craig yr Wrysgan. Walk up the road for approximately 1km, passing an incline, and then a boulder field, before a second prominent boulder field is reached below the crag.

Descent: There is an easy way down on the left side (facing in) of both crags.

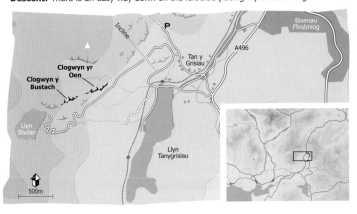

Clogwyn y Bustach

100m left of the descent path at the left side of the main crag lies the small, but perfectly formed Clogwyn y Bustach:

1. Flake Wall HVS 5a 36m
A minor classic, well worth the short walk to its base.
P1 5a 30m Ascend the left edge of the detached flake; at its top step left and continue up to a shallow groove V-groove. Go up this to reach a traverse that leads leftwards (bold) to a short crack. Scoot up the crack to a large ledge.
P2 6m The short wall leads to the top.
[D D Steward, T Kellett 21.09.55]

Clogwyn yr Oen

LLANBERIS +

OGWEN +

TREMADOG +

GOGARTH & LLEYN

LLANDUDNO +

Kirkus's
Climb
Direct →

2. Pinky VS 4c 80m

A delightful slabby strip leads to a steep and satisfying finale on P2.

P1 4b 44m Start at the base of the narrow pink-ish slabby strip, fringed by vegetation on either side. While not a great looking pitch it climbs well. Weave a line up through the initial bulge at 8m and continue up the pocketed slab to eventually gain a belay on the terrace.

P2 15m Scramble/walk rightwards to reach a belay below a tree in a steep corner groove.

P3 4c 21m Follow the steepening corner groove past the tree to a ledge on the left. Step back right into the strenuous crack splitting the headwall and 'keep-on-trucking' for the top.

[I G MacNaught-Davies, C W Brasher 15.04.53]

3. Kirkus's Climb Direct S 4a 60m

A classic and popular excursion providing sustained interest and a tremendous P3.

P1 4a 18m Start at the left side of the main slabby face at the base of a blunt rib. The route begins rudely up a steep wall, but soon relents with slabby ground and a pinnacle. Step across from its top onto a slab and trend up right to a jammed block cave belay.

P2 4a 11m Swing out right above a steep chimney and follow finger jugs rightwards on to the front slabby face. Continue up, in a less anxious state, to gain a large terrace.

P3 4a 23m The broad rib above is cleaved by a delightful slender groove on its left side; gain this and follow it to a sloping ledge. Move up to the right side of this and climb directly to reach a comfortable belay ledge.

P4 18m The slim groove leading up from the right side of the ledge leads on to easy slabs and soon after, a belay on top. Scramble up the ramp on the left to gain the descent path.

[C F Kirkus, C G Kirkus 1928]

Clogwyn yr Oen

4. Slack S 4a 90m

A fine route with an intimidating crux.

P1 21m Pad up the slab to the flake.

P2 20m Go up the right side of the flake and step onto the wall. Move left at the top of the wall to gain a crack; follow this up to a belay beneath the widest part of the overhangs.

P3 4a 12m Traverse beneath the overhangs then launch up the bold rib with gusto. Move up right to belay in a corner.

P4 18m Ascend the corner to a ledge, then move left to finish up another shorter corner. Scramble up to reach the top.

[I F Cartledge, J R Lees 13.11.60]

Pinky

Just above the steep start to P1 on **Kirkus's Climb Direct** S 4a photo: Si Panton ∧

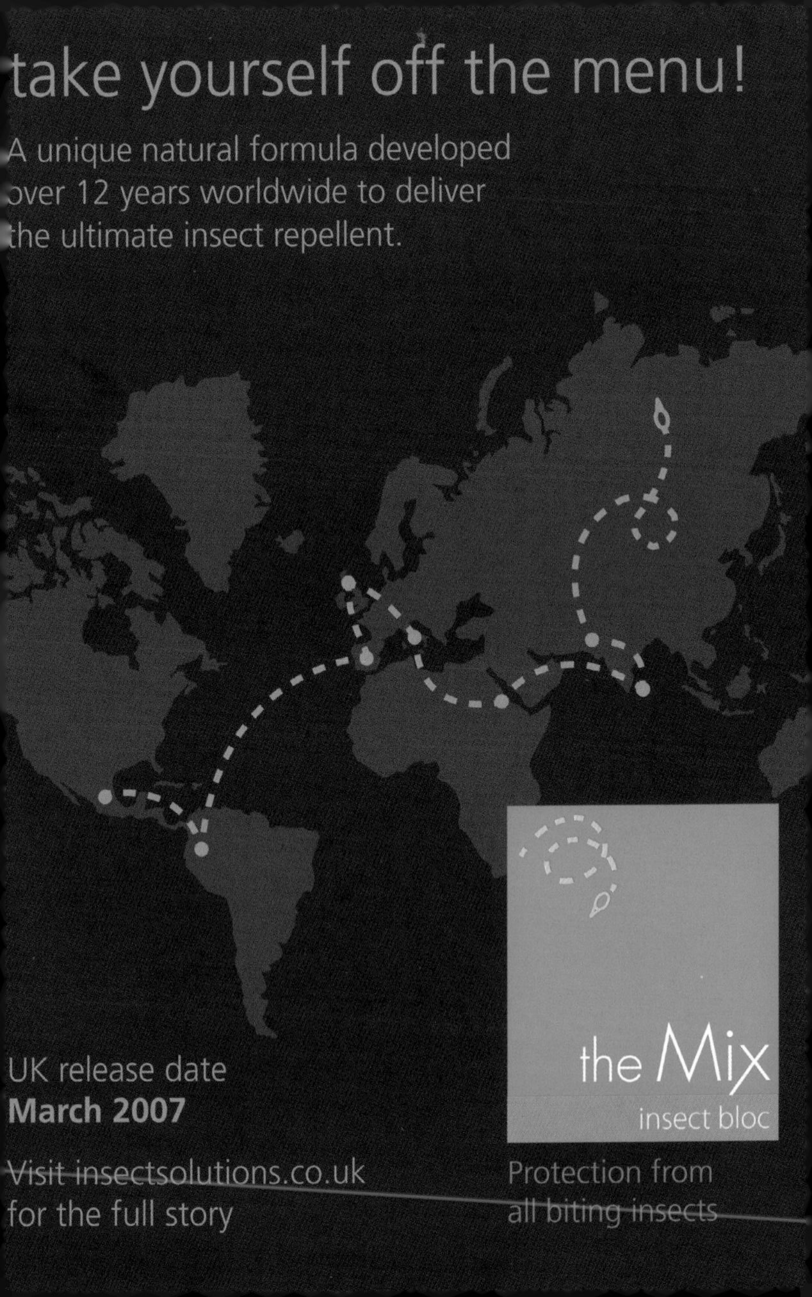
take yourself off the menu!
A unique natural formula developed over 12 years worldwide to deliver the ultimate insect repellent.
the Mix
insect bloc
UK release date
March 2007
Visit insectsolutions.co.uk for the full story
Protection from all biting insects

Gogarth & Lleyn

For many climbers the glorious sea cliffs of Gogarth are the pinnacle of the Welsh climbing experience. Here you can test yourself against a vast array of adventurous and sometimes serious routes. Gogarth definitely suits the more competent climber; many of the routes are tidal and loose rock is often encountered. There is little in the lower grades, and a degree of experience and composure is required to deal with the infamous Gogarth 'grip' factor.

Holyhead Mountain and, to a lesser extent, Rhoscolyn offer a less committing option for those looking for a more relaxed day at the crag.

The climbing style is defiantly traditional, and often multi-pitch. A large rack, prussiks and/or rope-ascending devices are advisable on all of the sea cliffs. Many of the approaches are made by abseil, which are safest when done with an extra static rope.

A copy of the tide timetable is also essential for any of the tidal cliffs. These can usually be picked up from the local climbing (or watersports) shops. There are also numerous online tidal prediction websites, which will help you plan your seaside adventure.

Seasonal Conditions: Gogarth is a useful bad weather alternative. When the mountain crags are besieged by rain, the weather out on the coast can be surprisingly benign. The cliffs are invariably west or south-facing suntraps, permitting climbing throughout the year. In fact in the mid-summer sun, it can be unbearably hot, especially on sections such as Main Cliff.

Getting There: Anglesey is served by a modern dual carriageway, which allows quick access to and from the Gogarth and Rhoscolyn area. Holyhead itself is also well served by the public transport network - see directions for negotiating Holyhead by car on page 353 (South Stack area) and page 386 (North Stack area).

Access Restrictions: A number of the cliffs are subject to a seasonal bird ban. Please read the intro sections of the individual crags for more details.

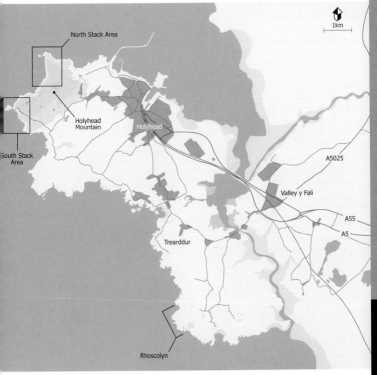

North Stack Area

Holyhead
Mountain

Holyhead

South Stack
Area

A5025

Valley y Fali

Trearddur

A55

A5

Rhoscolyn

1km

Looking across Red Wall to South Stack lighthouse photo: Si Panton <
Silvia Fitzpatrick and Lou Wilkinson taking shelter from the mid-summer sun on the Upper Tier photo: Ray Wood ∧

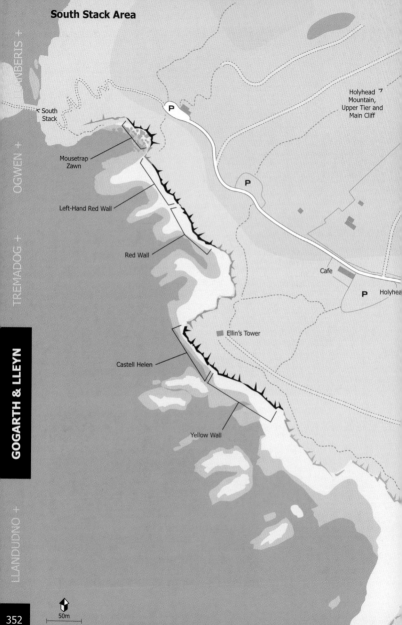

South Stack Area

South Stack

LLANBERIS +

OGWEN +

TREMADOG +

GOGARTH & LLEYN

LLANDUDNO +

Mousetrap Zawn

Left-Hand Red Wall

Red Wall

Castell Helen

Yellow Wall

Ellin's Tower

Cafe

Holyhead Mountain, Upper Tier and Main Cliff

Holyhea

50m

Getting to the South Stack Area: Take the A55 dual carriageway directly into Holyhead. Once in the town follow the road straight through, passing the large clock tower on its right side. Continue until you reach a left hand turn signposted for South Stack (Prince of Wales Road). Follow this road to a mini roundabout; turn left here up Walthew Avenue, as instructed by the South Stack signpost. Turn right at the next T-junction (again signposted) and follow the road out of Holyhead. Continue through open countryside for 2km until a signposted right turn presents itself. This leads directly up to the South Stack car parks.

∧ Streaky Desroy setting off on the top pitch of **The Moon** E3 5c, Yellow Wall photo: Mia Axon

Yellow Wall

Area:	**South Stack**
Style:	**Trad (2-3 pitches)**
Aspect:	**South-West**
Rock type:	**Quartzite**
Approach:	**5 minutes**
Altitude:	**20m**

Ludwig	E6
The Cow	E5
Dogs of War	E4
The Moon	E3
The Sind	E3
Creeping Lemma	E3
The Savage	E2

A steep and exciting crag criss-crossed by a herd of thrilling routes. In his Extreme Rock essay recounting an ascent of *The Moon*, John Kirk described Yellow Wall as "...a dusty, rotten chaos." Perhaps a little over-dramatic, but it's true that the rock quality is rather 'variable' in places. Although the featured routes are well-travelled and most of the loose stuff has already parted company with the cliff, occasional sections of soft dusty talc will be encountered. That being said, in general the rock feels more dependable than that which is typical to the looser sections of the nearby Red walls and Mousetrap Zawn. This is a good job really, because the angle of the cliff often dictates that you actually have to pull quite hard on some of those holds!

The geometry of the cliff is confusing; an array of intersecting diagonal angles serves only to disorientate the lonely leader and his/her anxious second. Surrounded by optical illusions it is difficult at first to tally the abundance of 'in-balance' positions that can be found, with the overwhelming steepness. Yet somehow, magic perhaps, it is possible to creep along slabby ramplines that dissect the bulging undercut rock like absurd stairways suspended in the air. Nonetheless, with the ever present exposure snapping at your heels, you will be especially thankful of the prussic loops clipped to the back of your harness, lest you part company with the crag and find yourself stranded, spinning slowly in space.

As far as a rack goes, volume and diversity is the key, especially if you fancy a pop at *Dogs of War.*

Conditions: As a south-west facing suntrap, the crag does dry quickly, except for the start of P1 on *The Cow* which is often damp. The routes are non-tidal, but a high tide does compromise the 'adventurous' approach to *Creeping Lemma.*

Approach: From a spike 30m south-west of Elin's Tower, arrange an abseil to ledges on a vegetated slope at the left side (looking in) of the crag. Scramble across to the base of your chosen route. (For *Creeping Lemma* see the route description for access details.)

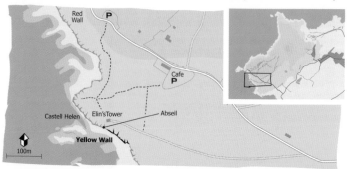

∧ Ben Bransby shuffling into the P2 crux on **Creeping Lemma**, E3 5c photo: Adam Long

⌐ Elin's Tower photo: Si Panton

Yellow Wall • South Stack

1. The Savage E2 5b 48m

An excellent outing, oft bypassed for the glories of the more famous adjacent routes, but well worth seeking out.

P1 15m From the base of the abseil line, easy climbing leads up to the base of the groove proper.

P2 5a 15m Overcome a pinnacle feature and continue up the groove, before moving out right on to the wall and climbing up to a small overhang capping the groove. Traverse right and pull onto the slab above. Belay further right below a short groove.

P3 5b 18m Go up the groove for a few moves; head diagonally leftwards, then upwards to reach a rightward trending weakness leading to the top, or follow a crack direct to finish.

[L E Holliwell, L R Holliwell 01.06.69]

2. The Moon E3 5c 80m

Quintessential Gogarth classic tiptoeing through spectacular territory.

P1 4c 15m Climb the steep juggy corner to a comfortable ledge.

P2 5c 35m Traverse out right along the diagonal band of slabs, moving up at 6m to gain and climb a steep wall rightwards, around an arête on to a narrow perched slab. Shuffle rightwards up the slab to gain a groove. Descend this and move right to a belay stance. (Don't forget to protect the second.)

P3 5b 30m Move up rightwards, then go left over some overhanging blocks. Climb up and follow the groove line to the top, all in a fantastic position.

[E Drummond, A Barley (4 pts) 17.06.71, FFA: J Allen, S Bancroft 1974 or A Sharp, B Hall 73/74]

3. The Cow E5 6a 67m

A steep and strenuous fight on P1 precedes an incredible P2, which takes a thrilling line through some impressive ground. A contender for one of the best pitches on Gogarth!

P1 6a 37m Move up to the overhanging crack. If it's damp, expect a battle (and perhaps an aid point!). If not, it's still a bit of a grapple! Either way, swarm up, then rightwards along the traverse line into a corner. Nip around the right arete and continue up to *The Moon* belay.

P2 5c 30m Move carefully through the overhang above the stance, then over a further roof to enter a groove, which leads to a slab and the top.

[D Pearce, P Trower 26.06.76/10.07.76, FFA: J Healey or P Gomersall 1980]

4. Ludwig E6 6b 52m

Another magnificent route, slowly building in difficulty to its awesome top pitch.

P1 5a 15m Move up to beneath the jutting roof and follow the highest ramp rightwards to take a belay below and to the right of a small cave in the bulging wall above.

P2 5c 10m Move left across the groove, then climb up to the right side of the small cave. Traverse out left and make tricky moves up an arête. Steep, but juggier, rock leads up right to *The Moon* belay.

P3 6b 27m Head left from the belay, then up and left again to the base of an attractive groove. Entry to the groove is guarded by a stiff move. Once past this initial test, zigzag up, picking the easiest line. The climbing is stubborn and pumpy, but reasonably protected if you can hang in there and find all the gear.

[M Fowler, M Morrison (3 pts) 07/08.08.78, FFA A Pollitt, S Andrews 10.05.84]

5. Dogs of War E4 5b 71m

A wild trip through some very challenging territory. Take a large rack as people have been known to run out of gear on the top pitch!

P1 5b 28m Follow the middle diagonal line leading rightwards (beneath *Ludwig*, but above *The Sind*), moving up a little when forced to, eventually reaching a belay on the *Creeping Lemma* traverse. A serious pitch.

P2 5b 43m Move carefully up steep ground on large but suspect holds, moving right to a bottomless recess (possible belay). Move right around the arête onto the steep upper wall. Climb up to ledges and finish direct.

[M Howells, P Trower (1 pt) 05.76]

Kalahari

Abseil

Direct
Finish

GOGARTH & LLEYN

6. The Sind E3 5c 74m

This striking diagonal line, slashing across the crag, provides a stunning and unforgettable route.

P1 5a 37m Follow the diagonal tramlines rightwards to reach a belay on the ridge.

P2 5c 37m The diagonal slab succumbs to some dusty shoulder udging in its lower parts, then cool steadiness in its upper section. A cracking pitch.

[J Brown, P Crew 28.10.66]

7. Creeping Lemma E2 5c 108m

A fantastic counter-diagonal to *The Moon* and similar in quality and difficulty too. It is common, and arguably preferable, to forego the rambling P1 by climbing P1 of *The Sind* instead. Purists wishing to embrace the full 'adventure experience' should take the low tide scramble approach: approximately 200m south-west of Elin's Tower a path drops steeply down leftwards (facing out) to sea level. Traverse back to the crag, passing through a tidal tunnel and scramble up to the base of the route. Alternatively, if the tide is high you could reach the same point by abseiling from a point close to the top of *The Sind*. (The abseil rope then provides a welcome back up to the poor belays.)

P1 4c 50m From a position above the cave (poor belays) traverse left across the grey wall along a series of ledges. After 35m a groove is reached. Follow this up right to belay on the crest of the ridge. Rope drag can be a real problem on this pitch, so make sure you extend all runners.

P2 5b 18m Climb easily across leftwards to the end of the ramp. Move left on to the slab and make alarming moves across an undercut corner and pull blindly round leftwards to gain easier ground and *The Moon* belay.

P3 5c 40m Move left and ascend a groove, then traverse left along a narrow perched slab. (This section being *The Moon* in reverse.) Move up and commit to a hard sequence leftwards underneath the overhang. The groove on the left leads to the top.

[A Sharp, S Humphries 10.74]

LLANBERIS +

OGWEN +

TREMADOG +

GOGARTH & LLEYN

LLANDUDNO +

∧ Looking south towards Penlas Rock photo: Si Panton

< Harry Pennells on the top pitch of **The Moon** E3 5c photo: Adam Long

Castell Helen

Area: South Stack
Style: Trad (1 - 4 pitches)
Aspect: South-West
Rock type: Quartzite
Approach: 5 minutes
Altitude: 0m (tidal)

Kalahari	E3
Atlantis/True Moments/Freebird	E2
North West Passage	E1
Lighthouse Arête/Blanco	HVS
Lighthouse Arête	VS
Rap	VS

A charming and relatively amenable introduction to the Gogarth experience. As the least intimidating of the South Stack sea cliffs, Castell Helen has always been a popular venue. It hosts a fine selection of mid-grade routes which can be accessed by a quick abseil. In contrast to the neighbouring Red and Yellow Walls, the rock quality is quite conventional, although there is an element of deterioration towards the cliff top. The routes are generally well protected and never overly steep.

Conditions: A sunny, south-west facing and exposed crag, which dries quickly. It is not unusual to grab a route here on a sunny winter's day. At low tide a rock platform is exposed beneath the base of the crag, however it is normal (assuming a calm sea state) to approach the routes even at mid – high tide by taking a belay above the water level.

Approach: Walk down in front of Elin's Tower to a cliff top ledge at the right side (facing out) of the crag. There is an abseil point on a short wall equipped with numerous pegs. Do back the pegs up when constructing your belay. A 60m abseil will easily get you to the large niche at the start of *Lighthouse Arete* (this is situated 8m above the low tide rock platform), or the small ledge at the base of *Rap* (situated just to the left of the right arête of the lower face). At low tides the rock platform beneath the cliff can be reached with the same 60m rope. Alternatively, it is possible to split the abseil at the halfway platform, although care is needed with pulled ropes getting tangled in the rocks beneath the sea surface. It should also be born in mind that because the easiest escape route is VS it is safest to leave your abseil rope in place.

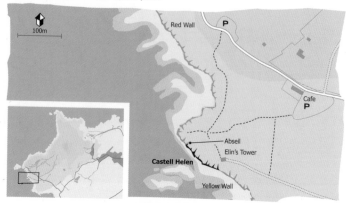

∧ Jon Ratcliffe enjoying winter sun on **Rap** VS 4c photo: Jethro Kiernan

∧ Small strong friends on the tide line photo: Ray Wood

Castell Helen

1. Lighthouse Arête VS 4c 72m

This charming excursion is the first true step in the Gogarth apprenticeship. Although a friendly enough route, it has a hint of the more chaotic adventures yet to be savoured.

P1 4a 20m Head out left from the niche and follow a diagonal line to a ledge on the arête.

P2 4c 25m Climb the crack directly above to reach a guano covered ledge below an overhang (good runners). Pull through the overhang into the hanging crack/groove and continue up to a ledge.

P3 4a 27m Trend up rightwards to reach and follow a broken ramp that leads back to the abseil point. Take care with the rock on this section.

[A G Cram, M Yates 08.10.66]

2. Lighthouse Arête Direct/Blanco HVS 5a 62m

A big satisfying pitch connecting the best parts of the two routes.

P1 5a 45m From the niche wander up the wall past a crack to a cone-shaped groove. Bridge up and pull out right to below the final overhang of *Blanco*. Turn the overhang on the right and continue, without much gear but on good albeit weird holds, up to a stance on the arête.

P2 4a 17m Climb the top section on P3 of *Lighthouse Arete*.

[Blanco: J Brown, D E Alcock 15.09.66]

3. Rap VS 4c 65m

A steep and open route with superb climbing; it feels quite hard for the grade.

P1 4c 28m From the small ledge at the base of the white wall, sprint up the wall on positive holds to finish up a steep groove leading to the middle of the platform.

P2 4b 37m Climb up the wall above the middle of the platform to reach a ledge. Step left to gain a line of holds, then move slightly back right to a crack and shallow groove, which leads up to the abseil point.

[P Crew, D Alcock 08.10.66]

P1 of *Pel* VS 4c provides a good alternative starting pitch to routes 3, 4 and 5 (see topo).

4. North West Passage E1 5b 70m

A fine route with a thrilling top pitch.

P1 5a 27m (Start as for *Rap*) Move onto the wall, trending leftwards initially, then heading directly up to a vague groove, which leads up to the left side of the platform.

P2 5b 43m From the right side of the platform move up to a horizontal break at 6m. Traverse rightwards for a few metres, then step up to the higher break. Move up left with difficulty into a short open groove. Climb the groove to a bulge then step left onto the front face of the pillar. A ledge and crack system leads directly to the top in a fantastic position.

[J Moran, A Evans, G Milburn, N Siddiqui 01.05.78]

5. Atlantis/True Moments/Freebird E2 5b 92m

A brilliant combination yielding a continuously interesting and exciting route.

P1 5a 28m To reach the start, either abseil directly down the corner, or traverse round from the ledge at the base of *Rap*. The corner provides a superb, sustained pitch leading to the right side of the platform.

P2 5b 30m Drop back down the corner for 3m, then foot-shuffle rightwards along the break for a few metres, before dropping down and hand-traversing out right to a rest at 12m. The wall above is difficult at first, but it gradually eases as a leftward trending line of better holds takes you across to a belay beneath the overhang.

P3 5b 34m Break through the overhang, where it narrows on the left, to gain a small groove. Traverse right on the lip of the overhang for a few metres, then head up and diagonally rightwards, eventually finishing up an easy groove.

[J Brown, D E Alcock 16.09.66/A Hyslop, D Knighton 01.05.78/A Evans, N Siddiqui, G Milburn, J Moran 27.03.78]

Abseil

GOGARTH & LLEYN

Pel

Castell Helen

6. Kalahari E3 5c 73m

An atmospheric and engaging trip, sneaking through some impressive territory on a less travelled part of the cliff.

P1 4b 10m To reach the start scramble across from the bottom of the *Atlantis* corner. Follow the gangway up right then pull through the steepness to reach a small ledge on the right.

P2 5c 45m Move awkwardly right onto the steep nose, and climb directly up through bulging rock to gain easier ground. Traverse diagonally rightwards to an arête and gain the groove above. Trend up rightwards to slabby rock and a belay below the headwall.

P3 5b 18m Climb up the groove then traverse out right to gain the top of the block. Finish directly up the thin crack.

[J Brown, P Crew (3 pts) 02.10.66/top pitch added by G Birtles, J Brown, B Ingle 1967]

Lee Roberts on the top pitch of **North West Passage** E1 5b photo: Jethro Kiernan ∨

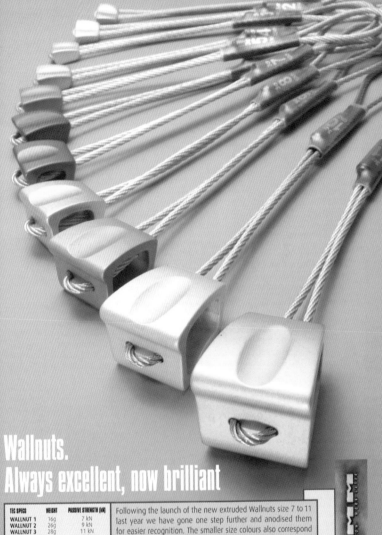

Wallnuts.
Always excellent, now brilliant

TEC SPECS	WEIGHT	PASSIVE STRENGTH (kN)
WALLNUT 1	16g	7 kN
WALLNUT 2	26g	9 kN
WALLNUT 3	28g	11 kN
WALLNUT 4	30g	12 kN
WALLNUT 5	34g	12 kN
WALLNUT 6	40g	12 kN
WALLNUT 7	40g	12 kN
WALLNUT 8	45g	12 kN
WALLNUT 9	50g	12 kN
WALLNUT 10	56g	12 kN
WALLNUT 11	68g	12 kN

Following the launch of the new extruded Wallnuts size 7 to 11 last year we have gone one step further and anodised them for easier recognition. The smaller size colours also correspond to DMM Peenut equivalent size and the labels too are orientated so you can clearly see the size when the nuts are hanging on your harness. Simple but brilliant!

Lighter, same strength and features, and easier to select! What more could you ask?

www.dmmwales.com

Red Wall ®

Area: South Stack
Style: Trad (1 - 5 pitches)
Aspect: West
Rock type: Quartzite
Approach: 5 minutes
Altitude: 20m

Rapture of the Deep	E4
Blue Remembered Hills	E3
Fantasia	E3
Redshift	E3
Television Route	E3
Red Wall	E2
Wendigo	E2

A mesmerising cliff, ineffably serious, yet utterly compelling. This vast sheet of plumb vertical, rusty red rock, hosts an impressive roster of adventurous routes. Parallel sandy troughs, gouged into the hard iron oxide crust, soar skywards. Within these dusty chimneys nervous climbers shuffle upwards, unloading slings onto bizarre gargoyles and clipping ancient stubs of ironmongery. Loose rock will be encountered, although much of the less-attached material has been shed from the popular routes. Out on the faces, a more conventional style of climbing is found. The rock is cleaner and seemingly solid, however complacency is likely to be punished, so be careful.

A large rack, including a full range of cams and perhaps a dozen slings, is sensible, particularly for the chimney routes.

Conditions: Sunny and west-facing, the crag can be expected to dry quickly after rain.

Approach: Abseil to the central promontory from stacked blocks, above a short slab. *Television Route* can be reached directly in one diagonal abseil. For the other routes, a grassy corner, 20m above the sea (the starting point of *Redshift*), can be reached by using a longer rope or a second abseil rope. From here, a roped scramble gains ledges at the base of the wall. It is also possible to abseil directly down the wall using an 80m rope.

Access restrictions: There is a bird ban from 1st February to 31st July.

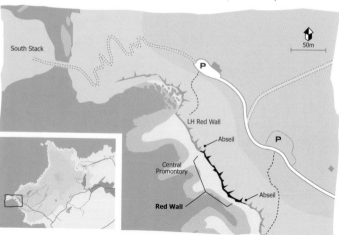

∧ Chris Parkin seconding P1 of **Blue Remembered Hills** E3 5c photo: Steve Long
↖ The upper section of Red Wall photo: Al Leary

Red Wall

1. Television Route (with the Safer Start) E3 5c 45m ®

Once upon a time a sacrificial lamb for the world of broadcasting, this route was beaten into submission with much ironmongery. It was later freed and is now recognised as a minor classic. Start from the right side of the large sloping ledge, by two loose spikes. Ascend to a peg, pass it on the left, until it is possible to move right to a sandy area below an overlap. Traverse right below the overlap to gain the main groove line. (A more direct start is possible, but it is very loose and scary.) Follow the groove, passing various rusting relics from the original aided ascent. Surmount a loose bulge and head leftwards to a plethora of pegs and an improvement in the rock quality. Move right into a groove beneath an overhang. Continue up the groove, past 2 overlaps, to a small ledge on the right. Climb the short wall, and finish up a groove, past the last remnants of scrap metal.

[J Brown, I G MacNaught-Davies (A1) Easter 1966, FFA: J Moran, B Wintringham, P Williams 08.78]

2. Redshift E3 5c 86m ®

A fine, yet challenging route, with a sense of relentless urgency on P2.

P1 5b 37m From the bottom of the 2nd abseil ascend slabby rock to gain leftward-trending cracks. Follow the cracks and, then head rightwards up to ledges and a large block belay.

P2 5c 37m Climb directly up, then weave right and then back left to reach a groove directly above. Follow the groove with sustained difficulties to a ledge on the left. Move up right to a sloping stance (junction with *Wendigo*).

P3 4c 12m Ascend leftwards into the continuation groove, which leads to the top.

[P Littlejohn, H Clarke 08.05.76]

3. Red Wall Escape Route VS 4c 116m ®

Not particularly recommended, but worth knowing about should your plans go awry.

P1 4c 20m Start from block belays on the right side of the wall. As for *Wendigo* P1.

P2 4b 30m Start initially as for *Wendigo*, but quit the upwards line and follow the diagonal break leftwards eventually reaching the sloping ledge at the base of *Television Route*.

P3 6m Stroll left and take a belay on the ramp.

P4 4b 45m Ascend the slabby, loose, grass-tufted ramp to the bottom of a slab.

P5 4a 15m The slab leads easily to the top.

[J Brown, D E Alcock 15.09.66]

4. Wendigo E2 5b 81m ®

A fantastic route following the most striking line on the wall. No real desperate bits, but pretty sustained, even the top pitch is a bit unnerving!

P1 4c 20m Start from block belays on the right side of the wall. Move left into the sandy shallow groove, and follow the easiest line of resistance to a sloping ledge.

P2 5b 50m Climb the obvious leftward-trending break above, to a shallow depression (possible belay). Continue up the emerging corner feature to reach a belay on the 3rd sloping ledge, on the left at the base of the top corner.

P3 4b 11m Move back right into the groove line and carefully pick your way to the top.

[J Brown, A J J Moulam 06.09.66]

5. Blue Remembered Hills E3 5c 73m ®

A fine open wall climb.

P1 5c 45m Start as for *Red Wall*, going up the shallow right-facing corner to the ledge, then move up for a few metres before gaining a groove on the left. At the top of the groove, step left and ascend the wall to a large flake (peg). Continue up until the line leads into *Wendigo* then follow this to the sloping ledge and poor belay (size 3 cam).

P2 5c 28m Trend rightwards past a downward-pointing flake, then move into a hanging groove which leads to a sloping ledge (peg on the right). Hanging flakes allow access to the groove above. From its top continue very carefully (much loose rock) to the top of the crag.

[G Tinnings, P Trower 01.08.80]

6. Rapture of the Deep E4 5b 70m Ⓡ

A demanding, yet deeply rewarding route. This is very much the unconventional end of the rock climbing spectrum. Expect soft rock, bizarre features and sustained difficulties. Start at the block belay, described previously.

P1 5a 25m Start as for *Red Wall*, going up the shallow right-facing corner to the ledge, then move rightwards across the steep wall to reach a diagonal quartz break. Follow this past 2 small bulges, to a recess. There is an old bolt belay and a loose spike.

P2 5b 45m Shuffle, squirm and tiptoe up the obvious sandy chimney, slightly to the right of the belay. You may see some pegs on the way.

[J Brown, B Wintringham, M Wintringham 13.09.78]

7. Red Wall E2 5b 77m Ⓡ

A true Gogarth classic. If you only do one route on this wall, let it be this.

P1 4c 34m Start at the blocky ledge on the right (further right than *Wendigo*). Go up a shallow right-facing corner to a ledge. Ascend the steep groove on the right, pulling round to a small stance on the right.

P2 5b 23m Shuffle up the diagonal line leftwards, until it turns tricky. Hard moves lead across the steep wall leftwards to gain a shallow chimney. Move up a metre or so to an alcove peppered with various bits of ageing ironmongery. A memorable belay position, I'm sure you will agree!

P3 4c 20m Continue up the steep chimney line, and follow the groove above moving right to finish.

[J Brown, P Crew 02.09.66]

8. Fantasia E3 5c 79m Ⓡ

A tremendous wall climb, which escapes out of *Red Wall*.

P1 4c 34m As for *Red Wall* P1.

P2 5c 45m Follow *Red Wall* for 10m, then move rightwards across a disturbingly sandy cave; from its right side pull round onto the red wall. Ascend directly, then trend left to reach a small hanging groove. From the apex of the groove, make bold and tricky moves leftwards to larger holds and easier ground leading to the top.

[B Wintringham, M Wintringham (1 pt) 28.10.78, FFA: J Moran, P Williams 1979]

Left-Hand Red Wall ®

Area:	**South Stack**
Style:	**Trad (1 - 3 pitches)**
Aspect:	**West**
Rock type:	**Quartzite/Siltstone**
Approach:	**5 minutes**
Altitude:	**20m**

Schittlegruber	E5
Heart of Gold	E5
Cannibal	E4
Pagan	E4
Deygo	E3
L-Hand Red Wall	E3
Anarchist	E1

A magnificent but, undeniably serious cliff. There is an abundance of excellent wall climbs on this tremendous sweep of rust coloured rock, which forms the sister wing to the neighbouring Red Wall. The climbing style shifts from strenuous and occasionally terrifying on the steeper and looser lower wall, to thin and elegant on the more compact rock of the upper pitches. Although much of the protection is reasonably conventional, it makes sense to carry a sizeable and diverse rack, including some large cams. The routes demand a cool and steady approach, and will probably be best appreciated by experienced climbers well versed in the vagaries of loose rock.

Conditions: As a west-facing suntrap, the crag dries quickly, although a few stubborn seepage lines have a tendency to linger in the lower breaks.

Approach: To access routes starting on the left side of the wall, abseil to the left-hand promontory from a huge spike near the left edge (looking in) of the wall. To reach the abseil block, cross the wall by the main car park and follow a vague path down to the cliff top on the edge of Mousetrap Zawn. Once on the promontory, a careful descent of the grassy ramp beneath the wall will land you beneath your chosen line. For *Anarchist* abseil to the central promontory from stacked blocks, above a short slab. If a spare rope is not used, care should be taken to ensure that the ropes pull through.

Access restrictions: There is a bird ban from 1st February to 31st July.

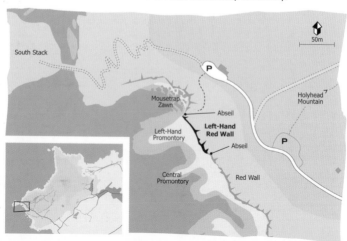

∧ Patch Hammond on **Cannibal** E4 5c photo: Ray Wood
↟ Ellin's Tower, South Stack photo: Adam Long

Left-Hand Red Wall

1. Cannibal E4 5c 43m ®
A fine sustained pitch with a fairly serious start. From the corner, traverse out right just above an overhang (peg). Climb up into a wobbly groove and exit leftwards from its top onto good grey rock (peg). Cruise upwards to a rest in the deep break, then step left, then pull up to some large bubble pockets which lead to a finish up a left-facing groove.
[J Moran, A Evans, P Williams, B Wintringham 06.08.78]

2. Schittlegruber E5 6b 56m ®
A mid '80s Pritchard classic featuring a worrying P1 and a physically taxing P2.
P1 5c 28m Start 8m up left from *Left-Hand Red Wall* where a vegetated groove leads out to join *Left-Hand Red Wall* at the small roof. Swing left and climb a hollow flake, and the wall above, then traverse right to the *Left-Hand Red Wall* belay.
P2 6b 28m Climb up leftwards to an overlap, then up to a ledge on the left, below a slanting groove. Follow the groove, breaking right at its end on to the hairy head wall.
[P Pritchard, N Harms 16.08.86]

3. Left-Hand Red Wall E3 5c 62m ®
Once again, an archetypal pitch combination; P1 is loose, but relatively steady; P2 is technical, but much less serious.
P1 5c 25m Start up a shallow groove, (a few metres above the main slanting overlap). At the roof, go right onto a slab, and move into a shallow rounded groove. A final hard section leads to the belay ledge.
P2 5c 37m Move right and ascend a flake crack to a small ledge. Traverse right (peg) into a shallow niche, then follow a diagonal crack above. Finish straight up the wall to the top.
[J Brown, P Crew (2 pts) 11.06.67, FFA: H Barber 1976]

4. Heart of Gold E5 6a 55m ®
Another elegant wall climb accessed by a strenuous traverse on P1.
P1 5c 17m Go up the initial groove of *Left-Hand Red Wall* for a couple of metres, then make a long pumpy traverse right across the bulging wall to a good resting niche. Above a diagonal crack leads rightwards to a hanging belay.
P2 6a 38m Move up to the overlap (peg), and climb the wall above with difficulty for 3m, before making a delicate traverse right to a short shallow groove. At the top of the groove move left to a good spike. (It is bolder, but arguably easier to reach this point directly.) Follow a diagonal crack rightwards to a niche, where a steep move leads into the diagonal crack of *Left-Hand Red Wall* P2. Finish up this route.
[M Fowler, P Thomas 16.08.78]

5. Pagan E4 5c 92m ®
A magnificent and intricate route that is sustained and quite serious.
P1 5b 21m Start about 25m above the sea, a few metres above where the grass ends. Follow the obvious traverse line right past a small ledge to gain an obvious dusty slanting chimney. Climb up on its right side and pull steeply right to a stance replete with various decaying ironmongery – a size 4 cam is a useful back-up.
P2 5c 28m Climb up for 3m on suspect rock, then move left along a dirty break. Climb the tricky wall above trending slightly right then left to reach a small ramp leading right to a fine hanging belay on a block at its top. (There is also an excellent belay in the bottom of the flake, at the start of P3.)
P3 5c 43m Traverse right along the flake to its end, then climb a depression rightwards to a sloping ledge. Follow the ledge back left until another depression leads up the smooth wall to a deep slot. Zigzag up left then right to gain a vague groove which leads to the top.
[P R Littlejohn, A Houghton 1973]

6. Deygo E3 5c 81m ®

The best line on the wall provides a memorable and challenging route that is both serious and strenuous in places.

P1 5b 21m As for *Pagan* P1.

P2 5b 21m Step right and climb the shallow chimney, moving left over a slight bulge (peg). Continue up the shattered crack to a square-cut ledge, then step right to and climb a groove (peg) to a small stance on easier ground.

P3 5c 24m Climb up above the belay for 3m (peg) to where the angle eases slightly. Follow the striking crack, past a few more pegs, to a belay on the ramp of *Red Wall Escape Route*.

P4 4a 15m The slab leads easily to the top.

[T Proctor, G Birtles (5 pts) 04.68, FFA: R Fawcett, J Heseltine 1973]

7. Anarchist E1 5b 45m ®

An excellent pitch which offers a relatively friendly introduction to the Red Wall experience.

P1 5b 30m From the base of the abseil traverse out left to a series of grooves, and climb up to a detached flake (peg). Climb the diagonal line (peg) then move up right (peg) to a crack, which leads to a belay on the ramp of *Red Wall Escape Route*.

P2 4a 15m The slab leads easily to the top.

[B Wintringham, J Moran 08.08.78]

Mousetrap Zawn ®

Area:	South Stack
Style:	Trad (3-4 pitches)
Aspect:	West
Rock type:	Quartzite/Siltstone
Approach:	5/10 minutes
Altitude:	Sea Level (semi-tidal)

Death Trap Direct	E5
Helmet Boiler	E5
Hysteresis	E4
Mantrap	E3
Mousetrap	E2
Primate	E2
The Green Slab	HVS

A profoundly adventurous crag breached by a range of daring and occasionally bizarre routes. Mousetrap Zawn is certainly a fascinating cliff, initially repellent, yet somehow compelling. The grotesquely folded rock stratum, a mesmerising and fantastical vision of metamorphic geology writ large, presents an intriguing medium upon which to climb. Up close the rock quality is rather 'variable'. In places it forms a soft dusty talc, in others, where the pancakes and gargoyles of iron oxide-rich rock occur, it inspires confidence and offers runners. Differential erosion has gouged deep diagonal troughs and chimney lines across the cliff face. Here you will be glad to find seemingly solid corrugated quartz fins protruding from the softer mutant sandstone.

Predictably, conventional protection is sparse; it makes sense to carry a sizeable and diverse rack, including large hexes, large cams and double your normal quota of slings. A steady and considered climbing method works best in this environment. Some holds simply cannot be trusted; careful weight distribution will help eliminate any undue stress on these less 'attached' features.

Conditions: As a west-facing suntrap, the crag does dry quickly, except for the *Hysteresis* wall, which retains lingering seepage often for days after rain. Most routes are non-tidal, though at high tide, access to *The Green Slab* may be compromised.

Approach: It is possible to approach all the routes at low tide from the lighthouse steps. A hole in the wall on the left-hand side is soon reached. From the next hole continue down the steps, hop over the wall and scramble down ledges to arrive at the base of the golden *Hysteresis/Primate* wall. For routes in the *Green Slab* and *Mousetrap* area it is less committing to abseil in from the large block at the top of Left-Hand Red Wall. A 90m rope will get you on to the boulders in the base of the zawn. Alternatively use 2 shorter ropes and make a changeover. To reach the abseil block, cross the wall by the main car park and follow a vague path down to the cliff top where a bird's eye view of your destiny awaits.

Access restrictions: There is a bird ban from 1st February to 31st July.

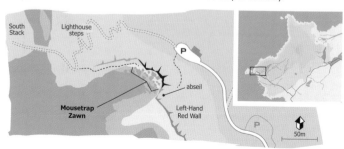

∧ Ben Bransby treading carefully on P2 of **Death Trap Direct** E5 5c photo: Ray Wood
↟ The South Stack lighthouse photo: Si Panton

Approach

Abseil

Mousetrap Zawn

1. Hysteresis E4 5c 89m ®

A tremendous route, striking a strenuous line up the centre of the horizontally banded, golden wall.

P1 5c 37m Climb easily up the centre of the wall for 6m and over a slight bulge to a reddish band. Move up through this to a horizontal break, and then climb up rightwards to gain the large guano-stained break. Trend leftwards through the upper bulge to gain a layback flake (crux) and pedal up this quickly to arrive at a decent belay ledge.

P2 5c 37m Move up into the large niche, and then move up and right then back left with a hard move to gain the sentry box. Continue up the wall and trend left to belay in a chimney.

P3 4c 15m Follow the unprotected arête to the top and belay well back from the edge.

[L E Holliwell, B Whybrow (3 pts aid) 31.10.71 Lawrie returned in 1973 and freed the route.]

2. Primate E2 5b 96m ®

Another fine route. A steep and wild first pitch precedes well positioned, but easier climbing.

P1 5b 34m Traverse out right to the arête and move up to a ledge. Swing around rightwards on to the overhanging face and climb diagonally rightwards for a few metres before cutting back up left to regain the front face; all very strenuous and trying. Move up past a ledge into a groove, which leads to a belay on a pinnacle.

P2 4c 25m Squirm up the entertaining groove above and exit rightwards on to the slabby wall right of the arête. Continue up, staying 3m right of the arête to a belay stance.

P3 4c 37m Climb to the top, following the left side of the arête.

[J Brown, I G MacNought-Davies (1 pt. aid 13.05.67]

3. The Green Slab HVS 4c 117m ®

A bold and rewarding route tackling the prominent green slab in the centre of the crag: quite serious, particularly in its upper reaches.

P1 4a 27m Start at the base of the massive open groove right of the bottom of the main slab. Climb the slabby, but steepening outer left wall of the groove to reach a crack; move up this a few metres until a traverse line leads out left to the arête. Step around (possible belay) and follow the crack feature up left wards, moving left into the dusty corner/groove. A high runner and a spike belay provide a less than perfect belay.

P2 4b 45m Move right onto the main slab and wander upwards through a series of funky rock features, eventually gaining a 5m left-facing corner groove. Move up the groove carefully to arrive at a belay stance on a corrugated shelf. Belay: thin threads left and right and a bomber hex just above the next ledge immediately above.

P3 4c 45m Traverse right for 5m and make worrying moves up the steep wall to gain a large diagonal trough (useful thread and spike to protect your second) that is followed leftwards (rather spectacularly) to an unnerving exit onto the upper muddy slopes. Continue up the slope (carefully) to reach a belay.

[S Wroe, D Crilly, P Braithwaite 05.06.65]

4. Helmet Boiler E5 5c 100m ®

A wild and intimidating route, sneaking through some outrageous terrain.

P1 4c 25m Start 6m to the left of *Mousetrap*, at the foot of a groove leading to an overhang at 12m. Climb up to a ledge level with the overhang, move left under this to a groove, which leads to a tricky belay at a steepening.

P2 5c 30m Ascend the pocketed right-hand wall above trending right to gain the arête which is followed to a peg beneath some overhangs. A horrifying traverse leads right for five metres to a lonely ledge where it is possible to pause and regain composure. Carefully exit from the ledge trending slightly right, peg, until a traverse line leads leftwards beneath overhangs (via a flake edge) to the edge of 'The Green Slab'.

P3 4b 30m Follow the edge of the slab to belay at its top.

P4 5a 15m Surmount a bulge, and go right over another bulge into a groove.

[M Fowler, A Saunders 09.09.84]

5. Mousetrap E2 5b 128m ®
A classic adventure breaking through some very impressive territory.
P1 5b 45m An intimidating and audacious lead. Start left of the large overhangs at a pillar left of a large grey groove. Gain the top of the pillar by a groove on its left and place the high side runner. Climb back down into the large grey groove and make committing moves rightwards across the wall to gain the hanging chimney. Move up this for a few moves before escaping out rightwards into another corrugated chimney. Quit this for another chimney to the right and continue up to easier ground and follow a slab leading rightwards to a large belay stance beneath the steep main wall.
P2 5a 46m Climb diagonally rightwards up the wall to gain a leftward-slanting groove. Pull up around a bulge to gain a further parallel groove and follow this to a break. Continue up the easy leftwards leading ramp line to belays at its top.
P3 5a 37m The steep red headwall looms above the ramp. Move up into a niche above the belay and step right on to the wall. Continue up diagonally right to gain a groove that is followed to the top.
[J Brown, P Crew (2 pts. aid) 09.10.66]

6. Mantrap E3 5b 119m ®
A superb route, focussing upon a short steep chimney that splits the centre of the attractive upper red wall. There is an independent start that scales the lethal tottering pillar to the right of the cave, but most people opt for a more agreeable start up *Mousetrap*.
P1 5b 45m As for *Mousetrap*.
P2 5a 24m Climb diagonally R-wards up the wall to gain a L-ward slanting groove. Pull up around a bulge to gain a further parallel groove and follow this to a break. (*Mousetrap* goes left from here up the ramp.) Move right to belay on a sloping ledge.
P3 5b 30m From the left side of the ledge, climb diagonally left, over a bulge, and up into the overhanging sandy chimney. Wriggle up this and out onto the red wall. Move right until you can climb straight up to reach a belay on the right.
P4 5b 20m Traverse right for 3m, move up and left over a bulge and trace a weakness rightwards onto easier ground.
[original P1 and P2: L E Holliwell, L R Holliwell 17.05.69. P3 and P4: L E Holliwell R J Isherwood 26.05.69 (1 pt aid – FFA unknown)]

7. Death Trap Direct (with the Direct Start) E5 5c 77m ®
A magnificent route that bluntly accepts the serious challenge of the prominent central slanting chimney in its entirety. Warthog pegs are recommended (for P1), as well as a double rack of cams and perhaps a dozen slings.
P1 5c 20m The Direct Start: This start gains the main slanting chimney at the earliest opportunity. Start by the right-hand side of the cave. Climb up right of the cave to a ledge on the left, level with the lip of the cave. Arrange warthog protection and make a long and committing span left onto the wall and left again to gain the main diagonal line. Climb up this to the *Mousetrap* belay.
P2 5b 45m Climb straight up the slanting chimney past a worrying steepening. Continue in the same line until the chimney steepens again, then climb straight up to enter an easier corner, which leads onto the slabby ramp on *Mousetrap* P2. Follow this to the same belay.
P3 5a 12m Surmount the bulge above the stance then go up to a right-facing corner and finish straight up.
[C Waddy, G Hughes 1988 Direct start: W Perrin, P Robins 2003]

Holyhead Mountain

Area:	Holyhead Mountain
Style:	Trad (single pitch)
Aspect:	South-West
Rock type:	Quartzite
Approach:	15 minutes
Altitude:	150m

Katana	E4
Sai Dancing	E3
Bran Flake	E2
Breaking the Barrier	E1
King Bee Crack	HVS
Bruvers	HVS
Tension	VS
Black and Tan	VS

A sunny crag with easy access and a relaxed ambience that contrasts markedly with the seriousness of the nearby sea cliffs. Although the atmosphere is friendly, the routes themselves pull no punches. True to the intense 'outcrop' style, they demand a physical and pushy approach. The rock is generally solid and clean.

Conditions: A quick-drying suntrap, even in winter!

Approach: From either of the small car parks at the end of the South Stack road a path or a track leads off right (the path and track soon join). Continue towards the microwave relay stations, and bear rightwards past them. The crag now presents itself a few hundred metres directly ahead.

Descent: For Yellow Wall, come down gullies on either side of the crag. For Quartz Wall, walk back rightwards to descend a short wall, then double back down a gully, which abuts the right side of the buttress.

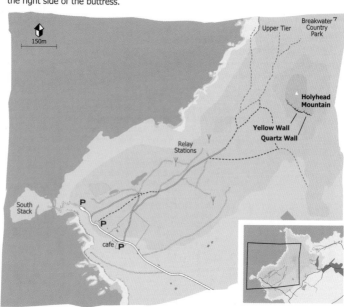

∧ Leanne Callaghan on the thin slabby wall of **Breaking the Barrier** E1 5b photo: Graham Desroy

⌐ Approaching Holyhead Mountain, showing the right side of the crag photo: Graham Desroy

Yellow Wall is situated at the right side of the broken escarpment that constitutes the Holyhead Mountain Crag.

1. Bran Flake E2 5b 30m
An urgent, pumpy pitch: requiring a forceful effort from the leader.
Ascend the outside of the chimney for 3m before stepping right to a scoop, which leads to a bulge. Pull through this leftwards to gain the steep crack; race up this to reach easy ground on the upper slab.
[K Robertson, S Robertson 31.01.81]

2. King Bee Crack HVS 5a 37m
An essential classic, tackling the appealing crack line. Initially climb the crack just right of the main crack to a small ledge at 5 metres, then move left and follow the main crack to a crux bulge that guards access to the easier upper slab.
[first ascent unknown]

3. Katana E4 6a 37m
The diagonal crack provides a superb and sustained outing. Climb the wall just left of the crack past an overlap to gain the crack, which is followed into the top of *King Bee Crack*.
[J Redhead, K Robertson 1982]

4. Sai Dancing E3 6a 37m
A brilliant direct line that swaggers up the crag at its highest point.
Start as for *Katana*, but continue directly up the wall to reach the halfway ledge in the groove on the right (which is taken in its entirety by *Penny* E3 5c). Climb up the groove past 2 old pegs, then head diagonally right (tricky) to a thin crack. Go up this to good holds and a peg, and then move diagonally left to climb an overhanging groove (also tricky). Finish up easy ground.
[M Gresham 18.06.88]

< Louise Thomas on **Katana** E4 6a photo: Ray Wood

Holyhead Mountain • Quartz Wall

Quartz Wall is situated 30m right of the prominent Yellow Wall (the right side of the crag).

5. Tension VS 4b 25m
This fine route is well supplied with runners and friendly holds.
Climb up the central corner to the large roof. Move left past a block and ascend a groove to a bulge. Large holds allow a swing left to gain the finishing crack.
[first ascent unknown]

6. Black and Tan VS 4c 28m
The striking diagonal line provides a great climb. Follow *Tension* to the roof, then trace the diagonal crack up rightwards beneath the roof, to a steep and daunting finale.
[first ascent unknown]

7. Breaking the Barrier E1 5b 25m
A delightful and intricate climb, which weaves a line up the centre of the attractive quartzy wall.
From a few metres right of *Tension*, move up and right to a large triangular foothold. Continue up the thin crack above, stepping right to follow another thin crack line to a good hold. Finish up a steep, shallow corner.
[J Donnelly 1980]

8. Bruvers HVS 5a 25m
The striking crack line proves to be somewhat brutal in execution, unless of course you have good technique!
[first ascent unknown]

∧ The thin slabby wall of **Breaking the Barrier** E1 5b photo: Ray Wood

Working up the corner on **Black and Tan** VS 4c photo: Graham Desroy ∧

Getting to the North Stack Area: Take the A55 dual carriageway directly into Holyhead. Once in the town follow the road straight through, passing the large clock tower on its right side. Continue until you reach a left hand turn signposted for South Stack (Prince of Wales Road). Follow this road to a mini roundabout; For North Stack go straight across this mini roundabout, and straight across the next mini roundabout. Then take the left turn immediately on the left (signposted Breakwater Country Park). Follow the narrow road over numerous speed bumps to the car park on the right at the end.

It is customary to approach the Upper Tier and Main Cliff from the South Stack car parks (see page 353 for directions through Holyhead to South Stack).

∧ Mia Axon venturing out on the final pitch of **A Dream of White Horses** HVS 5a, Wen Zawn photo: Graham Desroy

North Stack Area

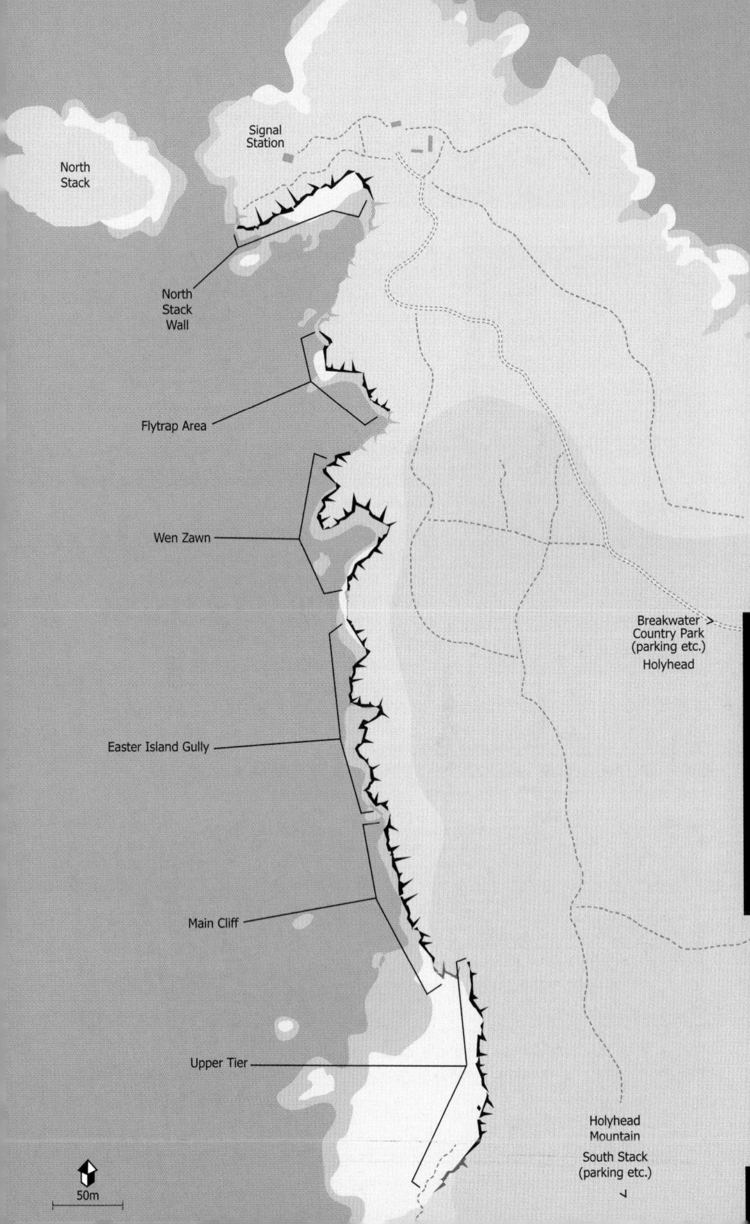

LLANBERIS +

OGW...

Signal
Station

North
Stack

North
Stack
Wall

Flytrap Area

Wen Zawn

Breakwater >
Country Park
(parking etc.)
Holyhead

GOGARTH & LLEYN

Easter Island Gully

Main Cliff

Upper Tier

Holyhead
Mountain

South Stack
(parking etc.)

50m

Upper Tier

Area:	**Gogarth Bay**
Style:	**Trad (1-3 pitches)**
Aspect:	**West**
Rock type:	**Quartzite**
Approach:	**20 + 10 minutes**
Altitude:	**100m**

Energy Crisis	E5
Run Fast, Run Free	E5
The Cruise	E5
Strike	E4
Winking Crack	E3

Fail Safe	E2
The Eternal Optimist	E2
The Strand	E2
U.F.O.	E2
Fifth Avenue	E1
Park Lane /	
Doomsville Connection	E1
Bloody Chimney	HVS
Central Park	HVS
The Gauntlet	HVS
The Ramp	HVS

Bezel	VS

A superb and popular section of Gogarth, with many striking and classic routes. It is non-tidal, but still a good deal more serious than the nearby Holyhead Mountain. The rock, although mostly solid, can be quite creaky and unnerving, even on the more popular lines highlighted here. Moreover, the approach path itself will be enough to unsettle the first time visitor. The routes on the left side of the crag are often done as extensions to one of the routes below on the *Emulator* section of Main Cliff. Mix and match however you desire.

Conditions: As a south-west-facing suntrap, the crag dries quickly.

Approach: From either of the small car parks at the end of the South Stack road a path or a track leads off right (the path and track soon join). Continue towards the microwave relay stations, and bear rightwards past them. (The Holyhead Mountain crag can be seen a few hundred metres directly ahead.) Once past the microwave stations keep following the left-hand branch on any splits in the main track. The path trends left and up to a blunt crest from where the Main Cliff and North Stack crags can be seen. Continue bearing leftwards and descending slightly, to reach a gearing-up spot at the top of a steep gully. Once you've racked up and hidden your rucsac from view, drop down the gully and follow a broken and occasionally collapsed path across the steep hillside beneath the crag. The routes are described from right to left, as approached from the descent gully.

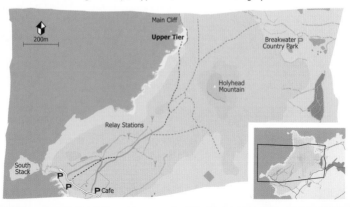

Descent: From the finish of all the routes scramble up to join a path contouring back across the upper slope above the crag. Follow it southwards to a heather and rock step. Just beyond the path divides; the right fork leads down to a short rocky gully dropping in to the gearing up area at the top of the approach gully. It is also possible to follow a gentler, but more circuitous route around to the left, then cutting back right to the gearing up area.

∧ Tal Niv bridged out on the Upper Tier classic **Strike** E4 6a photo: Phil Dowthwaite
↖ Shag Rock photo: Ray Wood

Upper Tier • Left-Hand

LLANBERIS +

OGWEN +

TREMADOG +

GOGARTH & LLEYN

LLANDUDNO +

390

1. Strike E4 6a 57m

A fierce pitch requiring an aggressive approach. At the bottom of the descent gully an obvious light coloured wall presents itself:

P1 6a 37m Climb up and make a hard move left establishing yourself on the line of the twin diagonal cracks. There is a poor rest in the middle of the next section, but it is normal to arrive at the final crux sequence (leading into the slabby groove above) pumped out of your brains. It is common to belay and abseil retreat from here. If you make it, continue up the slabby groove and wide crack on the right to reach a belay on top of the flake.

P2 4c 20m The obvious crack leads to the top.

[R Edwards, E Fry (5 pts) 24.05.66, FFA: P Gomersall, S Foster 1976]

The attractive wall to the left is taken directly by *Barbarossa*, an impressive route, which unfortunately is pushing E7 now that the peg has gone from the lower wall.

2. Bloody Chimney HVS 4c 60m

For some a fine route of great character. To others a perverse caving trip with an appropriate name!

P1 4c 22m From the foot of the slabby corner climb the crack and chimney to a sloping ledge.

P2 4b 18m Slide back into the chimney and press on past a large chockstone on the right until you pop out on top of the huge flake.

P3 4c 20m P2 of *Strike*.

[D E Alcock, D Potts 24.04.66]

3. U.F.O. E2 5b 60m

A good route with absorbing climbing.

P1 5b 25m Go up the slabby corner for 8m then follow a thin crack (a bit creaky) on the right wall, then continue up to a pinnacle. Descend rightwards to belay in the chimney.

P2 5b 35m Move back up to the pinnacle, then follow a line of grooves and cracks to a ledge. Up left is a crack, which leads to a niche and then the top.

[L E Holliwell, F Quigley, L R Holliwell 04.11.67]

4. Run Fast, Run Free E5 6a 68m

The pumpy crack on P2 provides a premier stamina test.

P1 4c 25m Climb the slabby corner for 15m, then head diagonally leftwards across the slab to belay below some short cracks.

P2 6a 43m Traverse back across the slab to reach the soaring crack line in the steep wall. Follow the crack leftwards past a pod, stepping right to a continuation crack which will take you to the top.

[D Knighton, J Girdley (2 pts) 27.10.78, FFA: P O'Donovan 1980]

5. The Cruise E5 6b 55m

Another strenuous and popular crack pitch.

P1 6b 37m Scramble up from the path to belay in a corner. Step left and go up the arête to a small ledge underneath the crack. Move into the crack and follow it past pegs to a brief resting position beneath the short chimney that guards access to the ledge above - medium sized cams serve to protect the inevitable tussle.

P2 4c 28m Easy slabs and vegetated ledges lead to the top.

[Originally with aid (*Nod*) by D Durkan, P Sandell 08.70, FFA: J Moran, P Williams, J Sonczak 1984]

6. Winking Crack E3 5c 67m

A notorious route with a gripping offwidth finish.

P1 5a 30m Scramble up from the path to belay on a large ledge. Move right and start up the first corner on *The Cruise*, traversing left around the arête and climbing up left to follow a groove until a block belay can be reached on the left.

P2 5c 37m Follow the crack to a ledge on the left where it divides. Continue up the left branch to a small overhang. Move left, then back right, before heading up the cracks to the final offwidth section. Summon every ounce of pent up aggression that you have within you and thrutch upwards with gusto (cowards and spoil sports can avoid this ultimate character test by striding out right on to the right arête).

[J Brown, A Cowburn (6 pts) 05.06.66]

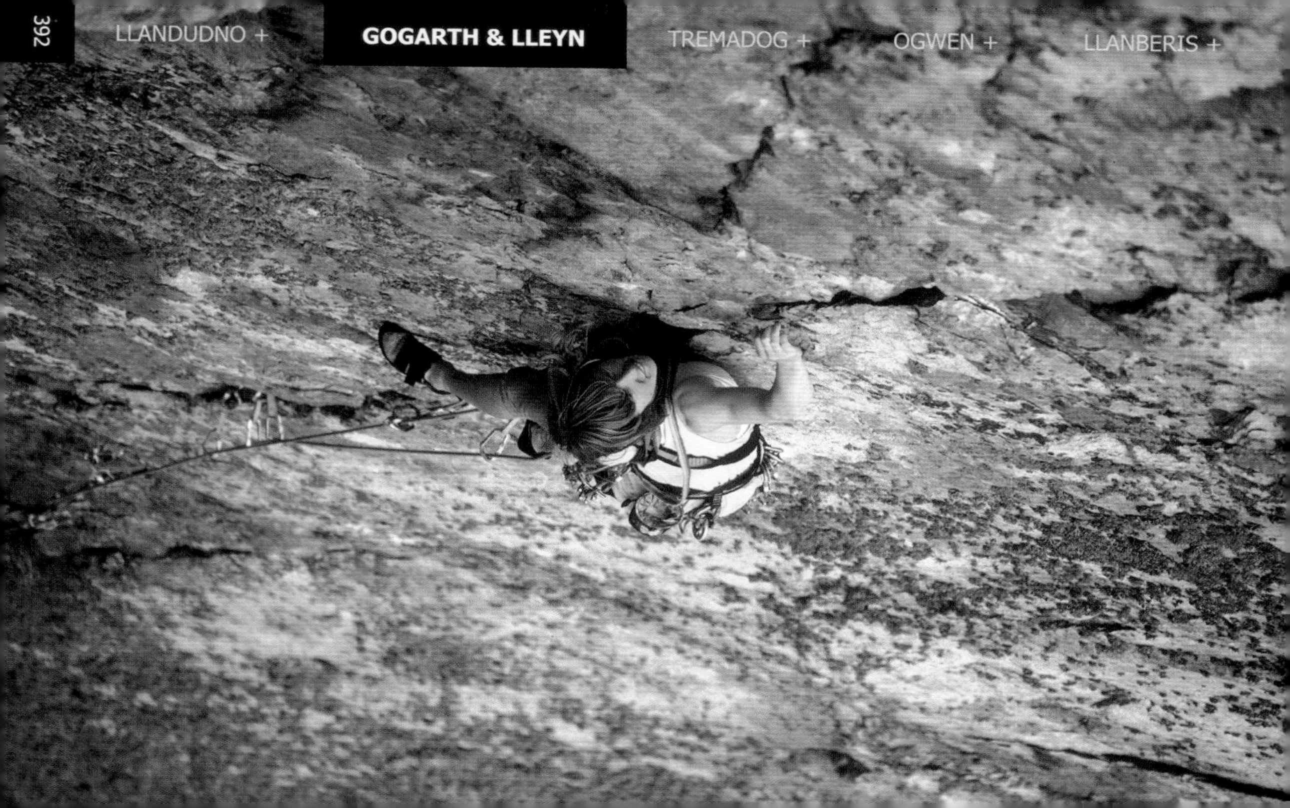

7. Fifth Avenue E1 5c 70m
A superb route, extremely varied and unrelenting 'til the very end.
P1 5c 40m Climb the chimney on the left side of prominent pinnacle (Shag Rock) until it is possible to move into the bulging groove that runs up leftwards. Layback the groove and gain the upper ramp via a precarious high step (crux). Follow the sustained ramp/groove (past a spike) to reach a spike belay below the upper wall.
P2 5b 30m The faint groove in the short wall proves to be steeper and harder than it looks. Scramble up for 25m to a big flake at a level/worn area.
[M A Boysen, M Yates 14.05.66]

8. Central Park HVS 5a 60m
An excellent route with contrasting pitches.
P1 4c 30m Start in a small niche at the left side of the short rock traverse on the path. Go up the slabby wall on the left to reach a shallow groove, leading to a ledge on the left. Move up right to gain and follow a leftward-trending line and steep groove to a wall. Ascend the wall and traverse back right delicately to reach a hanging belay at the base of the main crack.
P2 5a 30m Waltz up the crack to face a tricky section near the top. Belay on a ledge in a niche. Scramble up to a big flake at a level/worn area.
[P Crew, D E Alcock (10 pts) 14.05.66]

9. The Strand E2 5b 73m
A stunning and enticing pitch: sustained and well protected.
P1 5b 43m Move up right to gain the crack line, which is followed to a belay below a short slab. An abseil descent is often made from here.
P2 4b 30m A short slab leads to a scramble for 25m to a big flake at a level/worn area.
[E Drummond (1 pt) 01.10.67]

10. Park Lane/Doomsville Connection E1 5b 85m
A classic and popular combination.
P1 5b 30m Start initially as for *The Strand*, but trend up leftwards to below a bulge. Move up left with difficulty, then step back right into the crack which leads to the top of the flake.
P2 5b 25m The diagonal ramp trending up right proves to be harder than it looks. At its top a short crack leads up to *The Strand* belay below a short slab.
P3 4b 30m P2 of *The Strand*.
[L E Holliwell, L R Holliwell 22.10.67/M Yates, A G Cram, J Yates (2 pts) 19.05.67]

From the base of *The Strand/Parklane* a path drops down towards Main Cliff. A narrow, but reasonably obvious, continuation of the Upper Tier base path continues contouring across, then rises to reach routes 11 - 16:

11. The Gauntlet HVS 5a 50m
The attractive groove line left of the large yellow scar provides a superb route.
P1 5a 40m Follow the groove over a bulge then to a small ledge. Move left and follow the groove again, moving right into another groove leading to a stance on the right.
P2 4b 10m Move back into the groove on the left and finish up the steep corner crack to a broken ledge.
[P Crew, B Ingle 02.05.64]

12. The Ramp HVS 5a 55m
Another striking line yielding a fantastic route. Hard for the grade.
P1 5a 30m Climb up the pinnacle then step right on to a ledge. Ascend the corner, then climb the slab to reach spikes on the left. Move over a bulge and up to a large spike at the top of the ramp. Traverse left to belay below a steep corner.
P2 5a 25m Ascend the crack in the corner, then make blind moves right into the base of a bottomless chimney, which leads to the top.
[P Crew, J Baldock 24.04.66]

13. Energy Crisis E5 6a 58m

Wild, steep and pumpy! Thankfully this amazing route is well-endowed with protection (at least on the first pitch).

P1 6a 28m Blast up the steep wall to gain an undercut flake (useful kneebar). Swerve left across the wide crack with some improvised manoeuvres and keep on trucking (before the pump becomes overwhelming) for the belay on the ramp.

P2 5c 30m Make bold and tricky moves rightwards into the base of the hanging groove, which leads more easily to the top.

[P Whillance, D Armstrong 01.05.78]

14. Fail Safe E2 5b 53m

This funky route is steep and sustained, with just enough gear (including some slings for the spikes).

P1 5b 28m Follow the narrow slabs up left past a quartz spike to reach an overhang. Harder moves lead back right and up past small ledges to *The Ramp* belay.

P2 5a 25m P2 of *The Ramp*.

[D E Alcock, P Crew (1 pt) 07.05.66]

15. The Eternal Optimist E2 5b 47m

Another steep and engrossing route tackling the obvious corner crack leading up to an overhang.

P1 5b 37m A steep start gains the crack; follow it with the aid of some large holds on the left, and pull through the overhang with difficulty. Easier climbing and a wide crack leads to a ledge and belay on the left.

P2 4c 10m Finish up the wide crack on the left.

[A Sharp, S Humphries 06.02.75]

16. Bezel VS 5a 50m

A pleasant route with a short tricky bit on P2.

P1 4b 15m Climb up to the top of the pinnacle on the left then follow a diagonal crack up rightwards. Move left, then up to a small ledge at the foot of the groove.

P2 5a 25m Make a hard pull past the bulge, then continue up the groove until it is possible to gain ledges on the right.

P3 4b 10m The short crack on the left leads to the top.

[B Ingle, P Crew 25.04.64]

< Leo Houlding racing up **Energy Crisis** E5 6a photo: Ray Wood

Main Cliff

Area:	**Gogarth Bay**
Style:	**Trad (1-6 pitches)**
Aspect:	**South-West**
Rock type:	**Quartzite**
Approach:	**20 + 20 minutes**
Altitude:	**0 - 30m (mostly tidal)**

The most impressive cliff, not only at Gogarth, but arguably in the whole of the North Wales area. This magnificent swathe of overhanging rock rearing up out of the sea provides some of the most thrilling and fantastic rock climbs that you will ever do.

The lower two thirds of the cliff is blessed with solid fused rock, its heavily featured surface rounded back by the elements to leave a confusing array of open pinches, hidden undercuts and sloping cracks. On first acquaintance it can be hard to read, especially if a route is unchalked.

The quality of the rock deteriorates towards the top of the crag; the upper pitches typically involve some loose rock, which requires a careful approach.

The climbs are invariably unrelenting and deeply physical, demanding high levels of fitness. It's not uncommon to be wiped out for the day after completing one big route!

Although the crag is more conventional than the nearby South Stack cliffs, it is still advisable to carry a large rack.

Skinhead Moonstomp	E6
Citadel	E5
Dinosaur	E5
Hunger	E5
Mammoth Direct	E5
Positron	E5
The Camel	E4
Syringe	E3
The Assassin	E3
The Big Groove	E3
The Rat Race	E3
Aardvark	E2
Resolution Direct	E2
Emulator	E1
Gogarth	E1
Mestizo	E1
Nightride	E1
Cordon Bleu	HVS
Scavenger	HVS

Mia Axon out there on P2 of **Rat Race** E3 5c photo: Graham Desroy >

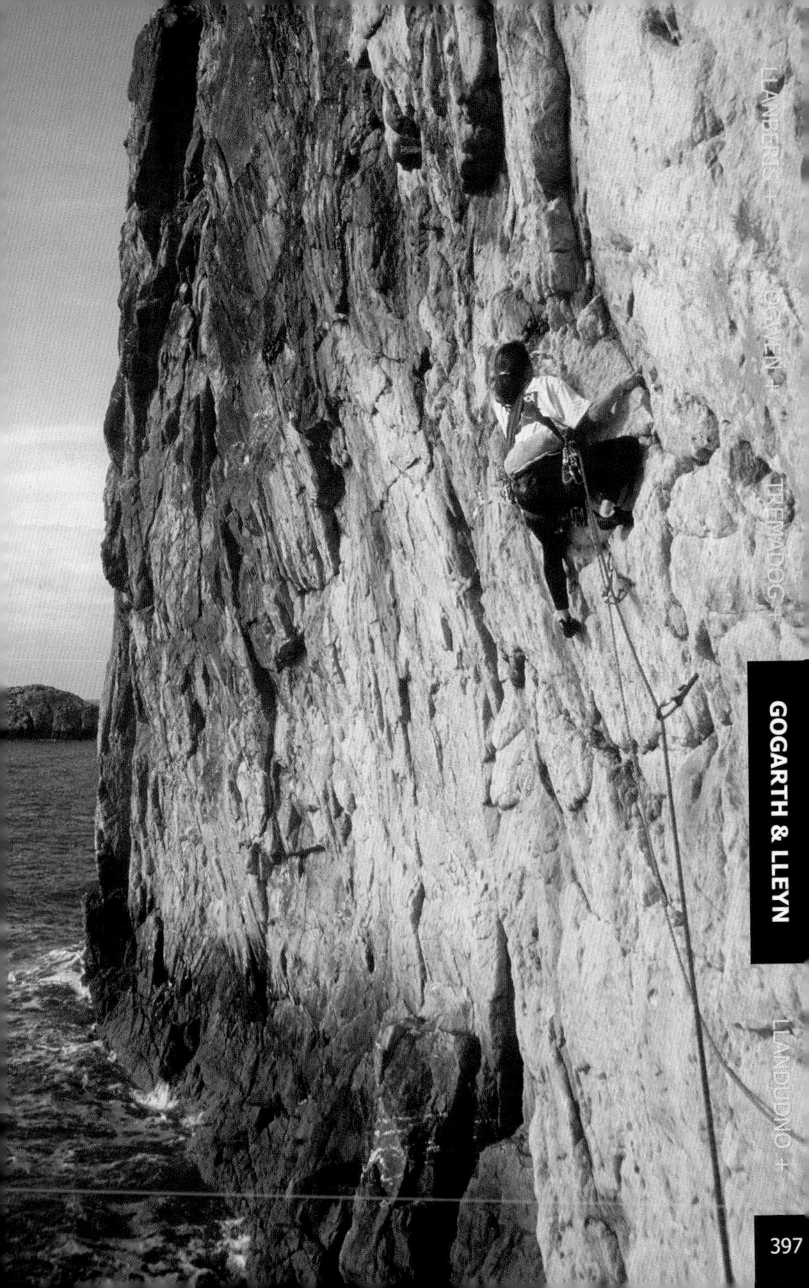

Main Cliff

Conditions: As a south-west-facing suntrap, the crag does dries fairly quickly. However, the best climbing conditions are a tricky call. It is quite common for the lower pitches to be plagued by dampness in the morning (especially on still days). The infamous Main Cliff 'toothpaste' effect makes an unwelcome addition to the already overwhelmingly strenuous nature of the routes. It pays to fill your chalk bag up, or play it smart and wait until the afternoon. Sunlight will help to burn off the moisture from the lower pitches, but may leave you burnt and frazzled as the crag heats up. Routes 1 - 6 can be done during any tide while routes 7 - 20 generally require low/mid tide to get around the pinnacle.

Approach: From either of the small car parks at the end of the South Stack road a path or a track leads off right (the path and track soon join). Continue towards the microwave relay stations, and bear rightwards past them. The Holyhead mountain crag can be seen a few hundred metres directly ahead. As you get closer follow a path bearing leftwards and descending slightly to reach a gearing up area at the top of a steep gully. Once you've racked up and hidden your rucsac from view, drop down the gully and follow a broken and occasionally collapsed path across the steep hillside beneath Upper Tier. From beneath the route *Strand*, a path leads down underneath the *Aardvark* wall.

Just beyond the base of *Emulator*, downclimb a 10m open corner on good holds. Traverse left on ledges to the base of the Pinnacle. At low tide make an exciting traverse leftwards around the foot of the pinnacle to reach ledges on the other side. Thereafter an obvious tidal traverse line runs across the base of the cliff.

Descent: From the finish of all the routes scramble up to join a path contouring back right across the upper slope, well above the top of the crag. Follow it southwards above the Upper Tier to a heather and rock step. Just beyond the path divides; the right fork leads down to a short rocky gully dropping in to the gearing up area at the top of the approach gully. It is also possible to follow a gentler, but more circuitous route around to the left, then cutting back right to the gearing up area.

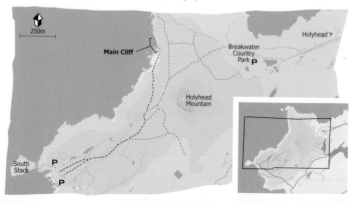

1. Cordon Bleu HVS 5b 144m

A thrilling 'sightseers' trip across the upper section of the Main Cliff. Although largely straightforward in technical terms (the crux wall being a notable exception), this is a serious and adventurous route cutting through some wild and exposed territory. To reach it break off from the normal approach path and head up to the base of *Bezel* on the far left-hand side of the Upper Tier. A steep grass slope leads down to an embedded flake belay on the edge of the Main Cliff. It is probably sensible to rope down this section, as a slip would end with dire consequences. It is also possible to reach the grass slope from one of the routes on the *Aardvark* wall.

P1 4a 38m Descend to an obvious traverse line leading out left onto the slabby face. Keep going until an arête is reached. Pass the arête and climb down a short chimney to a ledge – belay on the far side beneath P4 of *Gogarth*.

P2 4b 37m Climb down and move around the base of the massive flake to reach a corner on the other side. Go up this and traverse out left along the top of the flake traverse line to belay just beyond its apex.

P3 5b 20m The steep wall above blocks access to the corner above with a few powerful moves. Traverse left from the corner along the slabby ramp (not forgetting to place some decent runners to protect your second) to a small exposed stance.

P4 4b 25m Climb up the short chimney above and move across a slab to a large groove. Climb up this to a stance on the arête.

P5 4b 24m Move left and up behind a large flake. A short groove leads to the top.

[G Birtles, P Crew 21.05.66]

Routes 2 – 4 are often done in combination with one of the routes on the left hand side of Upper Tier. (See page 393)

2. Aardvark E2 6a 55m

A clean and popular test piece, with a hard, but well-protected, crux.

P1 6a 30m Start up the wall 5m right of the *Emulator* groove, reaching good holds that lead up left to a thin crack. Follow this with difficulty to gain the *Imitator* traverse. Climb up and follow the left-hand of 2 thin cracks past 2 small overlaps, then move right to good holds in the right-hand crack. Climb it to a small ledge and belay.

P2 4a 25m Easier ground leads to the grassy slope. Scramble up to a belay at the foot of *Bezel*.

[A Evans, G Milburn, B Wintringham, J Moran 23.07.78]

∧ Silvia Fitzpatrick on P1 of **Aardvark** E2 6a photo: Ray Wood
↖ Traversing in beneath Main Cliff photo: Ray Wood

Main Cliff

3. Imitator VS 4c 60m
A good climb; often linked with one of the routes above on the left side of the Upper Tier.
P1 4c 30m Start below the *Emulator* groove. Gain and climb the groove in the arête, thereafter making hard moves out right onto the slabby wall and then up to an obvious line of holds trending rightwards. Follow the traverse line until a short crack leads up to a belay.
P2 4b 30m The shallow groove on the left leads to a small bay. Step right and follow the arête to easy ground. Scramble up to a belay at the foot of *Bezel*.
[B Ingle, G Rogan 27.05.66]

4. Emulator E1 5b 45m
The striking groove line yields a classic pitch; satisfying and sustained! At its top scramble up to a belay at the foot of *Bezel*.
[P Crew, B Ingle 10.05.64]

5. Resolution Direct E2 5c 91m
A stunning route forcing an uncompromising line up the edge of the cliff.
P1 5b 43m Start on the left side of a bay of overhanging, creaky looking rock. Move up left and follow the crack in the arête, then up left into a clean-cut groove, which leads to a belay ledge on the left.
P2 5c 28m Climb the crack in the arête directly, passing a particularly trying section where it pays to spot your footholds before you launch into the sequence. The crack eases above and leads to a good flake and hanging belay in a fantastic position.
P3 5b 20m Bomb up the crack on the left and out onto the top of the block. A tricky groove up and left leads to an easier finishing crack.
[A Pollitt, H Clover 13.03.82]

6. Gogarth E1 5b 109m
An intricate and classic route building up to a dramatic finale on the exposed headwall.
P1 4b 18m Ascend the wide crack on the right side of the large pinnacle to gain a stance on its top.
P2 5a 18m Step down and traverse right across the steep wall to gain a shallow hidden groove. Climb up the groove, keeping left of a small overhang, then traverse back left to take a belay on the sloping ledge.
P3 4c 18m A short crack above the left side of the sloping ledge leads to easier ground. Climb directly to a ledge at the base of a large open groove on the left.
P4 4b 15m The pleasant groove leads quickly to a perched stance at the top of the huge flake.
P5 5b 40m Traverse out right onto the headwall to reach a ledge beneath a thin crack. Tussle upwards past a decidedly physical section to reach better holds. Continue to the top in the same direct line.
[B Ingle, M A Boysen (1 pt) 04.04.64]

7. The Rat Race E3 5c 116m
A challenging and exciting route. Start in the middle of the large ledge left of the Pinnacle. (If the tide cuts off the approach traverse around the base of the pinnacle, then do P1 of *Gogarth* instead.)
P1 5a 12m Ascend the wall, slightly right at first, then heading diagonally right to reach a belay on top of the Pinnacle.
P2 5c 30m Step left and follow the rising traverse line out leftwards, passing a tricky section to gain a chimney groove. Go up this to reach the curving overlap (usually damp). Ignore the rising pump in your forearms and follow a crack leftwards around the overlap to reach a steep slab. Pull up right to belay below an ominous looking chimney.
P3 5b 25m The overhanging chimney proves to be both a physical and psychological test. Do it quickly, before you get too pumped or scared (or both!). Exit right at its top onto the slab, and move up to belay on the flakey traverse of *Cordon Bleu*.

The Pinnacle

Approach to
Cordon Bleu

Bezel

Form

The
Strand

Approach path
beneath Upper Tier

Main Cliff

P4 8m Traverse down to belay at the base of the corner groove.

P5 4c 13m Romp up the corner to reach a perched belay stance on top of the huge flake (top of P4 on *Gogarth*).

P6 5a 28m Step down and head out left to reach a crack. Climb the crack, taking the right-hand branch where it divides, then move left across a rib to finish up an easier crack. A creaky South Stack-style pitch!

[M Howells, B Whybrow (1 pt) 23.07.66]

8. Positron E5 6a/b 105m

A magnificent and legendary route striking an audacious line through some breath-taking territory.

P1 5c 18m Start on the large ledge left of the Pinnacle, just left of *Rat Race*. Climb up rightwards into a scoop, then swerve back left to an obvious flake, and up left again to a small ramp on the arête. Pull over a small overlap and take a belay at the base of the chimney/groove on P2 of *Rat Race*.

P2 6a/b 12m Climb up left through the overlap and make a powerful layback move left from a slippy pinch, then pull round leftwards, below the next overhang, into the groove (this is *Alien*). Follow the groove more easily up to the *Rat Race* belay.

P3 6a 30m Step left, across the void, to the spike and eye the challenge ahead. A diagonal crack leads up left in an incredibly exposed position. Follow the crack, with a crucial shift from its left to right side, until a short traverse left gains a small overhang. Turn the overhang on the left and continue up more easily, stepping left into the groove of *Dinosaur* and follow it to a belay on blocks.

P4 5c 45m P3 of *Dinosaur*.

[A P Rouse, P Minks (5 pts) 03.71]

9. Skinhead Moonstomp E6 6b 108m

An outrageous and profoundly taxing route swaggering up the *Positron* headwall.

P1 6a 25m Ascend the corner left of the lower wall on *Positron*, surmounting a bulge on the left to gain a sloping shelf. Climb up into the overhanging corner above the shelf and traverse out right to a jug near the arête. Swing on to the arête to join *Positron*, pull over a small overlap and take a belay at the base of the chimney/groove on P2 of *Rat Race*.

P2 6b 43m The big lead! Follow *Positron* into the *Alien* groove. Go up the groove for a few metres then traverse out left and move up to a 'resting' position at the base of the looming wall. Climb up and right to gain the bottom of a blind flake. Race up the flake to its top, then continue up past a line of flat jugs to join the diagonal crack of *Positron*. Climb through the crux section of *Positron*, then head directly up to a small corner and a 'bucket seat' belay.

P3 5a 12m Climb up to belay on the apex of the slab on the *Cordon Bleu* traverse.

P4 5c 28m Move right and climb the crack system to the top.

[A Pollitt, S Andrews 12.05.84]

10. Dinosaur E5 6a 105m

A strenuous beast of a route, taking a very direct line up the cliff. The section after the chimney, on P1, feels quite committing. Take a big cam and avoid during humid conditions.

P1 6a 30m Start up the right-hand of 3 chimney lines. Climb up to the top overhang and make wild moves left to reach the arête. Continue up still very pumpy ground to reach a small stance.

P2 5b 30m Step right and follow the steep groove up the left side of the *Positron* headwall, all the way to reach a belay on blocks.

P3 5c 45m Climb the steep wall above to gain the corner above (as for *Cordon Bleu* P3). Traverse out right and up grooves in the arête, making an awkward exit up a shallow groove on the left. Scramble up the slope to reach a belay in the rock wall on the left, or belay on the last section of rock to avoid rope drag.

[P Crew, J Brown (10 pts) 19.06.66, FFA: R Fawcett 1980]

P3 of **Mestizo** E1 5b photo: Ray Wood >

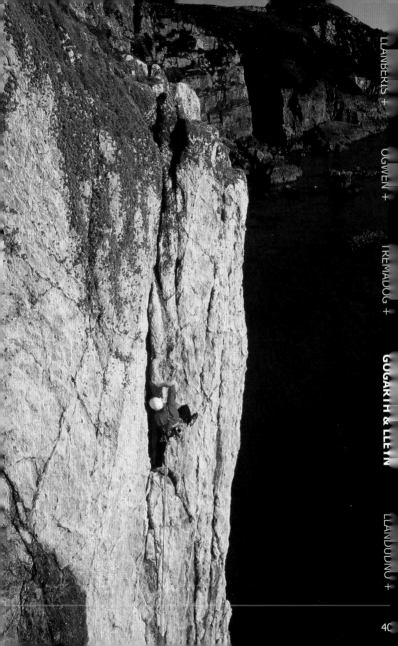

11. Mammoth Direct E5 6b 103m

Another exhausting test piece pushing up through some very steep and difficult terrain.
P1 6b 33m From the raised flat-top block beneath the chimney, move into it and climb up to a roof (large thread). Pull onto the wall, left of the cracks, to reach decent holds and gear. Move back rightwards before harder moves gain insecure holds in the funnel. Get pumped placing more mediocre gear then head up to belay on the left.
P2 5c 25m Move up past a small spike, then head up rightwards to a large blunt spike. Move back left and climb through a bulge. Continue up the easier groove, then move right to reach a belay on blocks.
P3 5c 45m P3 of *Dinosaur*.
[A Pollitt, M E Crook 26.05.84]

Adam Wainwright boxing clever on P1 of **The Camel** E4 6a photo: Ray Wood ∧

Streaky Desroy preparing to launch into the crux on P2 of **Positron** E5 6a/b photo: Mia Axon ∧

Silvia Fitzpatrick bridging up the chimney on P1 of **Mammoth Direct** E5 6b photo: Ray Wood ⚲

Main Cliff

12. Hunger E5 6a 90m

An impressive route with 2 big demanding pitches.

P1 6a 30m The red wall left of *Mammoth* is split by a discontinuous crack. Either climb this crack for 6m and move left, or start just left of the crack and climb direct to the same position. A sequence of fat, slopey pinches gives access to easier ground. Trend leftwards to the niche on *Citadel*. Traverse right for 3m and make some powerful, insecure moves through the roof, continuing up for 3m before moving right to a stance.

P2 5c 42m Climb up the wall to gain a good flake at 12m, then traverse right for 6m, nearly into the grove on *Mammoth*. Trend back up left, then up right to reach a crack line. Follow it to a stance on *Cordon Bleu*.

P3 5b 18m Climb carefully up the right-hand crack above, stepping left after 3m into loose grooves that lead to the top.

[P R Littlejohn, C King 08.06.78]

13. Citadel E5 6b 100m

An utterly stunning route, perhaps the best of the big E5s on Main Cliff.

P1 6b 40m Start a few metres left and down from *Hunger*. Move up the wall and bear leftwards to reach the undercut flakes which lead back right to a niche. Pull out left and make burly moves up past a small undercut, to gain a sloping ledge. Climb up right to belay on a long ledge below the soaring crack line.

P2 6a 35m Ascend the steep wall until a step right gains the crack proper. Work up the crack line, which turns out to be super sustained and pumpy as hell! Eventually, arms permitting, a belay is reached on slabby ground.

P3 4c 25m Climb up the easy groove then go up a loose groove on the right, to reach a belay on the other side of the ridge.

[J Street, G Hibberd (9 pts) 19.11.68, FFA: R Fawcett 1977]

14. The Big Groove E3 5c 113m

As its name implies, this excellent route tackles the huge left-facing groove that splits the upper part of the cliff.

P1 5a 43m Start 6m right of the large square block on the approach traverse. Move up to reach a line of rightward-trending flakes. Follow the flakes to a ledge beneath a short corner. Go up the corner for 3m, then move left into a left-facing corner leading to a ledge on the right. Ascend the short corner above to a large sloping ledge and a belay on the right.

P2 5c 18m From the left side of the ledge surmount a bulge to gain a corner, then head up right (hard) to reach a sloping ledge. Climb up and right to reach and follow the groove above, and its continuation crack/flake. Step left into a shallow niche and make insecure moves up this and on to the sloping ledge.

P3 5b 34m Move left and follow the sustained groove, with a tricky move near the top allowing access to a line of holds leading out left to a stance beyond the arête.

P4 18m Steady climbing leads to the top.

[P Crew, D E Alcock (1 pt) 18.06.66]

15. Syringe E3 5c 91m

A fine route, with engrossing and problematic climbing.

P1 5c 45m From the top of the prominent square block climb the grey wall to the overhang. Move right into a sentry box and make hard moves to pass the bulge at its top into the groove above. Follow the spooky groove to reach a decent-sized ledge on the left beneath the next overhangs.

P2 5c 28m Climb up the wall above, then move right and do battle with the steep and obstinate crack. The crack leads past a bulge to a groove, which in turn leads to a large ledge with a huge leaning block.

P3 4c 18m P3 of *The Assassin*.

[D Scott, R Gillies (7 pts) 11.06.66]

GOGARTH & LLEYN

The Pinnacle

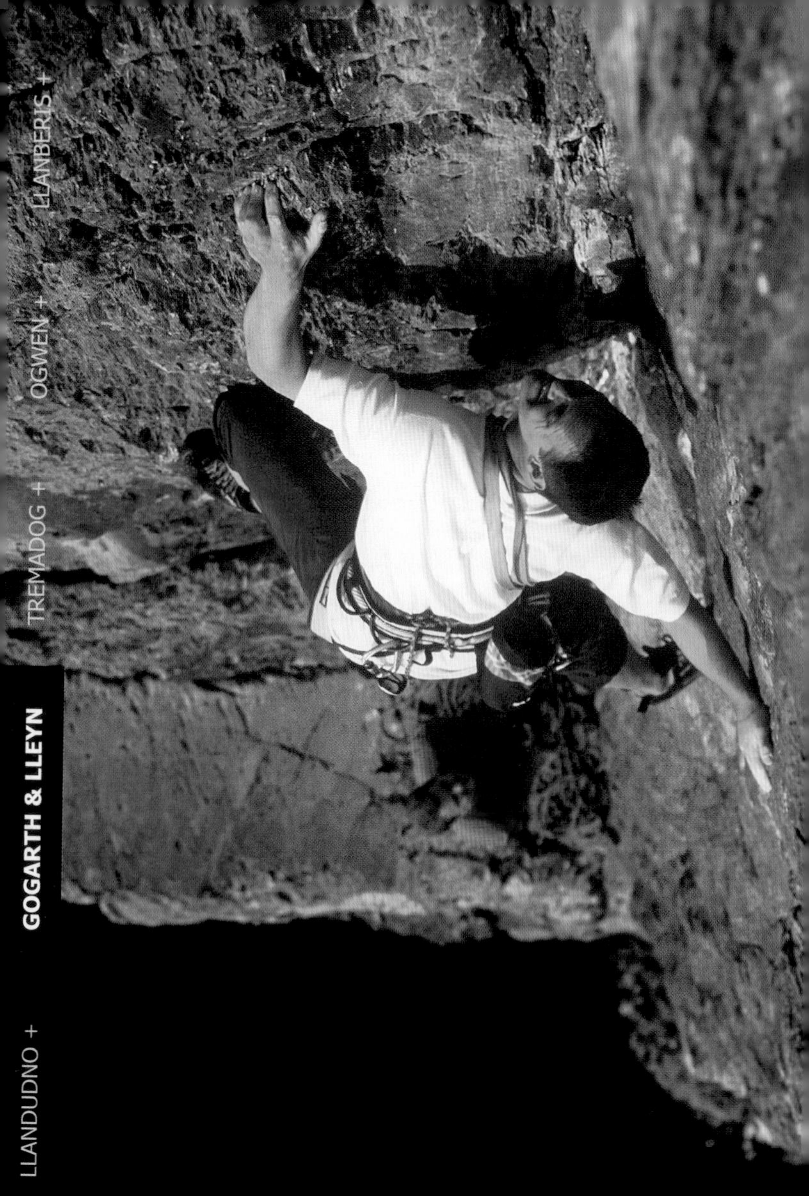

16. The Camel E4 6a 93m

A good old-fashioned Gogarth tussle: loads of gear and a full body pump guaranteed!
P1 6a 45m Start 2m right of the obvious corner, just left of *Syringe*. Follow the crack until 3m below the overhangs. Step left and pull into a bottomless closed chimney, then move right under a hanging fang and follow the crack over the roof. Continue up the groove above to gain the top of a large flake. Drop down right to a stance on *Syringe*.
P2 5b 30m Cross back over to the left side of the flake and trend up leftwards to the arête. Climb up to a sloping ledge where a steep crack leads to easy ground and a large ledge with a huge leaning block.
P3 4c 18m P3 of *The Assassin*.
[A Sharp, J J Zangwill 01.07.74]

17. The Assassin E3 5c 88m

An excellent route with a memorable crux at the top of this impressive wall.
P1 5b 30m Start up the wide, flaring crack 3m right of *Scavenger*. Ascend the crack, then trend rightwards, before climbing the steep wall to reach the left side of a ledge.
P2 5c 40m Go diagonally leftwards up the black wall overcoming a bulge to the left of a corner. Gain a crack on the left then climb diagonally right, continuing up an open scoop. Head up left and make a hard pull on a poor hold to gain easier ground leading to a sloping ledge. Go up a scoop, then easier cracks to a large ledge with a huge leaning block.
P3 4c 18m The left hand of the 2 cracks leads quickly to the top.
[J Moran, G Milburn, A Evans 11.06.78]

18. Scavenger HVS 5a 91m

A brilliant route in every sense. Superb rock, fantastic positions and interesting moves. Start below the right side of the big ledge 8m up on the front of the buttress.
P1 4c 8m Climb the steep wall on positive holds to the big ledge.
P2 5a 43m Go up the corner for 10m, then exit onto a ledge around the arête on the right. Move right to the bottom of a cracked groove – the highlight of the route. Float up the wonderfully exposed groove to reach a ledge.
P3 4a 40m Continue up more easily to broken ground, traversing left to exit up a grassy groove.
[M A Boysen, J Jordan 14.05.66]

19. Nightride E1 5b 92m

Another superb route with a steep and pushy P2.
P1 4c 14m From the right side of the deep bay (containing an overhanging chimney) trend diagonally up rightwards to gain the large ledge on *Scavenger*.
P2 5b 21m Climb up the corner for 3m, then follow the traverse line out left to the overhanging arête. Step up and right to reach a steep crack and race up it with a sense of urgency. A perched stance is soon reached.
P3 4c 27m Head up right and follow a wide crack to grassy broken area. Belay on the back wall.
P4 30m Scramble up to exit up a grassy groove.
[J Brown, G Rogan 26.02.67]

20. Mestizo E1 5b 55m

A terrific route sitting in splendid isolation at the very far end of the cliff.
P1 5a 12m From the left side of the deep bay (containing an overhanging chimney) make a low level traverse left to reach a stance at the base of the large corner.
P2 4c 23m Trend rightwards across the wall to gain a flake crack. Scoot up this to a ledge.
P3 5b 20m The upper crack provides a suitably intense finish. (It is possible to run P2 and P3 together.)
[T Taylor, P Jones 07.09.70]

North Stack Wall

Area: North Stack
Style: Trad (single pitch)
Aspect: South
Rock type: Quartzite
Approach: 15 minutes
Altitude: Sea Level (tidal)

| The Clown | E7 |
| The Cad | E6 |

The Long Run	E5
Blue Peter	E4
South Sea Bubble	E3

| Talking Heads | E2 |
| Nice 'n' Sleazy | E1 |

A prominent blank-looking wall of bleached quartzite sitting adjacent to the mind-boggling overhangs of Parliament House Cave. This smooth open face offers a collection of famously serious wall climbs and some fine mid-grade routes following strong feature lines. Although these routes are in effect easy access and single pitch, they do exude an unsettling air of seriousness. Protection is often spaced, or marginal, particularly on the harder routes, and the rock feels a little creaky, compounding the already bold nature of the climbing. A steady and considered approach seems to work best.

Conditions: A quick-drying suntrap. All routes left of *The Cad* are affected by high tides.

Approach: From the right side of Breakwater Country Park take the path past the left side of the small lake, then turn left and follow the path up a rising incline that runs through the quarries, taking the left fork where it divides. Further uphill the path divides again – follow the right fork down by some telegraph poles to reach the fog warning station on the North Stack promontory.

Access to the routes is via a 40m abseil from the telegraph pole by the side of the white wall. It is advisable to leave this rope in place for emergencies. Failing that *Green Gilbert E1 5a* (see topo) provides a possible escape route. At low tides it is also possible to reach the bottom of the zawn via a tunnel that runs underneath the promontory from sea level on its north side to emerge in the back left corner of Parliament House Cave. This normally involves some wading or swimming!

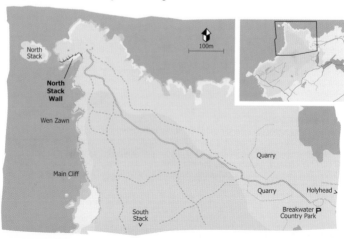

∧ **Blue Peter** E4 5c photo: Phil Dowthwaite
⤒ North Stack promontory photo: Si Panton

North Stack Wall

1. Blue Peter E4 5c 40m
This fine pitch is quite nerve-wracking, but ultimately steady. Move up to the overhang and pull through to the wall above. Trend up left to gain the flake crack, and follow it to a small ledge near the top of the wall. Step left and finish up the short groove.
[P Whillance, D Armstrong 02.09.78]

2. The Cad E6 6a 37m
A bold and sustained wall climb, with a big reputation and a controversial history. It is still possible to thread the head of the old bolt with a wire, but essentially the upper section of the route is pretty run out. Thin slings will be found helpful in protecting the lower section. Start 10m left of *The Clown* below a faint cracked groove running up onto the wall. Move up the crack and head up rightwards to some spike runners at 8m. Climb up and right to gain the undercut flake (in situ thread). Step left, then make difficult moves rightwards across the flake to reach a good foothold by the old bolt stud. Compose yourself, then head boldly up the wall past a blind break to reach a ledge. Easier climbing leads to the top.
[R Fawcett, C Gibb 17.09.78]

3. The Clown E7 6b 45m
The best of the hard routes on the face, cutting a counter-diagonal line to *The Cad*. Considered by the cognoscenti to be soft touch at E7, this is obviously still a formidable lead. Start below a left-facing flake crack/groove, with double overhangs at 8m. Climb up the groove to the roof (peg and size 1.5 cam) and make a burly pull through to gain the next roof. Surmount this and emerge onto the upper face. Traverse left (a reverse of *The Bells! The Bells!*) and move up to the undercut flake on *The Cad*. Step left onto the wall and move up to some undercuts. Make committing and reachy moves up to gain easier ground and a junction with the top of *The Long Run*.
[J M Redhead, D Towse, J Silvester 25.04.84]

4. The Long Run E5 6a 38m
A sustained outing requiring a cool and steady approach. The protection is never great, but the route can be made 'relatively safe' if the effort is made to search out runners. Start up *The Cad*, but break out left at 5m and move up to a thin flake crack. Climb this and the wall directly above to reach good holds at a point where the wall becomes steeper. Traverse right for 3m and surmount the bulge on dinky holds, before trending more easily up left to the top.
[P Whillance, R Parker, D Armstrong 30.09.84]

5. South Sea Bubble E3 5c 35m
A good route tackling the striking flake crack. Move up to the overhang and climb boldly leftwards through it to reach the bottom of the flake crack. Scoot up this to a large ledge. The remaining short wall provides an awkward finish.
[J Moran, S Horrox, A Evans, G Milburn 30.07.78]

6. Nice 'n' Sleazy E1 5a 35m
A very worthwhile pitch taking the obvious crack line, which eases towards the top.
[A Evans, G Milburn, J Moran 29.07.78]

7. Talking Heads E2 5b 37m
An excellent route, unfortunately only reachable at low tide. Start just left of *Nice 'n' Sleazy*, and traverse left just above the water until directly beneath the overhang higher up the wall. Ascend the wall, then follow a crack up to reach the right side of the overhang. Pull over and make an eye-popping stride out left to gain the final crack. The crack, although initially troublesome, soon eases.
[J Moran, G Milburn, A Evans, S Horrox 30.07.78]

GOGARTH & LLEYN

Green
Gilbert
E1 5a

Abseil
Approach

Flytrap Area

Area:	**North Stack**
Style:	**Trad (1-4 pitches)**
Aspect:	**South-West**
Rock type:	**Quartzite**
Approach:	**20 minutes**
Altitude:	**Sea Level (tidal)**

Arachnid	E4
20,000 Leagues Under the Sea	E3

The Flytrap	E2

An isolated section of the cliff with some exceptionally good routes. The atmospheric Flytrap sea cave is a classic feature of the area. A must-do experience for all Gogarth devotees.

Conditions: The crag has a sunny aspect and does dry quickly. However the inner sections of *The Flytrap* are often quite damp. Low tide and a calm sea are desirable for all of the routes.

Approach: From the right side of Breakwater Country Park take the path past the left side of the small lake, then turn left and follow the path up a rising incline that runs through the quarries, taking the left fork where it divides. Further uphill the path divides again. Follow the right fork down by some telegraph poles to reach the fog warning station on the North Stack promontory. From here walk over the top of Parliament House Cave and traverse the hillside to reach the promontory marking the southern entrance into the North Stack Wall zawn. Alternatively the promontory can be reached by walking across from the top of Wen Zawn.

For *Flytrap*, descend a short gully on the promontory and scramble down broken ground to a platform containing some blocks. Abseil 45m to sea level, then traverse across to the base of the route. It is also possible to abseil directly to the top of the first pitch. *Arachnid* and *20,000 Leagues Under the Sea* are best reached by abseiling directly down the wall left (looking in) of the *Flytrap* cave.

Possible escape routes include *Colditz* and *The Hitcher*, both of which are marked on the topo. It is also feasible to follow a slightly tricky sea level traverse at low tide from the base of *20,000 Leagues Under the Sea* round to Parliament House Cave.

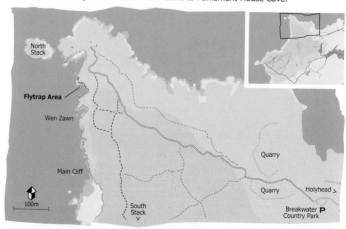

∧ Adam Wainwright and George Smith on P2 of **Flytrap** E2 5b photo: Ray Wood
↟ George Smith back and footing through the steepness on **Arachnid** E4 5c photo: Ray Wood

Flytrap Area

1. The Flytrap E2 5b 82m
An adventurous trip through some exciting territory. It's probably best if both members of the party are happy leading and seconding this sort of grade.

P1 4a 12m From the base of a pinnacle head up left on large holes to gain a ledge.

P2 5a 25m Descend for 5m from the left side of the ledge, then traverse left (slightly descending) on small, but positive holds until the bottom a black groove is reached.

P3 5b 25m Ascend the groove, which is often damp, then follow an obvious traverse rightwards. This is straightforward at first, but then becomes steep with a hard section passing a peg to gain juggy holds on the front face of the huge jammed chockstone at the top of the cave. The stance is just above.

P4 4b 20m Climb the right wall for 6m, then traverse the break rightwards for 6m to reach a crack. Finish up this.

[J Brown, P Jewell, D Cuthbertson (1 pt) 16.04.78]

2. Arachnid E4 5c 30m
An excellent pitch: well geared, yet taking in some rather steep and pumpy ground. Climb the cracked groove in the arête to the break. Swerve right, then chimney up underneath the roof, emerging on its left side to finish up the cracked groove on the left.

[G Smith, G Hughes 05.05.88]

3. 20,000 Leagues Under the Sea E3 5c 30m
Another brilliant pitch. As steep and pumpy as they come! Ascend the groove in the lower wall, then blast up the overhanging crack in the arête.

[M E Crook, D Kendal 29.07.87]

Adam Wainwright with Martin Crook (first ascensionist) on **20,000 Leagues Under the Sea** E3 5c photo: Ray Wood >

GOGARTH & LLEYN

LLANDUDNO +

Wen Zawn

Area: North Stack
Style: Trad (2-4 pitches)
Aspect: North-West
Rock type: Quartzite
Approach: 20 minutes
Altitude: Sea Level (tidal)

Conan the Librarian	E6
Metal Guru / Golden Bough Finish	E4
T Rex	E3
The Quartz Icicle	E2
The Spider's Web	E2
Toiler on the Sea	E2
Spider Wall	E1
A Dream of White Horses	HVS
Britomartis	HVS
The Concrete Chimney	HVS
Wen	HVS

A popular and atmospheric section of the Gogarth sea cliffs. Home to Gogarth's most famous route, *A Dream of White Horses*, which journeys up and across the huge white slab that defines the right side of the zawn. Directly opposite this impressive sheet of rock sits a promontory, which provides a perfect stadium viewpoint of routes on the main slab. The promontory is in fact an archway hollowed out by the erosive power of the winter sea storms. In rough seas the back of the zawn is a boiling cauldron of white water crashing back and forth; plumes of spray can be seen shooting right up the '*Dream...*' slab. Even on calm days the dark underside of the arch and the steep back wall of the zawn still exude a quietly menacing presence. If you've ever wondered what the 'Gogarth grip' was all about, chances are you'll find a little of it here.

The rock quality is predominantly good, but the final sections of all routes and the big traverse on P2 of *Conan the Librarian* are much less trustworthy and should be handled with care.

Conditions: The crag is mostly north-west-facing and does dry quickly once the afternoon sun swings around and burns the moisture off. Damp soapy rock is common on the first pitches of the slab routes in the morning. The chimney/layback on P1 of *T Rex* can be particularly traumatic if at all wet. For routes starting at the bottom of the zawn a low tide and a calm sea is essential.

Approach: From the right side of Breakwater Country Park take the path past the left side of the small lake, then turn left and follow the path up a rising incline that runs through the quarries, taking the left fork where it divides. Further uphill the path divides again – take the left fork again to a small col situated above Wen Zawn. A path leads down to the promontory.

At very low tide it is possible to abseil from the top of the promontory down the face immediately opposite Wen Slab. Skip across boulders at the base of the zawn to your chosen route. If you've missed low tide, or the sea is at all excitable, then it is normal to miss out the first pitches on the first 4 routes (*A Dream of White Horses, Wen, Concrete Chimney* and *Quartz Icicle*) and approach by abseiling in from the right shoulder of the slab. To reach the abseil follow a narrow path, which leads over the top of the slab, and scramble carefully down close to its edge to reach some blocks and an obvious abseil point. (Please remember that any rocks dislodged from the approach path are likely to endanger teams already climbing on the slab below!) Abseil diagonally down the slab for 40m to reach a series of ledges approximately 25m above the sea.

This abseil can also be easily continued down to ledges below the first pitches of '*Dream...*' and *Wen*. These ledges stay dry for a longtime after the boulder hop across the base of the zawn has been cut off by the tide.

For *Britomartis, Toiler on the Sea* and *Spider Wall* abseil down the line of a chimney (*The Trap* HVS 4c) on the seaward end of the promontory.

For *The Spider's Web* follow a vague path rightwards (facing out) from the main path leading down to the promontory until it is possible to abseil down a steep grassy gully and over steeper broken rock to reach ledges at sea level.

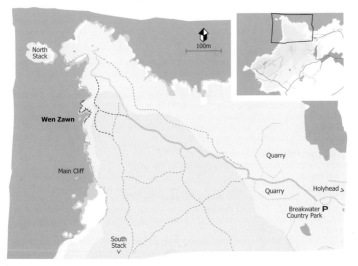

↑ Owain Jones topping out just in time as the rain arrives on **A Dream of White Horses** HVS 5a photo: Ray Wood

< Busy day in Wen Zawn, with the leader on P2 of **Concrete Chimney** HVS 5a photo: Al Leary

Wen Zawn

1. A Dream of White Horses HVS 5a 150m

The quintessential Gogarth adventure, requiring similar climbing abilities from both leader and second (this being especially pertinent on the final gripping pitch!). Make sure that all runners on this pitch are properly extended, or face horrendous rope drag and the likelihood of crucial runners popping out! Obviously it is vital that both members of the party are carrying prussik loops.

P1 5a 45m Start beneath a steep groove topped by a roof. Follow the left edge of the groove to the right end of the ledge on *Wen*. Continue up to a spike, then trend up right to a small corner.

P2 5a 25m A horizontal traverse line leads leftwards, past a difficult section, to a hanging belay in *Wen*.

P3 4c 35m Trace a line of flakes up left, passing a ledge at 15m. When the flakes run out, move across to good holds, then climb down and across a short broken chimney, to gain a belay ledge on *Concrete Chimney*.

P4 4c 45m Move out left and up to a roof. Traverse left beneath it and descend to make a nerve-racking move around a rib gains better holds. Climb up to some spikes then traverse left to to reach the final slab. Cross it daintily and climb up a bottomless groove, exiting leftwards. Scramble carefully up left to finish. There is a block belay well back from the edge.

[E Drummond, D Pearce 18/19.08.68]

2. Wen HVS 5a 100m

A superb direct route following the striking chimney/crack line that splits the slab.

P1 5a 25m Ascend the chimney, moving through the 'hole' to continue up a shallow groove. Belay just right of the crack line on ledges.

P2 4c 40m Follow the crack to a hanging belay at its widest point (passing the *'Dream..'* belay on the way).

P3 5a 35m Surmount the bulge on the left to gain a cracked corner leading up left. Make a tricky move left to a ledge, then follow it leftwards to belays on the back wall. (The final section of the crack can be climbed direct, but be warned, it is loose – both your second, and any other teams in the fall line are hardly likely to thank you!)

[J Brown, M A Boysen 08.05.66]

3. The Quartz Icicle E2 5b 87m

A brilliant route with some immaculate climbing.

P1 5a 25m As for P1 of *Wen*.

P2 5b 37m Climb up left to the start of the attractive diagonal quartz vein. Follow it past some thin moves just before it opens out into a crack. Continue to a belay in a broken chimney 6m right of *The Concrete Chimney*.

P3 5b 25m Trend diagonally rightwards through the *'Dream.....'* traverse, then traverse right to gain a small curving groove. Go up this and pull out right to reach a thin diagonal crack on the right side of a smooth slab. Climb up leftwards and finish up a crack leading to the traverse at the top of *Wen*. Traverse leftwards to belays on the back wall.

[E Drummond, B Campbell-Kelly P1: 09.11.68, P2: 31.08.69]

4. The Concrete Chimney HVS 5a 95m

Another fantastic route, thankfully not climbing the rubble jammed faultline itself! Hard for the grade.

P1 5a 25m As forP1 of *Wen*.

P2 5a 45m An obvious rising line leads leftwards to the arête overlooking the conglomerate packed chimney. Move up the slab to a thin crack, then ascend the wall on positive holds. Move left above the overhang and climb up the slab and short crack to belay in the chimney (as for *'Dream...'*).

P3 5a 25m Trend up left across overlapping slabs to gain an overhanging groove. Go up the groove and exit right at its top join the final bulge of the chimney proper. Scramble up to gain the *Wen* belay on the back wall.

[P Crew, J Brown 12.02.67]

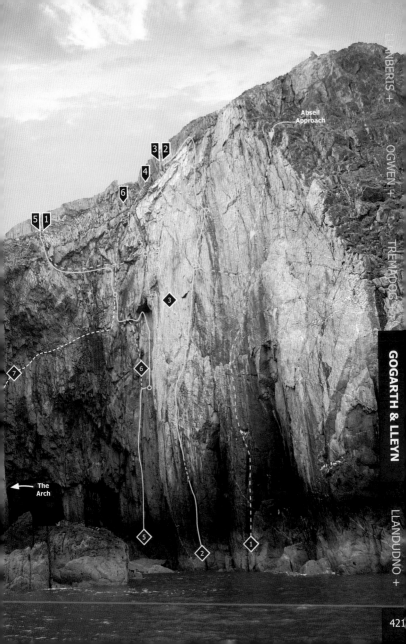

Abseil
Approach

The
Arch

Wen Zawn

5. T. Rex E3 5c 115m

A classic and inspiring excursion, featuring a memorable layback sequence on P1.

P1 5c 40m Start 10m left of the rubble jammed chimney. Wriggle up inside the flake (making use of the large cams you have remembered to bring), until forced to make a difficult and committing switch into a layback position on the outside. Head quickly up to a small overlap and 'thank god' runner. Continue up (a bit pumpy but well protected) to reach an obvious juggy traverse line leading out right across the open wall to a stance on the slab.

P2 5b 35m Climb up left passing a short steep wall to a slab. Cracks lead up left to a large overhang. Climb down and move leftwards, awkwardly and blindly at first, until easier ground leads to a stance.

P3 4c 40m Climb up to gain and follow the traverse on the final pitch of '*Dream...*'

[E Drummond, L E Holliwell, D Pearce, J Rogers (2 pts) 07/08.06.69, FFA: P Littlejohn 1971]

6. Metal Guru/The Golden Bough Finish E4 6a 65m

A brilliant direct version of the parent route, *T Rex*.

P1 6a 40m Start as for *T Rex*, but continue directly up the corner, to join and follow the final section of P2.

P2 5c 25m Climb up to gain the traverse on the final pitch of '*Dream...*', then go up the golden hued groove above, trending slightly left, then exiting right onto the finishing slab.

[S Long, C Parkin 13.08.89/E Drummond, C Dale 1973]

7. Conan the Librarian E6 6b 98m

An incredible route taking a stupendous line up the inside of the arch then out right across the impending back wall of the zawn.

P1 6b 28m Start at the base of the obvious open corner at the base of the arch opposite *T Rex*. Go up the crack just right of the corner, following it and the arête until a hard move can be made into the hanging corner on the right. Go up this with further difficulty, then traverse right on a juggy rail and up to a hanging stance in a groove.

P2 6b 45m (*The Janitor Finish*) Ascend the groove, with a hard move off the belay and exit right at its top. Follow a ramp across the back wall of the zawn to eventually join *T Rex* at the end of its P2. Mostly steady ledge-shuffling, but becoming a little pumpy towards the end.

P3 5c 25m *The Golden Bough Finish* (P2 of route 6).

[J Dawes, C Smith 08.86]

8. Britomartis HVS 4c 58m

A popular romp guarded by a difficult entry.

P1 4c 36m From the base of the abseil, climb down and make a tricky traverse left into the groove. Follow it up as it turns into a fine jug-ridden diagonal crack, all the way to a small stance high on the wall.

P2 4c 22m Move right and climb over a bulge to gain a good ledge. Head up right to finish up a steady groove.

[D E Alcock, G Rogan 11.02.67]

Wen Zawn

9. Toiler on the Sea E2 5b 62m
An excellent direct line up this fine wall.
P1 5b 37m Start as for *Britomartis*, but break out left from the groove/crack after a few metres, heading diagonally leftwards across the lip of the arch to gain the base of a steep crack. Sprint up the crack to the *Britomartis* belay.
P2 5b 25m Go up the thin crack above the stance, then snake upwards, first left, then back right across the upper slab to reach easy ground.
[G Gibson, D Beetlestone 03.04.80]

10. Spider Wall E1 5a 60m
A delightful route in a fantastic position.
P1 5a 45m Follow *Toiler on the Sea* to the base of the crack. Move up the crack for 4m then move out left for 2m and up to a flake, before stepping right and climbing a shallow groove up to the *Britomartis* belay.
P2 4c 15m Trend diagonally leftwards across into the groove, and follow it with care past some creaky holds to a ledge on the left.
[L E Holliwell, D S Potts, L R Holliwell 29.06.69]

∧ Sam Leary cruising up the steep crack on P1 of **Toiler on the Sea** E2 5b photo: Al Leary

Wen Zawn

LLANBERIS +

OGWEN +

TREMADOG +

GOGARTH & LLEYN

LLANDUDNO +

11. The Spider's Web E2 5b/A1 73m

A bizarre and exciting voyage across the underside of the arch. It can be freed at a very unconventional E5 6b, although most people plump for the aid climbing option. Both team members should carry prussiks/ascendeurs. From the base of the abseil descent, traverse across towards the arch to reach a sloping ledge on the arete

P1 15m Traverse right at sea level to gain the large chimney.

P2 5b 18m Circumnavigate the bulge rightwards and climb up a shallow groove. Move right again for 2m, then ascend the steep and difficult wall, trending right at the top to reach a small cave tucked up within the darkest innards of the arch.

P3 5a/A1 25m Ascend the chimney and move out to reach a cluster of pegs at its top. Pull one of the ropes through and descend it with your prussiks/ascendeurs. Place a nut behind the bottom of the overhang and use it to pull across to more gear on the lip. Move up using further aid to gain a small stance. The second should also be able to descend a similar rope set up to reach the lip, where the rope can be pulled through to be used as normal again.

P4 4c 15m Step down to the right and ascend a crack to a ledge in the groove. Move awkwardly leftwards into another crack which leads up and out to an easier finish.

[J Brown, P Crew (some aid) 08.68]

∧ Martin Crook spanned out on the immaculate P2 of **Quartz Icicle** E2 5c photo: Ray Wood

425

Easter Island Gully

Area: North Stack
Style: Trad (1-4 pitches)
Aspect: West
Rock type: Quartzite
Approach: 25 minutes
Altitude: Sea Level (tidal)

Ormuzd	E4
Supercrack	E3
This Year's Model	E3
Wonderwall	E3

Merchant Man	E2
Hombre	E1
Swastika	E1

| Phagocyte | HVS |
| Big Gut | VS |

A delightful section of the cliff sitting in isolation between its bigger neighbours Wen Zawn and Main Cliff, and sharing many characteristics of the latter, albeit on a smaller scale. The abseil approach to the tidal base adds an air of tension to any visit although in general the atmosphere is friendly and relaxed (assuming bad weather and a rising tide, which could cut off retreat to the abseil rope, don't catch you out!).

The routes are typically steep and strenuous, with ample protection. The rock is largely solid, but some deterioration should be expected in the upper reaches of all the routes.

Conditions: As a west-facing suntrap, the crag does dry quickly. However damp soapy rock is common in the morning (particularly at the base of the routes), before the sun has had the chance to burn the moisture off. The best combination for a visit is a low tide and a calm sea. Access to the routes is via a sea level traverse from the base of the abseil, which is obviously compromised by lively sea conditions or an incoming tide.

Approach: The cliff can be approached from the Main Cliff/Holyhead Mountain side, but is probably easier to locate from the top of Wen Zawn, the approach gully being the first one south of Wen Zawn. From the right side of Breakwater Country Park take the path past the left side of the small lake, then turn left and follow the path up a rising incline that runs through the quarries, taking the left fork where it divides. Further up hill the path divides again. Take the left fork again to a small col situated above Wen Zawn. Easter Island Gully lies up left from the col; a small path leads up to a second small col, just beyond the top of a heathery hill. From here a path leads down into the approach gully.

Descend the gully to a prominent pinnacle (said to resemble an Easter Island statue). From here a 35m abseil (trend right, facing out) will take you down steep grass (quite treacherous if wet) to a re-belay on a small rock platform at the top of *Supercrack*. A further 30m abseil will land you at sea level. Although you can scramble unroped down the upper grass section, and pull the ropes after reaching the base of the crag, it is definitely safer to leave an abseil rope in place in case of a forced retreat.

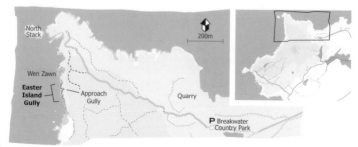

∧ Martin Crook romping up the lower crack on **Wonderwall** E3 6a photo: Ray Wood

↰ A local resident photo: Ray Wood

LLANBERIS +

OGWEN +

TREMADOG +

GOGARTH & LLEYN

LLANDUDNO +

428

Easter Island Gully

1. Supercrack E3 5c 30m
The line of the abseil provides a strenuous classic. Initially steep, then kicking back in angle slightly, but becoming decidedly problematic. A tricky move left, on good holds, just below the top adds further spice.
[L E Holliwell (2 pts) date unknown, FFA: A Sharp, C Rogers 17.08.74]

2. Wonderwall E3 6a 45m
A fantastic pitch snaking up the leaning wall immediately opposite the abseil. Climb the central crack in the wall, until an obvious transfer is made to the parallel crack on the left which leads up to overhangs. Pull past the steepness then swerve right to the base of a groove. Climb the groove with difficulty until good holds lead leftwards to a narrow ledge. Move back right to the arête and follow it to the top. *I Wonder Why* E5 6a finishes directly from the overhang, following a thin crack to ledges, then cracks above to gain a belay on the left.
[L E Holliwell, D S Potts (2 pts) 19.04.69, FFA: A Sharp, J Pasquil 1973/4, *I Wonder Why:* M E Crook, C Smith 06.86]

3. Phagocyte HVS 5a 45m
A superb and justifiably popular excursion.
P1 5a 20m Start at the base of a crack just left of the arête marking the right edge of the *Wonderwall* zawn. Muscle up the crack until a step right gains a small stance on the arête.
P2 5a 25m Climb up right and follow the steep groove before moving left to finish up the arête which eases towards the top.
[J Brown, P Crew 30.04.67]

4. Merchant Man E2 5b 45m
A good quality route with steep and pushy climbing on P1, then rather bold on P2.
P1 5b 20m Take the wall just right of the arête until it steepens, then race up the flying arête to the *Phagocyte* stance.
P2 5a 25m Climb up right and make bold moves up the vague arête to gain easier ground leading to the top.
[J Moran, G Milburn 06/07.05.78]

5. Big Gut VS 4c 52m
A good and varied climb that also provides a possible escape route for teams caught out by bad weather/rising tides.
P1 4c 15m Climb the obvious corner groove, just before the cliff juts out and runs steeply straight into the sea. Belay on the ledge.
P2 10m Wander up the broken corner on the left to reach another ledge.
P3 4c 27m Ascend the slabby groove to a small ledge; continue up the broken corner to the top.
[Joe Brown, D Alcock 08.01.67]

6. Hombre E1 5b 64m
A well-protected classic.
P1 5b 15m Start up *Big Gut*. From a few metres up the corner groove follow a line of quartz holds running out right to the arête. A small groove leads steeply to a belay ledge on the right.
P2 5b 37m Climb the groove, then finish up the steep crack above.
P3 12m A straightforward saunter up cracks leads to the top.
[J Brown, I G MacNaught-Davis (1 pt) 14.05.67]

7. This Year's Model E3 5c 60m
An excellent route taking the leaning wall above P1 of *Swastika*.
P1 5c 40m From the descending traverse on P1 of *Swastika* ascend a shallow crack/ groove initially bearing leftwards, then following a line of holds rightwards across the steep wall to gain a belay at the base of a ramp.
P2 5a 20m Finish directly up the crack.
[J Moran, P Jewell 13.06.78]

9

1 ◆

Abseil

3 ◆

4 ◆

2

5

6 ◆

7

8 ◆

Mestizo
(see Main Cliff)

8. Swastika E1 5c 62m

A wandering, but entirely absorbing trip.

P1 5c 15m From the base of *Big Gut* drop down a few metres and traverse onto the front of the buttress. Move rightwards up to a flake before descending rightwards to a stance.

P2 5a 10m Move out right from the bottom of the chimney (*Praetor* E1) and climb to a flake. Continue up rightwards to a ledge.

P3 5a 15m Climb straight up, then slightly right to a ledge on the arête, then up again to another ledge. From its left end pull decisively over as bulge and trend leftwards to belay in the groove (*Praetor*).

P4 5a 22m Traverse left for 3m and move onto a small slab. Ascend the steep crack above, stepping right to finish up a short corner.

[L E Holliwell, L R Holliwell 17.05.69]

9. Ormuzd E4 5c 33m

A wild and strangely compelling route tackling the rather intimidating cleft running up into the back of the cave and splitting the capping roof. Undoubtedly a character-building exercise. Large cams may be found to be useful.

P1 5b 18m Start from a small ledge below the steep wall left of the chimney. Ascend the left side of the wall for a few moves then traverse right into a shallow groove. Move up this a little way before slipping into the chimney on the right above the lower overhang. Continue up to a good stance.

P2 5c 15m Continue up the chimney then bridge out across the roof, eventually moving out on to the front face and finishing up the wide crack.

[J Brown, G Birtles, P Crew (1 pt) 04.02.67]

George Smith wondering if he'll get rope drag if he runs P3 and P4 of **Swastika** together! photo: Ray Wood ⋀

climbing walls

cave systems

rock sculpture

skateparks

- indoor
- outdoor
- mobile
- design
- manufacture
- installation
- maintenance
- matting

BENDCRETE

0800 146778 mail@bendcrete.com www.bendcrete.com

fiona roy on the 'evolution' climbing centre   photo : john hartley

Rhoscolyn

Area:	Gogarth
Style:	Trad (1-2 pitches)
Aspect:	South/South-West
Rock type:	Quartzite
Approach:	15 minutes
Altitude:	Sea Level (semi-tidal)

Dreams and Screams	E6
Jub Jub Bird	E6

Magellan's Wall	E5
Warpath	E5
Electric Blue	E4
Godzilla	E4
The Trail of Tears	E4
The Viper	E4
Centrefold	E3
The Mask of Red Death	E3

The Savage Sunbird	E2
The Sun	E2
The Wild Rover	E1
Icarus	HVS

Truant	VS

This accessible and sunny sea cliff has a range of top-class climbs and is an ideal introduction to the area. Rhoscolyn is a close cousin to the nearby adventurous cliffs of Gogarth. It shares the same rock type (quartzite), yet the atmosphere is a good deal less intimidating. This is due in part to the smaller scale of the cliff and the ease of access, but also because of the typically positive nature of the holds. Nonetheless, the routes still require a steady head to deal with the inevitable run-outs on slightly friable rock. Save for *Truant* the climbing is all on vertical or overhanging rock and the routes will generally demand a wide repertoire of trad climbing techniques. A combination of these with reasonable levels of stamina and a bold confident approach will pay dividends.

The rock is well-featured and normally allows for plentiful gear placements (take a big rack!). The blanker areas often have peg protection, although a lot of this is now old and of dubious quality. Belays at the top of some the routes can be quite difficult to find and care should be taken here.

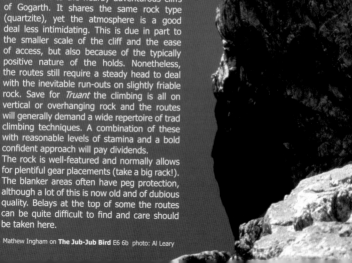

Mathew Ingham on **The Jub-Jub Bird** E6 6b photo: Al Leary

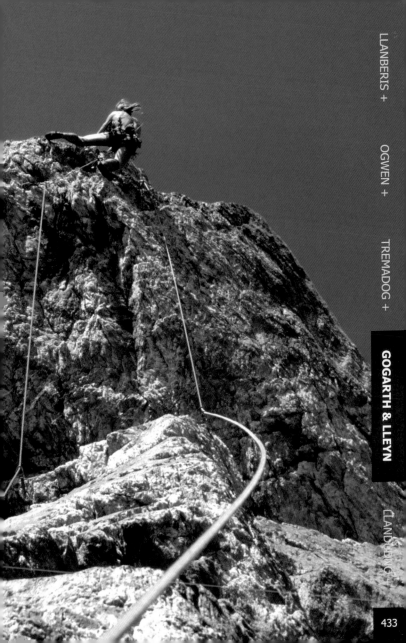

Rhoscolyn

Conditions: Because the cliff is generally south-facing and relatively sheltered it can be unpleasantly hot in summer. On the other hand it is quite possible to climb here in winter on sunny days with just a t-shirt. Seepage is not a major problem, except perhaps for the start of *Centrefold* and *Dreams and Screams*. However the quartzite does become very greasy in damp/humid conditions, particularly in Fallen Block Zawn.

Llawder and Sea Cave Zawn are non-tidal, but heavy seas can affect the starts of the routes. Fallen Block Zawn is tidal and access to most routes here is restricted for at least 2 hours either side of high tide.

Approach: Rhoscolyn is found on the western side of Anglesey by following the new A55 dual carriageway from the mainland until the Valley exit. Follow the old A5 into Valley and at the crossroads in the centre of the town turn left on the B4545 towards Four Mile Bridge. After the bridge take the first turning left towards Rhoscolyn and continue on narrow country lanes for about 2.5km until it is possible to park close to Rhoscolyn church. Please park considerately and take care not to obstruct local traffic.

There is a gated track about 25m to the left and slightly in front of the church. Follow this farm track past some houses and continue through a couple of gates until the old Coast Guard lookout post is visible ahead and slightly to the right. Once at the Lookout the red cliffs of Llawder are visible about 500m away to the west. Follow tracks across the fields until the crag is reached.

Access Resrictions: There is an occasional temporary bird ban affecting *Wild Rover* (see sign at crag).

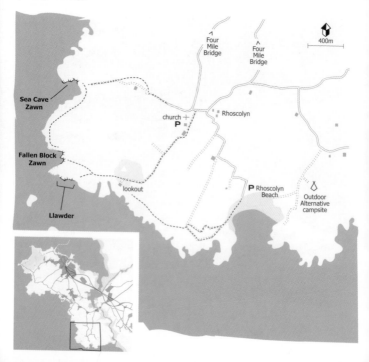

Llawder (The Red Crag) • **Rhoscolyn**

LLANBERIS +

OGWEN +

TREMADOG +

GOGARTH & LLEYN

LLANDUDNO +

The red rock of this cliff is formed from a mix of mudstone, shale and quartzite. This gives the routes here a slightly different feel to those just round the corner, in Fallen Block and Sea Cave Zawns, where the quartzite is much more predominant. The practical difference is that the climbing in Llawder involves more pulling on crimps and flatties and less squeezing rounded pinches.

The routes on Llawder are approached by the path that runs down from the right-hand side of the cliff. There is a convenient saddle halfway down which is a good place to gear-up.

1. The Savage Sunbird E2 5b 37m

A good route that requires a steady head. The climbing is technically quite reasonable, but it is sustained and the gear is both spaced and slightly hidden.

The route takes the clean stepped groove that is the first main feature on the right side of the face. Climb up to the large ledge at 6m and then continue boldly to good holds on a sloping shelf 3m higher. Teeter leftwards and then pull up on slightly suspect holds to another ledge. Continue up the groove, more easily now, before a final awkward exit.

[P. Williams, G. Peters 20.05.84]

Rhoscolyn • Llawder (The Red Crag)

2. Icarus HVS 5a 40m
The original route on this face up the huge open corner.
P1 4c 28m After belaying on the slab move left to climb the right-hand side of the large flake to gain a small ledge. Now move back right to ascend the slabby ramp and gain its right-hand edge. Continue more easily up to a nut belay at the foot of the big corner.
P2 5a 12m Fight up the crack with determination until horizontal ground is reached. The belays are well back from the edge.
[P. Buxton, D. Durkan 14.12.69]

3. The Sun E2 5c 44m
A brilliant climb up the prominent hanging corner left of *Icarus*, with unexpected exposure and isolation, and climbing that alternates between thuggish manoeuvres and technical delicacy. The corner is sometimes damp in its lower section, but this is normally easily avoided with some cunning bridging. Quite hard for the grade.
P1 4b 8m Start as for *Icarus*. After belaying on the slab move left to climb the right hand side of the large flake to gain a small ledge. Belay here.
P2 5c 36m Traverse leftwards to the arête and then make a committing move into the large, but hidden, corner system. Climb the corner with interest, but no serious difficulty until the overlaps are reached. The tenuous moves passing this section constitute the technical crux, but good holds soon arrive. Pleasant climbing now leads all the way to the top.
[P Williams, J. Moran 06.05.1984]

4. Warpath E5 6a 38m
An outstanding route that fires straight up the impressive overhanging wall on positive holds via a subtle line of weakness. It is a soft touch at E5, but going through the overlap requires commitment and the upper wall will spurn those lacking in stamina. Great climbing.
Start by belaying at the right-hand edge of the chossy ledge which lies about 8m left of the arête. Traverse up and right on slightly unstable rock to gain the base of the orange hour-glass slab. Climb this slab to its apex with increasing trepidation, as the overhanging upper wall looms ever closer. Swing onto the upper wall with conviction and pull upwards through a sustained section on good, but spaced incuts to reach a small ledge on the right arête. Relax slightly and continue up to finish slightly leftwards with more ease.
[J. Moran, P. Williams 12.05.84]

5. Mask of the Red Death E3 5c 42m
A good climb that starts as *Warpath* but then breaks out left from the hour-glass slab to attack the thin crack that splits the headwall.
P1 5c 25m Follow *Warpath* onto the orange hour-glass slab. Climb the slab for 5m until standing on good footholds and then step down slightly to pull into the groove on the left. Climb this to horizontal crack and bulge, pull through the bulge to gain a small belay ledge.
P2 5c 17m Move right from the belay to gain the crack and follow this with sustained and strenuous climbing to the top.
[P. Williams, T. Jadwat 19.05.84]

6. Wild Rover E1 5b 34m ℞
Enjoyable climbing up the right edge of the far wall.
Scramble up to the base of the wall with care. Start on the block in the centre of the face and climb up to gain a ledge after 10m. Move rightwards via the obvious horizontal crack to reach a flake on the arête. Move upwards and then left to a small ledge at the base of a groove. Step left again to finish up the centre of the wall past a flake.
[D. Durkan 05.08.1970]

Rhoscolyn ● Fallen Block Zawn

Although it adjoins the red walls of Llawder this crag has a very different feel. The huge boulders at the base of the round zawn cast a shadow over the routes, accentuating their steep and imposing nature. The rock is predominantly quartzite and tends to offer plenty of holds and reasonable gear, but the general steepness means that decent levels of stamina and confidence are needed to avoid flight time.

The amphitheatre of Fallen Block Zawn begins at the NW (far) edge of the Llawder wall. Routes in Fallen Block Zawn are normally approached by abseil from the right-hand side (looking out) onto the shoulder at the mouth of the small zawn. This is made more interesting at certain times of the year by nesting seagulls. At low tide it is also possible to make a sea-level traverse from Llawder (Red Wall) around the mouth of that zawn into Fallen Block Zawn.

7. Truant VS 4c 35m
A great little route that covers spectacular territory for the grade. The route follows the corner formed where the right-hand edge of the slab meets the back wall. The route is non-tidal as it can be accessed via ledges that are above the high water line, but the corner can stay damp longer than expected.
Climb the corner to a ledge and move up to a recess before moving left to good footholds. Continue to a second ledge and tackle the awkward bulge. Continue more easily to the top.
[D. Durkan, D. Birch 15.06.70]

8. Trail of Tears E4 6a 36m
Very good and varied climbing, with an evil offwidth tussle, preceding a wonderfully exposed upper section. Top tip: take care to avoid terminal rope drag on the upper arête. Start below and left of the overhanging fin that towers high above the centre of the zawn and gain a sloping ledge below the wide crack/chimney. Commit to this and fight up it to a hard section where a large cam comes in very useful; grunt past this in a primal fashion and gain the traverse line that leads to the side of the Fin. Bold, but steady climbing on good holds leads to a small ledge on the arête. The major difficulties end here, so relax and cruise up the slabby arête to the top.
[J. Healey, P Williams 23.05.84]

9. The Jub-Jub Bird E6 6b 40m
A pumpy and action-packed route covering some outrageous ground up the right side of the Fin feature. Ascend the groove and crack on the right side of the pillar. Move right onto the arête for a few metres to reach a rest and junction with *Godzilla*. After some moments of contemplation head out left across the disturbingly steep wall and layback wildly up to reach a good slot on the front side of the Fin. Go on up to reach a ledge and continue delicately up the right arête to the top.
[J. Moran, P. Williams, J. Sonczak 04.06.84]

10. Godzilla E4 5c 45m
Another big imposing route, striking a line up the compelling corner right of the Fin feature. Be sure to take a large rack of gear – you'll need it!
Climb up the corner and groove to reach a short traverse left, at 10m. Go up to a rest just beneath the fin (junction with *Jub-Jub Bird*). The large flake crack leads diagonally rightwards to a niche below the roof. Wriggle up, underneath the roof and break out on hollow flakes to gain an exciting bridged position on the lip. Pull quickly through steep ground to reach the upper groove with relief (remember to extend your slings under the roof).
[P. Williams, J. Healey, J. Moran 26.05.84]

11. The Viper E4 5c 40m
Very sustained, very pumpy and surprisingly intricate. The initial moves can be intimidating in humid or damp conditions.
Start in the centre of the steep wall beneath the prominent diagonal crack. Climb the bulge to gain the crack and easier ground before moving left slightly to a section of easier

climbing that leads to the roof and the most prominent hanging rock fang – The Vipers Head. Pull onto the head wall and then fight the pump up the ever-steepening crack/ groove before it is possible to exit right via a large flake hold. Then make a difficult step back left across a small corner to gain good holds and the easy finishing slab.
[D. Durkan, L. Costello (5pts) 19.06.70; FFA J.Moran, P. Williams 27.05.84]

12. Centrefold E3 5c 40m
A superb, well protected route, with interesting and varied climbing.
Start as for *The Viper*, pulling over the bulge to gain a rest and better holds. Move 3m to the right and climb the pleasant groove to a ledge. Continue up the steep corner crack system to an impasse where it is necessary to make a committing series of moves out right to gain a position below a short, steep wall. Climb this wall to good holds and gear below a small overhang and pull through this via a crack. Undercut rightwards on good holds to the finishing corner groove and teeter up this more easily to the top.
[J. Moran, P. Williams 05.05.1984]

13. Dreams and Screams E6 6b 41m
A totally brilliant and utterly physical climb, with a top crux section that is both hard and blind.
P1 5b/c 11m As for *Centrefold* to the top of the pleasant groove. Take a belay 2m to the right below the striking twin cracks.
P2 6b 30m Truck up the twin cracks for 15m, and then make an awkward manoeuvre left into a slanting crack. Trace this rightwards for 3m to an uncomfortable jam, and then swing right onto a hanging flake. Layback up this with haste to some decent holds over the bulge. (An alternative method is to reach and follow the first crack to the top.) An easy slab provides a suitable wind down from the fierceness that lies below.
[J. Moran, P. Williams 11.05.84]

14. Magellan's Wall E5 6a 48m
A tremendous route tracing a line across the lower lip of the concave wall to reach and climb its right arête.
P1 5b/c 11m P1 of *Screams and Dreams*.
P2 6a 37m Head right, then move up past the obvious undercut to reach a very small ledge. Move right and go up a shallow groove to gain good holds by a peg. Jugs lead right to the hanging rib. Climb this boldly, ignoring the pump in your arms, to reach a slabby finish.
[J. Moran, P. Williams 10.05.84]

∧ Rory Shaw on the top section of **Savage Sunbird** E2 5c photo: Rob Greenwood

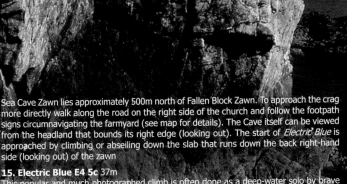

Sea Cave Zawn lies approximately 500m north of Fallen Block Zawn. To approach the crag more directly walk along the road on the right side of the church and follow the footpath signs circumnavigating the farmyard (see map for details). The Cave itself can be viewed from the headland that bounds its right edge (looking out). The start of *Electric Blue* is approached by climbing or abseiling down the slab that runs down the back right-hand side (looking out) of the zawn

15. Electric Blue E4 5c 37m
This popular and much photographed climb is often done as a deep-water solo by brave types. (It's actually a good deal less pumpy this way.)
Start on the left side of the cave and follow the obvious fault line rightwards to reach a slight recess above the apex of the arch. Trend up rightwards to finish in a recess just beyond the central pillar.
[S. Haston, T. Saunders 1983]

Adam Wainwright deep water soloing **Electric Blue** E4 5c photo: Ray Wood

Gogarth & **Lleyn**

Although of a lesser scale than Gogarth on Anglesey, the Lleyn Peninsula sea cliffs are, if anything, even more demanding. The approaches tend to be committing and the terrain on the crags requires high levels of skill and competence. The climbing is predominantly multi-pitch and very traditional. Volume is the key to a sea cliff rack – make sure you are carrying plenty of gear. Many of the approaches are made by abseil, which are safest when done with an extra static rope. Prussiks and/or rope ascending devices should be carried at all times.

The sea affects access to some of the routes, so it pays to know what the tides will be doing on the day of your visit. Tide timetables can usually be picked up from the local climbing (or watersports) shops. There are also numerous online tidal prediction websites.

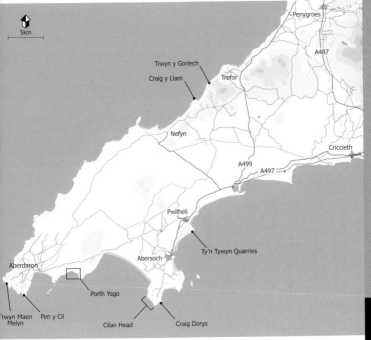

Seasonal Conditions: The Lleyn Peninsula is blessed with an unexpectedly warm and dry climate, given its position adjacent to the Snowdonia mountains. The featured cliffs are all west or south-facing suntraps, and thus climbing is possible throughout the year. Porth Ysgo is particularly popular as a winter bouldering venue.

Getting There: The popularity of tourist/surfing destinations such as Abersoch ensures that the roads on the Lleyn Peninsula have a tendency to clog with traffic on summer weekends. As a rough guide it takes approximately 45 minutes to get from Llanberis to Abersoch, given a relatively clear road. The remote nature of many of the crags precludes public transport as a viable approach option.

Access Restrictions: A number of the cliffs are subject to a seasonal bird ban. Please read the intro sections of the individual crags for more details.

Jason Pickles faces his fears on Craig Dorys photo: Adam Long <
The rugged coastline of Cilan Head photo: Ray Wood ⅄

LLANBERIS +
OGWEN +
TREMADOG +
GOGARTH & LLEYN
LLANDUDNO +

Trwyn y Gorlech

Area: Northern Lleyn
Style: Trad (9 pitches)
Aspect: West
Rock type: Granodiorite
Approach: 30 minutes
Altitude: 60m

Avernus	HVS

A large and adventurous cliff perched on the seaward shoulder of Yr Eifl, the prominent hill situated above the coastal village of Trefor. The featured route covers some fairly unconventional territory. Steadiness and route finding savvy are essential in an aspirant team, as is an affinity with the finer points of steep grass climbing technique. The compact lichenous rock, aside from being exceptionally slippy when wet, does not give much away in the shape of friendly runners. It is also rather loose in places.

Small wires and cams will be found useful, as will a largish hex for P7. It is normal practice to climb with your rucsac and follow the recommended descent route back to Trefor. (It is also possible to descend a steep grassy gully between Buttresses No. 2 and 3.)

Conditions: A sunny and exposed cliff, and consequently fairly quick-drying.

Approach: Park at the far end of the village of Trefor near the bottom of the Yr Eifl Quarry incline. Walk along a steep-sided dry valley, leading west to the beach. Turn southwards (left), passing some houses, and continue along the shoreline until you reach the furthest and largest buttress known as No. 5. Scramble up an earthy gully and traverse diagonally rightwards, with great care, across steep grass to the base of the route.

Descent: Go back from the cliff top and contour around the hillside above a small quarry. Continue across the slopes towards Trefor until you reach the top of Yr Eifl Quarry. Take a zigzag line down to the incline and follow this down to the parking area.

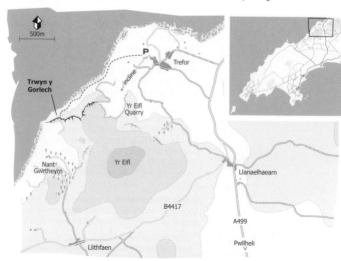

1. Avernus HVS 4c 250m

A big expedition with a serious feel. Protection is not overly abundant, and there is some steep grass and loose rock to negotiate. Still, this is a classic trip, and one you're sure not to forget in a hurry!

P1 12m Wander up easy ground to reach a large flake belay.

P2 43m Move up and go diagonally right for 5m. A grassy pull and a step left leads onto a rock rib. Romp up this on juggy holds, then head rightwards over a grassy section to another rocky outcrop with a capping overhang. From the right side of the outcrop make a step up left, then ascend the slab to a further grassy section. Belay on a large block beneath a short lichen-covered wall.

P3 4b 15m Ascend the wall above, passing a hollow flake and continuing on good holds, heading right to a belay underneath the barrier of overhanging rock.

P4 4c 23m Make an easy traverse left to reach a steep groove on the edge of the face. Go up this, and then trend diagonally right for 9m to gain a niche.

P5 4b 23m From a position just left of the belay, climb directly up for 11m to reach a grassy terrace. Traverse right for 3m, and then trace small grassy ledges diagonally rightwards to reach a belay on a narrow ledge in a corner, 3m left of the arête.

P6 4c 23m Go out right to the arête where a line of foot ledges leads up rightwards to a small V-niche. Move up and climb over the roof, and then continue up a rib for a metre or so, before pulling out onto a grassy ledge.

P7 4b 43m Climb directly via a ramp, and then up the 'honeysuckle slab'. Continue up the vague groove to reach easier ground.

P8 30m Wander up easy ground, heading rightwards.

P9 38m Ascend a groove on slopers for a short distance, then move right and go up another groove to reach block belays a long way back.

[G W S Pigott, A J J Moulam, W Craster 25.07.54]

↖ The Trwyn Gorlech headland photo: Al Leary

LLANBERIS +

OGWEN +

TREMADOG +

GOGARTH & LLEYN

LLANDUDNO +

445

Craig y Llam ®

Area: Northern Lleyn
Style: Trad (7 pitches)
Aspect: West
Rock type: Microgranite
Approach: 20 minutes
Altitude: Sea Level (non-tidal)

Fantan B	HVS

This huge guano-splattered sea cliff offers a committing and thoroughly adventurous day out for an experienced team. The cliff is hidden from view, and its immense scale does not become apparent until you are at least halfway up the route. The rock is loose in places and runners are difficult to arrange, even on the belays.

All in all, a serious proposition, where a good weather forecast is essential. It might also pay to have a couple of grades in hand, just to be sure!

Conditions: A sunny and exposed cliff, and consequently fairly quick-drying.

Approach: From the B4417 road to Nefyn, a small track leads off towards a disused quarry approximately 2kms after you leave the village of Llithfaen. Ignore a left turning and continue to an old gate just before the track splits and steepens. There is space for a couple of cars to park here. Walk along the track (ignoring the right split) past a couple of gates and houses until you reach the quarry. In the left corner of the quarry a cable leads down to a grass bank. It is possible to hand over hand down this and then scramble down very steep grass to sea level, however this method is both scary and potentially very dangerous. The safer method is to make an 80m abseil to gain the rocky ledges at the bottom of the grassy slope. From here you are really only seeing the approach pitches to the main event.

Access restrictions: There is a bird ban from 1st February to 31st July.

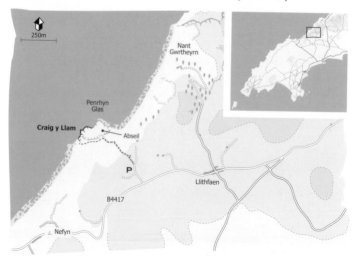

Craig y Llam

LLANBERIS +

OGWEN +

TREMADOG +

GOGARTH & LLEYN

LLANDUDNO +

1. Fantan B HVS 5a 230m ℞

A fine exposed adventure; more a mountaineering expedition than a sea cliff route. Escape would be very difficult, so be sure to leave yourself enough time. From the bottom of the abseil scramble across the guano-covered rock to find a belay of sorts near the right end, before the crag steepens.

P1 4a 40m Traverse right to an obvious pink ledge, with a peg and nut belay.

P2 4a 30m Head out right to an exposed position on the arete. A step up then leads to easier traversing rightwards to a poor belay on guano-covered ledges.

P3 4c 35m 15m Up and right is an obvious overhang. Move right for 8m until you are below them. Bold but easy climbing leads up and right underneath the overhangs to a perched block. Try and avoid pulling on it, and climb the wall right of this to a peg. Step left and climb the rake to another stance on the arete.

P4 4c 20m Above you, the cliff steepens. Make strenuous moves up and into a niche at the bottom of a prominent groove, peg. Make a bold step right round the corner, grovel right past a ledge at head height before climbing onto an amazing belay on a prominent nose of rock.

P5 5a 35m Pull directly out of the stance on big holds to enter a corner on the sloping ledge above. Step up onto a slab and traverse diagonally right under the bulges (2 pegs) to a jutting hold. Make steep moves to to gain a grass ledge, then go up a short slab to small grass ledge. Continue diagonally up left to belay on the arête.

P6 4b 40m Move out right onto the black wall, then trend back left to easier ground. Continue up to a cluster of blocks (or continue again to a big block on the ridge - 55m).

P7 30m Scramble along the alpine-esque ridge until you reach the sanctuary of a grassy meadow. From here it is possible to walk round the back of the quarry, and back down to your rucsacs.

[P Crew, I McNaught-Davis 04.04.66]

↖ Catrin Thomas on P4 of **Fantan B** HVS 5a photo: Al Leary

Trwyn Maen Melyn ®

Area: South-West Lleyn
Style: Trad (single pitch)
Aspect: West
Rock type: Gwyna Melange
Approach: 10 minutes
Altitude: Sea Level (non-tidal)

| Incredible Surplus Head | E3 |
| The Bardsey Ripple | E2 |

A short and alarmingly steep crag, with wonderful views of Ynys Enlli (Bardsey Island) off the tip of the peninsular. This tranquil place has a good feel about it. Sure, the climbing is quite wild and the rock friable in places, but the approach is very straightforward compared to some of the larger Lleyn crags.

Conditions: A sunny and exposed cliff, and consequently fairly quick drying.

Approach: Drive westwards out of Aberdaron, up the hill and take the first left turning towards Uwchmynydd. Follow the road for approximately 3km to a car park area where the road curves back right. From the car park take the vague path leading southwest down the valley towards the obvious small cove and site of St Mary's Well. (Legend has it that if you can manage to hold a mouthful of water from the well in your mouth, and climb to the top of Mynydd Mawr without spilling a drop, then whatever you wish for will be yours – none of the guidebook writers have tested this yet, but I'm sure it works.) About 100m along the right side (facing out to sea) of the cove the coastline turns right. At this point scramble down to the bottom of the crag.

Access Restrictions: There is a bird ban from 1st February to 31st July.

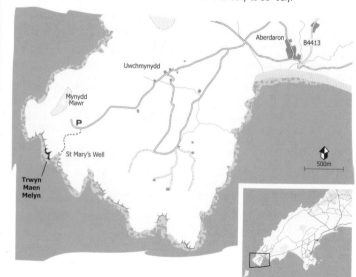

1. Bardsey Ripple E2 5b 35m ®

A wild trip along the quartz ripple that cuts a line across the crag.

At the right end of the crag is a chimney cave, start in this. Bridge and climb up the chimney until it is possible to commit to the left wall. Continue up and left into a groove, climb this exiting left at the top round a rib onto a ledge. From here step across the corner to the quartz 'ripple' that leads out left across the steep wall. Follow this on good holds in a great position, to finish up the far end of the crag.

[E Stone, G Griffiths 1991]

2. Incredible Surplus Head E3 5c 18m ®

A stunning and pumpy climb straight up the middle of the steep wall, via the 'head'. Start up a slab just to the left of a roof just left of the main corner. Climb up to good holds, and power up the wall to the head, finishing slightly left up the steepening ground to the top.

[G Smith, A Hopkins 1991]

⌐ Looking out to Bardsey Island photo: Si Panton

Pen y Cil

Area:	South-West Lleyn
Style:	Trad (2 pitches)
Aspect:	South-West
Rock type:	Meta-Dolorite
Approach:	20 minutes
Altitude:	Sea Level (tidal)

Catalyst	E5
Reactor	E5
Manx Groove	E3
Guillemot's Groove	VS

An intriguing and secluded sea cliff with some fine routes. The rock is good and solid, although the escape pitches are quite loose.

Conditions: A quick-drying suntrap. The routes are best approached at low to mid tide.

Approach: Drive westwards out of Aberdaron, up the hill and take the first left turning towards Uwchmynydd. Turn left again after 200m and follow the road for approximately 2km (ignoring the left turn after 1.5km), until it changes to a tarmac track ending at a fork. Park just up the left branch where there is room for about 4 cars (do not block the gates). Walk along the track, passing through a gate, and continue with the wall on your left, until a stile is crossed. Keeping left, continue again, passing through a gate to reach a second stile and the boundary of the Pen y Cil Nature Reserve. Go over the stile and walk down from the summit in a southerly direction for 300m to a grassy platform on the southern tip of the peninsula. Head west from here and drop down to a sloping grassy area. The zawn is situated down to the right (facing out); there is a prominent sea cave at its far side. Scramble down a gully on the east (near) side of the zawn and follow a traverse line (about D standard) across to the base of the routes.

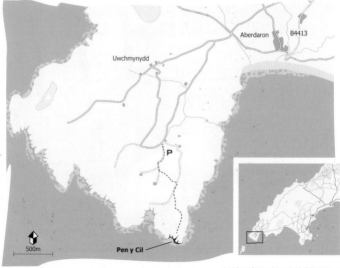

Local residents photo: Keith Robertson ʌ

1. Manx Groove E3 6a 70m

A superb, technical groove climb.

P1 6a 30m Ascend the black wall on the right for 6m, then head left into the groove and up the crack, making some tricky moves past a peg. Move right, and then back left to gain the top of the groove. Make a difficult move left across a slab to reach a big hold. Move up and jam around the left end of the roof to take a hanging belay on the slab above.

P2 4c 40m Go up the corner for 6m, then move right and wander carefully up loose ground to the top.

[R Edwards, P Sketcher (1pt) 07.04.67]

2. Guillemot's Groove VS 4c 67m

A fine and absorbing route.

P1 4c 37m Go up the short wall and enter the central groove. Follow it to its top and take a belay on the right.

P2 30m Wander carefully up loose ground to the top.

[R Edwards, P Sketcher 07.05.67]

3. Reactor E5 6a 64m

A superb, intense route up the left-hand crack line on the steep orange wall.

P1 6a 30m Come into the crack from the right and climb it until forced onto the left arete at 12m. Move up for a few metres, then back right to a quartz patch. Follow cracks up to a ledge.

P2 34m Wander carefully up loose ground to the top.

[P Littlejohn, M Hardwick 25.06.91]

4. Catalyst E5 6a 67m

The central crack on the orange wall provides another strenuous and sustained affair.

P1 6a 37m Climb the crack past some spikes in a shallow niche at 11m, to reach an open groove. Go up this, and head left to ledges.

P2 30m Wander carefully up loose ground to the top.

[P Littlejohn, C Baron 22.06.91]

Craig Dorys

Area: Cilan Head
Style: Trad (1-4 pitches)
Aspect: South
Rock type: Arenig Grit/Shale
Approach: 20 minutes
Altitude: Sea Level (semi-tidal)

Honeydew	E5
Byzantium	E4
The Mermaid Who Shed Her Glove	E4
Direct Hit	E4
Cripple Creek	E3
Knowing Her etc.	E2

One of the most notorious of the Lleyn Crags, yet one of the most convenient, with a gentle almost pleasant approach. Regardless of the amenable access, this is undoubtedly a very serious and challenging cliff. Even the featured routes, which are by and large the more conventional ones on offer, require steadiness, experience and the ability to deal with loose rock.

That said, if you can cope with the environment, you will appreciate these routes for what they are: classic climbs with much character. Have fun, but be careful.

Conditions: As a quick-drying, south-facing suntrap, climbing is possible here throughout the year. In fact in the summer, it can often be too hot. The routes on the Golden Wall are semi tidal, but only just.

Approach: From the one-way system in Abersoch drive out towards Bwlchtocyn and Cilan, until the road reaches a remote hamlet and a crossroads. Go straight across this and continue along the narrow winding road, taking the left fork at a bungalow. Park at Cilan Uchaf farm at the end of the road (there is a £2 charge). Walk along the narrow lane on the right, and follow the path up and to the right until it is possible to escape the field via a series of stiles. The descent to the crag is immediately down and left in a wide gully feature. Walk and scramble down an obvious path leading back left along the bottom of the Stigmata Buttress. Above, just before the steep scramble down to the beach is the right-facing corner of Cripple Creek, the only 'reasonable' route on this buttress. As you walk along the beach Byzantium Wall and Golden Wall become apparent.

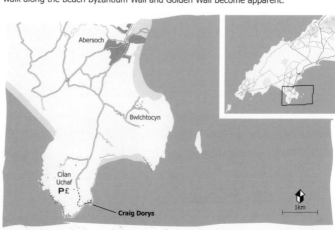

∧ Ben Bransby up on **Cripple Creek** E3 5b photo: Adam Long
↟ A cool footbath on a hot day? photo: Graham Desroy

Craig Dorys

LLANBERIS +

OGWEN +

TREMADOG +

GOGARTH & LLEYN

LLANDUDNO +

1. Cripple Creek E3 5b 37m

A good route guarded by an exceptionally loose start, which somehow doesn't feel that bad, probably because the rubble section is both technically straightforward and mercifully short (5m). Start, where the path drops down to the beach, by scrambling up to a wide ledge that runs across right to the base of the big corner line. There is a bollard belay up on the left. Climb the crack and move right to reach a ledge (easy, but terrifying). Above, more conventional climbing leads up the corner to the roof. Go around this on the right, and then finish leftwards.

[M Lynden, K Howett 06.82]

∧ Jack Gelderd on **Byzantium** E4 6a photo: Adam Long

Craig Dorys

LLANBERIS +

OGWEN +

TREMADOG +

GOGARTH & LLEYN

LLANDUDNO +

Golden Wall

2. Byzantium E4 6a 51m

This awe inspiring wall climb is somewhat reminiscent of *Right Wall* on Dinas Cromlech, albeit a slightly decaying version. Essentially an E4 5c with a V3/Font 6a boulder problem stuck on the top.

From the left side of the wall gain and climb the fault crack line breaking up and right, extreme care needed on the first section. From just before a pod in the crack make bold moves out left to reach a hidden peg in the wall. Wind you way up to the first break with relief and arrange gear. Surmount the break and move up to another break, steep moves over this lead to a small groove and some large blocks, pass these trying not to dislodge them onto your belayer and head up right, to a ledge below the final wall. The two pegs above are the only gear until the crux is over. So, summon all the courage you can muster, dig deep into your reserves, and power upwards to the top. Belay off fence posts and a boulder.

[P Littlejohn, M Hardwick 12.03.87]

Although the lower section of the wall is pretty solid, the rock deteriorates towards the top. Belays at the cliff top are hard to find; there are some fence posts well back from the edge.

3. Direct Hit E4 5c 34m
Another fine and bold wall climb. Make sure you've got plenty of cams on your rack. Start left of the cave; ascend for 6m, then left to a poor cam slot. Delicate moves lead up to a break; continue up to the next break (good cams). Trace the diagonal crack of *Mermaid* for a move or two, before stepping back right and heading directly up the wall. Finish more easily up the open groove above.
[P Littlejohn, M Hardwick 28.01.87]

4. The Mermaid Who Shed Her Glove E4 6a 36m
A superb route following the prominent diagonal crackline.
P1 6a 25m Climb up the groove at the back of the cave, then truck on up the leftward leading crack, slotting cams into the breaks as you go. Once the corner is reached, move up a further 3m to belay.
P2 4c 11m Continue up the corner to the top.
[R Kay, J Tombs 05.90]

5. Honeydew E5 6a 34m
An excellent if rather bold route. Ascend the rib at the right side of the shallow cave, then continue up, then left for a metre or so, before reaching up to a break. Move left along the break to a quartz crack, up into another break, then up and right to a thin ledge. Make a tricky move to a brown porthole, and continue boldly up the wall to a loose finish.
[S Haston, R Kay, C Bull 05.90]

6. Knowing Her/Fascinating Witches/
Scintillating Stitches/Knowing Her E2 5b 80m
A perverse but ultimately absorbing combination. A double rack of cams should be considered essential; an appreciation of the vagaries of Lleyn rock will also come in handy. The route starts up the slanting crack of *Knowing Her* up the right side of the Golden Wall, and can only be approached at low tide.
P1 5b 15m Follow the diagonal crack up and right until it is possible to reach a poor sloping ledge in the corner level with the first horizontal break. Construct an imaginative belay.
P2 5a 25m Traverse the lower of the horizontal breaks across to the other side of the wall. Move up the corner to belay on a good ledge on the left wall level with the next horizontal break.
P3 5a 25m Traverse the higher horizontal break back across the wall and take either a hanging belay in the corner or reverse back down to the sloping ledge belay.
P4 5b 15m Rejoin the upper crack of *Knowing Her*, heading up and slightly left to the top. Care needed with the rock on the last few metres. Belay well back on a pathetic spike, and take a braced stance.
Or, if you don't fancy all that, you could just climb *Knowing Her* in a single pitch.
[S Haston, M Howard 06.83/B Wright, D Ferguson, J Rothwell 07.06.92/D Ferguson, B Wright, M Rowlands 22.04.92]

< Jason Pickles on the bold **Honey Dew** E5 6a photo: Adam Long

Cilan ®

Area: Cilan Head
Style: Trad (2-4 pitches)
Aspect: South/West
Rock type: Sandstone/Shale
Approach: 15 - 25 minutes
Altitude: Sea Level (semi-tidal)

Other Realms	E6

Crow	E5
The Thoughts of Chairman Ray	E5
Vulture	E4
The Path to Rome	E3

Rastus	E2

The exciting sea cliffs of Cilan Head have a fearsome reputation, and rightly so. Whilst *Path to Rome* and *Rastus* offer a relatively amenable introduction to the area, beyond that lies some of the most adventurous sea cliff climbing around. Indeed, the harder routes described here are extremely committing and serious affairs. The approaches are also tricky and intimidating. Great care should be taken on the 'Orange' convex slopes on the cliff top. They are dangerously slippy when wet and unnervingly crumbly when dry. The rock itself consists of a challenging mix of shale and grit bands. The shale can be particularly unstable, demanding a very considered and steady approach. Experience and relatively equal ability within the team is essential; the routes are often just as harrowing to second as they are to lead. Prussiks/rope ascenders should be considered essential, as should an abseil rope to be left in situ during the climb. One thing's for sure, you won't want to pull your ropes down at the bottom of Cilan Main Cliff, even if you are a good swimmer! All that being said, these cliffs have tremendous atmosphere and character, and the featured routes are some of the best in the whole area. Just be careful out there, that's all.

Conditions: The crags all have a sunny aspect and thus, despite the odd seepage line, dry relatively quickly. *Path to Rome* and *Rastus* can be approached at any tide, but the other crags require low – mid tides.

The crux section (P1) of **Path to Rome** E3 5c photo: Rob Greenwood >

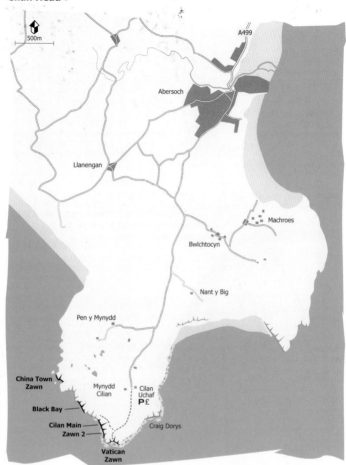

Cilan Head

A499

Abersoch

Llanengan

Machroes

Bwlchtocyn

Nant y Big

Pen y Mynydd

China Town Zawn

Mynydd Cilian

Cilan Uchaf P£

Black Bay

Craig Dorys

Cilan Main
Zawn 2

Vatican Zawn

Approach: From the one-way system in Abersoch drive out towards Bwlchtocyn and Cilan, until the road reaches a remote hamlet and a crossroads. Go straight across this and continue along the narrow winding road, taking the left fork at a bungalow. Park at Cilan Uchaf farm at the end of the road (there is a £2 charge). See the individual crag sections for further approach details.

Access restrictions: There is a bird ban on all the crags from 1st February to 31st July.

Path To Rome is the most travelled route on Cilan Head, and one of the easiest to locate as well. The rock is surprisingly good, horizontally banded grit, which yields a fine traverse line.

Approach: From the farm walk along the narrow lane on the right, and follow the path up and to the right until it is possible to escape the field via a series of stiles and reach open moorland. Follow a long straight path directly ahead (in a south-westerly direction) for approximately 230m until a sharp right bend is reached. Continue descending straight on, then head leftwards (south) for approximately 200m to reach a promontory from which you can view the crag to the south. Traverse across the grass slope above the crag and locate some rocky protrusions on the left-hand side (facing out) of the cliff. Make a short abseil to a ledge above and to the right of the large lower roof. There is some poor gear amongst the protrusions that will give a feeling of security, until better anchors can be arranged at the top of the cliff. It's a good idea to take 2 racks, with plenty of cams. You'll need a fair chunk of it for the abseil, and the rest will protect the big traverse pitch.

1. Path To Rome E3 5c 69m ®
This stunning diagonal traverse line provides one of best routes on the Lleyn.
P1 5c 46m The belay ledge provides a perfect viewpoint of the route ahead. Parallel tram lines run out left, across the crag and around the zawn. Follow these breaks left on the lip of the large lower roof, past an open corner, to a second open corner, capped by a small roof. Step up the corner then make a testing traverse leftwards around the bulge. Move up on better holds and continue the leftward traverse line into easier ground, eventually dropping down slightly to a belay 3-4m below the roof on the far left side.
P2 5c 23m Move diagonally left to gain the groove running up from the left side of the roof, and continue up, taking care with the loose/vegetated finish.
[D Jones, R Kay, P Evans 10.87]

LLANBERIS +

OGWEN +

TREMADOG +

GOGARTH & LLEYN

LLANDUDNO +

Cilan Head • Zawn 2 • Cilan Main

More good rock (by Lleyn standards) and an exciting route. Perhaps your first hereabouts?

Approach: From the sharp bend in the path mentioned in the Vatican Zawn approach continue straight on descending, and heading slightly rightwards, going down a prominent arête bounding the edge of the zawn. Descend the arête to a ledge and abseil down a groove line (*MGB* VS 4c) to a good ledge 12m above the sea.

2. Rastus E2 5b 55m ®
A superb route, although quite beefy for the grade.
P1 5b 45m Climb up the rightwards slanting groove, trending right around the bulge and continuing up to the roof. A hard move gains a ledge on the right, continue up the short wall until another hard move right gains a further ledge. Go up the groove to belay in the niche.
P2 4c 10m Climb the wall on the right to the top.
[C Jackson, J Street, B Andrew 02.06.68]

Cilan Main

A big bad cliff with a very serious feel.

Approach: From the sharp bend in the path mentioned in the Vatican Zawn approach, continue straight on descending, and heading rightwards towards 3 broken rocky bands running down the hillside. Traverse carefully across to the centre of the second rock bands, then descend down to a cracked ledge just below the cliff top. 8m to the right (facing out), a hidden peg and nut belay allows a 40m abseil to a sloping ledge at the left side (facing in) of the cliff.

A low or mid tide is required for access to *Vulture*.

Cilan Main • **Cilan Head**

LLANBERIS +

OGWEN +

TREMADOG +

GOGARTH & LLEYN

LLANDUDNO +

3. Vulture E4 6a 102m ®

An intimidating and serious route of much character, and one that should not be taken lightly. A fall on either the first, second, or third pitch could result in a serious accident for one or possibly both members of the team. The rock improves in the upper sections of the crag, but never reaches what one might refer to as an entirely solid state.

P1 5b 27m Start at the left side of the large overhang which undercuts the buttress. Climb up through bands of grit and shale, with only joke protection. Gear can be arranged in a crack out left before moving back right and up to a long narrow ledge. (runners up left will protect the second) Traverse right, and then move up to the horizontal terrace. There is a poor belay on old aid bolts (very decayed) and a wire.

P2 4a 15m Kick steps out right along the terrace, clip a solitary bolt, pray it will hold the weight of the quickdraw, and continue to another very poor belay on a dodgy spike and cam just where the terrace opens out below the roof.

P3 5c 35m Make a delicate and protection-free rightwards traverse until below the end of the roof. Blow it, and the whole team will probably be pulled off with you! Clip the insitu bong and place cams with much relief and size up the next section. Wild moves across a bottomless groove lead to a guano caked groove that heads up and slightly right to a sizeable ledge on the left. Traverse leftwards along the ledge to a larger ledge on the prominent nose of rock. At last, a more conventional belay: a peg, wires and cams.

P4 6a 25m Climb up to a broken ledge and traverse out left to an overhanging corner and good gear. Wild bridging leads to a hard and blind move into an easier final groove leading out right to the top. Phew, made it!

[J Street, C Jackson (1pt) 18.05.68, FFA: M Fowler, M Morrison 05.78]

4. Crow E5 6a 66m ®
Another entirely adventurous excursion, forging a path up the wall to the left of the large roofs.
P1 5b 18m Start 30m left of *Vulture* below a ledge with a perched block. A serious pitch, but one that is getting more solid with every ascent! Gain the ledge with the block on it via a groove on the left and a worrying bulge of choss.
P2 5c 18m Move right from the belay and go up into a groove. Continue up to gain a black corner and 2 ledges above. Good belay on the ledge above.
P3 6a 30m A tiring pitch. Continue up on good rock to a ledge underneath the line of overhangs. Move right into a steep groove and follow it to the arête on the right. Move left into a niche, and left again with difficulty to gain an easier final corner.
[K Myhill, K Jones (1pt) 10.70, FFA: M Fowler, M Morrison 20.05.78]

Black Bay

Another big bad cliff, featuring some rather challenging shale rock.

Approach: From the sharp bend in the path mentioned in the Vatican Zawn approach, turn right and follow the path for approximately 500m (in a north-westerly direction), until it is possible to drop down onto the promontory on the north side of the bay. This is the vantage point where the action shot (page 467) was taken from. Reverse your steps and locate an abseil point (stake, with a good nut above) around the point where the cliff changes from steep to a more relaxed angle. A 50m abseil will take you to a ledge system accessible at low to mid tide. The groove to the right (facing in) of the abseil line is *Curses*, a rather loose E4 5c.

5. Other Realms E6 6b 67m ⓡ

A hard, serious and utterly brilliant adventure. Expect loose, steep and committing territory and you won't be disappointed. That said, the belays are good and there is decent kit when it is most needed.

P1 5c 18m Stay clipped to the abseil rope and take a choice of belay positions: either on the tidal shelf at the cliff base, or on a ledge 6m up. Go up left to another ledge, then left again to reach some good wires in a recess. Move steeply up and left to gain a standing position on a small guano-covered ledge. Traverse left to belay on a ledge below a crack running up a compact wall. (A direct E6 6b pitch has been done up the lower crack leading to this point.)

P2 6b 34m Climb the crack to the overhang, and make a fierce move into the groove above. Continue up the groove and the same line above to reach a stance.

P3 5a 15m Climb up left and finish up slabby grooves.

[P Littlejohn, C Forrest 03.10.91]

< Harry Pennells on the top pitch of **Other Realms** E6 6b photo: Adam Long

Cilan Head • China Town Zawn

More radical and committing shale climbing for the seasoned ledge shuffler.

Approach: From the sharp bend in the path mentioned in the Vatican Zawn approach, turn right and follow the path for approximately 700m (in a north-westerly direction), until it is possible to descend down the large headland (Trwyn y Fulfran). Follow a path down, almost to the tip of the promontory. Leave your rucsacs here and climb down the rocks onto the promontory. A leftwards (facing in) traverse along a ledge just above sea level leads round to the base of the route.

6. The Thoughts of Chairman Ray E5 6a 70m ®

A magnificent rising diagonal line, just crying out to be climbed – fancy a shot?

P1 5c 20m Start just right of the cave. Move up to a traverse line and follow it leftwards past bulges to reach a decent belay ledge.

P2 6a 20m Drop down from the belay to follow the leftwards-leading diagonal line. This kicks in straight away with a crux section and some tricky protection. Continue on the same line, belaying before an a steep hanging arête.

P3 6a 30m Climb around the arête with difficulty, then continue on easier, but still loose ground to the top.

[Crispin Waddy, Frank Ramsey 1990]

Scramble
Approach

Harry Pennells seconding P2 on **Other Realms** E6 6b photo: Adam Long >

Ty'n Tywyn Quarries ®

Area: Llanbedrog
Style: Trad (2 pitches)
Aspect: South-East
Rock type: Micro Granite
Approach: 20 minutes
Altitude: 25m

Samurai	E2

This unique 'slab' climb, breaking through seven separate overlaps is situated in a series of quarries on the Trwyn Llanbedrog headland. The rock is compact and not overly blessed with runner placements.

Conditions: A quick-drying route with a sunny aspect.

Approach: Turn left off the A499 Pwllheli – Abersoch road (just before you reach the village of Llanbedrog) at the Llanbedrog service station on the left. Head down the road to a small village, and turn left just before St Pedrog's Chapel. Follow the road up and over the back of the headland. A track branches off on the left towards the beach; this leads to a car park. Walk left (facing out to sea) along the beach, if the tide is out. If it is in and not too rough, it is possible to traverse along the bottom of the cliffs fairly easily. The cliff opens out into a small bay (Microcosm Bay); access to Quarry 3, is via the middle of 3 ramps. Continue round for a further 200m to Quarry 4 where the route can be found.

Access Restrictions: There is a bird ban on the featured route from 1ˢᵗ April to 31ˢᵗ July.

Descent: Go across to the left (facing in), and descend the ramp between Quarries 3 and 4.

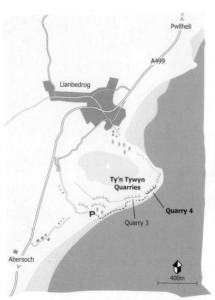

Approach to Quarry 3 and 4 from Microcosm Bay

∧ Pat Rainbird embroiled in the optical illusion that is **Samurai** E2 5c photo: Adam Long
⋏ Jellyfish on the beach at Microcosm Bay photo: Al Leary

Ty'n Tywyn Quarries

1. Samurai E2 5c 62m Ⓡ

An excellent route, and despite its appearance, predominantly an exercise in balance, with the overlaps being turned quickly.

P1 5c 25m On the lower slab is small tower. Move up to this and climb the corner on its right-hand side before rocking onto the next slab (peg). Traverse right, a little further than feels comfortable, and grovel over the next overlap to reach a thread in the lip of the next roof. Surmount this to reach another thread, and after another lip is turned, exit up the groove to a final traverse right to a ledge and peg belays.

P2 5b 37m Swing around the arête on the right to gain a narrow ledge with a flake crack at its right side. Climb carefully up for 3m to an ancient peg just left of a suspicious looking block. Climb gingerly over this and onto a slab on the right. Go directly up to the overhangs and traverse left, pulling over just before the arête is reached (possible belay). Head right for 5m, then follow easy slabs and grassy scrambling to an iron stanchion belay.

[J Brown, D Alcock (1 pt) 23.04.67]

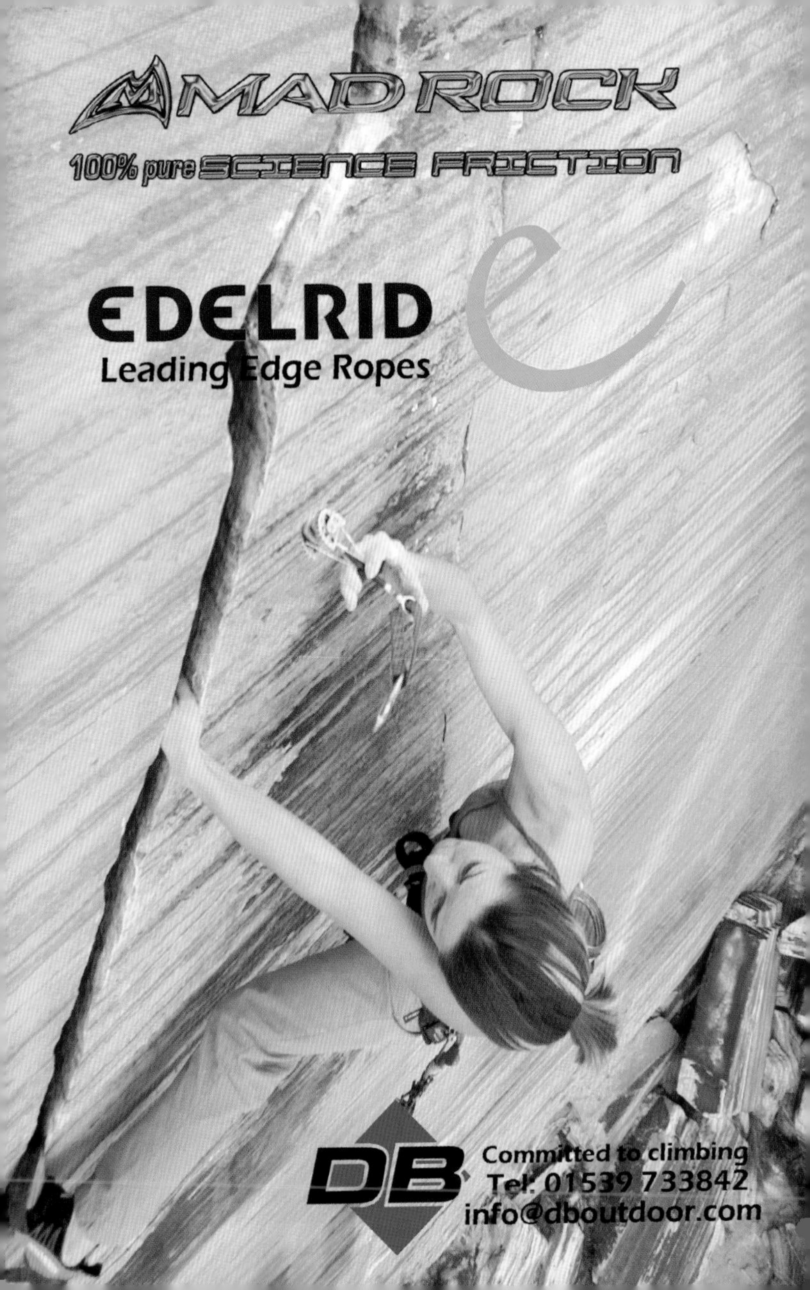

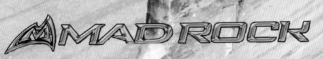

MAD ROCK
100% pure SCIENCE FRICTION
EDELRID
Leading Edge Ropes
DB
Committed to climbing
Tel: 01539 733842
info@dboutdoor.com

Porth Ysgo

Area: South-West Lleyn
Style: Bouldering
Aspect: South
Rock type: Dolerite/Gabbro
Approach: 15 minutes
Altitude: Sea Level (semi-tidal)

Porth Ysgo is a charming bouldering venue with over 100 problems all on wonderfully rough and clean rock. The superb climbing is complemented by the peaceful sea-bounded location. In short, this is a great place to get away from it all.

The full range of difficulty is on offer, with an abundance of easy problems upon which the casual visitor can potter. The landings are invariably rocky, in some cases frighteningly so. Bring a pad (or two) and a friendly spotter if you fancy a crack at any of the harder problems.

The rock itself is bullet hard, running from an ultra smooth, wave-and-pebble polished sheen on the lower boulders and undercut bases, to a 'rough-as-you-like' friction higher up. It is a real joy to climb on, if a little tough on the skin in warm temperatures.

Conditions: The aspect is sunny and open and the boulders dry quickly after rain, assuming there is a reasonable breeze. As you might expect on the Lleyn Peninsula, it is not unusual to be bouldering here in glorious sunshine in the depths of winter, whilst other parts of North Wales are blighted by damp and cold weather. Porth Ysgo truly does have a microclimate all of its own. The boulders are semi-tidal and a low tide visit is preferable, however there is plenty to do above the high tide mark.

Approach: Porth Ysgo lies just beyond the Rhiw headland that bounds the western side of the Porth Neigwl/Hell's Mouth bay (the surfing mecca just west of Abersoch). From Pwllheli take the Abersoch road but turn off at Llanbedrog, following diversion signs to Rhiw thereafter. From Rhiw drive towards Aberdaron, turning left when you see a Porth Ysgo signpost at a slightly offset crossroads junction. After 200m the road splits and it is possible to park in a small grassy lay-by. Go through the gate to the left and follow a path down a small valley (past various old manganese mine entrances) that opens out at the old winding house at the top of the grass inclines above the main boulder field.

If the layby is full (only room for 3 cars) drive further along the right fork to avoid some farm buildings in about 300m. Park around the back of the building on the left. There is a National Trust honesty box here. Follow the signpost down and trace the contouring path leftwards through a small kissing gate to reach the old winding house, as above.

Kim Leyland on the footless start of **Fast Cars** V5/Font 6c+ photo: John Coefield ∧

Porth Ysgo

LLANBERIS +

OGWEN +

TREMADOG +

GOGARTH & LLEYN B

LLANDUDNO +

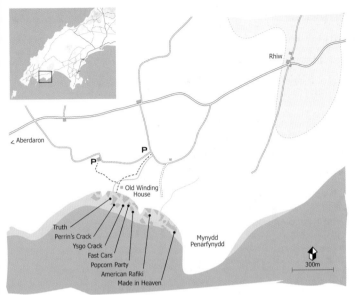

Rhiw

< Aberdaron

Old Winding House

Truth
Perrin's Crack
Ysgo Crack
Fast Cars
Popcorn Party
American Rafiki
Made in Heaven

Mynydd
Penarfynydd

300m

∧ Dave Parry topping out **Unmarked Grave** V3/Font 6a+ photo: John Coefield
↖ Rob Lamey demonstrating **Cured Weakling** V6/Font 7a photo: Lamey collection

The Llandudno area features a wide selection of limestone crags, from almost fully bolted sport venues such as Lower Pen Trwyn to the wildly adventurous expanse of Great Zawn over on Little Orme. Many of the routes mix in situ bolts with traditional gear placements; it is often worth taking some wires on, what might appear from the ground to be a full clip-up. In general there is a lack of easier sport routes (less than F6a), although Castle Inn Quarry (located in a pub car park) is a friendly option for those lacking the experience or skills required for the Marine Drive routes.

A copy of the tide timetable is also essential for any of the tidal cliffs. These can usually be picked up from the local climbing shops. There are also numerous online tidal prediction websites which will help you plan your day at the seaside.

Seasonal conditions: The coastal location of Llandudno affords it a relatively dry and warm weather system. If you have been rained out of the mountains it is always worth a look. Year-round climbing is possible, although seepage can be a problem on some crags. During hot weather it is possible to find shade, and if it rains, you can always retreat to the sheltered confines of Parisella's Cave or, failing that, the relaxed environs of the nearby Fat Cat pub in town.

Getting there: Llandudno is easily reached from the A55 dual carriageway, although the town itself is often snarled with traffic during the summer months.

Access restrictions: A number of the cliffs are subject to a seasonal bird ban. Please read the intro sections of the individual crags for more details.

A further restriction applies to the escarpment running along above the Marine Drive. No climbing is allowed before 6.00pm on all bank holiday weekends and during the school summer holidays (mid-July – first week in September).

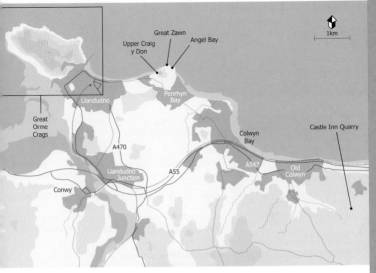

Mr. Parisella of Conwy, proprietor of the cafe by the gate house photo: Al Williams ∧
Climbers on the Mayfair Wall, Marine Drive photo: Phil Dowthwaite <

Mayfair Wall ®

Area:	**Marine Drive**
Style:	**Sport/Trad (1- 2 pitches)**
Aspect:	**East**
Rock type:	**Limestone**
Approach:	**0 minutes**
Altitude:	**75m**

Masterclass	F7c+
Oyster	F7c+
Needle in the Groove	F7b+
Plagued by Fools	F7b+
Bloodsports	F7b
Axle Attack	F7a+
Mayfair	F7a+
The Bearded Clam	F7a+
The Bloods	F7a+
Contusion	F6c
The Disillusioned Screw Machine	E6
Rapture	E4
Anchovy Madonna	E3
The Wall of Blutes	E3
Connor's Folly	E1

A fine selection of classic sport and trad routes, on an impressive sweep of rock. Without doubt the best section of the crags that sit above the Marine Drive. This is an ultra convenient venue, with a strong sense of history resonating from the early '80s. The rock is generally perfect, although there are some loose sections on the approach to the routes on the right-hand side. The climbing is typically sustained and technical, with the odd powerful move thrown in for good measure. As with many of the crags on the Ormes, it pays to carry a selection of wires on the sport routes.

Conditions: If you want sunshine you will have to make a morning visit. A fairly quick-drying crag, although persistent seepage is a problem on certain routes.

Approach: 50m beyond Parisella's cave an impending wall looms over the road

Descent: In situ bolt lower-offs.

Access restrictions: No climbing is allowed before 6.00 pm on all bank holiday weekends and during the school summer holidays (mid-July – first week in September). Please remember that the Marine Drive is a one-way road. If you do arrive by car, make sure that you park sensibly and do not block the road. The toll is currently £2.50 per car or £15 for a season ticket.

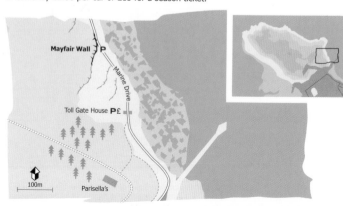

∧ Danny Cattell pulling through steep ground on **Mayfair** F7a+ photo: Alex Messenger
↑ An antique thread in the vicinity of ' **Disillusioned** ......' photo: Al Williams

47

Mayfair Wall

1. Axle Attack F7a+ 20m ®

A classic and historic testpiece, now polished but still superb. Follow the obvious line up right beneath the stepped overlaps to a semi-rest, then up into a shallow groove where a tricky crux awaits.

[M Griffiths, L McGinley (both led) 06.81]

Axle Attack was arguably the route that kick-started the Pen Trwyn new route boom. First climbed in 1981 by Mel Griffiths and Leigh McGinley after they had famously endured an axle-lifting training regime, it foretold of the 1983 gold rush. That year the Marine Drive was developed at a furious pace by a gang of cave-dwelling 'dole-boys' - some of whom (Moffatt and Moon in particular) went on to dominate the world climbing scene.

2. Bloodsports F7b 21m ®

A superb stamina test. Sketch up the lower wall, moving right to the base of the Bloods groove. Swerve left and attack the upper wall, which provides a sustained assault upon your wilting forearms.

[P Hawkins 07.88]

3. The Bloods F7a+ 20m ®

A fine route with an intense crux section. Climb up the small corner to gain the ledge beneath the bulge. Step left and blast up the steep little groove to reach easier territory.

[J Redhead, K Robertson, A Pollitt 07.08.82]

4. Contusion F6c 18m ®

A good open route with a fierce crux. Climb up to the mid-height bulge, which succumbs to a forceful pull. Continue up to a recess. The belay is up and left, but the final few moves to reach it are thin and reachy.

[G Gibson 22.09.84]

5. Mayfair F7a+ 22m ®

A fantastic pitch with 2 distinct cruxes. Climb straight up the wall then turn on the power to get yourself through the bulge. A brief rest allows some recovery beneath the steep top section, which presents a fittingly magnificent climax.

[R Edwards (some aid) 11.72/FFA J M Redhead, A D Newton 1982, although a youthful pairing of future hotshots, Andy Pollitt and Jerry Moffatt, climbed it free but with some rests in 1980]

6. The Disillusioned Screw Machine E6 6b 40m ®

A stunning route offering technical cruxes and a cool run-out to the top.

P1 6a 20m Climb up and over the bulge (clipping a couple of bolts on the way) to reach a flake. Step right and move up to the belay.

P2 6b 20m Traverse right past 2 sets of twin bolts. Reach blindly up right and execute a powerful pull to gain the large scoop above, then make further hard moves up leftwards onto the headwall (bolt). The top is in sight, keep it steady 'til you get there!

[J Redhead, A Pollitt (1 pt) 27.07.82/FFA A Pollitt, P Williams 14.06.83]

7. Masterclass F7c+ 15m ®

Another historic route tackling the crimpy headwall directly above the first belay on *The Disillusioned Screw Machine*.

[J Moffatt 08.83]

The following routes are all accessed via a creaky flake/corner. Whilst relatively straightforward it should be treated with respect or you risk landing flat on your back clutching a loose chunk of limestone!

8. The Bearded Clam F7a+ 30m ®

A dramatic route cutting through some awesome territory. Traverse easily left from the creaky flake and move upwards through the first bulge. Continue up left to gain a poor rest beneath the upper bulge. *Oyster* F7c+ powers out left up the hanging crack. Ignore its tempting line, and instead embark on a series of wild moves that take you rightwards into the hanging groove. Scoot up this placing a few wires and trend right to the lower-off.

[*The Bearded Clam:* A Pollitt P Williams, 16.06.83, Oyster: R Edwards (with aid) 11.72, FFA J Moffatt 08.83]

Mayfair Wall

LLANBERIS +

OGWEN +

TREMADOG +

GOGARTH & LLEYN

LLANDUDNO +

9. Needle in the Groove F7b+ 30m ®
A classic Fawcett route – both audacious and strenuous. Start as for *The Bearded Clam*, but break up directly towards the upper bulge (take some wires for this bit). Cross the bulge rightwards to gain the slender upper groove, which shows the way to the top.
[R Fawcett 06.83]

10. Rapture E4 6b 30m ®
Gain the scoop below the bulge from the *The Bearded Clam* traverse. A hard crux sequence leads out right and up into the groove above. At its top make an awkward step right onto a flake to finish.
[J Moffatt E Jones 17.06.83]

11. Plagued by Fools F7b+ 30m ®
A good route with difficulties concentrated around the steep nose. The crux is hard. It takes a direct line up the arête to reach the *Rapture* lower-off.
[G Gibson 07.11.87]

12. Anchovy Madonna E3 5c 30m ®
A justifiably popular excursion, sneaking up the perimeter of the main wall. Swagger up the initial bulging wall in a sufficiently convincing fashion and you will be rewarded with the delightful intricacies of the upper wall.
[A Pollitt, P Williams 17.06.83]

13. Connor's Folly E1 5b 20m ®
The attractive groove line at the top of the grassy bank just to the right is a corker. The slim groove in its left arête is *The Wall of Blutes,* a good technical E3 6a.
[Connor's Folly: J Connor and friends (1 pt) 11.72/FFA A Pollitt, N Clacher 06.08.82, *Wall of Blutes*: P Williams, R Fawcett, P Clark, A Grondowski, J Moffatt 03.07.83]

Plumbline Area ®

Area: Marine Drive
Style: Trad (single pitch)
Aspect: East/South-East
Rock: Limestone
Approach: 1 minute
Altitude: 75m

Gold Rush	E6
Flake Away	E5
Scary Canary	E5
Plumbline	E3
Precious Metal	E1

An attractive wall split by the atypical, continuous crack line of *Plumbline*. The harder wall routes are bold and fingery remnants from the transition years when bolts were only used as a last resort. They offer fine, adventurous challenges that will be remembered long after the belay chains are clipped. The area generally features good rock that varies from the vertical to the gently overhanging with the odd bulge thrown in for good measure.

Conditions: The crag receives the morning sun, but this disappears over the top of the crag by midday. It dries quickly, although *Plumbline* can stay damp longer than expected.

Approach: Continue along the Marine Drive from Parisella's Cave until 50m before the point where the road bends around the headland. The Plumbline Wall sits up above on a grassy platform.

Descent: In situ bolt lower-offs.

Access Restrictions: No climbing is allowed before 6.00pm on all bank holiday weekends and during the school summer holidays (mid-July – first week in September)

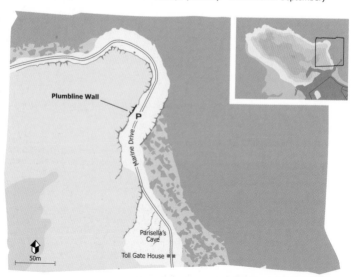

∧   Jordan Buys peering into the crack of **Plumbline** E3 5c photo: Alex Messenger

↖   The Marine Drive toll gate house, on the way up to the crag photo: Al Williams

Plumbline Area

1. Precious Metal E1 5b 18m ⓡ

50m left of the Plumbline Wall an eye-catching diagonal ramp forms the line of this superb route.

[F Crook, W Wayman 05.06.83]

2. Gold Rush E6 6b 18m ⓡ

A splendid, bold pitch in stark contrast to the bolt routes nearby. Climb with difficulty into the groove and continue upwards to cross the roof on its right before moving left to a rest on a ledge. Thin, necky moves rightwards gain a corner and gear. Cross the roof and climb leftwards to the belay.

[W Wayman, P Roberts, F Crook 27.10.82]

3. Plumbline E3 5c 18m ⓡ

The classic route of the area, which follows the continuous crack system with ever in-creasing difficulty. Start easily and follow the crack with optimism until the bulge slows everything down. Sustained and pumpy moves lead past this to the belay.

[R Edwards 08.73]

4. Scary Canary E5 6a 18m ⓡ

A very fine outing that defined an era with the single, prophetic bolt providing both wel-come relief and an indication of future trends. Gain the flake and continue with more dif-ficulty up and slightly right. Small wires give confidence for the moves to the bolt, where more difficult climbing gains a small flake, pockets and the belay.

[M Crook, K Howett, D Towse 04.83]

5. Flake Away E5 6b 18m ®

A good companion pitch to *Scary Canary* that is both harder and also features a contrasting climbing style with some quite powerful climbing through the bulges. Climb easily up the flake to gain a line of pockets that lead to the bulge. Pull rightwards through the bulge with urgency to gain a large flake hold. Now pull back left to easier ground and the finish.

[D Towse 03.83]

A superb F7b (Font 6c/V5) traverse can be made across the base of the Plumbline Wall, as Rich Betts demonstrates
photo: Betts collection

Firefly Wall ®

Area:	**Marine Drive**
Style:	**Trad/Sport (single pitch)**
Aspect:	**South-East**
Rock type:	**Limestone**
Approach:	**1 minute**
Altitude:	**75m**

Captain Fingers	F7b
You've Had Your Chips	F7b
Mr Chips	F7a

Private Investigations	E5
Firefly	E3
Klondike	E3
Pocket City	E3
Solid Gold	E3

A compact, undercut wall, featuring a range of superb and intense routes that seem to pack a disturbing amount of action into their relatively diminutive height. Don't be tempted to use a single rope for the trad routes as parallel runner placements are common. It is also is worth carrying some wires on the sport routes. The rock is good quality limestone, but some suspect holds will be encountered.

Conditons: Some morning sunshine, but generally this is quite a shady part of the crag. It does dry quickly, but persistent seepage can be a problem in places.

Approach: Continue along the Marine Drive from Parisella's Cave until just before the road bends around the headland. Firefly Wall sits up above on a grassy platform.

Descent: In situ bolt lower-offs.

Access restrictions: no climbing is allowed before 6.00 pm on all bank holiday weekends and during the school summer holidays (mid-July – first week in September).

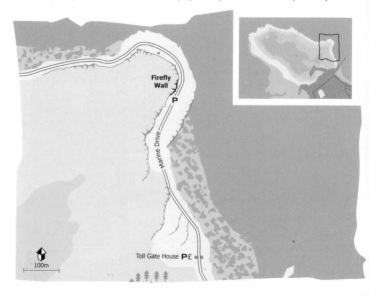

∧ Jon Ratcliffe getting stuck into **Mr Chips** F7a photo: Jethro Kiernan

↟ Llandudno Pier photo: Si Panton

1. Private Investigations E5 6b 15m ®
An excellent route with an unnerving and difficult start coming over the first bulge. Make a long move up from a fragile-looking 'handle' in the lumpy fossil-packed break to a 'hard-to-see' crimp, then place a wire with difficulty in the first pocket. Follow the twin cracks with pumpy, continuous climbing up through the bulges to the top.
[R Fawcett 1983]

2. Klondike E3 6a 18m ®
A fine technical route. Surmount the awkward initial bulge and traverse left, then move up to a big undercut pocket, before finishing directly up cracks above.
[W Wayman, F Crook 11.05.83]

3. Pocket City E3 6a 18m ®
A superb and sustained outing. Climb up through the lower bulge and continue directly up the wall trending leftwards through steep ground to reach the lower-off on the upper wall.
[A Pollitt, P Williams 30.06.83]

4. Solid Gold E3 6a 18m ®
A Marine Drive classic with a rather robust grade! Strenuous and pushy climbing leads up to the sloping ledge/ 'stuck-on blob'. Make a hard move to some crimps, fiddle in some gear whilst the pump grows in your arms, then tussle up into the corner and follow it to finish.
[W Wayman, F Crook 11.05.83]

5. Captain Fingers F7b 18m ®
A fierce and tricky clip-up (that feels more friendly with a few wires). Climb up the diagonal undercut/overlap, then make some very technical moves up and left. Continue directly before moving back right to the lower-off at the top of *Firefly*.
[A Pollitt, P Williams, M Crook 30.06.83]

James Lillie on the classic **Firefly** E3 5c photo: Jethro Kiernan **>**

6. Firefly E3 5c 18m ®
Another popular classic. Make strenuous moves on undercuts (that are often wet) through the bulge (bolt), then trend up left to reach the easier finishing groove.
[M Crook, D Towse 03.83]

7. Mr Chips F7a 18m ®
An appealing right-hand finish to *Firefly*, heading out right to climb the thin face on dinks and crimps.
[A Pollitt, P. Williams, J Moffatt 01.07.83]

8. You've Had Your Chips F7b 18m ®
A harder independent right-hand start is possible for *Mr Chips*. A difficult flash!
[M Griffiths 1995]

LLANBERIS +

OGWEN +

TREMADOG +

GOGARTH & LLEYN

LLANDUDNO +

487

Excursion Area ®

Area:	Marine Drive
Style:	Sport/Trad (single pitch)
Aspect:	North-East
Rock:	Limestone
Approach:	1 minute
Altitude:	75m

Barking Up The Wrong Tree	F7b
No Arc, No Bark	F7a+
Excursion Direct	F6c+
Call It Black	E5
The Visionary	E4
Clear White Light	E3
Excursion	E2

This excellent buttress commands a fine position on the headland above the first main bend on Marine Drive. The routes cover a wide range of grades and climbing styles, however all are of the highest quality.

The rock is mainly good and varies in angle from vertical to gently overhanging, with the left-hand routes being quite steeply undercut at the start.

Conditions: The crag receives the morning sun, but this disappears over the top by midday. It can be windier here than on Firefly Wall, due to its position on the corner of the headland. The crag dries quickly, although the darker rock on the left stays damp for longer.

Approach: Continue along the Marine Drive from Parisella's Cave until just after the point where the road bends around the headland. Excursion Wall sits up above the road.

Descent: In situ bolt lower-offs.

Access Restrictions: No climbing is allowed before 6.00pm on all bank holiday weekends and during the school summer holidays (mid July – first week in September)

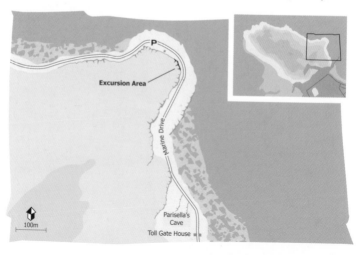

∧ Tony Shelmerdine on **Excursion** E2 5b photos: Alex Messenger

⏏ It goes without saying! photo Al Williams

Excursion Area

1. Barking Up The Wrong Tree F7b/7b+ 18m ®

A powerful and sequential series of moves straight off the ground leads to a long reach that gains massive holds and a rest. Good technical climbing waits on the upper wall. The original route is F7b and heads rightwards after the rest to join *No Arc, No Bark* at its last bolt and uses its belay. The more logical line is a bold F7b+ that heads straight up to use the last bolt and belay of *No Bark, No Dill*, which is the banned route on the left.
[G. Gibson 02.02.85]

2. No Arc, No Bark F7a+ 18m ®

Very good climbing. Pull rightwards out of the little corner with difficulty and go up and slightly leftwards to a rest in a recess. Move up on good holds until a long move starts a hard series of moves. Gain the last bolt on the left and move more easily to the belay.
[G. Gibson 19.01.85]

3. Excursion Direct F6c+ 18m ®

Pleasant climbing up the bolt line that leads straight to the *Excursion* belay. Crimp up the lower wall before manoeuvring left, then right in order to attack the bulge just right of the faint crackline. Pull into *Excursion* and follow it to the belay.
[T. Shelmerdine, A. Barnett 03.02.93]

4. Paint It Black E5 6a 18m ®

Good, committing climbing that starts midway between *Excursion* and *Excursion Direct*. Thin climbing up the initial wall joins Excursion at the base of the ramp. Gain the deep slot on the right and pass the bulge above to enter a shallow groove on the left. Break through the small roof on the right and continue rightwards to *The Visionary/Clear White Light* belay.
[G. Gibson 20.05.84]

A different kind of excursion on offer down at the beach front, Llandudno photo: Al Williams >

5. Excursion E2 5b 20m ®

A popular classic that follows the natural line of weakness to gain the top of the wall with sustained climbing and reasonable protection. Climb up and then leftwards to gain a ramp line. Follow this and from its end continue straight up to the belay.

[I. Alderson 09.05.81]

6. The Visionary E4 6a 18m ®

A good route in the same mould as *Paint It Black*, but a bit easier. Start up *Excursion* or slightly to its right if you want to climb new rock/avoid the crowds. At the height where *Excursion* moves left, pull rightwards to join *Clear White Light* at the bottom of a small corner. Climb the corner and exit up and leftwards with difficulty. Finish rightwards.

[A. Grondowski, P. Williams, A. Pollitt 05.07.83]

7. Clear White Light E3 6a ®

The original route takes a weaving line to minimise the difficulties. Climb the flake and head up towards parallel black streaks, moving left under them to gain a slot and small corner (junction with *The Visionary*). Exit the corner with difficulty, trend rightwards across the wall and then move up to a flake crack and the belay.

[K. Howett, D. Towse, S. Jenkins 01.12.82]

LLANBERIS +

OGWEN +

TREMADOG +

GOGARTH & LLEYN

LLANDUDNO +

491

Chain Gang Wall ®

Area: Marine Drive
Style: Trad (single pitch)
Aspect: North-East
Rock type: Limestone
Approach: 1 minute
Altitude: 60m

Foulish Goulish	E6
Olympus Trip	E6

Chain Gang	E5
More Genius	E5
Mr Olympia	E5
Precious Time	E4

Kanly	E2
Bauxed	E1

A superb leaning wall: compact and steep, it offers several hard testpieces that are among the best in the area. On the right side the rock is more featured; here are further excellent routes, at more amenable grades.

The climbing is generally a little more thuggish and less technical than on other Marine Drive sectors. A lot of the routes use bolts, but they have been used sparingly. So make sure you're carrying your trad rack too; these are not straightforward clip-ups.

Conditions: The crag receives very little, if any, direct sun. The sun does hit the road opposite the crag from late afternoon onwards and so it is possible to warm up there if it gets chilly belaying. When dry the rock offers excellent friction, but after rain it does take a little longer than other sectors to fully dry out.

Approach: Continue along the Marine Drive from Parisella's Cave around the headland. 50m further on Chain Gang Wall can be seen just right of a broken down look out, and directly above a prominent yellow phone box.

Descent: In situ bolt lower-offs.

Access Restrictions: No climbing is allowed before 6.00pm on all bank holiday weekends and during the school summer holidays (mid-July – first week in September)

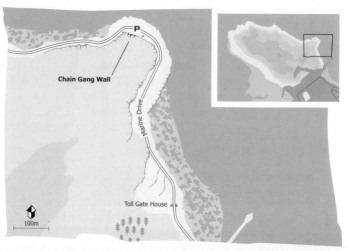

LLANBERIS +   OGWEN +   TREMADOG +   GOGARTH & LLEYN   LLANDUDNO +

492

∧ Silvia Fitzpatrick takes on **Mr Olympia** E5 6b, no contest! photo: Simon Marsh

↖ The phone box; a handy landmark, hopefully otherwise unused photo: Simon Marsh

Chain Gang Wall

1. Foulish Goulish E6 6b 18m ®
A fierce route that starts up the crack of *Mr Olympia* and then traverses a long way leftwards before heading upwards. Start below an obviously painful fist-jamming crack and pull up into this with difficulty. At the top of the crack move leftwards to an obvious incut jug. Hard moves left and up on thin crimps then allow slightly easier territory and the belay to be reached.

Mark Katz's F8b direct start encompasses a V7/Font 7a+ boulder problem called *Mr. Whippy* (which finishes at the prominent jug) before things become much harder passing the first bolt.
[G. Gibson 08.03.85]

2. Mr Olympia E5 6b 18m ®
A superb route, but hard for the grade. Start below the obviously painful fist-jamming crack and pull up into this with difficulty. Move leftwards at the top of the crack and break up the wall past 2 bolts. Hard moves back right at the second bolt lead to some large undercuts in an overlap. Pull over this on good holds and romp up to the belay.
[R. Fawcett, W Wayman, P Williams 06.83]

3. Olympus Trip E6 6b 18m ®
An excellent eliminate that seeks out trouble. Start as for *Chain Gang* at the small flake and follow this route to the poor rest from where *Chain Gang* launches upwards into its crux. Ignore this easy option and continue diagonally leftwards past a couple of bolts until it is possible to join *Mr Olympia* at the undercuts in the overlap. Pull over the overlap on good holds and romp up to the belay.
[G. Smith 1987]

4. Chain Gang E5 6a/b 18m ®
One of the best trad routes on the Orme. The crux involves quite a long reach and is probably 6a for the tall. Start at the small flake and pull up and left on good but spaced holds to a poor rest below a slight bulge. A long cross-through gains a good hold and more gear before a tiring series of moves leads to large undercuts in a flake. Easier, but still interesting, climbing remains.
[A. Pollitt, T. Freeman 24.11.82]

Silvia Fitzpatrick on **Mr Olympia** E5 6b photos: Simon Marsh

Chain Gang Wall

LLANBERIS +

OGWEN +

TREMADOG +

GOGARTH & LLEYN

LLANDUDNO +

▶ **5. More Genius E5 6b** 18m ®
A very good route that sees less traffic than *Chain Gang*, probably because it is harder, pumpier and bolder. It starts on the same small flake as *Chain Gang*, but continues straight up the wall until a delicate traverse rightwards gains a thin crack and assorted gear. Pumpy moves past the bolt give access to a poor rest and some bold, delicate climbing to reach the belay.
[G. Gibson 09.09.87]

▶ **6. Precious Time E4 6a** 18m ®
Good and varied climbing that starts 3m right of the *Chain Gang* flake and is possibly a soft touch at this grade. Step up rightwards until below the overlap and undercut this leftwards to gain a good hold at the end. A big rock-over gains reasonable holds and a position below the bottomless groove. Pull into this before moving slightly left to the belay.
[A. Pollitt, K. Robertson, J. Redhead 03.12.82]

▶ **7. Kanly E2 5c** 18m ®
This great little route shares the same start as the next route, *Bauxed*, at an open white groove just before the arête. The route is slightly bold, but the climbing is steady. Climb the groove to a move leftwards onto a small ramp. Move back slightly rightwards to an overlap, pull over this and go more easily to the belay.
[D. Towse 11.06.81]

▶ **8. Bauxed E1 5b** 18m ®
A fine climb at an accessible grade. Start as for *Kanly*, at the open groove just left of the arête, and follow this before moving rightwards onto the wall. Climb the wall on good holds before finishing slightly leftwards.
[G.Roberts, T. Cunningham 1979]

Yellow Wall ®

Area: Marine Drive
Style: Sport/Trad (single pitch)
Aspect: North-West
Rock type: Limestone
Approach: 0 minutes
Altitude: 75m

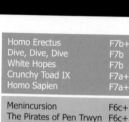

Homo Erectus	F7b+
Dive, Dive, Dive	F7b
White Hopes	F7b
Crunchy Toad IX	F7a+
Homo Sapien	F7a+

Menincursion	F6c+
The Pirates of Pen Trwyn	F6c+
String of Pearls	F6b+

Pen Trwyn Patrol	E4
Melkor	E3
The Gold Coast	E3

Pale Shelter	E1

Another popular section of this roadside crag, hosting a nifty selection of convenient sport/trad pitches. The only real drawback is the polish, which is evident on some of the routes. Needless to say, it pays to carry a selection of wires on the sport routes, particularly the sub F7a ones.

Conditions: A quick-drying wall blessed with glorious afternoon/evening sun (though the *Menincursion* wall does suffer from seepage problems).

Approach: 50m beyond Chain Gang Wall a large roof overhangs the road. Yellow Wall lies just to the right.

Descent: In situ bolt lower-offs.

Access restrictions: No climbing is allowed before 6.00 pm on all bank holiday weekends and during the school summer holidays (mid-July – first week in September).

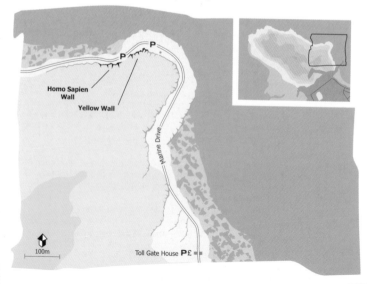

Homo Sapien Wall

Yellow Wall

Marine Drive

100m

Toll Gate House P£

∧ Rob Wilson cruising up **String of Pearls 6b+**   photo: Ray Wood

↰ The yellow Wall is a perfect venue at the end of a sunny day   photo: Al Williams

Yellow Wall • Dive, Dive, Dive • Yellow Wall

1. Dive, Dive, Dive F7b 18m ®
Break out left onto the wall from the easy ramp. Sustained climbing leads to the belay.
[A Pollitt 17.08.84]

2. Crunchy Toad IX F7a+ 18m ®
From a little further up the ramp climb directly up the crack. Short and sweet.
[S Lewis 24.08.84]

3. Melkor E3 5c 15m ®
An absorbing route taking the line of shallow scoops past an old in situ thread.
[D Towse, M Roberts 05.83]

4. Pen Trwyn Patrol E4 6a 15m ®
A superb trad route sporting a couple of bolts (the first of which is of limited use).
[R Fawcett, G Fawcett, A Pollitt, P Williams 25.06.83]

5. The Pirates of Pen Trwyn F6c+ 15m ®
An excellent, intense excursion breaking up from the lower cracked groove system to tackle the bulging wall. 'Sportingly' bolted (i.e. take some wires).
[R Fawcett, G Fawcett, A Pollitt, P Williams 25.06.83]

6. String of Pearls F6b+ 15m ®
A cracking pitch, one of the best at this grade hereabouts.
[D Towse, M Raine 19.06.83 – starting from *Pirates of Pen Trwyn*. Direct start: G Gibson 06.83]

7. Pale Shelter E1 5b 15m ®
A delightful route finishing up the attractive groove at the top of the wall.
[D Lyon, N Clacher 10.06.83]

The black wall to the right has numerous bolted routes, the best being *Menincursion* F6c+, which tackles the vague central scoop line. Start 4-5m right of the obvious crack, that splits the face, to a fingery finish over a bulge.

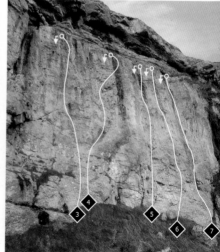

Approximately 100m further along above a prominent graffiti-tagged ramp (level with the 1100 mark), a clean undulating wall is dissected by the following classic clip-ups:

8. Homo Erectus F7b+ 15m Ⓡ
A bulging start (and a difficult 2nd clip) leads into a thin crack. Thereafter, continue up the wall above moving right to the belay.
[E Stone 1990]

9. Homo Sapien F7a+ 15m Ⓡ
This superb, technically sustained pitch is the archetypal Marine Drive sport route. Step left from the ramp into a shallow groove. Weave up the wall and finally move left to the belay.
[G Gibson 02.05.84]

10. White Hopes F7b 15m Ⓡ
Another sustained outing, but this time steeper and pumpier. Climb up the short diagonal groove then trend up rightwards to gain the hanging crack. Hard for the grade.
[A Pollitt, M Atkinson 16.08.84]

11. The Gold Coast E3 5c 15m Ⓡ
The obvious cracked groove system right of the graffiti tagged ramp provides another good route.
[I Carr, C Hardy 23.10.83]

∧ Chris Doyle on **White Hopes** F7b photo: Alex Messenger

Marine Drive Bouldering ®

Area: **Marine Drive**
Style: **Bouldering**
Aspect: **North-East**
Rock type: **Limestone**
Approach: **0 - 1 minute**
Altitude: **50m**

Conditions: The relatively mild coastal climate ensures that decent climbing conditions can be founds at all times of the year. Like the Carreg Hylldrem bouldering wall (down near Tremadog), the Parisella's Cave area provides a useful retreat if the weather closes in. However, seepage and dampness can be a problem during the winter months, particularly on still, wind-free days. That said, it is a rare that you won't find some climbable rock to play upon.

The landings at both places are good, but generally dusty; a pad is not essential (unless you fancy trying some of the highball lines in Parisella's) as long as you've got something to keep your feet clean.

Approach: Parisella's Cave sits in a conspicuous position just off the Marine Drive 100m along from the tollgate. Pill Box Wall is situated 50m beyond the headland, just right of a broken down look out, and directly above a prominent yellow phone box (Chain Gang Wall lies just to the right).

Access restrictions: No climbing is allowed on the Pill Box Wall area before 6.00 pm on all bank holiday weekends and during the school summer holidays (mid-July – first week in September). Please remember that the Marine Drive is a one-way road. If you do arrive by car, make sure that you park sensibly and do not block the road. The toll is currently £2.50 per car or £15 for a season ticket.

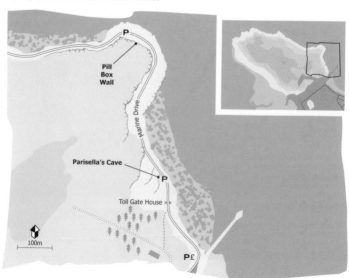

Parisella's Cave offers some excellent steep and finger-friendly bouldering. In fact, there are over 60 recognised independent problems and links spread between the Parisella's and Split Infinity caves, situated next door to the right. The grade range runs from V2/Font 5+/6a right up to V14/Font 8b+; basically, if you can boulder V5/Font 6c there will be plenty to go at.

Back in the early-mid '80s, Jerry Moffatt, Ben Moon, Martin 'Basher' Atkinson, Andy Pollitt and Tim Freeman hung out at this very spot. In between developing new routes on the Ormes they established a series of classic test pieces, such as *The Left Wall Traverse* (V7/8/Font 7a+/7b), which starts sitting at the back left corner and picks the easiest line of resistance, all the way out to exit on the left side of the cave. There are numerous radical lines crossing the central steepness, or, at a more reasonable level, breaking through the roofs on the right side.

Pill Box Wall lies around the headland just left of the Chain Gang Wall by the side of the broken down lookout. It is banned for routes, but at its base a steep section provides some splendid and rather powerful boulder problems. It can be greasy, but the rock is superb, so it is always worth a look. The best problem, *Pill Box Original* V6/Font 7a takes the obvious sitting start line right of the black stain to reach jugs in the break.

∧ Neil Dyer going for it on the first ascent of the rather highball **Upper Cut** V8/Font 7b photo: Si Panton

< Danny Cattell bouldering on Pill Box Wall photo: Alex Messenger

∧ Winter bouldering in the cave; flasks of tea and duvet jackets photo: Si Panton

LLANBERIS +

OGWEN +

TREMADOG +

GOGARTH & LLEYN

LLANDUDNO +

501

Lower Pen Trwyn

Area:	**Marine Drive**
Style:	**Sport/Trad (single pitch)**
Aspect:	**South-East**
Rock type:	**Limestone**
Approach:	**10 minutes**
Altitude:	**Sea Level (tidal)**

Mussel Beach	F8a
Statement of Youth	F8a
I've Been a Bad, Bad Boy	F7c

La Boheme Direct	F7b+
Libertango	F7b+
La Boheme	F7b
Mean Mother	F7b
Face Race	F7a+
Night Glue	F7a+
The Refrain	F7a+
The Pink Pinkie Snuffs It	F7a

Mad O'Rourke's Kipper House	F6c+
Under the Boardwalk	F6c
Kaffe Fasset	F6b
Skin Deep	F6a+
Skin Game	F6a+
Beauty is Only	F6a

Golden Pond	F5+

Jacuzzi Jive	E4
Twisting by the Pool	E4

Simply one of the best sports climbing venues in the UK. Lower Pen Trwyn (or 'LPT' as it is commonly known) hosts a very high concentration of quality climbing, but the really appealing factor is that, for once, there is a good range of routes across the grades from F5+ to F9a.

Most of the routes are fully bolted, although in the middle of the crag there are a couple of pure trad lines and several bolted routes that need the odd wire. When dry the rock has good friction and generally is of excellent quality. Despite this on still, humid days it can be exceptionally greasy.

Kaffe Fasset F6b photo: Phil Dowthwaite >

Lower Pen Trwyn

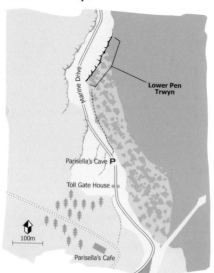

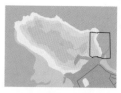

Conditions: The crag receives the morning sun, but this disappears by early afternoon. Conditions can be difficult to predict, and are largely dependant on wind and humidity levels. It is possible to get an indication of the conditions from the top of the descent path by looking at the colour of the rock at the steep left-hand end of crag; if the rock is light grey then conditions should be okay, but if it is dark grey then be prepared to drop your grade, or perhaps choose a different venue.

The crag is tidal, but access is possible for about 3 to 4 hours each side of low tide.

Approach: 150m past the Toll House at the entrance to Marine Drive a series of caves runs back up the hillside to the left. The lowest and deepest is the renowned hardcore bouldering venue, Parisella's Cave. Cross over the stone wall on the other side of the road and scramble carefully down the grassy descent gully. At the base of the slope, head left across the boulder beach to the crag.

Descent: In situ bolt lower-offs.

1. The Refrain F7a+ 20m

A fine, fully bolted sports route with a cruel crux section at the top. Start easily and then move right under the overlap, pull over and move back left to a rest. The next section escalates in difficulty until a hard undercut move allows a small edge to be gained over the bulge. Big holds and the belay follow.
[D Lyon 1988]

2. Under the Boardwalk F6c 20m

The classic introduction to the steeper routes is good, but getting polished. Climb up to the bulge and make a long move to pull over. Continue up to the base of the next corner groove and pull into it on good holds. Move up to the capping overlap and pull rightwards past it via an awkward mantelshelf move. The belay is immediately above.
[M Atkinson, A Pollitt 28.08.84]

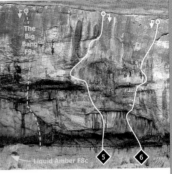

3. I've Been a Bad, Bad Boy F7c 22m

A great route with lots of good climbing and a very on/off finish. Fire through the polished and powerful starting moves to gain easy ground in the groove. At the top of this make a pumpy traverse leftwards until a thin series of pulls allow the upper groove to be gained. At the top of this pull out right and fire for the jug before barn-dooring off.

[M Pretty 19.08.88]

4. Mussel Beach F8a 22m

A power route. A hard move at the start gives access to big holds, some swinging around and an easing in angle. The ensuing work going through the bulge on undercuts and side pulls is difficult and only leads to some mediocre flatties. Control the pump and head up and left to the belay.

[M Pretty 09.07.88]

The crag continues to bulge out at an alarming angle. Various desperate routes break through the steepness including Jerry Moffatt's *Liquid Amber* F8c and one of the hardest lines in the UK, Neil Carson's *The Big Bang* F9a.

5. Statement of Youth F8a 22m

Ben Moon's classic F8a: at the time of its ascent, a state of the art route that defined the emerging sport climbing ethic. Go up easily to the famous traverse and heel hook across this to a hard move upwards. Once standing, work your way up the groove until a tenuous traverse right on undercuts gains the final groove and belay.

[B Moon 25.06.84]

6. Night Glue F7a+ 22m

An essential 'LPT' tick, perhaps the best route of its grade in the area. Pull onto the slab and teeter up this to the overlaps. Pull steeply through this section on good holds and then traverse rightwards and up to a ledge. Move up to a rest and then make some fingery pulls leftwards to a jug. Continue easily to the belay.

[A Pollitt 21.09.84]

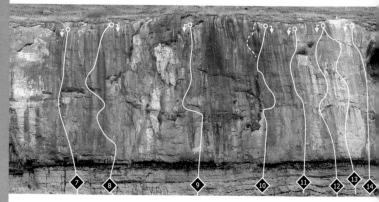

7. Jacuzzi Jive E4 6a 22m
A fine, fingery trad route. Climb up to the left-hand end of a small ledge at 12m. Continue up on some flakes and then go up the wall passing a bolt and a hard move at the top.
[D Lyon, C Lyon 21.07.83]

8. Twisting by the Pool E4 6a 22m
Climb up rightwards and then leftwards to enter the groove. Climb up to the bulge above and pass it on the left. Move back right and then take the excellent upper wall direct.
[D Lyon, C Lyon 03.07.83]

9. The Pink Pinkie Snuffs It F7a 22m
A good and popular sport route with two contrasting halves. The initial section involves steep wall climbing on good holds before a quick couple of moves left bring easier angled territory. Technical and fingery climbing now leads to bigger holds. Finish slightly rightwards up the final headwall.
[D Staniforth, R Curley 25.08.84]

10. La Boheme F7b 22m
One for the technicians. Great climbing with a sustained sequence to reach the belay. Start up the crack and at its top move out right onto the wall. At the break trend up and slightly leftwards to a bolt. Move right past this with some tenuous moves to reach and climb the faint crack line that leads to the belay.
[A Pollitt 28.06.84/]

10a. La Boheme Direct F7b+ 22m
A fine direct finish that is really quite hard. Eschew the final moves rightwards and blast straight up the wall. At the top move right to use the belay from the original route.
[P Hawkins 1990]

11. Libertango F7b+ 22m
Hard face climbing. Climb up on small flakes until the angle steepens and then move straight up before a slight move right to an area of lighter rock. Finish directly up via a hidden hold.
[A Pollitt, M Atkinson 15.06.84]

12. Mean Mother F7b 22m
A great route with a sustained crux section. Small wires are useful for the midsection. Climb easily until the angle increases and then make some increasingly difficult pulls to gain an open groove on the left. Continue up more easily, but still with interest to the belay.
[S Lewis, M Pretty 21.06.84]

13. Face Race F7a+ 22m
A popular route because the climbing is both very good and also reasonable for the grade. Take some wires for the first section. Climb the wall with a section on small, but positive holds at 2/3 height. Once past this push on to a rounded finish.
[S Lewis, M Pretty 16.06.84]

14. Mad O'Rourke's Kipper House F6c+ 22m
The crux leaving the cave is disproportionately hard compared to the rest of the route, but the climbing is still good. Take some wires for the first section. Climb up to the cave with one difficult move and then pull leftwards out of the top of the cave with difficulty.
[D Lyon 04.90]

15. Kaffe Fasset F6b 20m
A great little route with some strenuous climbing for the grade. Pull on to the wall and move quickly up the rough brown rock to a rest where the angle eases. Make some powerful moves on good holds to gain another rest in a corner system. Pull right out of the corner onto the face of the tower and then make the final few moves to the belay.
[C Tickell 1990]

16. Skin Deep F6a+ 19m
A good route with a steep and intimidating start. It may be prudent to take some wires for the first section especially in damp conditions. Pull through the rough rock at the start to gain the first bolt. Continue on good holds to a bulge, pull over via a flake and continue up the slab to the top.
[G Gibson 23.09.84]

17. Beauty is Only F6a 15m
Good climbing that is nicely balanced. A steep but straightforward start leads to a sustained few moves in the middle of the wall.
[G Gibson, M Jones 21.02.85]

18. Skin Game F6a+ 18m
Another worthwhile route with a steep start.
[G Gibson (solo) 17.03.85]

19. Golden Pond F5+ 18m
A suitable introduction to the delights of 'LPT'. The climbing is pleasant and steady.
[D Lyon 1995]

Matt Smythe on the classic **Night Glue** F7a+ photo: Al Leary ∧
Careful as you go photo: Simon Marsh ⌐↑

Wonder Wall ®

Area:	**Marine Drive**
Style:	**Sport/Trad (single pitch)**
Aspect:	**North**
Rock type:	**Limestone**
Approach:	**5 minutes**
Altitude:	**Sea Level (non-tidal)**

Laura	F7a+
Sweet Dreams	F7a
The Reflex	F7a

Clowns of God	F6c+
Heaven's Gate	F6b

A Cry of Angels	E3

Rainbow Warrior	VS

A neat little crag with a relatively straightforward approach; this is essentially a clean vertical wall situated above a non-tidal platform, accessed by abseil. The main attraction is the central quartet of superb sport routes, although there are a couple of interesting trad routes at either side of the crag. The sport routes are equipped with resin bolts (except *Laura* which is due to be re-equipped soon). That being said, a rack of wires might come in handy.

The rock is good quality, with a smooth flowstone finish evident in places. It offers the usual technical and sustained Pen Trwyn climbing style, albeit quite finger friendly considering the none-too steep angle (i.e. vertical).

Conditions: Early birds may catch some sun, but a more typical arrival time will find the crag resting in shade, moreover it can be very windy. Save it for a sunny day when it's too hot, or the tides are wrong for LPT. The wall does take some drainage, and is probably best avoided after heavy rain.

Approach: Park at the apex of the bend 250m beyond Hamburger Buttress and drop steeply down the depression below, trending leftwards (facing out) down the grass slope to find a single resin bolt on a flat sloping rock square. Abseil diagonally rightwards (facing in) from here down steepening grass to reach some ledges and three separate resin belay bolts (15m). Re-belay on the nearest one and abseil to the non-tidal (just) ledge at the base of the wall (25m).

Access restrictions: There is a bird ban on *Rainbow Warrior* from 1st March to 31st July.

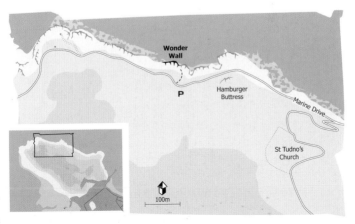

Wonder Wall

1. Rainbow Warrior VS 4c 25m ®
A useful escape route, but worthwhile in its own right as well. Climb the narrow groove to the ledge system; step right and continue up a further groove line to the top.
[N Clacher, D Lyon 05.84]

2. Heaven's Gate F6b 25m
A fine lower wall, but barely independent of the groove to its right (*Gibbering Wreck* HVS 5a) after the halfway break is reached. Nonetheless, a handy warm up for the other sport routes.
[K Smith 1992]

3. Clowns of God F6c+ 25m
A great route with a powerful crux on the upper wall; a hard independent start can be contrived past the first bolt, but it makes more sense initially to use the holds on *Heaven's Gate* (with your right, instead of left), swinging back left to move up to a ledge in the main break.
[D Lyon, N Clacher 15.05.84. Direct start: P Smith 1992]

4. Laura F7a+ 25m
A splendid, intricate route: thin and sustained climbing leads more or less directly up to and past the thin crack line above the main break.
[P Smith 25.05.92]

5. The Reflex F7a 25m
A sustained and fingery trip on marvellous flowstone rock: the classic of the crag. Follow the scoop up left to the break, and then trend up rightwards to gain another shallow scoop that leads boldly to the top.
[D Lyon, N Clacher 15.05.84]

6. Sweet Dreams F7a 25m
Another superb and unrelenting test of forearm stamina. After a slightly confusing start, clip the second bolt on *The Reflex*, step left and truck directly up the wall.
[D Lyon, N Clacher 15.05.84 – starting as for *The Reflex*]

7. A Cry of Angels E3 6a 25m
An interesting line, leading up to a hanging flake on the headwall. Muscle up the cracked wall or alternatively do the first section of *Sweet Dreams* to the break, then move up left, before making hard moves back right to gain the hanging flake.
[D Lyon 05.84]

∧ Silvia Fitzpatrick in a thumb-sprag press (far out!) on **The Reflex** F7a photo: Simon Marsh

Castell y Gwynt ®

Area: Marine Drive
Style: Trad/Sport (1-4 pitches)
Aspect: North
Rock type: Limestone
Approach: 10 minutes
Altitude: 50m

Hidden Sign	F7b+
Bittersweet Connection	E5
Cruella Deville	E5 (F7a+)
Plas Berw	E5
Pyschic Threshold	E5
The Exile	E5
New Dimensions	E4
Opal Moon	E4
Appian Way	E2/3

A dramatic and intimidating crag criss-crossed by a fascinating collection of classic multi-pitch trad routes and stunning sport pitches. Hidden from view it retains an air of mystery and intrigue quite at odds with the light-hearted roadside crags that line the Marine Drive. The sense of exposure on the crag is accentuated by its lofty position, perched as it is above a sloping grassy rake, beyond which a further hidden cliff plunges into the sea.

Steep and unforgiving, this is a not a place for those lacking in confidence or the ability to deal with relentlessly difficult ground. Even *Appian Way*, which manages to tip toe through some spectacular territory at a comparatively reasonable grade, is quite a forearm-wilting experience. The rock is mostly excellent quality although a little loose on the right-hand perimeter. There is a good deal of in situ gear, including many threads, bolts (both old and new) and pegs in varying states of decay. Nonetheless it pays to carry a comprehensive rack, including plenty of cams.

The sport routes are fully equipped with modern eco-bolts.

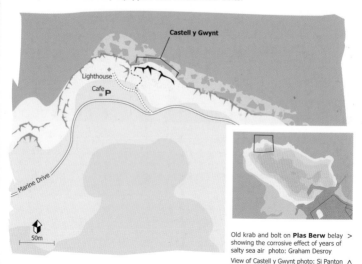

Old krab and bolt on **Plas Berw** belay > showing the corrosive effect of years of salty sea air photo: Graham Desroy

View of Castell y Gwynt photo: Si Panton ∧

Conditions: Castell y Gwynt is a cold crag. It gets virtually no sun and is one of the most exposed and windy venues on the Ormes. It also suffers from seepage, but perhaps not as badly as, say, Wonder Wall.

Approach: Park by the 'Rest and Be Thankful' café, walk back along the road and turn down the Lighthouse drive. Hop over the wall on the bend and walk down the grassy slope to reach a plateau on top of the crag. The descent gully lies over on the left (facing out). Scramble down it taking care, especially if the grass is wet.

Access restrictions: There is a permanent bird ban on *Opal Moon* from 1st March to 30th June. The rest of the crag is also subject to the same ban if peregrines are known to be nesting. Please check the notice board at the top of the descent gully for details of restriction extensions.

The Mini Finish

The Zippy Chicken Finish

1

7

5

6

7

6

Abseil approach to Opal Moon

Teenage Kicks E6 6b

Sidekick E6 6a

Central Pillar E6 6c (7b+)

Blast Peru E5 6b

The Long Goodbye E6 6b (7b+)

Bad Taste Direct F7b+

9

5

8

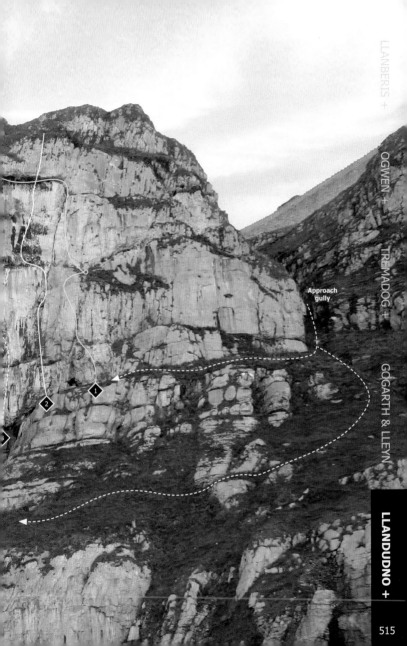

Approach gully

1

2

Castell y Gwynt

1. Appian Way/Watling Street E2/3 5c 88m ®

A memorable and head-spinning trip. Wild positions and a gradual increase in difficulty maintain an element of tension, right until the crux on P4. Take a full rack of cams up to size 4.

P1 5a 20m Start from the ledge up and right of the red-stained ledges beneath *Hidden Sign*. Gain the hanging groove from the right. Move up it for a few metres, before breaking out left and climbing up and right to reach a ledge and nut belays.

P2 5a 20m Pull up into the groove above and continue up astride the hollow-sounding pillar, to the top break. Now the fun really starts! Take a deep breath and make exposed moves leftwards around onto the front face. Continue leftwards along the break to reach a small stance (bolt and thread belay) common with *New Dimensions*.

P3 5b 18m Continue along the break past a series of tricky and increasingly pumpy sections to arrive at a foot ledge (massive thread) just before a steep arête.

P4 5c 30m Swing strenuously around the steep arête to a poor rest and continue along the break with difficulty, better holds and a kinder angle arriving just in time (for most!). At the left end of the break ramble up vegetated rock to reach bolt belays up and right.

[R Edwards, G Perry 03.77/R Edwards, F Smith 03.77]

2. The Exile E5 6a 40m ®

A fine example of a trad/sport hybrid, giving a big pitch cutting straight up to and through the roof that caps the *Appian Way* traverse.

Start steeply past a conspicuous pocket, pulling awkwardly into a narrow hanging groove. Continue more easily to the mid-height break. Hard moves lead up past a bolt and up to the *Appian Way* traverse. Pull directly through the small roof and make final tricky moves to reach the top.

[D Lyon, N Clacher, P Freeman 07.87]

3. Cruella Deville E5 6b (F7a+) 40m ®

An excellent route, almost a clip-up really. Start down the awkward step as for Hidden Sign. Climb the wall (wires protect, or clip the bolt on *Hidden Sign*) up to the twin threads in the break. Ascend direct up a shallow tufa groove, pulling over a smooth bulge to access the prominent right-facing corner to the *New Dimensions* belay. Abseil off, or continue up the 5b bolted line directly above the first pitch.

[D Lyon, D Summerfield, P Freeman 1987]

4. Hidden Sign F7b+ 35m ®

A dazzling sport climb. Start up on the red-stained ledges by a belay bolt. Ascend the flowstone wall trending slightly left to a rest. Gain and climb the hanging groove with difficulty, angling right to a lower-off near the top of the prow.

[S Lee, H Lancashire 05.96]

The line of bolts situated just left form a direct start to the route *Good Taste* E5 6b. This gives a F7b+ pitch overall.

5. New Dimensions E4 6a 52m ®

A fantastic and contrasting route; initially strenuous, then technical, and finally, steady, but very exposed.

P1 5c 27m Start towards the right-hand end of the main terrace, below and left of the red-stained ledges at the base of Hidden Sign. Scramble up to a small cave and follow an awkward crack out of it. Step right and move up to a small roof. Step right again and head up a bulging groove, before moving right once more to the base of another groove. Follow this, exiting left at its top to reach a bolt belay with threads above.

P2 6a 15m The black groove up and left proves to be a technical affair. At the main roof swerve right along the *Appian Way* break to reach a small stance (bolt and thread belay). Alternatively at the same grade, there is the Mini Finish: move right a few metres until a fun pull through the roof gains a bolt belay. Abseil off.

P3 5b 10m Trend up and left past old pegs to reach the top.

[R Edwards, T Jepson (3 pts) 11.10.75, FFA: R Edwards 1976]

Si Panton scooting along P2 of **Appian Way** E2/3 5c photo: Graham Desroy >

Castell y Gwynt

6. Plas Berw E5 6b 65m ®

A stunning route that accepts the challenge of the gloriously fat tufa left of *New Dimensions*. Unfortunately the 6b traverse on P2 is often wet and the in situ gear at this point is little more than 'ring pull pegs'. Many people just do the magnificent P1, then finish up *New Dimensions*.

P1 6a 20m From the initial wall of *New Dimensions*, break up left and boldly shin up the huge tufa to reach a good wire at its top. Traverse right to reach the *New Dimensions* belay.

P2 6b 15m Follow the obvious traverse line back left, with a short hard section moving beyond the top of the tufa, to reach a ledge and bolt belays.

P3 6a 20m Traverse out right onto the wall and follow flakes up to the main roof. Traverse right along the break, to reach the 2nd *New Dimensions* belay.

P4 5b 10m P3 of *New Dimensions*.

[J Redhead, K Robertson 29.08.79, P3 added: 02.10.79]

If you've got the fitness it is worth considering the following alternative extensions. No *Plas Like Home* E5/6 6b continues up the arête above the main tufa to reach the *New Dimensions* traverse. *The Zippy Chicken Finish* (E6 6b) adds a wild finish through the capping roof. Pull through the roof direct with a kneebar on the lip allowing you to grope further for the jug with the right hand. The top lies just above. A huge and exciting pitch, worth E6 6b.

7. The Bittersweet Connection E5 6b 45m ®

A majestic and pumpy route that swaggers up the crag to a thrilling exit over the capping roof.

P1 6b 30m Start as for *New Dimensions*, but almost immediately tackle the bulging wall on the left. Above the roof a difficult section leads past a bolt; continue up to the break (junction with P2 of *Plas Berw*) and head left to a belay.

P2 6a 15m Climb up to the roof (large thread) and breach it, taking note of the rather aged in situ gear as you go. Continue up loose ground to the top.

[J Redhead, K Robertson (1 pt and started from Central Pillar) 06.09.79, FFA: R Fawcett 14.09.82, right-hand start (as described) first climbed by D Lyon in 1988]

Central Pillar E6 6c (F7c+) scales the wall below the central belay and *Blast Peru* E5 6b takes the flowstone flake to its left. *The Long Goodbye* E6 6b (F7b+) is the mostly bolted route that leaves *Central Pillar* early on, pulling through the cave/roof and continuing up directly, all the way to the top.

8. Pyschic Threshold E5 6b 40m ®

This big challenging pitch is continuously steep and testing.

Start at a short arête beneath a small cave. Trend up right, then move back left onto the arête and up to the cave. Climb right through the roof to reach a rest. After a quick blow, press on up left past good pockets to reach a large niche. Pull over the bulge on the right and make a difficult move up left. Gain the thin crack above and follow it to a break. Continue up the wall trending left to reach the left end of the main break beneath the top roof. Ramble up vegetated rock to reach bolt belays up and right.

[R Edwards, P Williams (2 pts) 03.08.77 FFA: K Carrigan, D Hall 05.81]

The walls right and left of *Psychic Threshold* are taken respectively by *Sidekick* E6 6a and *Teenage Kicks* E6 6b.

9. Opal Moon E4 6a 35m ®

An exceptional route in a wild position.

From a nut belay 10m right (facing out) of the bolt belays at the top of *Appian Way/ Pyschic Threshold* a 35m abseil will get you to a small corner/cave. Climb rightwards to the arête and heave over the bulge on good holds to reach a bolt. Continue up the wall, trending first leftwards, then back right up a vague groove. Scramble up left then back right to reach the abseil point.

[D Lyon, D Summerfield 03.08.86]

Sure feet and trim beards all round photo: Graham Desroy

St Tudno's Upper Crag

Area: Marine Drive
Style: Trad (single pitch)
Aspect: West
Rock type: Limestone
Approach: 5 minutes
Altitude: 60m

Gritstone Gorilla Direct	E4
Gritstone Gorilla	E3
Limestone Lemur	E2

Gritstone Gorilla lives up to the promise of its name: a proper thug's route that responds best to a combative style. The other two variations offer a toned-down, or a cranked up version of the original classic. Situated on the central roofed section of St Tudno's Upper crag, the routes offer steep, pumpy climbing in an airy position above the sea. In fact, the perfect place to spend an evening. The rock is generally good quality, coarse-grained limestone, although extra care should be taken on all exits where the rock becomes looser. There are a few pegs scattered about, all old and of dubious quality. A full range of nuts and cams should be carried.

Conditions: The crag receives the afternoon and evening sun. The position of the crag on a corner of the headland means that it can be windy here, but the routes do dry quickly after rain.

Approach: Continue along Marine Drive to the Rest and Be Thankful Café. 130m beyond the café on the left-hand side is a large open area where you can park. Cross the road and go through the gate that is immediately opposite the picnic/parking area. The crag is clearly visible slightly down and right. It is approached via well worn sheep tracks.

Belaying and Descent: There is a single rusty belay bolt on the small buttress above the finish of *Gritstone Gorilla*. This can be backed up with natural gear. Walk off right (facing in) with care, until you regain the original approach path.

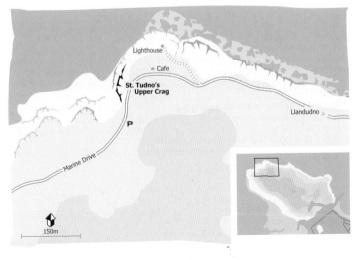

St Tudno's Upper Crag

LLANBERIS +

OGWEN +

TREMADOG +

GOGARTH & LLEYN

LLANDUDNO +

60m from the right-hand end of the crag is an area of roofs. The first route, *Gritstone Gorilla*, starts under the widest, steepest most featured section near a small recessed corner on the right.

1. Gritstone Gorilla E3 5c 25m

A power-stamina route that is harder than it looks and strenuous to protect. Start up the corner or slightly to the left and gain the hanging corner. Climb this on good holds until the roof, where an old peg can be clipped. A long reach left on a good side-pull gives access to the horizontal breaks in the roof. Pull leftwards out to the lip and then power back right to a flake crack in the headwall. Climb this with conviction to a rest below the final headwall. Undercut left more easily and pull into the corner crack that leads casually to the top.

[P. Williams, R. Edwards 20.09.77]

2. Gritstone Gorilla Direct E4 6a 25m

This variation blasts straight up the faint crack in the final headwall to create a very sustained route. Follow the original route through the roofs to the rest below the headwall; now pull straight up to a poor peg and pass this with difficulty via some fingery and slightly off-balance moves. Easy ground soon follows.

[D. Lyon, P. Freeman 1987]

3. Limestone Lemur E2 5c 25m

This route starts as for *Gritstone Gorilla*, but does the sensible thing and skirts rightwards to avoid the roof thuggery. Follow the original route to the roof and then pull right onto the arête with interest. Continue upwards to the break and then tackle the wide groove above with care.

[R. Edwards, P. Williams, P. Roberts 08.10.77]

∧ Silvia Fitzpatrick fighting hard on **Gritstone Gorilla** E3 5c photo: Simon Marsh

Upper Craig y Don

Area:	**Little Orme**
Style:	**Trad/Sport (single pitch)**
Aspect:	**West**
Rock type:	**Limestone**
Approach:	**15 minutes**
Altitude:	**75m**

Riptide	F7b

Doenitz	E5
Hydraulic Transmission	E5
Nimitz	E5
Frozen Moment/New Wave	E4
The Cruel Sea	E3

Hydro	E1

A delightful sunny crag overlooking Llandudno Bay. There is a fine selection of technical routes, both trad and some sport, all topped with resin anchor lower-offs.
Expect a mix of new and old in situ gear; wires should be carried on the sport routes.

Conditions: The sunny and open aspect means this is a quick-drying venue, which can be climbed on all year round.

Approach: The crag lies to the left of the main Llandudno - Rhos-on-Sea road on the landward side of Little Orme, above the eastern end of the main Llandudno beach. Park down the side road, at the point at which the dual carriageway section of the main road is reached (if travelling from the Llandudno side). Walk back along the road and go through the gate below Manor Crag. Follow the path up the right side of the crag. Just past a small quarry scramble up to reach a path leading westward along the top of Manor Crag. Follow this until it is possible to drop down and cross an old fence. Upper Craig y Don lies round to the right (facing out).

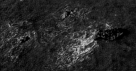

Dave Towse traversing the top break on **Hydro** E1 5b photo: Jethro Kiernan

Upper Craig y Don

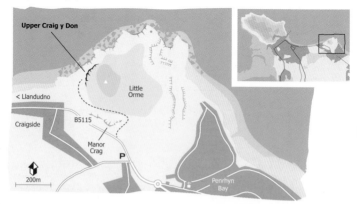

1. Doenitz E5 6b 27m

The open groove in the wall above the cave provides a grand route. Climb up the right side of the cave to reach the horizontal break above. Traverse left along the break, a bit slopey and awkward in places, to reach the open groove. Make crimpy and sequencey moves up, bearing left to reach the *Hydro* traverse line. Move left along the break, and ascend the headwall.

[K Howitt, D Towse (finishing up Hydro) 02.06.82, A Pollitt, K Howitt, D Towse (with independent finish) 06.06.82]

Glenda Huxter stretching for a clip on **Nimitz** E5 6b photo: Jethro Kiernan >

2. Nimitz E5 6b 27m

A cracking counter-diagonal to *Doenitz*. Follow Hydro until a thin traverse line leads out right past a thread to reach a resin bolt. Climb directly up the wall to the finish of *Hydro*.
[M Hammill, C Lyon 03.07.85]

3. Frozen Moment/New Wave E4 6a 20m

This neat link gives a very worthwhile variation on *Hydro*. Follow *Hydro* until it kinks left; climb directly up to the top traverse and step left for a direct finish up the headwall.
[M Hammill, C Lyon 07.07.85/M Hammill, C Lyon 27.06.85]

4. Hydro E1 5b 27m

The classic of the crag. Ascend easy ground left of the cave, turning left into a crack/ groove. Go up this to the upper break; then traverse right in a great position to finish up an easier flake.
[R Edwards, M Greasey 03.10.73]

5. Hydraulic Transmission E5 6b 24m

A splendid route with a fierce crimpy finish. Follow *Hydro* initially, but continue leftwards into a steep groove. Move right past a resin bolt and go up to the top break. A flake on the right leads up to another resin bolt. Finish with some desperate thin pulls back left to reach the lower-off.
[M Hammill, M Raven 26.06.85]

6. The Cruel Sea E3 6a 27m

A rambling start leads to a good finish. Start up *Hydraulic Transmission*, but continue along the diagonal line of to reach a thread at the left side of the top break. Pull onto the headwall and ascend directly past more threads to a lower-off.
[C Lyon, M Hammill 28.06.85]

7. Riptide F7b 18m

A nifty route with a bouldery roof section. Power through the roof with gusto and breeze up the upper wall to easier ground and a lower-off.
[D Lyon, P freeman, N Jowett 1987]

LLANBERIS +

OGWEN +

TREMADOG +

GOGARTH & LLEYN

LLANDUDNO +

525

Great Zawn ®

Area: Little Orme
Style: Trad/Sport (1 - 3 pitches)
Aspect: North
Rock type: Limestone
Approach: 30 minutes
Altitude: Sea Level (non-tidal)/75m

The Magic Flute	F7c
Old Sam	E3
The Hole of Creation	E3
The Glass Wall	E2
Quietus	E2

A deeply adventurous trip and/or something short and funky in a bizarre cave feature. Take your pick. Downstairs you will discover a stunning sheet of clean slabby rock set in a remote and committing position at the left side of the vast Little Orme sea cliffs, whilst upstairs, and by way of a contrast, a quirky rock orifice: *The Hole of Creation*. The latter offers a couple of steep, wacky routes with a grandstand view of Llandudno Bay.

Down below, the close proximity of the sea, and the obvious complexities of access and exit ratchet up the sense of adventure. Although the upper pitches have now become choked with grass, the lower slab presents an immaculate and remarkable sweep of beautiful rock.

The recommended approach to routes on the main slab requires four ropes in total. Two to climb with, one for the abseil, and a further rope to be pre-placed down the grassy upper section of the cliff.

Conditions: The crag receives little sun and does suffer from some seepage after rain. The routes on the main slab are not-tidal (the access traverse across the base of the slab sits above the high tide mark), nonetheless a calm sea is desirable.

Approach: Follow the seafront road in Llandudno Bay around the back of Little Orme (passing Upper Craig y Don and Manor Crag on the left) and continue down to a roundabout (Penrhyn Bay). Take the first exit left from the roundabout and turn left just after the garage into a housing estate. Turn either left or right at the first junction (both roads lead to the same point) and drive through the estate. Park at the end of the road, taking care not to block any driveways. Walk up the steps, turn right and head along to a flat grassy area below an incline leading up to the upper quarry. (Angel Bay lies straight ahead down a steep path) Turn left up the incline to gain the upper quarry. Skirt either side of the quarry and walk over the top to reach the old lookout. Walk down the grassy ramp below and left (looking out), then cut back left, then cut back left (pre-placing one of your ropes from the belay bolt marked on the topo if you are intending to do a route on the main slab) to reach a suitable base camp in the *Hole of Creation* cave.

Once you've geared up (and pre-placed your rope for the final pull out if you forgot to do it on the way in), scramble carefully down the slope until a mildly gripping traverse leads back right (facing out) to an abseil bolt. A 40m abseil leads down to a sloping ledge at the side of the main slab.

Access: A bird ban, running from 1st March to the 15th August, covers all routes in Great Zawn itself. *The Hole of Creation* and *The Magic Flute* are unaffected by this access ban.

Paul Donnithorne and Emma Alsford fully committed on P2 of **The Glass Wall** E2 5c   photo: Al Leary >
The old lookout   photo: Al Williams ∧

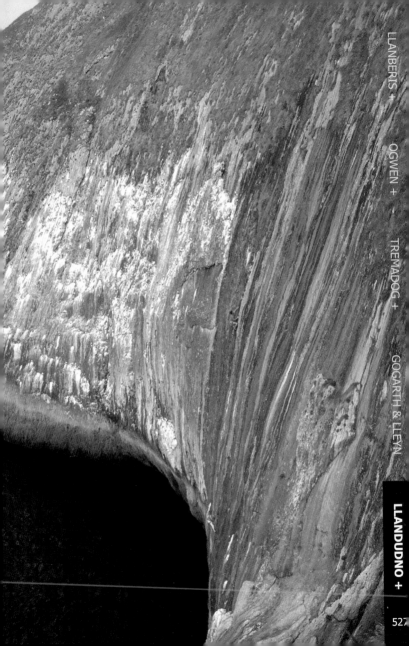

Great Zawn

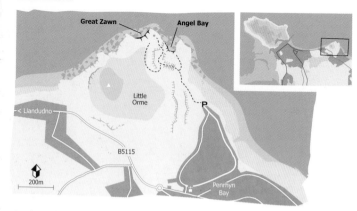

1. The Hole of Creation E3 6a 10m
A funky little route. Bridge and squirm up the back of the cave, going left around a convoluted bulge to gain the pod feature. Clip a monster thread above and make for the lower off at the top of *The Magic Flute*.
[P Williams, J Taylor 19.07.83]

2. The Magic Flute F7c 10m
The steep drainpipe tufa on the right wall of the cave is both powerful and tricky. 4 bolts to a lower off.
[G Smith 1988]

3. Quietus E2 5c 85m ®
A classic route following the narrow left facing groove line running up the centre of the slab.
P1 5c 50m Traverse across onto and along the ledge, then head up into the narrow groove. Climb the groove (2 pegs), then continue up to another peg. Go up first, then move left, before heading directly up to a small ledge.
P2 35m Pull out on your pre-placed rope.
[R Edwards, K Toms 04.04.71]

4. Old Sam E3 6a 87m ®
A superb, technical route in a committing position.
P1 5b 18m As for *Quietus* until beneath its groove, then keep traversing left, moving up initially, then following a thin and slightly descending line leftwards to gain a small recess.
P2 6a 34m Move straight up for 7m, then make tricky moves right to reach the bottom of a thin crack. Climb the crack past a thread, then trace another crack slightly leftwards, before trending rightwards to gain the small ledge on *Quietus*.
P3 35m Pull out on your pre-placed rope.
[C Lyon, D Lyon 13.06.81]

5. The Glass Wall E2 5c 88m ®
A very fine, but rather gripping excursion.
P1 5b 18m as for P1 of *Old Sam*.
P2 5c 34m Move up straight up for 8m then step left into a crack. Follow the crack and continue up the small groove above to a little roof. Move over this, and up the wall to reach a small ledge.
P3 35m Pull out on your pre-placed rope.
[R Edwards, I Pomfrett 24.08.74]

Hole of Creation

1 **2**

Approach

Upper pitches are now very grassy. Pre-place a rope to pull out on

Abseil

5 **4**

3

Angel Bay, mentioned in the approach description, is home to a fine collection of boulder problems. The steep wave-smoothed rock is well featured with water worn scoops and pockets that are a joy to climb on. The pebble beach offers a relatively friendly landing in most conditions, although it is not unusual for the pebble levels to shift by a metre in height after a storm. On occasion this does expose bare rock landings. The bouldering is tidal, and as such the rock can be a bit damp on still days. However, if you visit on a fresh breezy day, with a low-mid tide, you'll find plenty of absorbing problems to play upon.

Chris Davies on Bridey Arete V4/Font 6b photo: Si Panton >

Castle Inn Quarry

Area: A55
Style: Sport (single pitch)
Aspect: South
Rock type: Limestone
Approach: 0 minutes
Altitude: 100m

Cakewalk Direct	F6c
Route 3	F6c
The Cakewalk	F6c
School Mam	F6b
Route 2	F6a
Route 1	F5

A nifty little sport crag, rather fortuitously situated in the car park of a pub. The definitive convenience crag, which by dint of its 'clip-n-go' style has oft been decried as the climbing equivalent of fast food. This is partly true, and partly unfair. Yes, it is all very convenient, (but then so are the nearby Marine Drive routes), but the routes themselves are actually very good. The rock is solid, clean and in places offers some superb flowstone features. The climbing itself is invariably technical and interesting, both on the slabby front face and the steeper sidewall.

Try not to get too distracted by the adjacent pub, at least not until you've bagged a couple of routes, when the notion of a refreshing pint may be most attractive!

Conditions: A quick-drying and sunny crag.

Approach: Pull off the A55 at the Old Colwyn/Hen Golwyn junction. Turn left at the roundabout and continue on through Old Colwyn, bearing right towards Llysfaen. Turn right at the T-junction and drive up the hill, taking the 2nd right turning (a small lane) which leads in a few hundred metres to the quarry and pub on the left.

Access restrictions: The top of the quarry is an S.S.S.I so please avoid it by using the in situ lower-offs.

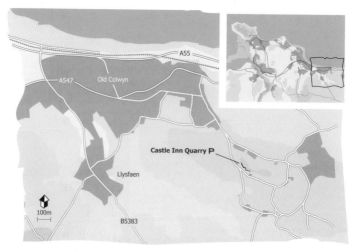

Castle Inn Quarry - the ultimate convenience crag! photo: Al Leary ∧

Finale F5 climbs the dirty crack line left of *School Mam*, whilst *The Outsider* F6c clips the same line of bolts, but keeps left of the crack.

1. School Mam F6b 24m
Start up Cakewalk direct and break out left to access some technical manoeuvres up the thin crack. (Can be started on the left as well.)
[G Gibson 20.05.84]

2. Cakewalk Direct F6c 24m
Start just left of the triangular recess and truck up the slab, making a fierce little crank through the roof to finish.
[T Shelmerdine, A Barnett 03.02.93]

3. The Cakewalk F6c 24m
The thin and fingery slab above the recess leads to a right-facing corner at the top.
[FA unknown, but finish climbed by A Pollitt, T Hodgson 31.08.82]

4. Route 3 F6c 23m
Perhaps the best route here. Starting just right of the recess, sustained technical climbing leads up the white-streaked slab.
[A Pollitt, T Hodgson 31.08.82 – first top-roped by C Goodey and friends in 1959!]

5. Route 2 F6a 25m
A further fine and slabby pitch, heading up past the long white streak.
[C Goodey, A Davies 1959]

6. Route 1 F5 25m
A great route, moving in from ledges on the right to climb some wonderful flowstone features up the arête.
[C Goodey, A Davies 1959]

To the right lie a number of lesser routes, worthy of inspection if you've ticked the front slab: *Cross Winds* F6c, *Solid 6* F6c, *Fuel Injected* F7b+ and *Secret Garden* F6c.

LLANBERIS +

OGWEN +

TREMADOG +

GOGARTH & LLEYN

LLANDUDNO +

531

Route Index

20,000 Leagues Under the Sea	416
Aardvark	399
Adam Rib	313
Africa Rib	338
Ampitheatre Buttress	252
Anarchist	373
Anchovy Madonna	479
Angel Pavement	311
Appian Way	516
Arachnid	416
Arête and Slab	195
Asahel	338
Astoroth	260
Astoroth Direct	260
Atlantis	362
Atomic Hot Rod	55
Aura	252
Avalanche/Red Wall/Longland's...	126
Avernus	445
Axle Attack	478
A Cry of Angels	511
A Dream of White Horses	420
A Midsummer Night's Dream	114
A New Austerlitz	71
Bananas	275
Barbarian	286
Bardsey Ripple	449
Barking Up The Wrong Tree	490
Bathtime	140
Bauxed	495
Beasts of the Field	103
Beauty is Only	507
Bella Lugosi is Dead	149
Belldance	142
Belle Vue Bastion	183
Bezel	395
Big Gut	428
Black and Tan	384
Black Spring	76
Blanco	362
Bloodsports	478
Bloody Chimney	390
Bloody Slab	120
Blue Peter	412
Blue Remembered Hills	368
Bochlwyd Eliminate	194
Boot Crack	190
Borchgrevinck	287
Bramble Buttress	296
Brant	39
Brant Direct	37
Bran Flake	383
Breaking the Barrier	384
Britomartis	423
Bruvers	384
Bungle's Arete	154
Byzantium	455
Cakewalk Direct	531
Californian Arete	170
Cannibal	372
Canol	31
Capital Punishment	216
Captain Fingers	486
Cardiac Arête 2	88
Carousel Waltz Variation	260
Catalyst	451
Cemetery Gates	54
Cenotaph Corner	53
Central Arête	229
Central Park	393
Central Route (Carnedd y Filiiast)	235
Central Route (Llech Ddu)	245
Central Sadness	170
Central Wall	317
Centrefold	439
Chain Gang	494
Chasm Route	199
Chimney Climb	195
Chimney Route	190
Chreon	60
Christmas Curry	270
Citadel	406
Clear White Light	491
Clogwyn y Person Arete	88
Clonus	259
Clonus Left Hand	259
Clowns of God	510
Clutch	296
Cneifion Arête	210
Cobweb Crack	50
Cockblock	38
Colossus	150
Comes The Dervish	142
Conan the Librarian	423
Condor	343
Connie's Crack	260
Connor's Folly	479
Continuation Crack	222
Contusion	478
Cordon Bleu	399
Crackstone Rib	44
Creagh Dhu Wall Direct	292
Creag Dhu Wall	292
Cream	276
Creeping Lemma	359
Crimson Cruiser	338
Cripple Creek	454
Crow	464
Crown of Thorns	30
Crucible	302
Cruella Deville	516
Crunchy Toad IX	498
Curving Crack	114
Cystitis by Proxy	154
Daddy Cool	280
Dawes of Perception	139
Day of Reckoning	299
Death Trap Direct	379

Demetreus 222
Devil's Kitchen Route 232
Devil's Nordwand 233
Devil's Staircase 232
Deygo 373
Diadem 204
Diagonal 74
Diapasan 65
Dinosaur 402
Direct Hit 457
Direct Route (Milestone Buttress) 190
Direct Route (Glyder Fach) 198
Dive, Dive, Dive 498
Dives/Better Things 51
Doenitz 524
Dogs of War 356
Doomsville 393
Double Criss 339
Dreams and Screams 439
Dwm 317
▶ Eastern Arete 308
East Wall Girdle 216
Efnisien 299
Electric Blue 441
Elliw 246
El Guide Direct 100
Emulator 400
Energy Crisis 395
Equinox 162
Erection 320
Erosion Groove Direct 47
Excursion 491
Excursion Direct 490
Extraction 272
▶ Face Race 507
Fail Safe 395
Falcon 284
Fallen Block Crack 89
Fantan B 447
Fantasia 369
Far from the Madding Throng 99
Fascinating Witches 457
Fear of Infection 101
Ferdinand 326
Fifth Avenue 393
Fingerlicker 286
Firefly 487
First Amendment 38
First Pinnacle Rib 183
First Slip 279
Flake Away 483
Flake Crack 207
Flake Wall 346
Flashdance 142
Flying Buttress 54
Foil 51
Fool's Gold 162
Forsinain Motspur 162
Foulish Goulish 494

Fratricide Wall 334
Freebird 362
Frozen Moment 525
▶ Gallop Step 323
Gambit Climb 88
Gamma 198
Gashed Crag 186
Geireagle 280
Geordie War Cry 163
German Schoolgirl 158
Get Close 201
Ghosts 84
Gin Palace 141
Glyder Crack 199
Gnat Attack 164
Godzilla 438
Gogarth 400
Golden Pond 507
Gold Rush 482
Gollum 71
Goose Creature 169
Great/Bow Combination 120
Great Balls of Fire 150
Great Feat 338
Great Gully 254
Great Wall 110
Grey Arête 228
Grey Slab 228
Grim Wall 278
Grim Wall Direct 276
Gritstone Gorilla 520
Gritstone Gorilla Direct 520
Grond 55
Grooved Arête 182
Groove Above 222
Guillemot's Groove 451
▶ Hangover 39
Hardd 330
Hawk's Nest Arête 201
Heading for Heights 317
Heading The Shot 174
Heart of Gold 372
Heather Wall 216
Heaven's Gate 510
Hebenwi 213
Helmet Boiler 378
Helsinki Wall 289
Herford's Crack 207
Hidden Sign 516
Holy, Holy, Holy 168
Hombre 428
Homicide Wall 225
Homo Erectus 499
Homo Sapien 499
Honeydew 457
Honeysuckle Corner 342
Hope 221
Horned Crag Route 125
Horse Latitudes 149

Route Index

Hunger 406
Hydraulic Transmission 525
Hydro 525
Hyndsight 201
Hysteresis 378
I've Been a Bad, Bad Boy 505
Icarus 436
Imitator 400
Incredible Surplus Head 449
Is it a Crime? 144
Ivy Sepulchre 54
Jabberwocky 302
Jack of Shadows 150
Jacobs Ladder 132
Jacuzzi Jive 506
Javelin 297
Javelin Blade 221
Javelin Buttress 221
Jelly Roll 114
Jubilee Climb 76
Kaffe Fasset 507
Kaisergebirge Wall 40
Kalahari 364
Kanly 495
Karwendel Wall 40
Katana 383
Kaya 199
Killerkranky 60
King Bee Crack 383
King Kong 331
King Wad 60
Kirkus's Climb Direct 347
Kirkus's Route (Craig Lloer) 238
Kirkus's Route (Craig yr Ogof) 305
Kirkus Direct 305
Kleinian Envy 141
Klondike 486
Knowing Her 457
Kubla Khan 176
Last Tango in Paris 142
Launching Pad 168
Laura 510
Lavaredo 334
Lazarus 221
La Boheme 506
La Boheme Direct 506
Left-Hand Red Wall 372
Left Edge 235
Left Wall 53
Leg Slip 279
Libertango 506
Lighthouse Arête 362
Lighthouse Arête Direct 362
Lightning Visit 334
Limestone Lemur 520
Llithrig 110
Llyn 204
Lockwood's Chimney 322
Longland's Climb 118

Long Kesh 92
Looning the Tube 169
Lord of the Flies 53
Lorraine 72
Lorraine Direct 72
Lost Boot Climb 228
Lot's Groove 199
Lubyanka 92
Ludwig 356
Mabinogion 30
Mad O'Rourke's Kipper House 507
Magellan's Wall 439
Main Wall 92
Major Headstress 150
Mallory's Ridge 309
Mammoth Direct 404
Manic Strain 141
Mantrap 379
Manx 213
Manx Groove 451
Marble Slab 195
Mask of the Red Death 436
Massambula 164
Masterclass 478
Mayfair 478
Mean Feat 338, 339
Mean Mother 506
Melkor 498
Memory Lane 52
Menstrual Discharge 141
Mental Lentils 139
Merchant Man 428
Merlin Direct 280
Meshach 278
Mestizo 409
Metal Guru 422
Micah Eliminate 270
Monolith Crack 206
Mordor 115
More Genius 495
Mousetrap 379
Mr Chips 487
Mr Olympia 494
Munich Climb 186
Mur y Meirwon 218
Mur y Niwl 252
Mussel Beach 505
Nea 36
Neb Direct 269
Needle in the Groove 479
Never as Good as the First Time 144
Never Never Land 176
New Dimensions 516
New Wave 525
Nexus 78
Nice 'n' Sleazy 412
Nightride 409
Night Glue 505
Nimbus 275

Nimitz 525
Noah's Warning 50
Non Dairy Creamer 339
North West Passage 362
Nosferatu 343
November 114
No Arc, No Bark 490
Octo 109
Old Holborn 47
Old Sam 528
Olympus Trip 494
One Step in the Clouds 275
One Step in the Crowds 292
Opal Moon 518
Ordinary Route 302
Original Route 221
Oriole 258
Ormuzd 430
Orpheus 32
Other Realms 465
Outside Edge Route 302
Overhanging Chimney 44
Overlapping Ridge Route 183
Overlapping Wall 44
Oxine 327
Pagan 372
Paint It Black 490
Pale Shelter 498
Paradise/Black Arête 125
Parchment Passage 50
Park Lane 393
Path To Rome 461
Pedestal Crack 115
Penal Servitude 216
Penamnen Groove 334
Pen Trwyn Patrol 498
Phagocyte 428
Phantom Rib 36
Phoenix 258
Pigott's Climb 110
Pincushion 286
Pinky 347
Pinnacle Arête 109
Pinnacle Rib Route 183
Pinnacle Ridge Route 241
Pinnacle Wall 252
Pinnaclissima 252
Plagued by Fools 479
Plastic Nerve 289
Plas Berw 518
Plexus 78
Plumbline (Craig y Gesail) 296
Plumbline (Marine Drive) 482
Poacher 327
Pocket City 486
Poetry Pink 154
Poor Man's Peuterey 287
Positron 402
Potency 316

Precious Metal 482
Precious Time 495
Pretty Girls Make Graves 99
Primate 378
Primitive Route 121
Princess 297
Private Investigations 486
Psychotherapy 139
Pull My Daisy 152
Pulpit Route 191
Pulsar 65
Pyschic Threshold 518
Quantum Jump 40
Quasar 40
Quietus 528
Rainbow Warrior 510
Rampart Corner 221
Rap 362
Rapture 479
Rapture of the Deep 369
Rastus 462
Reactor 451
Reade's Route 90
Rectory Chimney 90
Redshift 368
Red and Yellow and Pink and Green,
 Orange and Purple and Blue 152
Red Wall 369
Red Wall Escape Route 368
Rembrandt Pussyhorse 100
Resolution Direct 400
Resurrection (Dinas Cromlech) 53
Resurrection (Llechog).....................320
Ribstone Crack 46
Rib and Slab 32
Ride the Wild Surf 150
Rift Wall 32
Right Wall 53
Rimsky Korsakov 100
Riptide 525
Rocking Chair 205
Roc Ness Monster 60
Route 1 531
Route 2 (Lliwedd) 129
Route 2 (Castle Inn Quarry) 531
Route 3 531
Rowan Route 191
Rowan Tree Slabs 225
Run Fast, Run Free 391
Sabre Cut 51
Sacred Idol 65
Sai Dancing 383
Samurai 470
Samurai Groove 330
Satsuma Special 65
Scare City 162
Scarface Finish 245
Scarlet Runner 164
Scarlet Runner Direct 164

Route Index

Scary Canary 482
Scavenger 409
Schittegruber 372
School Mam 531
Scintillating Stitches 457
Scorpio 115
Scratch 286
Scratch Arete 286
Seamstress 174
Seams the Same 174
Sea Panther 30
Second Pinnacle Rib 183
Sexual Salami 288
Shadow Wall 47
Shadrach 278
Sheaf 119
Short Stories 176
Shrike 108
Sickle 37
Silhouette 115
Silly Arete 286
Skinhead Moonstomp 402
Skin Deep 507
Skin Game 507
Skylon 44
Slab Climb 205
Slab Climb Right-Hand 121
Slack 348
Slanting Buttress Ridge Route 130
Slape Direct 38
Slippery People 175
Slow Ledge Climb 76
Slug Club Special 174
Snake Connection 275
Snowdrop 260
Soapgut 190
Soap on a Rope 140
Solid Gold 486
Solstice 162
South Sea Bubble 412
Space Below My Feet 343
Spectre 36
Spectrum 36
Spider Wall 424
Spiral Stairs 52
Spitting Image 103
Splitstream 154
Spong 158
Statement of Youth 505
Sterling Silver 162
Strapiombo 287
Stratosphere 212
Strawberries 275
Strike 390
String of Pearls 498
Striptease 272
Stroll On 39
Stromboli 289
Sub-Cneifion Rib 209

Suicide Wall Route 2 216
Suicide Wall Route 1 218
Supercrack 428
Superdirect 74
Super Direct 190
Surplomb 39
Swastika 430
Sweet Dreams 510
Syringe 406
S S Special 37
T. Rex 422
Talking Heads 412
Tantalus 293
Television Route 368
Tennis Shoe 219
Tension 384
Tensor 292
Tentative Decisions 175
Ten Degrees North 78
Terminal Arete 129
Terminator 129
The Arête 222
The Assassin 409
The Atomic Finger Flake 276
The Axe 108
The Bearded Clam 478
The Big Groove 406
The Bittersweet Connection 518
The Bloods 478
The Bog of the Eternal Stench 33
The Boldest 118
The Boulder 118
The Burner 330
The Burning 169
The Cad 412
The Cakewalk 531
The Camel 409
The Carbon Stage 176
The Clown 412
The Concrete Chimney 420
The Corner 115
The Cow 356
The Cracks 72
The Cruel Sea 525
The Cruise 391
The Curver 316
The Dark Destroyer 157
The Dark Half 154
The Death Wisher 327
The Direct Route 74
The Disillusioned Screw Machine 478
The Eternal Optimist 395
The Exile 516
The Exterminating Angel 299
The Fang 272
The Flytrap 416
The Gauntlet 393
The Glass Wall 528
The Golden Bough Finish 422

Route Index

The Gold Coast 499
The Grasper 268
The Great Arête 245
The Great Corner 245
The Green Slab 378
The Green Wall 343
The Grimmett 252
The Groove 245
The Grooves 95
The Hand-Traverse 109
The Hole of Creation 528
The Hylldrem Girdle 330
The Iconoclastic Exit 299
The Jub-Jub Bird 438
The Kicker Conspiracy 60
The Long Run 412
The Magic Flute 528
The Mau Mau 157
The Medium 174
The Mermaid Who Shed Her Glove 457
The Mole 71
The Monster 55
The Monster Kitten 139
The Moon 356
The Mostest 107
The Nectarine Run 65
The Ordinary Route 219
The Overhanging Arête 95
The Parson's Nose 88
The Pink Pinkie Snuffs 506
The Pirates of Pen Trwyn 498
The Plum 271
The Quartz Icicle 420
The Rainbow of Recalcitrance 152
The Ramp 393
The Rat Race 400
The Reflex 510
The Refrain 504
The Savage 356
The Savage Sunbird 435
The Sind 359
The Skull 95
The Spider's Web 425
The Stebbing 103
The Sting 280
The Strand 393
The Sun 436
The Sweetest Taboo 144
The Sword 129
The Thing 50
The Thoughts of Chairman Ray 466
The Troach 115
The Viper 438
The Visionary 491
The Wall 84
The Wasp 292
The Weaver 275
The White Streak 342
The Wrack 194

This Year's Model 428
Toiler on the Sea 424
Torero 326
Touch and Go 297
Trail of Tears 438
Troubador 331
Trouble with Lichen 206
Troy 60
Truant 438
True Clip 158
True Moments 362
Tufty Club Rebellion 60
Twisting by the Pool 506
U.F.O. 390
Under the Boardwalk 504
Valerie's Rib 268
Valor 268
Vector 276
Vember 114
Vertigo 317
Via Media 132
Void 276
Vulcan 284
Vulture (Craig Bwlch y Moch) 280
Vulture (Cilan Head) 463
Wall Climb (Milestone Buttress) 190
Wall Climb (Clogwyn Bochlwyd) 194
Warpath 436
Watling Street 516
Waves of Inspiration 170
Weasels Rip My Flesh 101
Wen 420
Wendigo 368
Western Slabs 75
West Buttress Eliminate 119
West Rib 74
What a Difference a Day Makes 100
White Hopes 499
White Slab 120
Wildebeest 330
Wild Rover 436
Wind 40
Winking Crack 391
Womb Bits 110
Wonderwall 428
Woubits 107
Wrinkle 44
Yellow Crack 47
Yellow Groove 33
Yellow Wall 33
Yob Route 204
You've Had Your Chips 487
Y Gelynen 342
Zambesi 168
Zangorilla 47
Zarquon 320
Zigzag 31
Zig Zag Climb 206
Zukator 269

LLANBERIS +

OGWEN +

TREMADOG +

GOGARTH & LLEYN

LLANDUDNO +

Crag Index

Bochlwyd Buttress/Clogwyn Bochlwyd..... 192
Braich Ty Du 240
Bus Stop Quarry 160

Carnedd y Filiast 234
Carreg Alltrem 332
Carreg Hylldrem 328
Carreg Wastad 42
Castell Cidwm 314
Castell Helen 360
Castell y Gwynt 512
Castle Inn Quarry 530
Chain Gang Wall 492
Clogwyn Bochlwyd/Bochlwyd Buttress..... 192
Clogwyn Du 211
Clogwyn Du'r Arddu 104
Clogwyn Gafr 62
Clogwyn y Bustach/Gwynant 321
Clogwyn y Bustach/Moelwyns 346
Clogwyn y Ddysgl 86
Clogwyn y Geifr 230
Clogwyn y Grochan 34
Clogwyn y Tarw/Griben Facet 202
Clogwyn y Wenallt 324
Clogwyn yr Eryr 256
Clogwyn yr Oen 344
Cilan Head 458
Craig Aderyn 132
Craig Bwlch y Moch 266
Craig Cwm Du 312
Craig Cwm Trwsgl 298
Craig Ddu 28
Craig Dorys 452
Craig Lloer 236
Craig Pant Ifan 282
Craig y Bera 310
Craig y Castell 290
Craig y Clipiau 336
Craig y Gesail 294
Craig y Llam 446
Craig y Rhaeadr/Diffwys Ddwr 81
Craig yr Ogof 300
Craig yr Wrysgan 340
Craig yr Ysfa 248
Cwm Cneifion 208
Cwm Glas Bach 96
Cyrn Las/Diffwys Ddu 91

Dali's Hole Area 166
Diffwys Ddu/Cyrn Las 91
Diffwys Ddwr/Craig y Rhaeadr 81
Dinas Cromlech 48
Dinas Mot 66

East Face of Tryfan .... 1█
Easter Island Gully .... 4█
Esgair Maen Gwyn/Scimitar Ridge .... █
Excursion Area 48

Firefly Area .... 4█
Flytrap Area .... 41█

Glyder Fach Main Cliff 19
Glyder Fawr 22
Great Zawn 52
Griben Facet/Clogwyn y Tarw .... 20█

Holyhead Mountain 38
Homo Sapien Area 49

Idwal Slabs and Walls .... 21█

Llech Ddu 24
Llechog .... 31█
Left Hand Red Wall .... 37█
Lliwedd 12
Lower Pen Trwyn .... 50█

Main Cliff 39
Mayfair Wall 47
Milestone Buttress 18
Mousetrap Zawn .... 37█

Never Never Land 17
North Stack Wall 41

Pen y Cil 45
Plumbline Area 48

Rainbow Slab Area .... 14█
Red Wall 36
Rhoscolyn 43

Scimitar Ridge/Esgair Maen Gwyn .... 5█
Serengeti .... 17█
St Tudno's Upper Crag .... 51█

Trwyn Maen Melyn .... 44█
Trwyn y Gorlech .... 44█
Ty'n Tywyn Quarries .... 46█

Upper Craig y Don .... 52█
Upper Tier .... 38█

Vivian Quarry .... 13█

Wen Zawn 418
Wonder Wall 509

Yellow Wall/Gogarth 354
Yellow Wall/Marine Drive 496
Y Garn .... 30█

LLANBERIS +

OGWEN +

TREMADOG +

GOGARTH & LLEYN

LLANDUDNO +

Advertising Directory

Ground Up would like to thank all the advertisers who helped to support this guidebook:

LLANBERIS +

OGWEN +

TREMADOG +

GOGARTH & LLEYN

LLANDUDNO +

Acknowledgements

The success of the North Wales Rock guide rests upon the shoulders of many people, but most significantly with a core group of contributors and researchers: Al Leary, Rob Wilson, Graham Desroy, Simon Marsh, Mark Reeves and Pete Robins. This book would not have been possible without their valuable input and relentless enthusiasm for the job in hand. Vital feedback and advice has also been drawn from a large pool of active climbers. The following 'local experts' have been especially helpful: Jon Ratcliffe, Dafydd Davis, Jez Stephenson, James McHaffie, Noel Craine, Rich Betts, Neil Dyer and Adam Wainwright.

I am greatly indebted to the following group of photographers who put forward a range of inspiring images, often obtained in very difficult circumstances; much of the credit for the visual impact of this book lies with them: Ray Wood, Jethro Kiernan (www.onsight. com), Alex Messenger (www.snowfire.com), Al Leary, Graham Desroy, Rob Wilson, Simon Marsh, Al Williams, Adam Long (www.adamlong.co.uk), John Coefield (www. beardownproductions.com), Phil Dowthwaite, Steve Long (www.safetysteve.co.uk), Matt Tuck, Mia Axon, Gruff Owen (www.exposure-therapy.com), Rob Greenwood, Paul Houghoughi, Rob Lamey, Andy Godber, Gav Foster and Rory Shaw.

Thanks are also due to the following people: Mike Hammill for geology advice; Ian Lloyd Jones and Pete Rowlands from St Davids school, Llandudno for taking us on a boat trip to the Ormes to snap crag shots; Gareth Williams (www.goseafishing.biz) for the boat trip to Gogarth; Keith Robertson and Anne Vowles for the crag shot of Pen y Cil (check out Keith's website www.fachwen.org for some stunning landscape photography); Dave Ferguson for the Cilan Head crag shots and Andy Newton for the Rhoscolyn crag shots; Ted Silvester for the loan of the Caban camera equipment and Simon Marsh, Streaky, Andy Newton, Rob Wilson, Al Leary, Mike Raine, Jez Portman for proofing duties and in particular Mark Hundleby for his eagle eyed attention to detail.

And for various reasons the following people deserve my thanks: Clive Davis, Simon Jones, Crispin Waddy, Matt Perrier, Chris Davies, Pete Griffiths, Dave Evans, Mark Richardson, Steve Dunning, Andy Bruce, Lee Roberts, Sam Leary, Chris Rowlands, Dave Simpson, Ollie Wright, Cath Wilson, Ritchie Pullen, Silvia Fitzpatrick, Dave Towse, Glenda Huxter, Alex Williams, James Lillie, George Smith, Paul Barker, Chris Doyle, Tony Shelmerdine, Liam Desroy, Rachael Barlow, Pat Littlejohn, Mike Bailey, Martin Kocsis, Chris Parkin, Ron James, Gareth Davies (SNPA), Elfyn Jones (National Trust), Ken Latham and Paul Sivyer (Parc Padarn), Guy Keating (BMC), Anita Grey and Mark Dicken.

Although this guide has been extensively researched out on the crags, I recognise that the existing framework of North Wales climbing guidebooks provided a valuable base of reference material. In view of this, special thanks are due to all the people who have helped to develop this remarkable range of books: The Climbers' Club guidebook authors (Iwan Arfon Jones, Nick Dixon, Kelvin Neal, Mike Bailey, Dave Ferguson, Pat Littlejohn, Bob Wightman, Paul Jenkinson, Martin Crocker, John Sumner, Terry Taylor, Elfyn Jones, Mike Rosser, Dave Wrennall and Andy Newton) and the many local climbers who have contributed to the roster of CC guidebooks for the North Wales area. Also the CC Publication sub-committee (in particular: Ian Smith, John Willson, Bob Moulton, Simon Cardy, Mike Rosser, Don Sargeant and Richard Wheeldon), Alan James (Rockfax) for his 1997 North Wales Limestone guide, Tony Shaw (Mynydd Climbing Club) for his 1997 Crafnant guide, Iwan Arfon Jones for the 1999 Slate guide and of course, Ron James, Paul Williams and Steve Ashton for the groundbreaking selected guidebooks they produced in the '70s and '80s.

A big thank you is also due to Mark Lynden (www.matrix10.net) who instigated the initial design concept, and most of all to Al Williams, the designer, who worked tirelessly, refining and developing the design concept of the book and whose measured judgements and supportive presence kept the project on track through some difficult times.

And finally a very heartfelt thank you to my wife Clare, and my kids, Cadi and Charlie, for supporting me and tolerating my obsessive tendencies (once again).

Simon Panton Nov 2006

Acknowledgements

From above clockwise:
Graham Desroy on topo of Lliwedd photo: Al Leary
Al Williams and Slim photo: Williams collection
Simon Panton on The Upper Tier, Gogarth photo: Al Leary
Rob Wilson in Vivian Quarry photo: Jethro Kiernan
Pete Robins on Cloggy photo: Al Leary
Al Leary on Clogwyn y Grochan photo: Si Panton
Simon Marsh at Bariloche (Argentina) photo: Silvia Fitzpatrick
Mark Reeves on the Sickle Ledge, The Nose, El Capitan photo: Reeves collection